S0-FCQ-600

Arms and the Man

History of Warfare

Editors

Kelly DeVries

Loyola College Maryland

John France

University of Wales Swansea

Michael S. Neiberg

University of Southern Mississippi

Frederick Schneid

High Point University North Carolina

VOLUME 68

Arms and the Man

Military History Essays in
Honor of Dennis Showalter

Edited by
Michael S. Neiberg

BRILL

LEIDEN • BOSTON
2011

Cover illustration: Finnish soldiers with *Panzerfausts* at the battle of Tali-Ihantala on the Karelian Isthmus, 30 June 1944. Photo: SA 155340.
With kind permission of The Finnish Defense Forces, Photographic Centre.

This book is printed on acid-free paper.

Library of Congress Cataloging-in-Publication Data

Arms and the man : military history essays in honor of Dennis Showalter / edited by Michael S. Neiberg.
   p. cm. -- (History of warfare ; v. 68)
 Includes bibliographical references and index.
 ISBN 978-90-04-20668-7 (hardback : alk. paper) 1. Military history. 2. Military art and science--History. I. Neiberg, Michael S. II. Showalter, Dennis E. III. Title. IV. Series.

D25.5.A77 2011
355.009--dc22

2011007831

ISSN 1385-7827
ISBN 978 90 04 20668 7

Copyright 2011 by Koninklijke Brill NV, Leiden, The Netherlands.
Koninklijke Brill NV incorporates the imprints Brill, Hotei Publishing,
IDC Publishers, Martinus Nijhoff Publishers and VSP.

All rights reserved. No part of this publication may be reproduced, translated, stored in a retrieval system, or transmitted in any form or by any means, electronic, mechanical, photocopying, recording or otherwise, without prior written permission from the publisher.

Authorization to photocopy items for internal or personal use is granted by Koninklijke Brill NV provided that the appropriate fees are paid directly to The Copyright Clearance Center, 222 Rosewood Drive, Suite 910, Danvers, MA 01923, USA. Fees are subject to change.

PRINTED BY A-D DRUK BV - ZEIST, THE NETHERLANDS

CONTENTS

List of Contributors vii

Introduction 1
   Michael S. Neiberg

Loving the German War Machine: America's Infatuation
   with Blitzkrieg, Warfighters, and Militarism 5
   William J. Astore

'Clash of the Titans': Law vs Security in World War II Britain 31
   Mary Kathryn Barbier

Military Cultures, Military Histories and the Current
   Emergency 63
   Jeremy Black

Manstein, the Battle of Kharkov, and the Limits of Command 83
   Robert M. Citino

The Question of Medieval Military Professionalism 113
   Kelly DeVries

Modern Soldier in a Busby: August von Mackensen,
   1914–1916 131
   Richard L. DiNardo

Winning and Losing: France on the Marne and on the Meuse 169
   Robert A. Doughty

The Forgotten Campaign: Alsace-Lorraine August 1914 193
   Holger H. Herwig

"Total War, Total Nonsense" or "The Military Historian's
   Fetish" 215
   Eugenia C. Kiesling

England's "Descent" on France and the Origins of Blue-water Strategy 243
  Robert McJimsey

Conclusion 259
  Dennis Showalter

List of Books by Dennis Showalter 267

Select Bibliography 269

Index 273

LIST OF CONTRIBUTORS

William J. Astore
Professor of History, Pennsylvania College of Technology

Mary Kathryn Barbier
Associate Professor of History, Mississippi State University

Jeremy Black
Professor of History, University of Exeter

Robert M. Citino
Military History Center, University of North Texas

Kelly DeVries
Loyola University Maryland and Honorary Historical Consultant, Royal Armouries

Richard L. DiNardo
USMC Command and Staff College, Quantico, Virginia

Robert A. Doughty
U.S. Military Academy (Retired)

Holger H. Herwig
Canada Research Chair in Military and Strategic Studies, University of Calgary, Canada

Robert McJimsey
Professor of History, Colorado College, 1968–2004.

Eugenia C. Kiesling
Professor of History, United States Military Academy, West Point

Michael S. Neiberg
Harold K. Johnson Professor of Military History, United States Army War College

Dennis E. Showalter
Professor of History, Colorado College

INTRODUCTION

Michael S. Neiberg

I had the great pleasure of sharing a city, if not a department, with Dennis Showalter for eight years. Dennis was by then a legendary visiting professor and frequent guest lecturer at the United States Air Force Academy, my first job out of graduate school. Dennis had also served in similar positions at West Point and the United States Marine Corps University. In 1998, when I showed up in Colorado Springs, Dennis had just returned to his home department at Colorado College. Over those eight years, I benefited from his friendship, his advice, and his library. It is an honor for me to able to present this festschrift to him as a humble token of my thanks for all that he did to help me become the scholar I am.

I knew Dennis by reputation, of course, long before I came to Colorado. I had read virtually everything he had written and admired the logical, careful way Dennis had of analyzing difficult problems. His *Tannenberg: Clash of Empires* and *Railroads and Rifles* had become must reads for anyone who wanted to understand warfare in the 19th and 20th centuries. As I was to learn, however, Dennis's interests ranged well beyond military history, including a deep love of baseball (our friendship has survived not only political disagreements, but his attachment to the New York Yankees as well), country music, and even the television program *Buffy the Vampire Slayer*, at a conference on which Dennis once presented a paper.

At our first meeting, a chance encounter in the hallway, Dennis asked me what I was working on. I told him that my dissertation was revised and about to be sent to Harvard University Press for consideration. Dennis offered to read it and I scurried back to my office to get the manuscript like a young undergraduate eager to show the professor that I belonged in his class. Dennis had the manuscript back to me within a few days with thoughtful commentary and suggestions. He also attached a copy of the letter he had written to the press urging them to publish the book. I soon came to depend on this kind of energy, encouragement, and criticism from Dennis, who never shied away from telling me where he thought I was wrong, but always at the same time brought out the best in what I could write.

As this small anecdote shows, one of the most amazing qualities of Dennis is his willingness to give his time to other scholars. I am constantly astounded at the number of books whose acknowledgements page thanks Dennis for his time and effort. He has also been a mentor to generations of young officers who have pursued graduate-level work and publication in history as part of their career development. He has been, in the words of William J. Astore, a "force multiplier" for the use of history as an analytic tool inside the defense community. That Dennis is a generous scholar who is always reaching his hand to others, from high school students to generals, will come as no surprise to anyone who knows him.

Dennis takes as much care with undergraduates as he does with his fellow scholars. I remember somewhat sheepishly asking him if I could "audit" his course on coalition warfare, then being offered at USAFA in conjunction with that year's symposium. I filled two notebooks while watching a master teacher use everything from folk songs to *I Love Lucy* references to explain complex problems to a classroom full of cadets, and I never saw him use any lesson plan more sophisticated than a Post-It note with a few words scribbled in Dennis's distinctive handwriting. I can think of few greater compliments for a teacher than to note that five members of the USAFA faculty "audited" Dennis' course on the Holocaust. We five, all experienced educators, sat stunned by the intelligence, the grace, and the wit with which Dennis handled this important and difficult subject.

Anyone who regularly attends the annual meeting of the Society for Military History knows the role Dennis has played in that organization. Having once served as the Society's president, Dennis played a key role in making it the positive intellectual environment it is today. He has brought that same level of energy and dedication to the International Society of First World Studies that he helped to create and to projects like the journal *War in History*. He was also responsible for keeping military history relevant and important. Even as much of the profession was abandoning operational military history, criticizing it as "drum and trumpet" analysis, Dennis was (re-)investing it with heavyweight research, incisive analysis, and delightful writing. Insofar as there has been a renaissance of late in operational history, it has been of his making.[1]

---

[1] That last sentence belongs to Robert Citino, who suggested it to me in an earlier draft of this introduction.

I also had the chance to tour the western front with Dennis in 2003, an experience I will never forget. I learned more in those few days than I had in many years of study on the topic. My most powerful memory of the trip remains watching Dennis discuss the war with a young Canadian park ranger at Beaumont-Hamel in the same tone he would have used in discussing it with a group of specialists. It was all part and parcel of Dennis's egalitarian manner and his desire to learn as well as teach at every opportunity.

This festschrift is a bit different from most in that it is not a collection of work by Dennis's graduate students. Having spent his career at Colorado College and in various military schools, Dennis has not had any graduate students of his own (I often wonder how much stronger our field might be today if he had). Fortunately, however, it fell to us, those who so greatly admire him and his work, to put together this book in honor of his career and how much his mentorship and friendship has meant to us. As editor, I asked Dennis for a list of people whose contributions he would like to see in this book. The response from the authors he named was immediate and enthusiastic, my favorite response being Rob Citino's "Mike, you know I'd do anything for my godfather."

As editor, I gave the authors no more guidance than to write an original piece of scholarship that honored Dennis and would stand the test of time as solid historical study of some aspect of the problem of warfare. The results have surpassed my wildest dreams; my colleagues have produced work that will be of interest to scholars across time, subdiscipline, and topic. Collected here are a wide array of subjects that span the centuries. They come from some of the very best scholars working in military history today, all of them influenced and encouraged by Dennis. Also included is a posthumous essay by Dennis's friend and colleague, the late Robert McJimsey. I then gave these essays to Dennis and invited him to write a response; that response appears at the end as the book's conclusion.

Before yielding the floor to the authors of this compilation, I would like, on behalf of the contributors, to thank Julian Deahl and the staff at Brill for seeing the value of this book. Thanks to their efforts, this book will remain a tribute to Dennis for as long as people are reading military history.

LOVING THE GERMAN WAR MACHINE
AMERICA'S INFATUATION WITH *BLITZKRIEG*, WARFIGHTERS, AND MILITARISM[1]

William J. Astore

Why do people have a fixation with the German military when they haven't won a war since 1871? – Tom Clancy[2]

Ever since I was a boy, I have been interested in the German military, especially the *Wehrmacht* of World War II. I recall building many models, not just German Panther and Tiger tanks, but famous Luftwaffe planes as well. True, I also built American tanks and planes, Shermans and Thunderbolts and Mustangs, but the German models always seemed "cooler," a little more exotic, a little more predatory. And the German military, to my adolescent imagination, seemed admirably tough and aggressive: hard-fighting, thoroughly professional, hanging on against long odds, especially against the same hordes of "godless communists" that I knew we Americans in the 1970s were facing in the Cold War.

Later, of course, a little knowledge about the nightmare of Nazism and the Holocaust went a long way toward destroying my admiration for the *Wehrmacht*, but – to be completely honest – a residue of grudging respect still survives. I no longer have my models, but I still have many of the Ballantine illustrated war books I bought as a young boy for a buck or two, and which often celebrated the achievements of the German military, with titles like *Panzer Division*, or *Afrika Korps*, or even *Waffen SS*.[3]

---

[1] An early version of this chapter appeared under the title, "American Blitzkrieg: Loving the German War Machine to Death," posted on February 18, 2010 at http://www.tomdispatch.com/archive/175208/. I wish to thank Tom Engelhardt and Mike Neiberg for their comments and encouragement.

[2] Quoted in Joel Achenbach, "War and the Cult of Clausewitz: How a Long-Dead Prussian Shaped U.S. Thinking on the Persian Gulf," *The Washington Post*, December 6, 1990, *Style* pages D1 and D4.

[3] Major K. J. Macksey wrote *Afrika Korps* (1968) and *Panzer Division: The Mailed Fist* (1968); John Keegan wrote *Waffen SS: The Asphalt Soldiers* (1970). I still own these dog-eared books (and many others in the Ballantine's Illustrated History of World War II series).

As the Bible says, we are meant to put aside childish things as we grow to adulthood, and an uninformed fascination with the militaria and regalia of the Third Reich was certainly one of these. But when I entered Air Force ROTC in 1981, and later active duty in 1985, I was surprised, even pleased, to discover that so many members of the U.S. military shared my interest in and enthusiasm for the German military. To cite just one example: As a cadet at Field Training in 1983 (and later at Squadron Officer School in 1992), I participated in what was known as "Project X." As cadets, we came to know of it in whispers: "Tomorrow we're doing Project X: It's really tough ..."

A problem-solving leadership exercise, Project X consisted of several scenarios and associated tasks. Working in small groups, you were expected to solve these while working against the clock. What made the project exciting and more than busy-work, like the endless marching or shining of shoes or waxing of floors, was that it was based on German methods of developing and instilling small-unit leadership and teamwork. If it worked for the Germans, the "finest soldiers in the world"[4] during World War II, it was good enough for us, or so most of us concluded (including me).

Project X was just one rather routine manifestation of the American military's fascination with German methods and German military mystique. As I began teaching military history to cadets at the Air Force Academy in 1990, I quickly became familiar with a flourishing "Cult of Clausewitz." So ubiquitous was Carl von Clausewitz and his book *On War* that it seemed as if we Americans had never produced our own military theorists. I grew familiar with the way *Auftragstaktik* (the idea of maximizing flexibility and initiative at the lowest tactical levels) was regularly extolled.[5] So prevalent did Clausewitz and

---

[4] Max Hastings, "Up Against 'the Finest Soldiers in the World,'" *The New York Review of Books*, April 3, 2008, 18–20 [Review of *The Day of Battle: The War in Sicily and Italy, 1943-1944*, by Rick Atkinson]. In *Overlord* (1984), Hastings characterized the German Army as "the most professionally skilled army of modern times," an accurate statement if professionalism is viewed narrowly as mastery of fighting tactics. Contrast this view of German mastery with Kenneth Macksey, *Why the Germans Lose at War: The Myth of German Military Superiority* (London: Greenhill Books, 1996).

[5] Here, war is seen as a creative activity in which skills and determination, rather than materiel factors, decisively influence the course of events, an idea captured in Germany's Field Service Regulations of 1933: "Leadership in war is an art, a free creative activity based on a foundation of knowledge. The greatest demands are made on the personality." See David M. Keithly and Stephen P. Ferris, "*Auftragstaktik*, or Directive Control, in Joint and Combined Operations," *Parameters* 29 (Autumn 1999): 118–33.

Auftragstaktik become that, in the 1980s and 1990s, American military thinking seemed reducible to the idea that "war is a continuation of politics" and a belief that victory went to the side that empowered its "strategic corporals" at the fighting level.

A Case of Wehrmacht Penis Envy

American idolization of German methods and techniques, even "warrior" codes of thinking and behaving, has come at high cost. It has consigned the United States to unreflective conformity and imperial decline, just as it condemned the German Reichs in both world wars. Paradoxically, after 1945 the U.S. military sought to define itself as the successor to and inheritor of German military excellence at operational and tactical levels, while at the same time embracing the "war as a continuation of politics" meme of Clausewitz. A cult of Clausewitz came to exist, and continues to persist, that sees war as politics vitalized, a cult that (in part) explains the growing ascendancy, and now dominance, of the Department of Defense (DoD) and Pentagon vis-à-vis the Department of State, a dominance that works to keep the U.S. in a state of perpetual rearmament, even when we are not at war.[6]

The U.S. military's belief in war's creative power and its inherent controllability, the extolment of a post-draft "all-volunteer" (read: professional) military, and an affinity for *Blitzkrieg*-like "shock and awe" military action as a way to cut complex geo-political knots: all are traceable to an unreflective affection for and admiration of Prussian/German military models and methods.

Interestingly, the U.S. military's fascination with all things German is in historical terms a relatively recent phenomenon. In *Patton and Rommel* (2005), Dennis Showalter noted that before World War II, American military men looked not so much to Germany as they did to France for military inspiration.[7] Napoleon Bonaparte was a favorite of U.S. Civil War generals like George McClellan. France was America's

---

[6] See James Carroll, *House of War: The Pentagon and the Disastrous Rise of American Power* (Boston: Houghton Mifflin, 2006). The Pentagon budget was *twelve* times the size of the State Department's in 2008, admitted Secretary of Defense Bill Gates. See Stephen Gain, "The American Leviathan," *The Nation*, September 28, 2009, available at http://www.thenation.com/article/american-leviathan.

[7] *Patton and Rommel: Men of War in the Twentieth Century* (New York: Berkley Caliber, 2005), 23–24.

"arsenal of democracy" in World War I, with officers like George S. Patton forming "a fraternity of arms" with their French counterparts.[8]

In the immediate aftermath of Germany's defeat in World War II and the Nuremberg trials, many Americans held German military models in suspicion. The U.S. Congress, for one, resisted President Harry S Truman's proposal for a more tightly integrated and powerful defense staff due to its evocation of the powerful Prussian general staff.[9] Critical post-war accounts, such as Telford Taylor's *Sword and Swastika* (1952), condemned Germany's military elite for its alliance with Nazi totalitarianism, blaming the co-joined product for its "desolation and devitalization of Europe."[10] Senior American generals like Dwight D. Eisenhower won praise precisely because they were not, in the words of Alistair Cooke, "bristling with a long tradition of military chauvinism." Eisenhower's superiority as a leader, Cooke claimed, was in part because he was something more than a "practiced old warrior," something more than an Erwin Rommel.[11]

But as memories of Nazism faded and Americans confronted their very own Soviet menace, Germanic military exploits began to be elevated and mined for lessons in a downsizing U.S. military. Historians like Martin van Creveld and Russell Weigley[12] contrasted a U.S. Army approach to warfare that they claimed stressed materiel abundance and managerial efficiency as war-winning determinants to a German military that had relied on vitalism, spirit, morale, and other intangibles.[13] Such intangibles, they suggested, kept the German military machine running even when most of its gears had ground down, a lesson they suggested was largely lost on an increasingly materialistic U.S. military.

---

[8] Robert B. Bruce, *A Fraternity of Arms: American and France in the Great War* (Lawrence: University Press of Kansas, 2003).

[9] Elizabeth Kier, *Imagining War: French and British Military Doctrine Between the Wars* (Princeton: Princeton University Press, 1997), 22. Kier cites a study by Paul N. Stockton here.

[10] Telford Taylor, *Sword and Swastika: Generals and Nazis in the Third Reich* (New York: Simon and Schuster, 1952), vii.

[11] *General Eisenhower on the Military Churchill: A Conversation with Alistair Cooke* (New York: W. W. Norton, 1970), 14.

[12] Russell F. Weigley, *The American Way of War* (New York: Macmillan Publishing, 1973); Martin van Creveld, *Fighting Power: German and U.S. Army Performance, 1939-1945* (Westport, CT: Greenwood Press, 1982). With respect to Creveld, see the probing review essay by David Schoenbaum, "The Wehrmacht and G. I. Joe: Learning What from History?" *International Security* 1 (Summer 1983): 201–07.

[13] D.E. Showalter and Horst Fuchs Richardson, *Sieg Heil! War Letters of Tank Gunner Karl Fuchs, 1937-1941* (Hamden, CT: Archon Books, 1987), 134.

Similarly, Trevor N. Dupuy suggested the U.S. military after World War II had not learned enough from Germanic models, although the object lesson for Dupuy was not Germanic vitalism but rather its institutional excellence as represented by the "genius" of the same general staff Telford Taylor had roundly condemned as hopelessly compromised by Nazism.[14]

These and similar critiques highlight the point that the U.S. military and its civilian masters, although quite critical of German military culture and its fixations in the immediate aftermath of World War II, soon came to admire German accomplishments so fervently that one could speak, as John Mearsheimer pithily noted, of an American military establishment that by the 1970s was exhibiting an embarrassing case of "*Wehrmacht* penis envy."[15]

Early signs of such envy were caught in *About Face*, an American bestseller in which U.S. Army Colonel David Hackworth commented at length on the post-war U.S. military's infatuation with all things German. Among items big and small, it led to the Army's green "Class A" uniform and the M-60 machine gun (based on the German MG-42), the larger trend being the Army's post-Eisenhower decision to favor vitalistic elite forces enabled by the latest technology over a mass conscript force enabled by a patriotic call to arms.

Similarly, Paul Fussell noted how in World War II the Yanks knew "where it counted their arms and equipment were worse than the Germans' .... They knew that their own tanks ... were ridiculously under-armed and under-armored, so that they were inevitably destroyed in an open encounter with an equal number of German Panzers." A common illustration of emasculating German superiority is to juxtapose a puny American Sherman tank from 1942 (or an even punier pre-war British light tank, as Fussell does) to a German "King Tiger" tank from 1944; the lesson of "Heinz's gun was far bigger" certainly evokes a sense of phallic adulation, though for every heavy King Tiger crawling across the battlefield there were roughly 100 medium Shermans motoring about.

---

[14] T. N. Dupuy, *A Genius for War: The German Army and General Staff, 1807–1945* (Englewood Cliffs, NJ: Prentice-Hall, 1977).

[15] Daniel P. Bolger critiqued the enthusiasm of "maneuverists" in the U.S. Army in "Maneuver Warfare Reconsidered," in *Maneuver Warfare: An Anthology*, ed. Richard D. Hooker Jr. (Novato: Presidio Press, 1993), 19–41, on 27. Herein, Bolger attributed the phrase "Wehrmacht penis envy" to Mearsheimer.

But "quantity has a quality all its own" is a telling proverb for Russians, not Americans.[16] And most American military men conveniently forgot how much the "cutting edge" *Wehrmacht* was dependent throughout the war on horses for mobility and logistics.[17] Elite, tactically innovative, "special" forces and cutting edge technology became the answer, a formula for victory tested and found wanting in the jungles and highlands and rice paddies of Vietnam. Rather than focusing on a fundamentally misguided grand-strategic vision about the perils of dominoes falling, the U.S. military decided to do more of the same, only better, and this time with a thoroughly professionalized, non-conscript force.

Loving the Alien

Among the more disturbing aspects of an over-hyping of Germanic military models and modes of thinking is their inappropriateness to America's strategic situation and needs. Germany and the United States, as Dennis Showalter has noted, exist at opposite ends of a geopolitical spectrum. Germany's central position in Europe, together with the centrality of war in Prusso-German culture and related desires for more "living space," impelled Wilhelmine and Nazi Germany to adopt a frontloaded, operational/tactical focus to its wars.[18] The relative isolation of the U.S. (granted by the Atlantic and Pacific Oceans) and persistent isolationist tendencies within American politics and culture impelled (or should have impelled) the U.S. to take a top-level, grand-strategic focus. In Showalter's pithy description, "For the U.S. military to admire Germanic methods and modes of thinking uncritically is like a squirrel envying a turtle."[19]

Why did the U.S. squirrel seek to emulate the Germanic turtle? For since the 1970s, if not earlier, the U.S. *has* neglected to define a grand strategic vision even as it has focused on achieving a "revolution in

---

[16] David Hackworth, *About Face: The Odyssey of an American Warrior* (New York: Simon and Schuster, 1989); Paul Fussell, *Wartime: Understanding and Behavior in the Second World War* (Oxford: Oxford University Press, 1989), 10–11, 268.

[17] See R. L. DiNardo, *Mechanized Juggernaut or Military Anachronism?: Horses and the German Army of WWII* (Mechanicsburg, PA: Stackpole Books, 1991, 2008).

[18] D. E. Showalter, "German Grand Strategy: A Contradiction in Terms?" *Militägeschichtliche Mitteilungen* 58 (1990): 65–102.

[19] Personal communication to the author.

military affairs" based on operational/tactical prowess and technical innovation. One truly wonders why the negative example of Germany in 1918 and 1945 failed to provide a compelling narrative against repeating the narrowly tactical and technical fixations that contributed to the utter defeat of two Germanic empires.

Recall that the Prussians won decisively, almost too easily, in 1866 against Austria and again in 1870–71 against France.[20] Recall too that interpreting the reasons for victory is sometimes as difficult, perhaps more so, than explaining those for defeat. It is fair to say that Prussia fell in love with "force multipliers" like railroads and rifles[21] while at the same time putting its faith in front-loaded wars in which operational and tactical virtuosity would overcome the longest of odds. Thus Germany entered World War I with the same basic philosophy it had used at Königgrätz and Sedan: Win the decisive battle through operational/tactical excellence achieved by peerless professionalism at the point of attack.[22]

Whether on the Western Front in 1914–18 or the Eastern Front in 1941–45, the decisive battle eluded Germany, a fact that soon revealed its bankrupt approach to grand strategy. The resultant strategic dilemma in both world wars was a protracted, two-front struggle against the longest of odds, odds that even the most energetic "can-do" warrior spirit could not overcome. Ironically, Germany had ignored the key Clausewitzian lesson that operational and tactical successes are ultimately meaningless if they fail to generate the conditions required for strategic success.

Compare this to the United States' experience in Vietnam or during and after Desert Storm in 1991 and Operation Iraqi Freedom in 2003 and one sees disturbing parallels. In Vietnam, lightning-quick mobility and superior firepower at the point of attack never translated into decisive victory. In Iraq, tactical and technological virtuosity in the hands of narrowly competent war managers against a symmetrical (and ultimately inferior) opponent led to seemingly quick and decisive victories, but the latter proved illusory when events at higher

---

[20] D. E. Showalter, *The Wars of German Unification* (London: Hodder Arnold, 2004).

[21] D. E. Showalter, *Railroads and Rifles: Soldiers, Technology, and the Unification of Germany* (Hamden, CT: Archon Books, 1976).

[22] D. E. Showalter, "From Deterrence to Doomsday Machine: The German Way of War, 1890–1914," *The Journal of Military History* 64 (2000): 679–710.

geo-political levels spun out of control. The result was strategic paralysis in the U.S. and, whether in Vietnam or in the recent cases of Iraq as well as Afghanistan, unexpectedly long and debilitating wars, ultimately ending in costly defeats (or in pyrrhic victories that lacked closure).

Such is the tragic if predictable result of a country too willing to embrace that which is alien to it. For what could be more alien to a democratic republic than to embrace the warrior methods and mystique of the Germanic Reichs? Why would the United States, founded on the citizen-soldier ideal, an ideal that became "a defining characteristic of American history for over two centuries ... [that] anyone with sufficient intelligence, good will, and preliminary education" could arrive at a suitable level of competence in the profession of arms,[23] come to idolize Prussian war theorists and German military prowess, even when the latter was inseparably connected to and driven by Nazi ideology during World War II?[24] Why indeed?

Reading Clausewitz Selectively

> Clausewitz spoke almost directly to the American experience [in Vietnam], like no one else did. Clausewitzian theory is going to define and determine the conflict in Iraq [in 1990–91]. Whether we realize it or not. – Colonel Harry Summers Jr.[25]

Selectivity was not just applied to recalling the composition and thrust of the *Wehrmacht*; Clausewitz was also selectively read by the U.S. military. The first clear sign of a "cult of Clausewitz" in the U.S. Army appeared soon after the Vietnam War, linked as it was to the Army's internal critiques of its flawed strategy and desultory military performance. The cult served to revive the spirit and sense of purpose of a deflated but newly "all volunteer" (or professionalized) U.S. military. Senior U.S. military leaders came to embrace the idea of war – not as "all hell," as General William T. Sherman famously opined – but as a

---

[23] D. E. Showalter, jacket blurb for Michael S. Neiberg, *Making Citizen-Soldiers: ROTC and the Ideology of American Military Service* (Cambridge: Harvard University Press, 2000).

[24] On Nazi ideology and its pervasiveness within the ranks, see Omer Bartov, *Hitler's Army: Soldiers, Nazis, and War in the Third Reich* (Oxford: Oxford University Press, 1991).

[25] Achenbach, "War and the Cult of Clausewitz," D4.

vitalistic act, one in which well-trained leaders could impose their will on events. And so too did many of their civilian overseers.

For these officers and leaders, war was viewed not as destructive but constructive. It was not the last resort of democracies, but the preferred recourse of "creative" warlords who demonstrated their mastery of it by cultivating such qualities as flexibility, adaptability, and quickness. One aimed to get inside the enemy's "decision cycle," the so-called OODA loop[26] – the U.S. Air Force's version of Frederick the Great's *Auftragstaktik* – while at the same time cultivating a "warrior ethos" within a tight-knit (post-draft) professional army that was to stand above, and also separate from, ordinary American citizens.

A highly selective reading of Clausewitz and a growing idolization of the fighting power and techniques of a World War II-era German military were telling manifestations of a growing militarism within an American society that remained largely oblivious to the slow strangulation of its citizen-soldier ideal. At the same time, through a selective reading of its past the post-Vietnam American military set the stage for the glorification of a new generation of warrior-leaders. Old "Blood and Guts" himself, the warrior-leader George S. Patton – the commander as artist-creator-genius – was celebrated; Omar N. Bradley – the bespectacled GI general and steadfast soldier-citizen – was neglected.

Not coincidentally, a new vision of the battlefield emerged by the 1980s in which the U.S. military aimed, without the slightest sense of irony, for "total situational awareness" and "full spectrum dominance," goals that, if attained, promised commanders the almost god-like ability to master the storm of steel, to calm the waves, to command the air. In the process, any sense of war as thoroughly unpredictable and enormously wasteful was lost. In this growing infatuation with military prowess, the U.S. celebrated its ability to *Blitzkrieg* its enemies, promising rapid and decisive victories that would be largely bloodless (at least for the U.S.).

Among the many lessons conveniently neglected, however, was this: The proto-*Blitzkrieg* of the Kaiser's military in 1918, or the Nazi

---

[26] Popularized by John Boyd, an influential Air Force fighter pilot and tactician, the OODA Loop (Observe, Orient, Decide, Act) was spoken of in almost religious terms when I was in the Air Force. Countless times I heard: "We must get inside the opponent's OODA loop if we are to prevail." Success in war was thus expressed in terms reminiscent of a knife fight between fighter jocks. See Grant T. Hammond, *The Mind of War: John Boyd and American Security* (Washington, D.C: Smithsonian Institution Press, 2001).

Blitzkrieg of 1939–42, ended in both cases with Germany thoroughly thrashed by opponents who continued to fight even when the odds seemed longest. What a remarkable, if not to say bizarre, turnabout! The army and country the U.S. had soundly beaten in two world wars (with a lot of help from allies, especially, of course, the Soviet Union in 1941–45) had become a beacon for the U.S. military after Vietnam.

A further irony here, as David Schoenbaum has noted, is that the U.S. military would have been a good deal better off if its people had actually read Clausewitz in full, "rather than continue to gaze in wonderment at those guys in field grey, who did not even have to read him in translation, and who still managed to get him so disastrously wrong."[27]

How did this come to pass? How did the U.S. manage to get Clausewitz so disastrously wrong?

The New (American) Masters of Blitzkrieg

Busts of the Prussian Clausewitz reside in places of honor today at both the Army War College at Carlisle Barracks, Pennsylvania, and the National War College in Washington, D.C.[28] Clausewitz was a complex writer, and his vision of war was both dense and rich, defying easy simplification. But that has not stopped the U.S. military from simplifying him. Ask the average officer about Clausewitz, and he will mention "war as the continuation of politics" and maybe something about "the fog and friction of war" – and that is about it. What is really meant by this rendition of Clausewitz for dummies[29] is that, though warfare may seem extreme, it is really a perfectly sensible form of violent political discourse between nation-states.

Such an officer may grudgingly admit that, thanks to fog and friction, "no plan survives contact with the enemy." What he is secretly thinking, however, is that it will not matter at all, not given the U.S.

---

[27] Personal communication to the author.

[28] A statue of Frederick the Great, proponent of *Auftragstaktik*, also has a prominent place of honor at the Army War College in Carlisle, PA.

[29] When I was at the Air Force Academy in the early 1990s, a one-page primer of Clausewitz's theory circulated within the History department. Few officers (myself included) had the time to read *On War* in full. Even fewer, perhaps, sought to challenge an emerging orthodoxy that viewed Clausewitz as offering a road map (however unclear) to military success.

military's "mastery" of *Auftragstaktik*, achieved in part through next-generation weaponry that provides both "total situational awareness" and a decisive, war-winning edge.

Highlighting this faith in masterly quick wars achieved in part with next-generation weaponry was an article penned by Condoleezza Rice in 2000. Rice, soon to become President George W. Bush's National Security Advisor, claimed the U.S. military held a "commanding technological lead" that translated to "a battlefield advantage over any competitor." All that was needed to complete an American "revolution in military affairs" was to make this military force even more lethal, primarily by making it "lighter" and "more mobile and agile," in part by equipping it with radically new weaponry as "force-multipliers."[30]

The emphasis on speed, agility, and defeating the enemy through dislocation – what later became known as "shock and awe" against Iraq in 2003 – reflected a collective understanding of *Blitzkrieg* as a formula to replicate (and improve upon) the stunningly rapid German conquests that occurred during the opening stages of World War II. After all, what else was American "shock and awe" than an overwhelming show of force that was intended to paralyze the enemy? A paralysis[31] effected by instilling fear and terror, a visceral experience of mind-freezing intensity due to the sheer scale and rapidity of destruction and the sense of helplessness generated thereby. Think of German *Stukas* with screaming sirens raining precision death from the skies – or volleys of American precision guided munitions (PGMs) and cruise missiles doing the same three generations later over Baghdad.

Small wonder that President Bush, Vice President Dick Cheney, and Secretary of Defense Donald Rumsfeld were eager to go to war in Iraq in 2003. They saw themselves as the new masters of *Blitzkrieg*, the new warlords (or "Vulcans," to use a Roman term that was popular back then),[32] the inheritors of the best methods of German fighting power and efficiency, now enhanced by the added lethality of American technological know-how. A book cries out to be written to capture the zeitgeist of this moment, perhaps with the title: "Quest for

---

[30] C. Rice, "Promoting the National Interest," *Foreign Affairs* 79 (2000): 45–62.
[31] "Shock and awe" was also intended to produce paralysis by "decapitation" of the enemy's leadership, but U.S. efforts to target Saddam Hussein's leadership in the opening days of Operation Iraqi Freedom failed to find their targets.
[32] James Mann, *Rise of the Vulcans: The History of Bush's War Cabinet* (New York: Viking Penguin, 2004).

Decisive Victory: From Quagmire in Vietnam to *Blitzkrieg* in the Middle East, 1975–2003."[33]

This quest for, and belief in, German-style lightning victory through relentless military proficiency is best captured in Max Boot's gushing Neo-Conservative tribute to the U.S. military, published soon after Bush's self-congratulatory and self-adulatory "Mission Accomplished" speech in May 2003. For Boot, America's apparent victory in Iraq had to "rank as one of the signal achievements in military history." In his words:[34]

> Previously, the gold standard of operational excellence had been the German *blitzkrieg* through the Low Countries and France in 1940. The Germans managed to conquer France, the Netherlands, and Belgium in just 44 days, at a cost of 'only' 27,000 dead soldiers. The United States and Britain took just 26 days to conquer Iraq (a country 80 percent of the size of France), at a cost of 161 dead, making fabled generals such as Erwin Rommel and Heinz Guderian seem positively incompetent by comparison.
>
> This spectacular success was not achieved easily, however. It required overcoming the traditional mentality of some active and retired officers who sniped relentlessly at Rumsfeld right up until the giant statue of Saddam fell in Baghdad's Firdos Square on April 9, 2003. Winning the war in Iraq first required rooting out the old American way of war from its Washington redoubts.

The so-called "old American way of war," based on materiel and numerical superiority, of caution and patience and exit strategies, had given way in Max Boot's mind to a "new" American way of war that made even past German masters of lightning war – the Rommels and Guderians – appear as rank amateurs. Yet how likely is it that future military historians will celebrate American General Tommy Franks and elevate him above the "incompetent" Rommel and Guderian? Such praise, even then, was more than hyperbolic: it was absurd. And in its very absurdity, it was revelatory of a stunning American hubris.

Throughout history, many Americans, especially frontline combat veterans, have known the hell of war. It is one big reason why the U.S. had traditionally been reluctant to keep a large standing military.

---

[33] Riffing off of Robert M. Citino, *Quest for Decisive Victory: From Stalemate to Blitzkrieg in Europe, 1899–1940* (Lawrence: University Press of Kansas, 2002).

[34] Max Boot, "The New American Way of War," *Foreign Affairs* 82 (July/August 2003): 41–58; available at http://www.foreignaffairs.com/articles/58996/max-boot/the-new-american-way-of-war.

But the Cold War, the strategy of containment, and illusions about imitating and then surpassing the German *Wehrmacht* changed everything. Many in the U.S. military (and outside of the military) began to see war not as a human-made calamity but as a creative science and art. This new breed of warlords were not so much "Vulcans" (even if they reveled in that label) as they were disciples of *Blitzkrieg* Americanized, forever in search of force multipliers that promised rapid and decisive victories achieved through an almost Prussian mania for tactical excellence.

How had this paradigm shift occurred? Reeling from a seemingly inexplicable and unimaginable defeat in Vietnam, the U.S. officer corps used Clausewitz to crawl out of its collective fog. By reading him selectively and reaffirming its faith in military professionalism and precision weaponry, it convinced itself as well as its civilian leaders and admirers to believe it had attained mastery over warfare.[35]

Forgotten was the fact that Clausewitz had compared war not only to a rational political process but to a highly risky, and highly unpredictable, game of cards. Call it the ultimate high-stakes poker match. Even the player with the best cards, the highest stack of chips, does not always win. Guile and endurance matter. So too does nerve, even luck. And having a home-table advantage does not hurt either.

But none of that seemed to matter to a U.S. military that aped Germanic models while over-hyping Germanic successes. The result? A so-called "new American way of war" that was simply a desiccated version of the old German one, which had produced nothing but catastrophic defeat for Germany in both 1918 and 1945 – and disaster for Europe as well.

Perhaps we should not be surprised, then, that American efforts in Iraq, Afghanistan, and elsewhere are contributing to the decline of the American empire, as well as bringing disaster to ordinary Iraqis and Afghans caught between overweening American militarism and the cruel realities of war.[36]

---

[35] During the Clinton years, Secretary of State Madeleine Albright once asked, "What's the point of having this superb military you're always talking about if we can't use it?" She might have been better served to ask whether this military was as superb as it claimed. More fundamentally, she might have asked whether building and using even a "superb" military was truly in the best interests of the nation.

[36] Besides the writings of Andrew Bacevich, see Nir Rosen, *Aftermath: Following the Bloodshed of America's Wars in the Muslim World* (New York: Nation Books, 2010), and Nick Turse, ed., *The Case for Withdrawal from Afghanistan* (New York: Verso, 2010).

Warrior-States: The German Reichs (and The United States)

It often comes as a shock to Americans, but the U.S. Army was not the world's best in the field either in World War I or in World War II. And thank heavens for that. That dubious distinction falls to Kaiser Wilhelm's army in 1914, and to Hitler's *Wehrmacht* in 1941. Even toward the end of World War II, the American army was still often outmaneuvered and outclassed by its German foe. Because victory has a way of papering over faults and altering memories, few but professional historians today recall the many shortcomings of the U.S. military in both world wars.

But that is precisely the point: The American military made mistakes because it was often ill-trained, rushed into combat too quickly, and handled by officers lacking in experience. Put simply, in both world wars it lacked the tactical virtuosity of its German counterpart.

And here is the question to ponder: At what price virtuosity? In both world wars, the Germans were the best soldiers because they had trained and fought the most, because their societies were geared, mentally and in most other ways, for war, and because they celebrated and valued feats of arms above all other contributions one could make to society and culture. Being "the best soldiers" meant that senior German leaders – whether the Kaiser, Field Marshal Paul von Hindenburg, that Teutonic titan of World War I, or Hitler – always expected them to prevail. The mentality was: "We're the world's best military. How can we possibly lose unless we quit – or those (fill in your civilian traitors of choice) stab us in the back?"[37]

If this mentality sounds familiar, it is because it is the one we Americans have imbibed and internalized over the last three decades. German warriors and their leaders knew no limitations until it was too late for them to recover from ceaseless combat, imperial overstretch, and economic collapse. Today, the U.S. military, and by extension American culture, is caught in a similar bind. After all, if we truly believe ours to be "the world's best military" (and, judging by how often

---

[37] On the stab-in-the-back myth that emerged in the closing stages of World War I, see W. J. Astore and D. E. Showalter, *Hindenburg: Icon of German Militarism* (Dulles, VA: Potomac Books, 2005), 80–81, 102–03. On stab-in-the-back myths in recent American culture, see W. J. Astore, "The Enemy Within: Finding American Backs to Stab," posted at TomDispatch.com on November 6, 2007 and available at www.tomdispatch.com/post/174859.

the claim is repeated in the echo chamber of the mainstream media, we evidently do),[38] how can the U.S. possibly lose in Iraq or Afghanistan? And, if the "impossible" somehow happens, how can the American military be to blame? If America's "warfighters" (indeed, our *heroes*)[39] are indeed "the best," someone else must have betrayed them – appeasing politicians, lily-livered liberals, duplicitous and weak-willed allies like the recalcitrant Iraqis or the corrupt Afghans or the peacenik Dutch, you name it.

Today, the American military is arguably the world's best, at least in terms of its advanced armaments and its ability to destroy. But what does it say about American military and civilian leaders that they are so taken with this form of power? And why exactly is it so good to be the "best" at this? Just ask a German military veteran – among the few who survived the wars, that is – in a warrior-state that went berserk in a febrile quest for its own version of "full spectrum dominance."

But is it truly fair to claim that the U.S. is a warrior-state? To answer this, a good place to start is with troop veneration. A cult of the warrior often covers up a variety of sins. It helps, among other things, to hide the true costs, and often the futility, of the wars being fought. At an extreme, as the war began to turn dramatically against the Nazis in 1943, Germans who attempted to protest Hitler's failed strategy and the catastrophic costs of his war were accused of (and often executed for) betraying Germany's "heroes" at the front.

The United States is not a totalitarian state, so surely it can hazard a few criticisms of its wars and even occasionally of the behavior of some of its troops, without its people facing charges of stabbing the troops in the back and aiding the enemy. Yet such is not the case in contemporary American political and cultural discourse. The one unforgivable sin in America today is *not* to "support our troops," as so many magnetic ribbons remind Americans to do. Supporting the troops often extends to granting them unquestioned "hero" status in American society, even if all they have done to this point is don a uniform and complete basic training. My local post office proudly displays a photo collage of young American troops labeled "Our Hometown Heroes." As I journey

---

[38] During his pep talk to U.S. troops in Afghanistan in December 2010, President Obama praised the U.S. military as "the finest fighting force that the world has ever known." Such hyperbolic statements go virtually uncriticized in American culture.

[39] On the dangers of assigning hero status to all American service members, see W. J. Astore, "The Harm in Hero Worship," *Los Angeles Times*, July 22, 2010, A23 (Op-ed).

through downtown Williamsport, Pennsylvania, I see photo placards on posts celebrating a particular "hometown hero" for his or her decision to enlist in the military. At college graduation ceremonies I have attended, the graduates who receive by far the loudest and longest round of applause are those who have joined the U.S. military.

Having made a career of service in the U.S. military, I think this sentiment is precisely backwards. It is a *privilege* to serve; it is a *privilege* to defend the U.S. Constitution and all it represents. Making a special virtue out of military service is not a practice I associate with a representative democracy that enshrines individual liberties. Indeed, boasting about having the world's finest fighting force (not just the finest now, but the finest *ever*, according to President Barack Obama)[40] echoes more than faintly the bombast and arrogance of Nazi Germany.

Loving the (Sanitized) German Wehrmacht

There is a mystique that surrounds the German military (especially the *Wehrmacht*) that remains quite powerful in the United States. Admirers praise the Germans for their tactical skill and relentless efficiency, while ignoring or dismissing their unbounded ambition and utter ruthlessness. On reading an earlier version of this chapter, an American military man wrote to me of *Wehrmacht* soldiers as "consummate professionals." When I pointed out the war crimes of the *Wehrmacht*, he dismissed these as irrelevant. What mattered to him was Germanic fighting power, and that alone. Such people refuse to connect the obsessive militarism of Nazi Germany – a fanatical focus on technique and "hardness" divorced from restraint and morality – to the amorality and often the utter brutality of Nazi methods and practices. They celebrate Germany's tactical "brilliance" while denying (or failing to see) the murderous efficiency and barbarism that accompanied it.[41]

---

[40] For a transcript of Obama's speech from December 2010, see http://www.nytimes.com/2010/12/04/us/politics/04prexy-text.html.

[41] At my current institution, I had a student come to class wearing a *Schutzstaffel* (SS) Death Head's insignia on his collar. When I attempted to explain to him the horrendous crimes of the SS, he dismissed these as much exaggerated. Perhaps this student was engaged in a form of in-your-face taboo-breaking, as manifested in Dennis Showalter's words by "outlaw bikers wearing Nazi helmets and regalia, through the legions of souvenir collectors, to the buyers of the detailed unit histories of the SS offered by certain specialized publishers." Ronald Smelser analyzes this disturbing phenomenon in *The Myth of the Eastern Front: The Nazi-Soviet War in American Popular Culture* (Cambridge: Cambridge University Press, 2007).

Well into the 1980s, and in some quarters even today, the myth of the *Wehrmacht's* "clean shield" – of honorable soldiers fighting as cleanly as they could given the primitive nature of the Eastern Front – was advanced, protected and sustained. Even the *Waffen* SS largely succeeded in depicting itself as "soldiers like the rest," as Dennis Showalter notes.[42] While scholarly studies are now available that debunk and disprove the myth of the *Wehrmacht's* clean shield, much of this material remains "virtually unknown outside academic circles," Showalter concludes.[43]

What remains far better known are all those Ballantine war books, some of them written by German officers, such as Heinz Guderian's *Panzer Leader*. They were everywhere in the 1960s and 1970s, even at book racks in Rexall drug stores, recalls Philip Wohlstetter. In his words, they provided "Sanitized versions of the Eastern front campaign (with the *Einsatzgruppen* and the exterminations edited out) prefaced by admiring intros from American generals, one soldier honoring another."[44]

Such sentiments were reinforced by admirers such as B. H. Liddell Hart, who offered a thoroughly professional and morally observant corps of German leaders in *The Other Side of the Hill* (1948), published in the United States as *The German Generals Talk*. And talk they did, of honorable and skillful military campaigns betrayed by Hitler's meddling and micro-managing, of a massive and anonymous Red Army that could have been overcome if only the "Bohemian Corporal" had deferred to his much wiser field commanders. To American military men, this theme may have proved attractive indeed, vexed as they were with containing their own "red menace" while keeping their own meddling civilian masters in check.

---

[42] See Showalter's brilliant response to "Which Side? Selective Memory" on the H-Net Discussion Network, July 25, 2006, available at http://h-net.msu.edu/cgi-bin/logbrowse.pl?trx=vx&list=h-war&month=0607&week=d&msg=1cE7F1aNRm/SyujeewsTCw&user=&pw=.

[43] See, for example, Omer Bartov, *The Eastern Front, 1941–45, German Troops and the Barbarisation of Warfare* (New York: Palgrave, 1985, 2001); Stephen G. Fritz, *Frontsoldaten: The German Soldier in World War II* (Lexington: The University Press of Kentucky, 1995); Ben Shepherd, *War in the Wild East: The German Army and Soviet Partisans* (Harvard: Harvard University Press, 2004); and most importantly Wolfram Wette, *The Wehrmacht: History, Myth, Reality* (Harvard: Harvard University Press, 2006).

[44] Wohlstetter, personal communication to the author. For a concise exposé of Guderian's checkered career, see Russell A. Hart, *Guderian: Panzer Pioneer or Myth Maker?* (Dulles, VA: Potomac Books, 2006).

Hollywood as well played an important role in painting a flattering picture of the "Good German Officer": noble, high-minded, playing Bach or Beethoven on the gramophone in refined settings even as German troops rampaged. It was as if those high-brow and noble soldierly archetypes were at several removes from the ignoble and indecent SS/Gestapo/Nazis, but who were nonetheless forced to follow orders from those same deranged, black leather-jacketed goons. In many cinematic re-creations, one was left with the impression that the Nazi Party's apparatus had disembarked from a UFO to exert an alien mastery over a tragically resistant breed of decent and honorable warrior-aristocrats. In various films you see versions of the latter raising an eyebrow, either resignedly or quizzically, to carry out yet another reckless or foolish or brutal order of the Führer. Such cinematic images suggested these men were both above the fray but also victims of a cruel twist of fate in that they were "forced" by their oath of office to carry out such distasteful orders hailing from such a disreputable source.

And the inflated hero worship – notably in the film "Valkyrie," starring Tom Cruise – of the far-too-late and politically naïve attempt to kill Hitler and take over: Why, one may ask, should we celebrate such "men of honor," men who had been all-too-happy only a year earlier to strut like *Übermenschen* when it all seemed to be going their way? Movies like "Valkyrie" are Hollywood kitsch and hogwash of the highest order – and are no less dangerous for this fact.[45]

The reality was far different. The truth is that the *Wehrmacht* and especially its senior leaders were, almost to a man, supporters of Hitler and his cruelly expansionist designs. Some may have been more pragmatic than others; some may have worked quietly to moderate the worst excesses of Nazism; some may have truly suffered from a sense of misplaced and seemingly irreversible loyalties;[46] but nearly all went along, and those few who expressed concerns were either cowed or bribed into silence.[47]

---

[45] A hearty thanks to Marten Hutt for sharing his thoughts with me on Hollywood's role in advancing the "clean shield" and "good German soldier" archetype.

[46] See, for example, Christopher Sykes, *Tormented Loyalty: The Story of A German Aristocrat Who Defied Hitler* (New York: Harper & Row, 1969), about Adam von Trott.

[47] Norman J. W. Goda, "Black Marks: Hitler's Bribery of His Senior Officers during World War II," *Journal of Modern History* 72 (2000): 413–52; Gerd R. Ueberschär and Winfried Vogel, *Dienen und Verdienen: Hitlers Geschenke an seine Eliten* (Frankfurt: Ficher Taschenbuch Verlag, 2000).

One simply cannot separate German military excellence in World War II from the horrific ideology to which it pledged allegiance. Nevertheless, many Americans apparently believed (and continue to believe) that such separation is tenable. Perhaps this was attributable in part to the presence of so many German "experts" who came to this country after World War II to work on U.S. governmental projects as diverse as rocketry to computers to strategy. But the purposes to which the *Wehrmacht* was put – and its ready acquiescence to and complicity in war crimes – cannot help but leave behind a toxic residue, one that, if ignored in a febrile pursuit of warrior excellence, will eventually erode the American citizen-soldier ideal, leaving in its place an ideal of a hard warrior-elite that is profoundly antithetical to democracy.

The Emerging American Cult of the Warrior

In a seminar I attended at the U.S. Holocaust Memorial Museum in 2002, Henry Friedlander highlighted the adjectives used by the German SS to describe its best operatives: action words like "relentless," "decisive," "tireless," and "powerful," and character words like "loyal" and "direct" and "simple."[48] At that time, I was a lieutenant colonel on active duty, and I had seen those very words, and similar superlatives, used in our efficiency and performance reports in praise of American officers. Any military, of course, is going to favor men and women of few words and much action – "Type A" hard-chargers in U.S. military jargon – but the bias against thoughtful, contemplative, cautious, and compassionate operatives, a bias inculcated by the SS,[49] appears to be taking hold within the U.S. military.[50]

---

[48] On the use of fanatical words and similar "hard" superlatives in Nazi Germany, see Otto Klemperer, *The Language of the Third Reich* (London: Continuum, 1957, 2006).

[49] One thinks here of the young SS officers' contempt for their "weak" commander, Major Wilhelm Trapp, who spoke haltingly and with some pain of Police Battalion 101's mission to kill thousands of defenseless civilians, as depicted in Christopher Browning's *Ordinary Men: Reserve Police Battalion 101 and the Final Solution in Poland* (New York: HarperCollins, 1998).

[50] Consider the sentiments expressed by U.S. Army Colonel Dan Williams in September 2010 that "War does change you, I believe in a better way, a noble way. A decade of combat has made us very hard. It has made us an incredibly strong Army. I believe we do have a warrior class in this country." In David Wood, "In the 10th Year of War, A Harder Army, A More Distant America," posted on Politics Daily on 9/9/10; available at http://www.politicsdaily.com/2010/09/09/in-the-10th-year-of-war-a-harder-army-a-more-distant-america.

Viewed from a different angle, if the Germans were "the finest soldiers in the world" in World Wars I and II, why had American doughboys and dogfaces come up short? Along with the need for tougher and more realistic training, American military leaders seemed to conclude that a new ethos had to be inculcated: the idea of soldiers as hardened "warriors"[51] (even as "warfighters"). Such an ethos was concomitant to a more general admiration for the warrior spirit of the German military: a sort of spiritual "force multiplier" that would enable American forces to prevail even when they were outnumbered (as doubtless they would be if facing a full-fledged Warsaw Pact invasion).

Ever since 9/11/2001, American troops have been celebrated as "warfighters," even occasionally as members of "Generation Kill," judging by an HBO series by that title. Meanwhile, U.S. politicians, from presidents on down, are remarkably proud of declaring the U.S. military to be "the world's best." Open up any American defense publication today and you cannot miss advertisements from defense contractors, all eagerly touting the ways they "serve" America's warfighters. Listen to Congressional testimony and you will hear the by now obligatory incantation about America's troops being the best in the world.

All this is, by now, so often repeated – so eagerly accepted – that few in America seem to recall how against the American grain it really is. If anything, it is far more in keeping with the bellicose traditions and bumptious rhetoric of Imperial Germany than of an American republic that began its march to independence with patriotic Minutemen in revolt against King George. A small but meaningful act against creeping militarism would be for Americans collectively to repudiate the "world's best warfighter" rhetoric and re-embrace instead a tradition of reluctant but resolute citizen-soldiers.

Until recent times, the American military was justly proud of being a force of citizen-soldiers. It did not matter whether you were talking about those famed Revolutionary War Minutemen, courageous Civil War volunteers, or the "Greatest Generation" conscripts of World War II. After all, Americans had a long tradition of being distrustful of the

---

[51] America's soldiers and airmen are reminded they are "warriors" in "creeds" that many of them (and their families) display with pride. Here's an excerpt from the *Airman's Creed* (2007): "I am an American Airman./I am a Warrior./I have answered my nation's call.//I am an American Airman./My mission is to fly, fight, and win./I am faithful to a proud heritage,/a tradition of honor,/and a legacy of valor." The Army's *Soldier's Creed* (2003) makes the same point about the need to be a warrior first and foremost.

very idea of a large, permanent army, as well as of giving potentially disruptive authority to generals.

America's tradition of citizen-soldiery was (and could still be) one of the great strengths of this country. Let me give you two well-known examples of such citizen-soldiers. Eugene B. Sledge served in the U.S. Marines during World War II, surviving two unimaginably brutal campaigns on the islands of Peleliu and Okinawa. His memoir *With the Old Breed* is arguably the best account of ground warfare in the Pacific. After three years of selfless, heroic service to his country, Sledge gladly returned to civilian life, eventually becoming a professor of biology. His conclusion – that "war is brutish, inglorious, and a terrible waste" – is one seconded by many a combat veteran.

Richard (Dick) Winters' exploits were captured in the HBO series *Band of Brothers*. He rose from platoon commander to battalion commander, serving in the elite 101st Airborne Division during World War II. A hero beloved by his men, Winters wanted nothing more than to quit the military and return to the civilian world. After the war, he lived a quiet life as a businessman in Pennsylvania, rarely mentioning his service and refusing to use his military rank for personal gratification.

Sledge and Winters were regular guys who answered their country's call. What comes across in their memoirs, as well as in the many letters I have read from World War II dogfaces, was the desire to win the war, return home, hang up the uniform, and never again fire a shot in anger. These men were war-enders, not warfighters. Indeed, they would have been sickened by the very idea of being warfighters.

Where did this warrior and warfighter trope come from? In a post-Vietnam military, American elites decided that creating a professional caste of "warriors" was preferable to relying on civilian conscripts. The former promised to be more tractable than sullen draftees, thus more reliable, especially during long and unpopular wars. With fraggings, work stoppages, and other manifestations of unit disintegration[52] in Vietnam fresh in their minds, America's senior leaders sought to eliminate the tensions that had boiled over when a restless and alienated class of draftees met warrior cadres of career officers and NCOs. And the most direct way to do this? Eliminate the draftees by abolishing the draft, as was in fact done in 1973.

---

[52] Cincinnatus [Cecil B. Currey], *Self-Destruction: The Disintegration and Decay of the United States Army during the Vietnam Era* (New York: W. W. Norton & Co., 1981).

An all-volunteer (fully professional) military eliminated alienated and disaffected draftees, but at the cost of separating the military from American society at large,[53] even as that society increasingly celebrated and idolized its troops. After the terrorist attacks of 9/11/2001, Americans readily accepted a permanent state of war fought by America's heroes as necessary for its security, as well as for vengeance against its enemies. The very separation of the military from the rest of society, and of society from the realities of war – a new form of American isolationism, as I have argued elsewhere[54] – worked to facilitate perpetual war, as did the fact that Americans had come to believe that war was creative politics, as opposed to so much waste and murder.

The result, as Andrew J. Bacevich has argued, was a new American militarism that extolled military power and its own virtuosity even as it failed to recognize limits to this form of power.[55] Meanwhile, a deliberate de-politicization of military service (an idea captured by the phrase, "Happy to be here, proud to serve"), which supplanted the World War II-era idea of fighting for noble causes (such as FDR's Four Freedoms), was itself supplanted by an increasingly politicized military.[56] The result: Americans continue to applaud the troops as warriors while watching them become more and more ideologically driven along partisan political lines. Thus their resemblance to Prussianized elites with hands collectively grasping the levers of power continues to grow.

The term "warfighter" – a combination of "warrior" and "war fighting" – suggests a person who lives for war, who spoils for a fight.

---

[53] Sounding the alarm was Thomas E. Ricks, "The Widening Gap Between the Military and Society," *The Atlantic* 280 (July 1997): 66–78. See also Ricks, "Is American Military Professionalism Declining?" *Proceedings* [U.S. Naval Institute], 124 (July 1998): 26–29; Adam Clymer, "Sharp Divergence Found in Views of Military and Civilians," *The New York Times*, September 9, 1999, A16; and Bradley Graham, "Civilians, Military Seen Growing Apart: Study Finds Partisan Armed Forces 'Elite,'" *Washington Post*, October 18, 1999, A17. Such concerns were linked to the military's not-so-veiled contempt for its then commander-in-chief, Bill Clinton, and his alleged record of draft-dodging during Vietnam.

[54] Astore, "The New American Isolationism: The Cost of Turning Away from War's Horrific Realities," posted on TomDispatch.com on 10/31/10; available at http://www.tomdispatch.com/blog/175314.

[55] Andrew J. Bacevich, *The New American Militarism: How Americans Are Seduced by War* (Oxford: Oxford University Press, 2005); also *The Limits of Power: The End of American Exceptionalism* (New York: Metropolitan Books, 2008).

[56] Andrew J. Bacevich, "Warrior Politics: The U.S. Military Is Becoming More Politically Assertive. This Is Not A Welcome Development," *The Atlantic* 289 (May 2007): 25–26.

Certainly, the United States has fought its share of ruthless wars. But traditionally our soldiers have thought of themselves as civilians *first*, soldiers second. Equally as important, the American people also thought of their troops that way.

Why are Americans, with so little debate, casting aside an ethos that served them well for two centuries for one that straightforwardly embraces war and killing? Have we not hugged the Germanic example so closely to our breastplates that we can no longer separate ourselves from it?

Concluding Thoughts

In seeking to create the world's most effective military, the U.S. military and its civilian overseers aped German methods and modes of thinking, trumpeted *Blitzkrieg* as a fail-safe strategy for victory rather than as one among many operational approaches to war, selectively (mis)read Clausewitz, and embraced militarism to a degree heretofore unparalleled in American society. Among the many unintended consequences are an empire in a state of perpetual war and a government that dedicates more than half of its discretionary spending to matters of national defense and homeland security.

But what if the unintended consequence *is* the intended one? What if the end goal was (and is) an ever-growing military-industrial complex, a complex that thrives off an open-ended state of perpetual rearmament and war? Such a seemingly radical interpretation deserves a hearing; for one thing, it is consistent with President Dwight D. Eisenhower's famous warning fifty years ago about the emergence of this "complex" and its potential for misplaced power.

Put differently, did certain powerful elements in U.S. society learn all-too-well how effective Germanic exploitation of fears and war-fevers had been, and still could be? In World War I, the Kaiser and conservative elements within Germany used war to stifle political debate and socialist critiques, effectively declaring a political "truce within the castle walls," ostensibly to present a united front against the enemy. In World War II, Hitler blamed "alien" elements (most notably, an international Jewish conspiracy) for bringing war to Germany, then redefined the war as "total" (therefore ruling out any possible debate, let alone opposition), stoking Germanic fears (which, in the end, proved all-too-real) of a barbarian flood from the east.

Close scrutiny of Wilhelmine and Nazi Germany may provide parallels to the dilemma America finds itself in today. Ordinary German citizens, whether in 1914 or 1941, were not told by their government that Germany was waging wars of aggression. Rather, they were told these were defensive wars to deter and punish aggressors as well as to secure Germany's future. A few Germans saw through the propaganda, but they lived in societies in which the people's will was disconnected from that of the state and its leaders. If compelled to choose between an anti-war position that seemed hopeless and participation in a collective effort that could make them feel less isolated, German citizens mostly chose the latter.

A similar dynamic is at work in American society today. As of December 2010, a majority of Americans remain skeptical whether the Iraq war was worth it, and they oppose the war in Afghanistan, yet they continue to support rising defense budgets and open-ended war. Told that their nation faces an implacable, terroristic enemy bent on their destruction; kept isolated from the true costs of these wars; resigned to the belief that these wars will continue whether they want them to or not, the American people have acquiesced to endless war and a government consumed by military priorities.

By the time ordinary Germans knew they were in for endless war – wars that curtailed their already limited choices and personal freedoms even further – they were in far too deep to extricate themselves. By that point, their leaders had called for no retreat and no negotiation, especially since the latter could be seen as a sign of weakness, as a betrayal of the sacrifices of the troops, and also as a de facto admission of the poor decision-making, perhaps even the criminality, of this same leadership.

Today, Americans are witnessing something similar. The argument is invariably made that the U.S. simply cannot afford to lose or even to withdraw fully from Iraq or Afghanistan. Again and again, when decision points are reached, the seemingly inexorable logic of "surging" or doubling down comes into play. Such logic has the added benefit of perpetuating elite rule that is accountability-free, along with ever-expanding resources and authority granted to the guarantor of eventual victory: the U.S. military-industrial complex.[57]

---

[57] See W. J. Astore, "Doubling Down in Afghanistan: Why We Refuse to Fold a Losing Hand." TomDispatch.com, Nation Institute, June 3, 2010. Available at http://www.tomdispatch.com/post/175256.

To this end, arguably the most important function of *Blitzkrieg*-oriented war is to keep the homefront buffered from war's painful realities until a point of no return has been achieved.[58] Did American elites learn the enabling aspects of this form of war? By isolating the people from war and its horrors, and by elevating American warfighters and celebrating American heroes in uniform, did they not also arrogate unprecedented power for themselves, as measured by the "Patriot Act" and ever-surging defense budgets?

After two calamitous defeats, today's Germany has succeeded in turning its back on war. Precisely because those disasters did not befall America, precisely because the United States emerged triumphant from two world wars, the country became both too enamored with the decisiveness of war, and too dismissive of its own unique strength. For America's strength was not military élan or wonder weapons or tactical finesse (these were German "strengths"), but rather the dedication, the generosity, even the occasional ineptitude, of its citizen-soldiers. Their spirit was unbreakable precisely because they – a truly democratic citizen army – were dedicated to defeating a repellently evil empire that reveled fanatically in its own combat vigor.

Looking back on my youthful infatuation with the German *Wehrmacht*, I recognize a boy's misguided enthusiasm for military hardness and toughness. I recognize as well the seductiveness of reducing the chaos of war to "shock and awe," to *Blitzkrieg* and warrior empowerment. What amazes me, however, is how this astonishingly selective and adolescent view of war – with its fetish for lightning results, achieved by elevating and empowering a new generation of warlords, warriors, and weaponry – came to dominate mainstream American military (and civilian) thinking after the frustrations of Vietnam.

Unlike a devastated and demoralized Germany after its defeats, the United States decided not to devalue war as an instrument of policy after Vietnam, but rather to elevate and embrace it. So we marched forward, seeking decisive victories, yet like our masters the Germans, we found victory to be elusive.

---

[58] Though evidence also suggests the Nazi leadership "insinuated" knowledge of the Holocaust and other atrocities among ordinary Germans, thereby making these citizens complicit in the horrific crimes of Nazism. See the review essay by Benjamin Schwarz, "Co-Conspirators," *The Atlantic* 291 (May 2009): 79–82.

So, I have a message for my younger self: Put aside those models of menacing German tanks and predatory planes. Forget those glowing accounts of Rommel and his *Afrika Korps*. Dismiss *Blitzkrieg* from your childish mind. There is no lightning war, America. There never was. And if you will not take my word for it, just ask the Germans.

'CLASH OF THE TITANS': LAW VS SECURITY IN WORLD WAR II BRITAIN

Mary Kathryn Barbier

Historians generally discuss cross-purposes in war in international contexts – for example, the Soviet-Anglo-American grand strategy of World War II.[1] When considering wartime cross-purposes in government contexts, strategy is generally the common issue as with Britain's Great War debate between Westerners and Peripheralists, a debate that occurred again in a different context during the Second World War.[2] Other contexts exist, however, for cross-purposes. They permeate lower levels of the government as military and civil agencies vie for resources and power from combinations of self-interest and principled differences about how best to achieve the general goal of victory.

Such competition, conducted within understood parameters, can not only be fruitful, but also necessary. Perhaps the best example during the Second World War was the competition for resources between the Allied military and the London Controlling Section (LCS). One group was garnering resources – people, equipment, food, transportation vehicles – to mount the invasion of France while the other required the same resources to perpetrate a deception operation to cover that invasion. The two had to work together in order for the invasion to succeed.[3] Unlike totalitarian governments, a democracy faces a particular

---

[1] See Gerhard Weinberg, *A World At Arms: A Global History of World War II* (Cambridge: Cambridge University Press, 1994); Williamson Murray and Allan Millett, *A War to be Won: Fighting the Second World War* (Cambridge: Belknap Press, 2000); Richard Overy, *Why the Allies Won* (New York: W.W. Norton & Company, 1996); Mark Stoler, *Allies and Adversaries: the Joint Chiefs of Staff, the Grand Alliance, and U.S. Strategy in World War II* (Chapel Hill: UNC Press, 2000); Mark Stoler, *The Politics of the Second Front: American Military Planning and Diplomacy in Coalition Warfare, 1941–1943* (Portsmouth, NH: Greenwood Press, 1977).

[2] See Mark Stoler, *The Politics of the Second Front: American Military Planning and Diplomacy in Coalition Warfare, 1941–1943*; Donald L. Miller, *The Story of World War II* (New York: Simon & Schuster Paperbacks, 2006); Jon Meacham, *Franklin and Winston: An Intimate Portrait of an Epic Friendship* (New York: Random House, 2003).

[3] See Thaddeus Holt, *The Deceivers: The Allied Deception in the Second World War* (London: Weidenfeld & Nicolson, 2004); Roger Hesketh, *The D-Day Deception Campaign* (London: St. Ermin's press, 1999); Mary Kathryn Barbier, *D-Day Deception: Operation Fortitude and the Normandy Invasion* (Westport, CT: Praeger Security International, 2007).

set of problems, however, when a government agency systematically stretches the law to its breaking point, or perhaps beyond, which can result in a conflict with a legal system designed to uphold the law.

During World War II, Britain devoted significant resources to its intelligence services. Indeed, historians might describe intelligence as the crucial element in Britain's survival during the dark years of 1940–42.[4] Deception operations, ranging from creating imaginary divisions to planting forged documents, were a key component of wartime intelligence. Determined to utilize every resource, Britain's intelligence services employed resident aliens as agents – generally Germans who volunteered to serve Britain both directly against the Axis and to expose pro-Nazi sympathizers who threatened Britain from within.

Historians have discussed agents' high-risk roles in larger deception operations, such as Mincemeat and Fortitude. Being "blown," or exposed, was a constant risk followed by often fatal consequences. To date, however, few scholars have investigated "own goals" or incidents where agents were in danger of being "blown" because of the activities of another government agency. Using previously untapped primary sources, including the minutes of Twenty Committee (which was in charge of the double agents), court records, and double agent files, along with some secondary accounts, I will discuss one case. It involved agents of military intelligence, one of them a double agent put in jeopardy when called to testify against a JP (Justice of the Peace, in this case, Benjamin Greene) who was challenging his arrest for his Nazi sympathies. The results illustrate what can happen when a nation's legal system and its intelligence service are at counter purposes. In this case, a "clash of the titans" occurred – no less spectacular and no less significant for being subterranean.

Setting the Stage: Fear of Fifth Column and Regulation 18B

In 1915, William Le Queux published *German Spies in England: An Exposure*, which fueled or, some might argue, started the spy scare in England during the Great War. Although he was a novelist, Le Queux

---

[4] See Thaddeus Holt, *The Deceivers: The Allied Deception in the Second World War*; F. H. Hinsley, *British Intelligence in the Second World War* (Cambridge: Cambridge University Press, 1979–90); John Hughes-Wilson, *Puppet Masters: Spies, Traitors, and the Real Forces behind World Events* (London: Weidenfeld & Nicolson, 2004).

wrote a convincing exposé, or it appeared as if he had because much of the British public, as well as the British government, seemed to treat his claims seriously. He suggested that all naturalized and un-naturalized Germans living in England were suspect, especially if they worked in certain jobs, such as barbers, watchmakers, nannies, and hotel clerks. Relying, he claimed, on personal knowledge, he cited cases of German spies who were ignored by the authorities despite reports by local citizens.

A quarter-century later, the six-week German offensive that resulted in the defeat of France and the Low Countries had a similar impact. Only a few years earlier, the Nationalists had claimed that they had four columns outside Madrid and a "Fifth Column" of sympathizers in the city. Now fear of a Fifth Column operating in Britain gripped the country. Other rumors of a Fifth Column flooded the country. A "Fifth Column" purportedly "working behind the lines" was responsible for the rapid German victory, according to one rumor. The British minister in the Netherlands, Sir Nevile Bland, sent a warning back to his homeland that the "enemy in our midst" threatened his countrymen. The War Cabinet took seriously his alarm about a "sleeper cell" of enemy alien Fifth Columnists waiting for a signal to rise up and engage in sabotage and attacks against both the military and civilians.[5]

This apprehension added impetus to the counter-espionage work of Britain's intelligence organizations in the years leading up to the war. The outbreak of hostilities in 1939 gave impetus and a sense of urgency to their counter-espionage efforts. Internally, intelligence officials focused on the segments of society that they feared posed a genuine threat to the survival of the Britain at the same time that the nation faced very real external menace.[6] They aggressively pursued segments of society perceived as outside of "acceptable" wartime parameters. Although they questioned and in some cases detained "enemy aliens," MI5 operatives also investigated British nationals, particularly those who had come to their attention prior to the outbreak of hostilities – those who engaged in pro-Nazi or pro-Communist activities. Naturally, after May 1940 their attention turned increasingly to pro-Nazi groups

---

[5] Nigel West, *MI5: British Security Service Operations, 1909–1945* (New York: Stein and Day Publishers, 1981), 118; Christopher Andrew, *Defend the Realm: The Authorized History of MI5* (New York: Alfred A. Knopf, 2009), 223–224.
[6] Ibid.

and their members. Doubly caught in MI5's web were pacifists, like Ben Greene, who had connections to Germany.

As the threat of invasion by the Germans loomed and the nation's resources became strained, the counter-espionage work of Britain's intelligence organizations gained new importance. When things looked bleakest in 1940–41, the nation increasingly relied upon the intelligence services to provide the security that the nation and its citizens demanded. However, no matter what the demands placed on the intelligence services were, they generally had to operate within prevailing law. As is the case with the military, the activities of the intelligence services were intended to support, but also to be limited by, civil power. While those limitations were reduced during wartime, the "Golden Thread of British Justice" – the presumption of innocence – was supposed to prevail.[7] Unfortunately, the lines became blurred when threat to the nation outweighed the rule of law. Consequently, regulations were issued that broadened their powers and allowed actions that would not be acceptable during peacetime. A. W. Brian Simpson does an excellent job of analyzing the creation of the system of "executive detention" and the steps taken that legalized such actions by the British government and security services, including MI5.[8]

The practice of detention during wartime was not necessarily a new concept. In 1866 and 1867, for example, Britain implemented the Habeas Corpus Suspension Acts in Ireland, which permitted the government to "hold individuals on treason charges without bringing them to trial," but as the situation in Ireland eased, so did the government's use of detention.[9] It was not until World War I, however, that the executive revived detention policy with a Defence of the Realm Act, Regulation 14B, under which "disloyal British subjects" could no longer avoid "legal" detention. British citizens under normal circumstances were entitled to the fundamental right of a trial; what they discovered, however, was that under certain circumstances that right could be suspended. Simpson argues that Regulation 14B, which in many respects was the precursor to Regulation 18B, represented the British

---

[7] The concept of the "Golden Thread" was first articulated in a 1935 murder trial and became familiar through John Mortimer's British television series 'Rumpole of the Bailey' in which he trumpeted the "Golden Thread of British Justice."
[8] See A. W. Brian Simpson, *In the Highest Degree Odious: Detention Without Trial in Wartime Britain* (Oxford, Clarendon Press, 1994), 1–50.
[9] Ibid., 3.

government's reaction to two important factors – "a fear of a Fifth Column" and a realization that the lack of evidence against its members meant little likelihood of conviction in court. Both of those fears seemed to have returned with the tensions and threat of conflict by the late 1930s.

Regulation 14B, which allowed the executive to usurp power given to Parliament, did not stand unchallenged. Two immediate cases questioned its validity. The regulation withstood those challenges, but there were others. In some situations, the courts refused to intervene.[10] Because the courts in effect upheld or refused to hear challenges to Regulation 14B, a precedent of sorts was in place before the institution of Regulation 18B approximately 20 years later. What neither the challengers nor the courts seemed to address was who – Parliament, the Home Secretary, MI5, or the Courts – determined which citizens and resident "enemy aliens" were dangerous. This issue would arise indirectly during the case in which Benjamin Greene was detained under Regulation 18B.

In the post-World War I period, there seemed to be less need for detentions, but the policy was not just shelved. Instead, discussion about revising it occurred. In 1925 the War Emergency Legislation Sub-Committee of the Committee of Imperial Defence received the task of assessing the government's detention policy. Both the Home Secretary and MI5 weighed in on the nature of future detention policy. Under the leadership of Lord Chancellor Cave, the committee drafted a regulation that reflected MI5's request for an expanded policy, but failed to issue its final recommendation. As tensions flared and Italian troops invaded Abyssinia, war loomed on the horizon, and Sir Claud Schuster chaired an interdepartmental committee tasked with recommending a policy in the event of war. Influenced by German military expansion into the Rhineland in 1936, the committee recommended "an entirely unrestricted power of detention." On 1 September 1939, the recommendation of Schuster's committee became the law called Regulation 18B.[11]

According to Simpson, Regulation 18B, which was a Defence Regulation.

> enabled the government to imprison citizens thought to be dangerous to national security without charge, trial, or term set, under what Herbert

---
[10] Ibid., 5–7, 12–14, 24–26, 44–49.
[11] Ibid., 42–43.

Morrison, who administered the system during most of the war, described as "a terrible power".[12]

The purpose of this regulation was to thwart "future harm;" as such, it allowed the government, and those representing the government, to act preemptively, in effect to identify and eliminate by whatever means necessary – in the case of people, through detention – anything deemed to be a threat to the internal security of Britain during this time of crisis, during the war 1939 to 1945. The fear was that, if allowed to roam free, certain identifiable people *might* engage in activities that would endanger the nation; therefore, the regulation permitted their detention until such time as the Home Secretary, or a committee if an incarceration was challenged, determined that these people no longer constituted a threat to the well-being of the nation. Because the Home Secretary had to sign off on a detention, it was, as Simpson reiterated, "typically imposed as a result of an administrative decision, taken in private, by state officials, without any form of prior trial."[13] With the institution of Regulation 18B, which gave the Home Secretary broad powers to detain those who threatened Britain's internal safety, the stage was set for the incarceration of Benjamin Greene.

Setting the Trap: Greene vs MI5 and the Home Office

Before introducing Greene, however, it is necessary to provide some background on the two government agencies, along with key officials, who were involved in the Greene case, starting with MI5 which gathered the information and provided it to the Home Office, which made the final decision. In the early 1920s the newly instituted MI5's job was to do the Special Branch type of work, not handle the legal end. It uncovered sabotage and subversive plots, but then it had to turn their intelligence over to the law and order branch, which arrested and prosecuted the suspects. Recruiting and managing the agents who gathered the appropriate information became the rule.

Into all of this came Major Charles Henry Maxwell Knight, a former naval officer, who in 1924 joined the "club" and reiterated its mission when he said: "The proper function of M.S. lies in the recruitment and operation of agents who are trained for the purpose of penetrating

---

[12] Ibid., 1.
[13] Ibid., 1.

subversive political bodies, and for the investigation of suspicious individuals or groups of individuals."[14] This mission guided Knight and the way in which he approached his job. Ironically, particularly in light of his efforts to protect Britain from subversive elements, such as from pro-Nazis, his political positions were somewhat in line with those espoused by the British Fascists (BF), which, one would have thought, would have put him at odds with his new employers, if not in 1924, then in 1939, if he still held those views. As Christopher Andrew noted, "Like a majority of the BF, however, his views were those of die-hard conservatives rather than the radical right."[15] Perhaps his earlier views were what drove Knight in his efforts to identify those who threatened Britain internally. Perhaps, unlike, Greene, he recognized that times had changed, and he did, too.

Knight took to his new position like a duck to water. In addition, when possible, he persuaded close friends such as Dennis Wheatley to join the pool as well. Before it was all over, he exerted significant influence on MI5. Knight enjoyed the "cloak and dagger" aspect of the organization, and occasionally his friends provided him with information and gave his agents cover. He appeared willing to use whatever means were necessary to achieve the endgame, and he was good at his job.[16]

Knight's focus was on thwarting subversion. To achieve that end, he recruited agents from various backgrounds, including refugees. These agents received orders to infiltrate political organizations, such as the Communist Party of Great Britain, the British Union of Fascists, the Peace Pledge Union, and the British People's Party. He did not hesitate to pursue those he deemed a threat to Britain's security, even if they were British citizens. He often acted as if pro-Nazi British citizens posed the greater threat because they were committing disloyal, treasonous acts, even if only in what they advocated, not necessarily in what they did. He viewed men like Benjamin Greene, who appeared to be pro-Nazi as well as a pacifist, as dangerous threats to Britain's security, particularly during wartime, and seemed to focus his efforts on

---

[14] Maxwell Knight, 'History of the Operations of M.S. (Agents) during the War 1939–1945,' p. 1, KV 4/227, The National Archives of the United Kingdom (TNA, formerly the PRO), Kew, England; Christopher Andrew, 123.

[15] Andrew, 124. According to Andrew, Maxwell Knight later claimed that he joined BF under orders from his superiors. Andrew, 123.

[16] Nigel West, 44–45; Anthony Masters, *The Man Who Was M: The Life of Maxwell Knight* (Oxford, UK: Basil Blackwell, 1984), 70–75, 110.

defusing the peril. Therefore, he used his agents to gather evidence against those who most endangered the country's internal safety.

Gathering evidence was only the first step; the next was deciding what to do with it. When sufficient intelligence about a particular individual, individuals, or organizations had been gathered, it was turned over to the Home Office, which decided whether or not to proceed. In some cases, the recommendation was arrest and detention. The person who had to sign off on the detention of enemy aliens and British citizens under regulations, such as 18B, was the Home Secretary. In 1939 that man was Sir John Anderson, Viscount Waverly. A "brilliant politician," Anderson was perhaps best known among Londoners for backyard air raid shelters.[17] He had served in several government posts until his appointment as permanent undersecretary, a position he held until 1932 before being sent to India. Upon his return to Britain five years later, Anderson was elected to the House of Commons and held several positions, including membership on a "committee to prepare for the evacuation of nonessential workers in the event of war."

When World War II broke out, Anderson accepted the positions of Home Secretary and Minister of Home Security, which he held until 1945. During his time as Home Secretary, he became noted, and received much criticism, for his position regarding the detention of enemy aliens and British citizens deemed a threat to the nation and the war effort. In the beginning, under Anderson's orders, tribunals examined the cases of "enemy aliens" and ordered the internment of a small number of the refugees. Under his direction, however, the number of detainees drastically increased during the summer of 1940 when the nation feared German invasion. It was also during this time that the British security services, with the help of Anderson, targeted citizens who were members of pro-Nazi or pro-Communist organizations, such as the British Union of Fascists and the British People's Party. As Home Secretary, Anderson was involved in the case of Ben Greene.[18]

Benjamin Greene, JP, who is one of the principal actors in this case, was born in Sao Paolo to a British father and a German mother.

---

[17] In 1938, Neville Chamberlain put Sir John Anderson in charge of ARP (Air Raid Precautions). In that capacity, he directed William Patterson, an engineer, to design an affordable shelter that citizens could build in their gardens. Within a very short time, approximately one and half million Brits had received 'Anderson shelters.' http://www.spartacus.schoolnet.co.uk/2WWandersonshelter.htm

[18] Keith Laybourn, *British Political Leaders: A Biographical Dictionary* (ABC-CLIO online, www.abc-clio.com , 2010), 7–8; West, 127.

When reasons for his detention were considered, the nationality of his mother seemed to suggest to Knight and others that Greene might be "pro-Nazi," rather than "pro-British." It did not help that she was, according to the "Secondary Advisory Committee," publicly vocal about her pro-German views despite the fact that she had not lived in Germany since she was quite young. In addition, Greene's brother Edward and his sister Katherine participated in his later political activism, and his sister Barbara lived in Germany and was involved with a German official. Interestingly enough, however, Greene was detained, while his siblings who remained in Britain were not, partially perhaps because Edward Greene did not fall for a trap that was set out for him. There does not seem to have been an effort to entrap Katherine Greene. Perhaps as a woman, she was not deemed a threat.

Although he had suspicious family members and although his cousins, including the novelist Graham Greene, wanted nothing to do with him or his family during his time of difficulty, Greene's education was typically British. Following his family's return to England and his early preparatory schooling, he continued his studies at Berkhamsted Grammar School, where his cousins were educated and where the Head Master was Charles Greene, his uncle. Upon completion of his education at Berkhamsted, Greene enrolled at Wadham College, Oxford, in 1919. Because he suffered a "religious crisis," the nature of which remains unclear, he withdrew from Wadham before finishing his studies; however, after this time, he became openly affiliated with pacifist groups, in particular, with the Quakers. After the First World War, he engaged in relief work in several European countries affected by the conflict, including Germany, Austria, Poland, and Russia, with groups such as the "Quakers, the Save the Children Fund, and the American Relief Administration." These experiences had a great impact on Greene, particularly in light of his "religious crisis."

Beliefs and convictions, which developed in the early 1920s, provided the driving force behind his actions by the 1930s. While his participation in pacifist activism was not unreasonable in the early 1930s, by 1939 the rules had changed, even if Greene had not. Returning to Britain in 1923, he became active in the Labour Party. Subsequently Ramsay MacDonald hired him as his secretary. Greene then decided to work for his father in his coffee enterprise; his duties took him to New Orleans for a time. Upon his return to Britain, he set up shop in Berkhamsted – first as an employee of an insurance company and then as a sales manager for a subsidiary of the Hudson Bay Company – and became more active in the political scene – first on the Berkhamsted Urban District Council for six years and then on the Hertforshire County Council for two.

Around this time, Greene became involved in various activities, including national politics, as he unsuccessfully ran to represent Gravesend in Parliament in 1931 and again in 1935, and in promoting an end to war. By 1938, several factors – his unsuccessful election bid, his disagreement with MacDonald's position on frontiers, and his inability to feel at ease within the party – led to his withdrawal from the Labour Party.

Greene simultaneously became involved in promoting an end to war. In 1935 he traveled to the Saar as Deputy Chief Returning Officer for the League of Nations because of the plebiscite. When he returned to the region a year later, he did so for two reasons. First, he was charged with "returning" the plebiscite documents and, second, as a Quaker representative investigating alleged atrocities that British newspapers had reported. In November 1938 he returned to the continent as a Quaker investigator to ascertain the situation in Germany following *Kristallnacht*. Distressed by what he saw, he attempted to initiate a cooperative effort by the British and German governments to create a "selective emigration scheme," but his efforts came to naught.[19]

Greene's experiences in relief work and in his investigations into alleged atrocities had a profound impact on him, and, as Simpson states, "his commitment to pacifism became more intense." His opposition to war guided his actions, his speeches, and his publications, and it apparently blinded him to the danger in which he placed himself by being different during a time of great tension and threat, by acting outside of the acceptable paradigm of loyal British citizens as set by the government, by MI5, by society. Greene became associated with and worked for organizations or groups whose views reflected his own, including the Peace Pledge Union. In 1939, although he later

---

[19] 'REPORT OF FIRST ADVISORY COMMITTEE,' dated 30th August 1940, signed, H. G. Hart, Secretary, p. 6, TS 27/522, TNA; 'SECOND STATEMENT OF CASE against BENJAMIN GREENE for SECONDARY ADVISORY COMMITTEE,' dated 3.6.41, signed S. H. Noakes, p. 9–10, TS 27/522, TNA; 'REPRESENTATIONS TO H.M. SECRETARY OF STATE BY BEN GREENE,' dated 4 September 1941, signed Ben Greene from Brixton Prison, p. 1, TS 27/522, TNA; Masters, 143–145; Simpson, 341–345. Unfortunately, the documents are not clear about why Greene was returning the plebiscite documents, to whom he was returning them, or who sent him to return them. One can only assume that he was sent by the League of Nations.

supposedly disassociated himself from the group, Greene became treasurer of the newly formed British People's Party, which was founded by Lord Tavistock and John Beckett and which was on MI5's "watch list." His involvement with these organizations, in conjunction with speeches that he made and articles and pamphlets that he published brought Greene to the attention of MI5, which set out, according to some analysts, to entrap Greene and succeeded in bringing about his detention under Regulation 18B.[20]

Focused on his anti-war efforts in the late 1930s, Greene seemed unaware that he had come to the attention of MI5 and that it had begun to build a case against him, and while some of his activities might have been innocent, they, examined in conjunction with other factors, presented a picture of a pro-Nazi, anti-British individual who appeared willing to help the Germans should they successfully invade Britain. As such, he was dangerous. According to the information compiled against him, Greene's questionable activities dated back as early as May 1936 when he corresponded with a German official and organizer of German and English boys' camps, the "Anglo-German Circle," which was around the same time that he began to receive German newspapers in what was viewed as an excessive number.

Greene then seemed to operate below the radar until September 1938 when he signed a "Joint Peace Manifesto" promoted by a number of groups, including the Peace Pledge Union. Founded by Rev. Dick Sheppard, the Peace Pledge Union was one of the largest pacifist groups of the 1930s and was committed to getting its message out and attracting the most people to its cause as possible. In addition, that same year (1938), Greene traveled to Germany, supposedly in connection with the "German refugee problem." In early 1939 he entered into some correspondence with Germans that MI5 found to be somewhat suspect. Contacting an employee of the German Ministry of Propaganda, Greene initiated a conversation regarding his peace plans. The men were soon on a friendly footing, which raised a "red flag." During the course of their correspondence over the next several months, Greene mentioned his work as secretary for a periodical bulletin called the "Peace and Progress Information Bureau." According to the "Original Statement of Case against Benjamin Greene for First Advisory Committee," the newsletters, which were published by this

---

[20] Simpson, 343–345; Masters, 144–145.

group until August 1939, were both pro-German and anti-British, or at least critical of British treatment of Arabs in Palestine.[21]

1939 was an extremely busy year for Greene. As noted earlier, in that year, MP John Beckett and Lord Tavistock, along with Ben Greene formed the British People's Party (BPP). Tavistock served as President, Beckett as Secretary, and Greene as Treasurer. BPP promoted peace and "other legitimate political ends," among which were "the right to security and social justice, the abolition of usury and adoption of social credit, and the abolition of land speculation." BPP circulated its literature, much of it pro-German and pro-Nazi in nature; Greene was largely responsible for one publication in particular, *The Truth About the War*, which was released in December 1939.[22]

In the summer of 1939, as BPP treasurer, Greene sent out appeals for money to be used in the organization's campaign "to avoid war and bring about much needed social regeneration."[23] While under normal circumstances that action might not have been suspect, the fact that Greene sent funding requests to two Germans who left Britain with the outbreak of hostilities was. In addition, Greene began to make speeches, the nature of which MI5 found problematic. In September, for example, at a meeting of the British Council for Christian Settlement in Europe (BCCSE), Greene, in addition to being critical of British policy, apparently praised Adolf Hitler. During the next month, however, Greene decided to leave the BPP and sent a letter to that effect to Beckett. Although he was no longer an official member of the BPP, Greene continued to make speeches that appeared to be supportive of the group and their views.[24]

The actions of the BPP continued to fall under the watchful eye of MI5. The head of MI5, Sir Vernon Kell, approached the Home Office in

---

[21] 'ORIGINAL STATEMENT of CASE against BENJAMIN GREENE for FIRST ADVISORY COMMITTEE,' dated 12.7.40, p. 1, TS 27/522; 'REPORT of FIRST ADVISORY COMMITTEE,' dated 30th August 1940, signed H. G. Hart, Secretary, p. 6; 'SECOND STATEMENT of CASE against BENJAMIN GREENE for SECONDARY ADVISORY COMMITTEE,' p. 10; David C. Lukowitz, 'British Pacifists and Appeasement: The Peace Pledge Union,' *Journal of Contemporary History* 19 (January 1974): 115–127.

[22] Simpson, 138–139.

[23] 'ORIGINAL STATEMENT of CASE against BENJAMIN GREENE for FIRST ADVISORY COMMITTEE, p. 1.

[24] 'ORIGINAL STATEMENT of CASE against BENJAMIN GREENE for FIRST ADVISORY COMMITTEE, p. 1; 'SECOND STATEMENT of CASE against BENJAMIN GREENE for SECONDARY ADVISORY COMMITTEE,' 10–11.

January 1940 about the organization and, when a list of detainees under Regulation 18B was compiled, suggested that Greene and Beckett be added. Unbeknownst to Greene, MI5 was keeping track of him, as he continued to give speeches.[25] With the outbreak of war, security concerns intensified. The "Phony War" did nothing to alleviate the tensions that existed in the halls of the Home Office and the Security Services.

While Kell was notifying the Home Office of his concerns, Greene addressed the Parliament Christian's Committee meeting.[26] A month later, at a BCCSE meeting, he gave another speech and supported the group's resolution opposing using bombs against German civilians because of the possibility of reprisals and because of the impact bombing would have on both civilian populations. Then in March when Greene spoke in Wellingborough apparently as a "representative" of BPP, it was reported in the *Northamptonshire Evening Telegraph*. Throughout this time, even though he was technically no longer a member of BPP, Greene remained in contact with the other founding members, a fact which was of some interest to MI5, which continued to make a case against the JP.[27]

In fact, a conversation between Sir Claud Schuster, Permanent Secretary to the Lord Chancellor, and Sir Alexander Maxwell, Permanent Under Secretary (PUS), Home Office, about Greene commenced in mid-January 1940. Maxwell suggested that Greene's associations with the BCCSE made him unsuitable to continue in his position as a Justice of the Peace. Suggesting that Greene's presence on the Commission was troublesome to the other members, Schuster vehemently concurred and recommended that the Home Office continue to keep Greene under surveillance.[28] At the end of March, Knight decided that the time had come for action. Because MI5 needed more direct evidence in order to act against Greene, however, he decided to turn to one of his agents, who would give Greene the opportunity to incriminate himself.

Enter Harald Kurtz. According to Maxwell Knight, Harald Kurtz was a "genuine refugee," a German Jew, who was vehemently anti-Nazi.

---

[25] Simpson, 345.
[26] The Parliament Christian group was similar politically to the BCCSE.
[27] 'Extract from "NORTHAMPTONSHIRE EVENING TELEGRAPH,"' TS 27/522.
[28] Letter from Maxwell to Schuster, dated 5th February, 1940, LCO 2/1454, TNA; Letter from Schuster to Maxwell, dated 6th February, 1940, LCO 2/1454.

The two men became acquainted in June 1938 at which time Kurtz became an MI5 agent. As Knight attested in a written statement, "Since June 1938, Kurtz has worked for me on many occasions, in all of which he has given me complete satisfaction, and I have never had the least occasion to doubt the accuracy of his reports or his loyalty to this country."[29] He was born in Germany, and his parents remained there. In fact, his father, Kurtz admitted, was pro-Nazi and supported Hitler's regime. He had two brothers, one of whom was in Civil Service, the other probably a naval officer.

In 1937, Kurtz visited England for the first time while on holiday from his studies in languages and history at Geneva University. Although it was possibly a bit impulsive, it was then that he realized that he wanted to live in England. In fact, he managed to stay in the country and lived off "private money" before obtaining work for a wholesale bookseller. He then gained employment as a "private secretary to Lord Noel Buxton," but he left that position in 1938 after meeting and agreeing to work for Maxwell Knight, which he did for the next several years. Apparently his work for MI5 not only provided Kurtz with a regular salary, but he also held his position there for a longer time than had been the case with his previous employments.

Because he was a refugee, Kurtz was able to perform a specific function for MI5, or rather for Knight, in investigations of members of the British Union of Fascists, the British People's Party, and other similar organizations. He willingly allowed himself to be interned for months at a time. During his incarceration, he gathered information about the other inhabitants of the facility, which MI5 used in building a case in support of their continued detention.[30] His family's pro-Nazi stance gave Kurtz credibility with the internees in the camps although his work demonstrated the reality of his views. To an outside observer, however, there seem to be some discrepancies, or perhaps omissions, in the story of Kurtz's background. Was he truly Jewish? If he was, then it wouldn't make sense for his family to be pro-Nazi and safe in Germany. What, then, was Kurtz's motivation in working for the

---

[29] 'STATEMENT of CHARLES HENRY MAXWELL KNIGHT, Major, attached to the General Staff (Directorate of Military Intelligence),' p. 1, undated TS 27/522, TNA.

[30] 'STATEMENT of CHARLES HENRY MAXWELL KNIGHT, p. 1; Masters, 111; 'REPORT OF THE SECOND ADVISORY COMMITTEE, dated 18th September 1941, Ref. G.4/4, signed, Williams, Secretary, p. 18–19, TS 27/522, TNA.

British? Apparently Kurtz did not want to be sent back to Germany, where life might not have been pleasant, whether he was Jewish or not. What better way to remain a free man in Britain than to work for MI5?

At the time of the Ben Greene affair, Kurtz, who had just been released from internment assignment, was in his late twenties. Because of his knowledge of the BPP, Knight assigned Kurtz the task of getting in touch with the organization in general and with Greene in particular. He was to drop the name of a mutual acquaintance – Fraulein von Binzer – as a way of starting a conversation with Greene. After several attempts via letters and phone calls to Greene's place of business, Kurtz was finally able to arrange a meeting, which occurred on 22 March 1940 at his flat. According to Knight, Kurtz reported that he felt that he had succeed in convincing Greene that he was pro-Nazi, which did not make the other man uncomfortable.

Satisfied with the results, Knight ordered Kurtz to meet with Greene again. In early April both Kurtz and Greene attended a meeting at which Lord Tavistock among others spoke and at which John Beckett presided. After the meeting Kurtz approached Greene and met his sister Katherine. Following Knight's instructions, Kurtz contacted Greene again and requested another meeting, which was set for 24 April and at which Kurtz set the stage for the introduction of an associate, per his orders.

Enter Fraulein Gaertner. Friedericka Gaertner, née Stottinger, Alien Registration No. 611918, was an Austrian by birth, but, according to her own statement, "a German subject." Born in Raitham and later employed as a stenographer in Vienna, she married a German and emigrated to Palestine with him. The marriage soon ended, and she came to Britain to stay with her sister who was married to Sir Stewart Menzies' brother.[31] A 29-year-old divorced woman at the time she testified in writing against Greene, Gaertner provided information under her maiden name Stottinger.[32] As she stated and Maxwell Knight confirmed, the two met in April 1938, at which time she "offered my

---

[31] Sir Stewart Menzies was the Chief of SIS, Secret Intelligence Service. As noted above, Gaertner's sister was married to his brother Ian. Later Menzies facilitated Gaertner's introduction to employment as a double agent with the Double-Cross (XX) Committee.

[32] 'STATEMENT OF FREDERICKA STOTTINGER, of 5 Spring Street, Paddington, W.2.' undated, TS 27/522, TNA; From B.5.b. to B.2. (Mr. White), dated 13.9.39, KV 2/1275, TNA.

services to the British Military Intelligence Department. Since that date, I have been employed by this Department in connection with counter espionage work."[33] What was her motivation? Although she was no longer married, Gaertner's ex-husband was German and Jewish, which suggests that it would not necessarily be safe for her to return to her homeland. In addition, her sister lived in Britain, which is why she moved there in the first place. Finally, her brother-in-law's brother was connected to British intelligence. Gaining a job with British intelligence would serve two purposes: to allow her to evade detention as an enemy alien and to live an exciting life operating in certain social circles as a double agent working for the British while pretending to be loyal to Germany.

Before the outbreak of war in Europe, she avoided interment as an "enemy alien," thanks to three men – Sir Stewart Menzies ('C') because she was a friend of his younger brother and Dennis Wheatley, an Oxford Don,[34] as a favor to the third man, Maxwell Knight (MI5). In fact, Menzies recommended, in May 1938, that she obtain a German passport and that she "mix with the German colony in London" as a way to help the British intelligence services although she was expected to get a "real" job in order to support herself.[35] Apparently, Menzies believed that his sister-in-law's sister could contribute to the war effort by helping the secret services. His recommendation regarding her actions was just the first step in putting Gaertner in position to do just that.

Gaertner did indeed find gainful employment. Based on a recommendation and request from Knight, Wheatley hired her as his secretary or "part-time research assistant" – as cover for her primary job with MI5. When MI5 officials considered utilizing Gaertner, her "very

---

[33] 'STATEMENT OF FREDERICKA STOTTINGER,' p. 1; 'STATEMENT of CHARLES HENRY MAXWELL KNIGHT,' p. 1.

[34] Dennis Wheatley was a member of the London Controlling Section (LCS) during World War II. The LCS designed deception plans that provided cover for several military operations, including the invasion of Normandy in June 1944.

[35] Confidential note signed by Sir Stewart Menzies, dated 18th May, 1938, KV 2/1280, TNA; Memorandum with information about Gartner's passport and registration, undated, KV 2/1280; Memorandum entitled 'GELATINE,' dated 18.5.1941, signed W.E. Luke, KV 2/1275, TNA; APF, 'X' (iii) VI, 'TRICYCLE, BALLOON, AND GELATINE,' undated, unsigned, p. 2, KV 2/1278, TNA. It is interesting to note that in some of the documents, Gaertner's name is omitted, and her real name is not provided in the brief description of the files related to her listed in the TNA's catalogue. Perhaps this has something to do with her connection to Sir Steward Menzies.

considerable personal attractiveness"[36] was mentioned. In his "History of the Operations of M.S. (Agents) during the War 1939–1945," Knight devotes pages to the use of women as agents. While he admits that an over-sexed agent, whether male or female, would not be a good one (obviously nobody informed James Bond of that fact), he did contend "that a clever woman who can use her personal attractions wisely has in her armoury a very formidable weapon."[37] Armed with her good looks and training, such as it was, MI5's newest recruit was ready to hit the ground running.

Posing as a pro-Nazi, Gaertner toured the London social circuit where she gathered information against the "Nazi front organizations" that were the target of Maxwell Knight's investigations. MI5 targeted the British Union of Fascists and the British People's Party and utilized agents such as Gaertner in their efforts. She successfully identified several "pro-Nazis" who were subsequently detained under Regulation 18B. In addition to working for Knight, Gaertner, using the code name Gelatine, became a part of a double agent network that provided primarily fictitious information to the Germans and was one of the networks that ultimately participated in Operation Fortitude, the deception scheme that supplied cover for the Normandy invasion in June 1944.

In mid-May 1941, Knight agreed to release Gaertner, "who had good contacts in political circles," from "any investigation work;" that would allow MI5 to utilize her talents more productively as a "double agent." She was employed as a secretary by Dennis Wheatley and, although she had been working for MI5, the Germans were unaware of that fact. To get established as a double agent, she could volunteer her services to the Germans when approached by an established double agent. The reality was, however, that Gaertner was working for the British, and, in fact, she reiterated her loyalty to Britain in a written statement

---

[36] Memorandum dated 30.5.38, signed B.5b, based on an interview of Gaertner that Captain Guy Liddell recommended, KV 2/1280, TNA; Letter from Maxwell Knight to Dennis Wheatley, dated 5th January, 1939, KV 2/1280, TNA; Letter from Maxwell Knight to Dennis Wheatley, dated 11th January, 1939, KV 2/1280, TNA; Letter from Maxwell Knight to Dennis Wheatley, dated 26th January, 1939, KV 2/1280, TNA; Letter from Maxwell Knight to Dennis Wheatley, dated 30.1.39, KV 2/1280, TNA; Masters, 71–75. See also Hervie Haufler, *The Spies Who Never Were: The True Story of the Nazi Spies Who Were Actually Allied Double Agents* (New York: NALCaliber, 2006), 39–40.

[37] Maxwell Knight, 'History of the Operations of M.S. (Agents) during the War 1939–1945,' p. 20.

while at the same time questioning the loyalty of British citizen Ben Greene.[38]

On 28 April the dinner orchestrated by Harald Kurtz took place with Ben Greene and Friedl Gaertner in attendance. According to Gaertner, Greene freely expressed his views about the war, National Socialism, which he thought would be the salvation of the Empire, and his peace movement. Then, according to both Kurtz and Gaertner, Greene suggested that he had seen a man whom he knew was a S.A. member, but that he had not reported the German to the police. This claim, if true, was quite damning.[39] Because all loyal British citizens and residents were expected to report suspicious characters, particularly during wartime, Greene's failure to do so could be construed as suspect at the very least or treasonous at the very worst. For MI5, with Greene's failure to report a possible German S.A. member, combined with his pro-Nazi comments to their agents, they had all that they needed to approach the Home Secretary.

The Home Office decided that MI5 had compiled enough evidence to justify Greene's arrest and subsequent detention. In addition, it did not need consent from the courts authorizing the next step. Consequently, on 22 May 1940 the Home Secretary signed the order based on "hostile associations." When he learned that he was being sought by the police, Greene presented himself to Scotland Yard on the evening of 24 May 1940 at which time he was arrested and sent to Brixton Prison.[40] Tensions were high. Less than two weeks before the Home Secretary signed the arrest and detention directive, German troops had invaded Belgium and France. The "Phony War" was over; the "real" war was on. Three days after Greene's arrest, Operation Dynamo – the evacuation of British and French troops from Dunkirk – began. Neither the Home Office nor the Security Services seemed willing to take any chances and appeared committed to protecting the

---

[38] Memorandum entitled 'GELATINE,' dated 18.5.1941, signed W. E. Luke, KV 2/1275; APF. 'X' (iii) VI, 'TRICYCLE, BALLOON, AND GELATINE,' undated, unsigned, p. 2, KV 2/1278; Masters, 71–74; West, 198–199; J. C. Masterman *The Double-Cross System: In the War of 1939 to 1945* (New Haven: Yale University Press, 1972), 96.

[39] 'STATEMENT of CHARLES HENRY MAXWELL KNIGHT, Major, attached to the GENERAL STAFF (Directorate of Military Intelligence), p. 2–3; 'SECOND STATEMENT of CASE against BENJAMIN GREENE for SECONDARY ADVISORY COMMITTEE,' p. 12–13; 'STATEMENT of FREDERICKA STOTTINGER, of 5 Spring Street, Paddington, W.2., p. 1–3.

[40] 'REPRESENTATIONS TO H.M. SECRETARY OF STATE BY BEN GREENE,' p. 6, TS 27/522; Simpson, 345–346.

internal security of the nation. Benjamin Greene was committed to contesting his "illegal" detention.

Pursuing Legal Avenues: Greene vs MI5 and the Home Office

A discrepancy in the "Reasons for Order," or the justification for Greene's arrest, combined with varying accounts of events raised questions. Although the original order signed by Anderson noted "hostile associations," a "Reasons for Order" issued in July claimed "acts prejudicial" as justification for the actions taken by the Home Office. While initially, the discrepancy did not negate the Home Office's case nor gain the release of Greene, it did become an issue later, particularly when he decided to take the Home Secretary to court. Two separate Advisory Committees reviewed Greene's case, evaluated the written and oral testimony, and arrived at different conclusions. In the first instance, the Committee decided that there was sufficient evidence to warrant his continued detention; in the second case, the Committee gave more credence to Greene's testimony than Kurtz's or Gaertner's and recommended his release. Although it opposed it, MI5 could not prevent Green's release because the Home Office accepted the recommendation.

When the first decision was rendered in August 1940, the threat of a German invasion contributed to a heightened sense of peril, and it would have been perfectly reasonable for the Committee to choose not to take any chances regarding the release of questionable characters. By the time of the second decision in late December 1941/early January 1942, however, invasion no longer seemed imminent, and Britons could take a more reasonable approach to their wartime situation.

As soon as he was able, Greene contested his detention, but he did not know the reason for his arrest until *after* he filed his appeal. Greene apparently had a limited amount of time in which to file his appeal to the Advisory Committee, but the lack of paper, pens, and ink pots, a small number of which were shared by 60 prisoners, delayed Greene's appeal. According to a statement that he submitted to the Secretary of State in September 1941,

> I only got my copy of the detention order on June 1st after my solicitors had made representations to the Home Office. This matter has some importance as at Brixton Prison I was told that I had to make my appeal

to the Advisory Committee within three days of my arrest which I did in complete ignorance of the reason for detention.[41]

Although their final report would not be released for a month, the First Advisory Committee issued a statement in mid-July that provided a brief litany of Greene's activities from the early 1930s when he was "Secretary of the Hemel Hampstead Divisional Labour Party" to his speech in Northamptonshire in March 1940, stating:

> The above represents the main outlines of what may be termed Greene's official activities, but there remains to be considered the far greater question of his secret opinions, actions and intentions in relation to the War.

The Committee noted its willingness to consider information that had to be handled "with some discretion," meaning the statements from Kurtz and Gaertner, which were briefly summarized in its account. Perhaps the most troubling part of Greene's actions related to his supposed recommendation that Kurtz make the acquaintance of his associate in Ireland, Meydrick Booth. A potential meeting between Kurtz and Booth was not the issue. As far as the committee was concerned, the rest of Greene's recommendation was.

> He suggested that Kurtz should try to get a post in the Ministry of Information, saying that he would find it an excellent cover and that he would have some qualifications for the job.

Although it did not say it explicitly, the committee seemed to be suggesting that Kurtz, should he get a position with the Ministry of Information, could provide useful information to Booth, "whom he [Greene] described as an ardent friend of Hitler's." The implication was that Greene was orchestrating "treasonous activities," which was troublesome although the committee waited several weeks before issuing its report and recommendation.[42]

The report issued by the First Advisory Committee on 30 August 1940 was more formal. After noting the members of the committee, it stated clearly the position of the Secretary of State:

> The Secretary of State has reasonable cause to believe that you have been recently concerned in <u>acts prejudicial</u> to the public safety and the defence

---

[41] 'REPRESENTATIONS TO H.M. SECRETARY OF STATE BY BEN GREENE,' dated 4 September 1941, signed BEN GREENE, Brixton Prison, p. 6, TS 27/522.

[42] 'ORINIGAL STATEMENT OF CASE AGAINST BENJAMIN GREENE for FIRST ADVISORY COMMITTEE,' dated 12.7.40, unsigned, TS 27/522.

of the realm, and in the preparation and instigation of such acts, and that it is necessary to exercise control over you.[43]

"Necessary to exercise control over you" translated into "detention." Following statement of the State's justification for Greene's arrest and detention, the committee presented the evidence for that justification as well as Greene's explanation of his actions and noted the inaccuracies in the accused's initial testimony before the committee and his subsequent written amendment of that deposition. The committee, obviously bothered by Greene's inability to "get his facts straight," asserted that it found "it difficult to believe that his memory, which appeared in other connections to be excellent, failed him as suggested." It also admitted that Greene confessed to other activity not in the record at that point and identified the charges that they found most troublesome – awareness of Beckett's pro-Germany publications, correspondence with people in Germany after the outbreak of hostilities, associations with German agents to whom he offered help, and certainty that Greene would not stop these activities despite the state of war between Britain and Germany. Some of the charges were based solely on the statements given by two foreign MI5 agents. Ultimately, the committee concluded that the continued detention of Greene, as requested by the Home Secretary, was warranted.[44]

> Having considered carefully all the circumstances, the Committee are unable to regard GREENE'S assurances and promises as a sufficient safeguard, and accordingly recommend that the detention of Benjamin GREENE should be continued.[45]

It is perhaps not surprising that the First Advisory Committee issued such a decision at the end of August 1940 – just a couple of weeks after the start of the Battle of Britain. The First Advisory Committee, because it had no confidence in Greene's assurances that he would not do anything against the British war effort, could not afford to release Greene and others like him. According to Simpson, Greene finally learned of the First Advisory Committee's decision in October 1940. That did not mean, however, that Greene was willing to accept his continued

---

[43] 'REPORT OF FIRST ADVISORY COMMITTEE,' dated 30th August 1940, signed H.G. Hart, Secretary, p. 5, TS 27/522; letter to The Under Secretary of State, Home Office, dated 30th August, 1940, signed H. G. Hart, Secretary, LCO 2/1454, TNA.
[44] Ibid., p. 5–7.
[45] Ibid., 8.

incarceration. Greene's removal as Justice of the Peace became official a month later.[46]

In the midst of the First Advisory Committee's proceedings, Greene's brother Edward had become involved and hired a solicitor, Oswald Hickson, who chastised the committee for failing to list the allegations against Greene or identifying the agents who had provided evidence against the pacifist. Perhaps not surprisingly, MI5 was hesitant not only to identify Kurtz and Gaertner, but also to allow them to appear before the committee, probably because that would hinder their ability to continue their work for the security services if their participation in the case became common knowledge.

In May 1941 the Division Court heard a habeas corpus application filed on behalf of Green in March. Although he had legal representation, Greene, wishing to present his own case, petitioned the justices, who consented. One of the issues proved to be the mistake in the "Reasons for Order," which possibly suggested carelessness on the part of the Home Office in preparing the documentation for detentions. Other contributing factors were Greene's connections, his past political activities, and the seriousness of the allegations against him. At issue as well were the agents' accounts being used in the case. The number of habeas corpus cases pending in the Divisional Court provided additional pressure on the justice system to get the Greene case "right."

Greene's habeas corpus application hinged on two contentions. First, he challenged "acts prejudicial" and used an account of his life as evidence that the "Reasons for Order" was not justified. Second, citing a sworn statement from Anderson that an error regarding the "Reasons for Order" had been made, Greene alleged that the mistake "prejudiced" Anderson and requested that the court investigate "the basis for his detention." During the proceedings although he agreed that the Home Office admitted responsibility for the error, the Attorney-General argued that discovering the cause of the error was indeterminable. Weighing all the evidence, the Justices decided that the Home Office was not prejudiced against Greene by the mistaken "Reasons for Order," but because Greene "thought the Home Secretary had changed the grounds for the order," they recommended another review of Greene's detention by a new committee, a recommendation that the Home Office did not oppose.[47]

---

[46] Simpson, 351–352.
[47] Ibid., 356–360.

Perhaps the Home Office was confident that a different committee would reach the same conclusion as the First Advisory Committee. After all, the nation was still at war. German planes continued to bomb British cities, especially London. Although a German invasion no longer appeared imminent, it was still crucial to minimize the internal threats to security and safety. Surely, the Second Advisory Committee would also recognize that Greene could not be trusted, posed a potential threat to the nation's internal security, and, consequently, warranted continued detention as the best way of "exercising control" over him.

On 3 June 1941 the Second Advisory Committee issued the "Second Statement of Case against Benjamin Greene" that began with a recap of events, including the detention order based on "hostile associations," the "incorrect assumption" that the basis for the order was "acts prejudicial," and Greene's application for a "writ of habeas corpus." The committee acknowledged the failure of Greene's appeal and the recommendation of the Justices for a new hearing by the Advisory Committee. While similar to the "First Statement of Case against Benjamin Greene," issued by the First Advisory Committee, this document provided a bit more detail about the pacifist's activities before and during the early part of the war, including evidence of Green's pro-German behavior, participation in the BPP, and speeches that he gave after resigning from the organization. It also listed the evidence – particularly letters – that demonstrated Greene's continued close connection to BPP in general and, more specifically, to Beckett and Tavistock, after his departure from the group. Then the committee got to the crux of the case. "[T]here remains another matter to be considered, namely his secret opinions, actions and intentions in relation to the War."

At this point, however, the committee's statement referred to the content of Greene's meetings with Kurtz and Gaertner and Greene's suggestions to Kurtz with regard to Meyrick Booth and "spying." Thus the Second Advisory Committee, chaired by Sir N. Birkett, set out the case under review. It would spend months gathering statements and interviewing witnesses – Greene and Kurtz in particular – before rendering its recommendation in mid-December.[48] Questions of security, the war effort at home and abroad, and testimony credibility, among others, came into play. Perhaps most challenging was their need to determine Greene's "secret opinions, actions, and intentions."

---

[48] 'SECOND STATEMENT OF CASE against BENJAMIN GREENE for SECOND ADVISORY COMMITTEE,' dated 3.6.41, signed S. H. Noakes, p. 9–14, TS 27/522.

The Second Advisory Committee's job was made more difficult by the fact that MI5 did not initially want to let Kurtz or Gaertner testify before it. At issue was future work of the two agents, in particular of Gaertner, who had begun work as a double agent as part of an established spy ring led by Dusko Popov, codenamed Tricycle. Protecting the identity of the double agents was of such concern to the Twenty (XX or Double-Cross) Committee that it articulated a policy during a meeting held on 6 November 1941. Although the resolution was adopted with regard to another double agent, it could be, and probably was, invoked with regard to Gaertner, codenamed Gelatine. The adopted resolution stated:

> When action is to be taken or contemplated which is likely to compromise an agent through whom Service information has been passed to the enemy, the D.'s of I. should be given time to consider whether the effect is likely to be serious from their point of view, and opportunity should be afforded to them to make representations to M.I.5 or M.I.6 as the case may be.[49]

MI5 and MI6 probably relied upon this resolution in refusing to allow Gaertner to appear before the Second Advisory Committee; therefore, they could only refer to her written statement. The Security Agencies did not, however, prevent Kurtz from being questioned by the committee.

MI5's motivation had shifted in ways that reflected an equal shift in securities issues and in the war effort. While the internal threat had eased, the external one had not. Certainly, by 1942 the XX Committee was utilizing all of its available double agent resources to deceive its German enemies. These double agents provided information to the Germans in a critical effort to persuade them to reach intended conclusions with regard to upcoming Allied operations in North Africa, Sicily, Italy, and, ultimately, in France. Protecting the double agents was crucial; MI5 and MI6 refused to allow the Second Advisory Committee to interview Gaertner, a double agent. Because Kurtz was not operating as a double agent, it was not necessary to shield him from the committee.

While the Second Advisory Committee was gathering information and questioning witnesses, Guy Liddell, MI5's Director of

---

[49] Twenty Committee, Minutes of the 45th Meeting of the Committee, held on Thursday, 6th November 1941, p. 3, KV 4/64, TNA.

Counter-Espionage, consulted with Maxwell Knight about the situation and expressed his concerns. In October the two men discussed the problems caused by Oswald Hickson's successful entrapment of Kurtz, who apparently lied rather than reveal that he was a MI5 agent. According to his diary, Liddell "suggested to Max [Maxwell Knight] that it might be a wise move to ensure that no Parliamentary Question was put down on the Order Paper about Kurtz since once this was done an answer would have to be given, and Kurtz's name would have been exposed."[50] A couple of weeks later, he reacted to Hickson's petition to the Advisory Committee for access to their transcripts and notes related to the Greene case, and although Sir Alexander Maxwell agreed to the solicitor's request, Liddell was opposed to such a move for two reasons. First, he thought that a problematic precedent could be set and that "the official notes of the Advisory Committee should not be allowed to pass into the hands of a private individual." He was quite adamant on this point. In addition, he recognized the impact that the release of "official notes" would have on the looming discussion about Regulation 18B.[51]

A reversal of Regulation 18B could undermine MI5's efforts to guarantee the nation's internal safety during wartime. At the end of November, some of Liddell's fears were realized as Kurtz's name, not "the material witness," was indeed entered on the Order Paper, and the agent was publicly exposed. As Liddell noted, "[T]his incident amply justifies his [the Director-General] contention that information and agents should on no account be forced to appear before the committee."[52] Kurtz's usefulness to MI5 appeared to be over.

Throughout this period, Greene remained interned at Brixton Prison. Perhaps as evidence of his impatience with his prolonged incarceration, he decided to contact the Secretary of State directly in September 1941 in order to plead his case. In his communication, he provided an explanation of his trips to Germany beginning in 1933, his contacts with the Home Office, his meeting with Sir Samuel Hoare, his contact with Mr. Bohle of Germany, and his family connections to hostile nation and acknowledged activities and speeches that he had given that he had forgotten to enter into the record for the First Advisory

---

[50] Nigel West, ed., *The Guy Liddell Diaries*, Volume 1: *1939–1942, MI5's Director of Counter-Espionage in World War II* (London: Routledge, 2005), 185.
[51] Ibid., 191–192.
[52] Ibid., 197.

Committee. He also provided an account of his interaction with Kurtz and Gaertner in the spring of 1940 and contested Kurtz's version of events. In addition, claiming to be suspicious of Kurtz and Gaertner, Greene asserted that he had telephoned Scotland Yard, voiced his reservations about the pair, and provided Kurtz's address. Despite their assurances, Greene claimed that he did not hear from Scotland Yard again until the day of his arrest. He did admit that he saw Gaertner and Kurtz once more between his report to the police and his own arrest, but noted that it was not an arranged meeting. He then denied the charges leveled against him and suggested that he attempted to entrap Kurtz. Greene admitted "that I may have expressed admiration for certain aspects of the Nazi system in my endeavor to extract from him [Kurtz] exactly where he, a German refugee, just released from detention, stood."[53]

Greene's efforts to entrap Kurtz backfired, and he, not the German, ended up in Brixton Prison. His "representations" to the Secretary of State did not, however, bring the matter to a conclusion. Instead the Second Advisory Committee's investigation continued. In fact, Greene's brother Edward lured Kurtz to his solicitor's office where he apparently retracted the statement that he had provided to the First Advisory Committee.[54] Hickson formally entered this into the record with the Second Advisory Committee; the 'new' Kurtz statement muddied the waters.

Recognizing that the Greene case had sparked public attention and that the "legal proceedings" had been lengthy, the Second Advisory Committee finally issued their report on 16 December 1941, reiterating the reason for Greene's detention under Regulation 18B and itemizing the justification for the Home Secretary's order. The committee also discussed Greene's responses to the allegations and analyzed the evidence provided by Kurtz and Gaertner. The committee definitely favored Greene's account over those provided by Kurtz and Gaertner, concluding:[55]

> That the statements and actions of Ben Greene have been misunderstood is quite plain; that some of them have been distorted is equally plain; and

[53] 'REPRESENTATIONS TO H.M. SECRETARY OF STATE BY BEN GREEN,' dated 4 September 1941, signed BEN GREEN, Brixton Prison, p. 1-6, TS 27/522.
[54] 'MINUTE OF INTERVIEW WITH MR. H. KURTZ AT OFFICE OF PLAINTIFF'S SOLICITOR,' dated 21st October 1941, TS 27/522.
[55] 'REPORT OF SECOND ADVISORY COMMITTEE,' dated 16th December 1941, signed Williams, Secretary, TS 27/522; Simpson, 367-369.

that deficiencies have been supplied by Kurtz, either by way of inference or assumption, is plain, too.[56]

The committee questioned the validity of Kurtz's testimony, particularly in light of the events in Hickson's office in which he recanted his original statement. MI5, in particular, took issue with the committee's dismissal of Kurtz's testimony and with the committee's suggestions that it lacked credibility. The committee went a step further, accused Kurtz of being "guilty of very considerable lying," and examined his testimony in great detail. In comparing Greene's and Kurtz's versions of their meeting on 24 April, they concluded "that the explanation of Green was the more credible." In almost every instance in which the accounts of the two men diverged, the Committee discounted Kurtz and sided with Greene.

In almost every respect, the Second Advisory Committee rejected the evidence provided by MI5 and the Home Office for Greene's detention under Regulation 18B and at times suggested that parts of the story did not ring true. For example, Greene claimed to have contacted Scotland Yard about Kurtz and Gaertner. Although Scotland Yard apparently had no record of the report, the Committee concluded that it did not make sense for the pacifist to contact the police if he knew that the two were agents and was planning to work with them. Despite the lack of corroboration from Scotland Yard, the committee believed that Greene actually notified the police.[57]

Ultimately, two important factors weighed heavily in the committee's decision. It was not given the opportunity to question Gaertner and, consequently, was reluctant to give her statement much credence. In addition, it did not buy Kurtz's testimony because of its discrepancies and because of his "confession" to Hickson. While it claimed to take the statements of the two agents seriously, the committee ultimately accepted Greene's testimony as more credible. The Second Advisory Committee admitted that it did not discount his past associations with Beckett and the BPP or his sister's connection to Beckett's wife, but decided that Greene's continued detention was unwarranted and "recommended" his release. Its recommendation came down to its inability to interrogate Gaertner, which weakened the Home Office's case. The Second Advisory Committee was clear when it emphasized

---

[56] Ibid., 19.
[57] Ibid., 20–26.

this in the final paragraph of their lengthy report while at the same time admonishing the unnamed MI5 for putting the Home Office in an untenable position:

> The Committee finds there is no substance in these charges, and regret profoundly that the original Committee was not allowed to see Kurtz or Gartner [sic]. Even now the present Committee have not seen Gartner [sic], but are not disposed to accept the written statement of Gartner [sic] as it stands, in view of Greene's evidence and the evidence of Kurtz: despite the evidence of Major Knight that he regards them both as witnesses of truth and worthy of confidences. The Committee feels that the rule that only in exceptional circumstances can agents be seen and examined by the Committee is most unsatisfactory. It leads to possible injustice, and places the Home Secretary in a most difficult position. If the Committee have come to a right conclusion in this case, as they think they have upon the evidence, Greene is entitled to be freed from charges which amount to treason, and not to labour all his life under the cloud which otherwise will remain.[58]

Both the Office of the Home Secretary and MI5 registered their opinions about the Second Advisory Committee's recommendation. At this point, perhaps because the overall wartime situation was different in early 1942 than it had been in May 1940, the two offices responded in different ways. F. A. Newsam reviewed the Second Advisory Committee's report and made his recommendation to the Home Secretary in early January 1942. He briefly reviewed the work of the committee, acknowledged that, as chair of the committee, Sir N. Birkett thoroughly interrogated Kurtz, and bemoaned the fact that he was unable to question Gaertner. Newsam admitted that the committee found Greene a more credible witness than Kurtz and that the evidence did not support the allegations. Consequently, the committee concluded "that the evidence of Greene who denied all these allegations was to be believed and that he was entitled to be acquitted of what they described as 'terrible allegations.'"[59] Newsam stated that, whether or not MI5 wanted to accept it, based on Greene's convincing testimony, Kurtz and Gaertner had lied. Consequently, he saw no reason not to accept the Second Advisory Committee's recommendation to free Greene. He agreed with the committee's assessment of Greene as a "woolly-headed type," but honest. If his assurances to the committee were to be accepted,

---

[58] Ibid., 30

[59] F. A. Newsam's comments on 'THE CASE OF BENJAMIN GREENE,' dated 4th January, 1942, p. 32, TS 27/522; Simpson, 369.

then Greene "would not be a danger if released." According to Newsam, he, Mr. Hutchinson and Mr. Hoare were in agreement and advised the Home Secretary to follow the Second Advisory Committee's recommendation "that Benjamin Greene should be released unconditionally."[60] Newsam's assessment ended with a caution:

> This case illustrates vividly the possibility of injustice being caused to persons who are detained wholly or mainly on the evidence of agents employed by the Security Service and the desirability of ensuring that information supplied by such persons is subjected to the closest examination. This matter ought to be taken up urgently with the Security Service.[61]

David Petrie,[62] Director-General of the Security Services, on the other hand, vehemently disagreed and wrote a letter to that effect to Sir Alexander Maxwell two days later. Both the security division that handled the case and the legal division, according to Petrie, advocated the continued detention of Greene. Challenging the legal system, he argued that Second Advisory Committee demonstrated bias and unfairly expected Kurtz to remember the exact details of a statement that he wrote 18 months prior to his interrogation without having the opportunity to review it. Because Kurtz's responses to it deviated some from his original statement, the committee chose to discount it, but Petrie argued that certain facts were incontrovertible, that "Kurtz did hold a series of essentially treasonable conversations with Greene, and that the latter listened to them with every appearance of acceptance."[63] Concerned that "the strictness of Kurtz's examination is in curious contrast with the Committee's facile acceptance of Greene's denials," he suggested that MI5 would have no incentive to cooperate with the committee in the future. There was perhaps some justification for Petrie's accusation. Finally, Petrie reaffirmed his recommendation that the Home Secretary reject the advice of the Second Advisory Committee and order that the detention of Greene under Regulation 18B remain in effect.[64]

---

[60] F. A. Newsam's comments on 'THE CASE OF BENJAMIN GREENE,' dated 4th January, 1942, p. 31–35; Simpson, 369.

[61] Ibid., 35.

[62] Sir David Petrie became 'Director-General of the Security Services in November 1940.' West, 14.

[63] 'Comments of M.I.5. on Report of Second Advisory Committee, dated 6th January, 1942, signed D. PETRIE, to Sir Alexander Maxwell, p. 36, TS 27/522. See also Guy Liddell's Diary entry on 18 January 1942, p. 214; Simpson, 369–370.

[64] Ibid., 36–38.

Three days later, Maxwell noted the Home Secretary's decision to release Ben Greene under specific conditions. The Home Secretary wanted Greene kept under surveillance, and upon release, Greene had to keep the police apprised of where he was living. Some of the conditions that were listed for his detention – "hostile associations," German mother, family in Germany, contacts with Germans and with the BPP – provided justification "to exercise some supervision over him."[65] On 16 January 1942 Maxwell informed Sir Claud Schuster that the Home Secretary had suspended Greene's detention order and authorized his release based on the conditions listed above.[66] On the same day Maxwell corresponded with Greene and informed him of the conditions of his release as ordered by the Home Secretary.[67]

After almost two years of detention at Brixton Prison under Regulation 18B, Greene was finally a free man. Despite his release, Greene did not feel completely vindicated and within two months decided to file suit against Sir John Anderson requesting "damages for libel" and "false imprisonment." Although he was allowed to sue Anderson, Greene had little likelihood of success since he had to prove that the Home Secretary was lying when he told the committee that he "believed" the evidence against Greene when he signed the order of detention under Regulation 18B. Petrie agreed to let Kurtz and Gaertner testify although the latter was to be referred to by initials or an assumed name in order to protect her identity since she was still active as a double agent. Apparently, Greene proved to be a "poor witness," and Kurtz was a better witness for the defendant than for the plaintiff. Because there was concern that, if Gaertner were allowed to testify as a witness for the plaintiff and she corroborated Kurtz's testimony, further damage would be done (the final nail placed in the coffin of Greene's case), Greene and his solicitor decided to drop their case against Anderson. It was finally over.[68]

---

[65] Memorandum, dated 9th January, 1942, signed A.M. (Sir Alexander Maxwell), LCO 2/1454; Simpson, 371–372.

[66] Letter to Sir Claud Schuster from Sir Alexander Maxwell, dated 16th January, 1942, LCO 2/1454; Simpson, 371–372.

[67] Letter to Benjamin Greene from Sir Alexander Maxwell, dated 16th January, 1942, LCO 2/1454; Simpson, 371–372.

[68] 'IN THE HIGH COURT OF JUSTICE KING'S BENCH DIVISION, 1942 G. No. 257, BETWEEN BENJAMIN GREENE, Plaintiff, and THE RIGHT HONOURABLE SIR JOHN ANDERSON, Defendant, TS 27/522; Simpson, 372–376; Note from Oswald Hickson to Fredericka Gaertner informing her that her presence in court was required under a subpoena that she had received on 22 June 1942, dated 27th January, 1943, KV 2/1280, TNA.

Conclusions

What happened to Ben Greene was, in some respects, tragic, but perhaps understandable given the circumstances. During times of upheaval, unfortunately, injustice happens, and mistakes are made as a result of excessive zeal. The question is how soon is the injustice reversed or rectified. As has happened in the past – the internment of Japanese-Americans during World War II or, more recently, the detention of terrorist suspects at Guantanamo Bay – situations or events are seen in an absolute (i.e. black and white) context. The powers that be do not seem to see the shades of gray, and sometimes the result is injustice, albeit an understandable one.

Here was a man who was engaged in questionable activities, at least according to Maxwell Knight and his colleagues at MI5, at a time of crisis and threat to national security. An avowed pacifist, Greene, whose mother was German, had relations and other connections in Germany. His views had been shaped by his experiences on the continent after World War I. He was committed to trying to create a world in which war did not exist. Some of his German, as well as British, contacts were questionable, if not before 1939, then certainly after the outbreak of hostilities. He was associated with the British People's Party and made speeches, the content of which was open to interpretation, but seemed to be pro-Nazi. Greene's behavior appeared to be outside the paradigm that was acceptable during wartime, and he seemed to be oblivious to the changing situation at home. Knight, on the other hand, was not, and he considered Greene to be a threat. Consequently, Greene was on MI5's radar.

Investigating a possible Fifth Column that could threaten Britain's internal and external security, MI5 focused its attention on suspicious organizations, such as the British Union of Fascists and the British People's Party. It cast its net wide and caught suspects who posed or potentially posed threats to the nation's safety. MI5's authority came from Regulation 18B, which was passed at a time of great crisis and which granted the Home Secretary broad powers to detain those in the country who were deemed a threat. With the end of the "Phony War" and the invasion of Belgium and France, the war heated up. The Home Secretary signed the order for detentions, including Greene's, when the war in France was going poorly and the evacuation of British and French troops from Dunkirk was about to begin.

By the time the First Advisory Committee reached its decision to recommend the continued detention of Greene, the Battle of Britain was underway. Because of the dire circumstances and the looming German invasion of Britain, the committee seemed willing to give more weight to the written testimony of two MI5 agents than to that of Greene, despite its inability to question Kurtz. Identifying its lack of faith in his assurances to do nothing to hinder the war effort or to help the Germans should they actually invade, the First Advisory Committee approved the action taken by the Home Office against Greene.

Why, then, did the Second Advisory Committee do the exact opposite? By the time the Second Advisory Committee came into the picture, approximately a year had passed. Although the Germans were still dropping bombs on London, the Brits had basically "won" the Battle of Britain, and the nation no longer feared a German invasion. While a year earlier it was acceptable for MI5 agents to gather information that resulted in the detention of British citizens, that was no longer the case in late 1941/early 1942. The imminent danger had eased, and the country felt less willing to tolerate the activities of MI5 agents against its citizens. In addition, it is possible that Greene's highly connected friends put pressure on the government to reverse itself in a case that had garnered public interest. Consequently, the Second Advisory Committee repeatedly sided with Greene over Kurtz and rejected Kurtz's testimony and his and Gaertner's written statements against Greene. Unlike the First Advisory Committee, it found Greene to be a more credible witness than Kurtz despite Knight's witness to his and Gaertner's reliability. What the Second Advisory Committee seemed also to be rejecting was the broad powers that the Home Office had exercised under Regulation 18B a year earlier. It is possible that the committee was concurring with Judge Rolfe, who is 1842 said in *Winterbottom v Wright*, "Hard cases ... are apt to introduce bad law."[69] As the possibility of the nation's demise receded, the committee eased the heavy hand of government and, to some extent, rejected MI5's argument for continued vigilance. At the end of the day, for Benjamin Greene, in the "clash of the titans," law defeated security.

---

[69] Quoted by David Rubin, "Law's Blindfold," in *Conflict of Interest in Professions*, eds. Michael Davis and Andrew Stark (Oxford: Oxford University Press, 2001), 40.

MILITARY CULTURES, MILITARY HISTORIES AND THE CURRENT EMERGENCY

Jeremy Black

'Military history is arguably the last stronghold of what historiographers call the "Whig interpretation" ... [it] sees the development of warfare as progressive'. Dennis Showalter's perceptive comment of 2002[1] drew valuable attention to the culture of military history, which, in turn, offers a useful angle on one of the leading concepts in military studies and history, the cultural turn in military history. Culture in military history focuses on perception and expectations, especially the perception of opportunities, of problems, of options, and of success. The variety of issues and concepts summarized as the cultural aspects of war is a subject has attracted considerable attention over the last decade, offering a different way of assessing capability to that focused on weaponry.[2]

The theme here is that culture is dynamic, not static, as both a reality and an analytical process. Cultural influences emerge clearly in the writing of history, including military history. Thus, culture needs to be tackled as a dynamic and problematic phenomenon whereas the standard approach in military history is to employ less refined concepts of culture as an overarching, one-dimensional and fixed set of objective ideas, a practice long challenged within the social scences.

While some scholars, therefore, have argued in favour of the need to consider particular cultural elements, especially the way in which understandings of appropriate military conduct, victory, defeat, and casualty, are all culturally conditioned, others have sought to employ cultural issues in warfare as explanatory factors in large-scale, overall or synoptic theories allegedly explaining military history. This approach

---

I have benefited from the opportunity to discuss some of these points provided by invitations to speak at the University of Oxford and to ICAP and from the comments of Michael Neiberg and Patrick Porter on an earlier version.

[1] Dennis Showalter, "Europe's Way of War, 1815–64," *European Warfare 1815–2000* (Basingstoke: Palgrave Macmillan, 2002), 27.

[2] Patrick Porter, *Military Orientalism: Eastern War Through Western Eyes* (London: C. Hurst & Co. Publishers Ltd., 2009).

includes (although it is not limited to) the eloquent, if somewhat simplistic, account of Western military success that in part reflects the misleading looseness of cultural definitions, an account seen in particular in the work of Victor Davis Hanson such as his *Carnage and Culture: Landmark Battles in the Rise of Western Power* (New York, 2001). This cultural interpretation, however, risks the danger of an ethnographic exceptionalism that can strike critics as racist. Hanson's work also offers an interesting parallel to that of Samuel P. Huntington.[3] Indeed, it can be seen as a consequence, or even rationalisation, of the latter for military historians.

Culture is a much employed term for, aside from the culture of society as a whole, including why people fought and how they responded to the issues of conflict, on which there has recently been excellent work for the American Civil War, there is also the organizational culture of particular militaries, a topic that overlaps with sociology. This category, which includes issues such as hierarchy, discipline and the responsiveness of subordinates to responsibilities, illustrates the widespread applicability of the concept of culture and of related terms and vocabulary.

There is also the concept of strategic culture, employed to discuss the context within which military tasks were "shaped", a concept that overlaps with that of strategic landscapes, and a topic that interacts with issues raised in international relations studies. For example, it has been argued that China's strategic culture was primarily defensive and focused on protecting its frontiers, but there has also been a critique of the notion of a defensive, Confucian, strategic culture, and, in its place, an argument that there have been longstanding expansionist strands in Chinese strategic culture, notably at the expense of steppe peoples.[4] This issue is seen as of considerable pertinence at present, although it may also be asked how far a discussion of Chinese warmaking in say the eighteenth century is of relevance today, in what is a very different political context, both domestic and international, as well as with regard to the nature of war.

---

[3] Samuel P. Huntington, *The Clash of Civilizations and the Remaking of World Order* (London: The Free Press, 1996).

[4] Alastair I. Johnston, *Cultural Realism: Strategic Culture and Grand Strategy in Chinese History* (Princeton: Princeton University Press, 1995); Hans Van de Ven (ed.), *Warfare in Chinese History* (Leiden: Brill, 2000).

This use of culture approximates to earlier and current discussions of distinctive ways of war, in particular the notion of American exceptionalism.[5] With reference to ideas of national exceptionalism, the concept of strategic culture, however, does have to address the fact of the heavily-contested character of national interests, as well as the issue of consistency in the policies of particular states. Thus, there have been competing strands of thought within the evolution of the American army.[6] It is necessary to identify and probe the problem of plurality and diversity within strategic cultures. For example, there is the question of the strategic culture of individual military services, which, in part, are shaped by their assessment of their domestic role.

As a related issue, there has been considerable scholarly interest of late in symbolic aspects of the military and of war – although, by their nature, it is difficult to assess the relative importance of these aspects. Yet, a past failure to give due weight to the cultural contexts of warfare has ensured that much military history has devoted insufficient weight to these symbolic aspects, which include modes of fighting as well as a ritualisation of combat and conflict that can affect, as well as reflect, tactical, operational and strategic goals.

It is also possible to present wars in a "cultural" context different from the more "realist" conventional wars of the rivalry of states, and do so not least by emphasizing psychological elements in the causes and conduct of war. This emphasis on non-"realist" and non-materialist factors is especially important in understanding the causes of war. Rather than treating the latter in terms of rational drives and/or the operation of an international system, it is possible to draw attention to the cultural drives that make war welcome and desirable or, at least, less threatening.[7]

Cultural imperatives and weaponry have also been linked for much more recent times, as in the argument that the B-17 bomber embodied the dreams of glory of American air power enthusiasts, or Rachel Holloway's account of President Reagan's "reinvigoration of

---

[5] Hans R. Guggisberg, "American Exceptionalism as National History?" in *Bridging the Atlantic: The Question of American Exceptionalism in Perspective*, eds. Elisabeth Glaser and Hermann Wellenreuther (Cambridge: Cambridge University Press, 2002), 265–76.

[6] Brian M. Linn, *The Echo of Battle: The Army's Way of War* (Cambridge, Massachusetts: Harvard University Press, 2007).

[7] Jeremy Black, *Why Wars Happen* (London: Reaktion, 1998).

the technological sublime".[8] Indeed, the role of cultural assumptions in the response to the whole idea of air power, and the extent to which these assumptions varied within the organizational cultures of particular militaries, are clearly important to particular national cultures of air power.[9] There is no reason why this approach should not be more generally applied.

"Culture", however, is a term so widely and loosely used[10] as to have its analytical value at least in part compromised, a point that requires discussion whenever culture is deployed as a descriptive or, even more, explanatory category. Furthermore, the idea has been politicised in that the notion of a specifically Western Way of War, moreover a particularly successful one, has become an aspect of the American culture wars, as with the bitter debate over the views of Victor Davis Hanson. These views apparently influenced Dick Cheney[11] and greatly helped Hanson's career. For some commentators, the notion of a Western Way of War is a hostile response to political correctness and multi-culturalism in American education. That view, however, is overly simplistic: it ignores the wider resonances of the subject, not least discussion outside the USA, as well as the extent to which concern, both there and elsewhere, with cultural issues was a response to conflict with non-Western forces, especially the experience of the Korean and Vietnam Wars. Thus, the stress on the cultural dimension is, in part, a result of an awareness of multi-culturalism in global military affairs.

To take another approach, there is a contemporary political aspect to this discussion, as belief in the special effectiveness of a Western cultural type of war-making has provided encouragement to those encouraging American interventionism, such as Hanson, and will presumably continue to do so. The notion of a specifically Western Way of War,

---

[8] R. Holloway, "The Strategic Defense Initiative and the Technological Sublime: Fear, Science, and the Cold War," in *Critical Reflections on the Cold War: Linking Rhetoric and History*, eds. Martin J. Medhurst and H. W. Brands, (College Station, TX: Texas A&M University Press, 2000), 225.

[9] Malcolm Smith, "'A Matter of Faith': British Strategic Air Doctrine Between the Wars", *Journal of Contemporary History* 15 (1980), 423–42; Stephen L. McFarland, *America's Pursuit of Precision Bombing*, 1910–1945 (Washington: Smithsonian Books, 1995).

[10] For example in Martin van Creveld, *The Culture of War* (New York: Presidio Press, 2008).

[11] Barton Gellman, *Angler: The Cheney Vice Presidency* (New York: Penguin Press, 2008), 249–50.

however, flagrantly simplifies the West, and thereby ignores diversity within the West, including what has been a frequent reluctance to engage in battle; and this notion also simplifies the non-West. Thus, for example, the dichotomy of a Western preference for open battle versus Oriental trickery that is offered, is doubly flawed, and is an aspect of the divide between the sometimes oversimplified notions of culture used within military history and the more promising approaches elsewhere within the intellectual marketplace.

The looseness, and therefore flexibility and extendability, of the cultural interpretation of war, however, can in itself be instructive, as it encourages a focus on the impact and role of ideas and assumptions. These, in turn, affect the very process of military history. For example, the study of combat styles has been seen as indicating the possibilities that a borrowing from other disciplines offers military history.

Furthermore, returning to more functional considerations of the cultural dimension, the varied nature of assumptions affecting military capability and its assessment encourages a departure from the more structured ranking of militaries that arises when the focus is on weaponry and organization. In practice, these issues are not separate, as cultural factors help to explain why particular weapons, such as firearms, or organizational systems, for example conscription, are adopted or discarded in individual states (or cultures) with contrasting consequences. These factors have been employed to discuss developments such as the abandonment of the use of the gun in seventeenth-century Japan.

More generally, even though "culture" is used somewhat loosely as an analytical term, it provides a way to bring together the varied dimensions of warfare – organisation and tasking, "war and society", and the "face of battle"; each of which indeed has a cultural dimension, and a dynamic character to that as well. An emphasis on culture also offers a more relativist mode of explanation in military history, notably by comparing the strategic and organizational cultures of competing states and their militaries, rather than by measuring them against an absolute or universal scale of technological capacity or proficiency, as in the attempt to assess which is the "best" army in the Second World War. For example, views on military promotion, and the related practices, reflect cultural factors. Thus, in the Second World War, the British army showed a tendency in promotions to value personal recommendation over specialist expertise or operational experience, a value that matched the nature of the norms in British society.

The pursuit of the idea of the "best" army, or of better armies, as in the work of Max Hastings on 1944–45, reflects problems with the idea of employing cultural classification in the shape of national distinctiveness, as it is unclear that differences at the aggregate, national, level are more pertinent than variations within armies, for example between élite *Wehrmacht* units and the bulk of the German divisions, which tended to be far less well equipped and to fight with less determination. This stress on an élite can be discussed in functional military terms of the allocation of troops and *matériel*, but also reflected the assumptions of the *Wehrmacht* and the ideology of the Nazi regime, each of which can be discussed in cultural terms.

The relativist approach needs to be open to the variety of military cultures across the world, past and present (and, planners note, future as well); and this openness means not only an interest in non-Western developments, but also an understanding of their variety and complexity – as well as the avoidance of misleading approaches to the respective capability of West and "non-West", and to warfare between them.

This openness challenges model-based approaches that emphasize apparently scientific analysis, and that are designed to demonstrate universal laws; and which, as a consequence, focus on a limited and readily-defined group of conflicts and military systems. Such an openness to the variety, and importance, of cultures therefore is at variance with the pronounced dominance of Western assumptions, paradigms and examples in military history. Thus, one instance of "cultural" analysis limits another, which is a consequence of the widely-ranging nature of the use of the language of culture. In short, the cultural approach also relates to the practice of military analysis, its subject, content and themes, and this should be an important theme in discussion of the cultural angle.

Across both time and space, the cultural specificity of particular types of warfare emerges as a building block for analysis, indeed the key building block. As such, this specificity displaces attention from a crudely functionalist account of military capability, effectiveness and success, one based on the appropriate use of resources and technology and on the maximisation of the latter. Instead, the idea of the appropriate is discussed in terms of the assumptions and ideology, in short culture, of particular societies.

Military history, of course, is not in some fashion separate to contemporary discussion about war, nor to the general currents of historical thought. Indeed, the combination of both help shape it, although any account of that shaping has to allow for the partly autonomous nature of the particular discipline and of the writers, publishers and readers involved in it. Indeed this interplay requires an explicit discussion, because there is a misleading tendency to push these factors to the background. Instead, the perception and analysis of military history are both products of shifting perceptions. Thus, culture is both an analytical construction (or, rather, a number of different constructions), and also a perception that reflects changing moods.

The historical moment for the modern cultural assessment is clearcut; although there were also earlier such assessments that are of considerable interest and that provide valuable insights on recent and current developments. This historical moment is that of the last decade and, in particular, of the unravelling of the confidence displayed in the 1990s about the extent to which embracing and shaping technological developments provided the opportunity for carrying through a Revolution in Military Affairs (RMA) that constituted a paradigm shift in military capability and effectiveness, in short a transformation.

The belief in the RMA was particularly strong in the USA but was also embraced elsewhere. It accorded with ideological drives and demands of the period, but also with specific political and military requirements, and with the struggle (debate is too mild a word) over resources within the military and the related military-industrial complex. These factors were interrelated which underlines the problem with separating out only one theme for analysis.

Before considering these points, a note on the mixed relationship between academics and the RMA is relevant. In part, there were the issues of influence and relevance, issues that also play a role in discussion of cultural factors today. The wealthiest military, that of the USA, sponsors conferences and also treats history as an important aspect of its military education, not only for those entering the military but also for internal promotion, especially to, and in, command ranks. Without suggesting any undue influence, this situation obviously affects the nature of academic discussion in the USA. There are related pressures elsewhere, including in Britain. Indeed, cultural factors serve there as an explanation of how best to compensate for a relative lack of resources.

Moreover, the "space" for would-be objective academic debate is limited in many countries, in part because military analysis has not developed in the universities, a situation that owes much to an anti-militaristic ethos,[12] and in part because the pressures within, and from, the military are very much for analysis to accord with current doctrine. The extent to which this is the case is underplayed in anglophone discussion, because the cultural norm in most English-speaking states is one of free enquiry; but, aside from the limitations in practice in anglophone states, this situation is not more generally relevant.

As far as the USA was concerned, the belief of the 1990s and early 2000s in the RMA made historical and cultural aspects of military analysis appear far less relevant, if not completely irrelevant. The belief that a paradigm shift in capability had occurred, or was occurring, or would occur – and there was a disturbing lack of precision on these points – was, at once, historical and cultural in nature and a denial of such factors. In practice, belief in *the* RMA, or *a* RMA, and, again, there was a lack of precision, represented another iteration of a pronounced trope in Western culture, namely that which put an emphasis on machines and, in doing so, reflected and sustained the assumption of a hierarchy of military proficiency defined by technology. There was a definition of a past ages in terms of their material culture, notably the Stone, Bronze and Iron Ages, and a stress on past revolutions in capability stemming from new technologies, notably the stirrup, gunpowder, steam and nuclear.

This approach, however, represented a limited account, and, in part, a serious misreading of capability and proficiency, and indeed of military history. The approach was one that became particularly strong with industrialisation, which itself demonstrates the contingent nature of intellectual analyses and cultural moods; but was already in play earlier, not least with the self-conscious awareness of differing military forms that can be seen with, and from, the European Renaissance of the fifteenth century. This awareness helped underline both the possibility of major change through time and also the extent to which this change could be linked with a powerful cultural relativism between competing societies.

---

[12] John Lynn, "The Embattled Future of Academic Military History," *Journal of Military History* 61 (1997), 775–89; Victor Davis Hanson, "The Dilemmas of the Contemporary Military Historian," in *Reconstructing History: The Emergence of a New Historical Society*, eds. Elizabeth Fox-Genovese and Elisabeth Lasch-Quinn (London, 1998), 189–20; "Military History: A Forum on the State of the Field," *Historically Speaking*, X/5 (Nov. 2009), 10–19.

A crucial point in the last was the reading, indeed rereading, of the longstanding clash between Christendom and Islam. Although, in practice, conflict was not continual, this clash could be read in existential terms, indeed, to employ Samuel Huntington's phrase from the 1990s, as a clash of civilisations. As a consequence, there was a particular concern among European commentators to explain how best to protect Christendom from the advance of Islam. The latter owed much to the extent to which Christendom appeared to be in retreat from the twelfth century on, repeating the earlier cataclysm seen with the original Islamic advances in the seventh and eighth centuries. Jerusalem, a key reality, as well as symbol, of Christianity, lost in the seventh and regained again at the close of the eleventh century, was conquered anew for Islam in 1187, and the Crusader states in the Near East were finally extinguished with the fall of Acre in 1291.

By then, Byzantium, the Eastern Roman empire, was a fraction of its one-time strength, and, in the fourteenth century, the Ottoman Turks invaded the Balkans, turning back to finish off Constantinople (Istanbul) itself in 1453. Subsequent Ottoman progress was not without checks, for example at Belgrade and Rhodes, but, seemed inexorable and, indeed, an apocalyptic threat. By 1520, when Suleiman the Magnificent came to the Ottoman throne, the Ottomans were in control of most of the Balkans and had recently conquered the Mamluk empire, adding Egypt, Syria and Palestine to their dominions. The 1520s brought the total defeat of the kingdom of Hungary and in 1529 the Ottomans besieged Vienna.

This advance, like the brief occupation of Otranto in southern Italy in 1480–81, proved the limit of Ottoman capability, but, like many measures of military effectiveness, the question of how best to respond to the Ottomans coincided with the rebirth of interest in the Classical past during the Renaissance. That renewal encouraged a search for ready reference between the periods, a search dramatically seen in Albrecht Altdorfer's depiction of the victorious Macedonians of Alexander the Great at the battle of Issus (333 BC) as modern European warriors.

This search led to an adoption of the Classical Greeks' account of their confrontations with Persia, notably the Persian invasions of 490 and 480 BCE. These invasions were presented in terms of resistance to a brutal and expansionist power and, crucially, a power with far greater military resources, both on land and at sea. A far from nuanced account of Persian power was presented. In reality many Greek states did not resist the Persians in 480 BCE, and some allied with Xerxes, but that was not a narrative welcome in the Renaissance, other than in suggesting the need for vigilance against backsliding in the Christian camp.

For the Renaissance, the emphasis again was on virtue rather than weaponry, although it is dangerous to use generalisations for movements such as the Renaissance or the (later) Enlightenment without noting a diversity of tendencies and variety of circumstances. Nevertheless, whereas gunpowder was shared with the Ottomans, this was not the case, it was claimed during the Renaissance, of the Christian virtue displayed in resistance to them. Thus, culture served as an explanation both of conflict and of respective capability. At the same time, this cultural dimension did not lead to a reliance on zeal nor on any sense of superiority. Instead, there was a determined attempt to employ information and experience as aspects of a clearly understood learning curve. If this does not apply the term culture overly loosely, this process can be seen as a key aspect of the Western response. It was seen, in particular, with ballistics and fortification, as well as in the use of information to help conceptualise and understand the working of a multipolar international system.

It would be mistaken to imagine that this process was solely seen with the West, and, if less is known about its characteristics and extent in other cultures, the situation is better than was the case even thirty years ago.[13] Moreover, non-Western powers could make effective use of information, which is a key constituent of power. Not only Ming China and Tokugawa Japan, but also Mughal India and several other societies boasted information systems that in significant respects vied with those of the West until at least the eighteenth century.

The Chinese information system proved highly effective in planning the deployment of power in the eighteenth century, against both Tibet and the Dsunghars, into the Eurasian "Heartland" to employ a later term which has a cultural resonance. Chinese usage of information rested on an effective communication system. Aside from improving the flow of information, and, crucially, providing the predictability that made the use of information an integral part of planning, the communication system – roads, canals and, fundamentally, depots,

---

[13] Brett D. Steele and Tamara Dorland (eds.), *The Heirs of Archimedes: Science and the Art of War through the Age of Enlightenment* (Cambridge, Mass: MIT Press, 2005), esp. 87–133.

made it possible to move large quantities of resources. As a result, Eastern China was able to support power projection into the "Heartland" by moving resources to the internal frontier, a movement that, in part, rested on cultural/ideological assumptions about a necessary superiority.

Thanks to an effective system, Indian rulers accumulated information about the situation both within their own territories and externally. This system was to be taken over the British in a process that needs to be considered alongside their understanding and, thus successful use, of military labour markets and local economic and financial systems.

The Ottomans benefited from the presentation of information in a relatively sophisticated fashion, both on the empire and on lands further afield. Ottoman land and revenue surveys and descriptions of frontiers afforded the Ottoman government knowledge of its resources, as well as helping to delineate the otherwise porous frontier of the empire.

The context within which the relationship between West and non-West was judged changed from the 1680s. Whereas the Ottoman failure at Vienna in 1529 was one essentially arising from the problems of campaigning at the distant edge of empire and was not marked by the defeat of the main Ottoman army, the situation was very different in 1683. Furthermore, whereas Ottoman failure in 1529 did not prevent advances and successes over the following decade, the situation was radically different after 1683. This was true both in the early years, and also in the century 1690–1790 as far as the trend of success was concerned: Ottoman successes occurred but could not reverse the key Western triumphs.

This context lessened the need for any Thermopolyae complex in which vulnerable and greatly-outnumbered forces relied on willpower in mounting resistance, although this theme appealed to Western public opinion as with the prominence given the successful British defence of Rorke's Drift against Zulu attack in 1879, and to equivalents for other countries. Instead, the emphasis now was on how best to advance and to secure advances, an emphasis that encouraged a more technocratic approach. Moreover, an aspect of this was provided by the conviction that Western superiority pertained both in knowledge and in its application; and this superiority was regarded both as utilitarian and as providing evidence of superior moral worth. The conviction of such superiority needs underlining as the modern tendency to counterpoint technological and moral factors needs to be reconsidered in light of the worth placed on technology and, indeed, the extent to which it is in part a social construction.

The latter point can be highlighted by assessing the cultural aspect of the information systems that were central to Western capability and power-projection, while accepting that such an analysis risks a new Whiggism. Thus, a relative lack of commitment to maritime activity and naval power in the eighteenth century impoverished the non-Western powers, not as land powers at the time but in so far as information acquisition and assessment were concerned. In particular, navigational/astronomical methods and empirical, knowledge-based practices of organising new, and reviewing existing, information were important to the West, and were increasingly integrated from the late-eighteenth century. The issues of that era were confronted in the West within the context of an intellectual culture organised on the basis of a self-conscious rationalism devoted to the new.[14]

War helped enhance the drive for information as its different levels involved particular requirements. The tactical dimension required an understanding of terrain, both the details and what they entailed. The operational dimension necessitated an appreciation of territory and such questions as what resources could be obtained from particular areas. The strategic dimension required a grasp of the relationship between control over territory and the understanding of how best to conceptualise and achieve the goals of victory. Operations at sea led to pressure for an increase in information, not only charting of waters and coasts, but also currents and winds, and on a global scale.

The representation and reproduction of such information also became regular and more fixed. Thus, the density of the information matrix was enhanced in response to specific requirements and, once enhanced, became normative. In turn, this process encouraged the idea that information definition and acquisition were both dynamic processes.

On the world scale, the West became clearly distinctive for an interest in information both divorced from spiritual references and set in the guiding context of global information systems. This separation was

---

[14] Daniel R. Headrick, *When Information Came of Age: Technologies of Knowledge in the Age of Reason and Revolution, 1700–1850* (Oxford: Oxford University Press, 2000).

natural in a society increasingly impressed by the idea that authority should take scientific form. This development was seen in the long-term impact of Cartesian thought and, subsequently, in the major attempt in Britain to reconcile revealed religion with the insights gained by Newtonian science – a science with Europe-wide prestige. This understanding of religion ensured that it did not act as a break on new systems of understanding, nor as an ideology of conservatism.

In turn, science was both institutionalised at the state level in Europe and inserted into education systems. In the nineteenth century, Western spiritual renewal, in the form of evangelicalism, was largely compatible with utilitarianism and scientific attitudes. The debate over geological knowledge and the Darwinian controversy are both instructive.

Although science offered apparently fixed answers, the process of scientific exposition entailed an inherent changeability stemming from new validation. For example, advances in measurement encouraged higher standards of accuracy and precision. There was a continuous process of improvement and testing. Thus, in naval capability, the period from 1850 to 1910 brought the testing of new systems of armament, propulsion, firepower and communications, as well as experimentation with underwater and aerial warfare. The characteristics of particular combinations of material for use in armour, e.g. nickel-steel, were tested, as were oil-fired engines. The change in information systems from 1810 to 1910 was a greater transformation than in any previous century.

More generally, the emphasis on observation, experimentation and mathematics, seen also in astronomy, chemistry, physics and other branches of science, provided encouragement for information-gathering and for the use of data to help both decision-making and cycles of testing policies or products, and then amending them. As a consequence, there was a relative strengthening of Western capability and effectiveness,[15] not least through the borrowing of Western concepts of information by non-Western states such as Japan, which thus affirmed Western norms in measurement, for example of the Meridian and of time.

The development of formal intelligence processes, systems and institutions ushered in a new world of information acquisition and analysis.

---

[15] Daniel R. Headrick, *Power Over Peoples: Technology, Environments, and Western Imperialism, 1400 to the Present* (Princeton, NJ: Princeton University Press, 2010).

Information became Intelligence in a reflection of military value and use.

Information was also a crucial adjunct to international capitalism, for example to the search for raw materials and, more generally, comparative advantage, to integrated production systems, and to multinationals. The role of capitalism was a product of the long-term relationship between information and commercial élites. In trading states, the levers are controlled by complex commercial élites interested mostly in controlling flows and nodes. Surplus value comes from tapping into, creating, and controlling flows of raw materials, goods, capital and labour (usually skilled). States are funded by taxes on these flows.

In territorial states, in contrast, much smaller élites, composed mostly of landowners, control the levers and are interested primarily in extracting surplus values from direct ownership or taxation of land. Non-Western states were essentially territorial powers, with limited élites extracting tax revenue from land, rather than commercial powers extracting revenue from trade flows. Once (some) Western powers understood how to restructure their organisation around these flows, they were quickly able to surpass the ability of territorial states to generate surplus, and the latter began an increasingly steep relative decline; the situation in the nineteenth century.

The techniques available to the West were only very slowly or poorly adopted by most non-Europeans, and the contrast provided a dynamic edge to the Information Revolution. In historical order, this had a long genesis but was particularly important in the nineteenth century. Thus, double-entry bookkeeping, the development of national debts, atlases stressing routes and ports (nodes and flows), and insurance, were followed by packet boats (commonly used outside Europe from the 1820s), the telegraph (first terrestrial, then submarine), limited liability companies, and radio.

Within the West, the consequences of the Enlightenment and the American and French Revolutions included the changing understanding and use of information to advance power both internationally and domestically. "Rationalism" as statecraft cannot be divorced from political contexts, nor these contexts from the reconceptualisation of states and societies in terms of malleable entities that could, and should, be directed by information; the last very much seen with the French Revolution. These ideas contributed to the growing development of a specifically Western information system, notably in comparison with the situation elsewhere and with reference to key issues at the point of contact, both in warfare and in imperial control.

The discussion of the understanding, and therefore, use of information as a form of cultural history underlines the wide-ranging and porous nature of the cultural definition, which poses a major problem in terms of analytical rigour, if not value.

There is again a marked danger of adopting a Whiggish approach, but such Whiggism was itself a cultural characteristic (and product), and, at times, a resource or problem. Western capability as an aspect of an advancing and allegedly superior civilisation was a theme that linked the post-Vienna (1683) situation to the confidence seen by American commentators from the Second World War to the Vietnam War. This is a long period, however, and chronological qualifications must be added.

Moreover, the relationships between military cultures (in the sense of assumptions about the use of power) and general cultural characteristics, are complex, not least in terms of the endorsement of technology as a proof and enabler of virtuous, and thus necessary, power. In addition, in particular circumstances, societies can be defined as both offensive and defensive. There is also the question whether both characteristics in practice entail a response to circumstances that is as much about perception as reality, with defensive societies more likely to resort to a cultural pessimism. The latter, however, did, and does, not have simply one manifestation. In particular, such pessimism can encourage a defiant search for elements that might be likely to redress what appear to be adverse circumstances. Both technology and cultural factors can be seen as redressing elements. That technological accounts of military proficiency can arise from both optimistic and pessimistic analyses indicates the complexity of the situation being addressed when the culture of war is considered.

This complexity underlines the conceptual poverty, or at least limitations, of much modern discussion of military history. There is a tendency to revert to the same, very small, group of thinkers, both in military and in naval history, and that is not terribly helpful because the usual suspects, whether Clausewitz or Cobbett, Jomini or Mahan, Sun Tzu or Mao, were writing with reference to the particular contexts of their time and indeed were very much guided by their own experiences. It is important to understand military writers as products of their place and time. This is especially true of Clausewitz. The alternatives are even grimmer, notably supposedly timeless searches for universal truths of leadership, strategy or whatever.

Each approach suffers because it finds it difficult to explain change, which, more generally, is a problem with the cultural theme. Indeed "the culture of war" is essentially a static concept. As such, those who employ it face the problem of deciding how best to understand change, and notably without resorting to Whiggish platitudes. Is it to be assumed that change in a military system is a constant process as it adjusts to circumstances? Alternatively, is it the case that the idea of a culture of war implies a fundamental conservatism, and that change is only accounted for from the pressure of external forces, notably if there are serious discontinuities in the context and, more particularly, if a serious defeat is involved?

Of course, a perception of failure does not have to lead to a change of course as it can result, instead, in a determination to avoid the recurrence of similar problems. Arguably, this is the case with the American army after Vietnam, as the lesson learned was one of focusing on the Cold War in Europe and not on counter-insurgency operations in the Third World. The customary approach is to argue that this was a mistake as the army should have trained for such operations, the resulting mistake helping to lead to serious problems from the aftermath of the conquest of Iraq in 2003 onwards. Such an approach is seductive but also entails problems. First, there is the assumption, in this case as in others, that success can be ensured provided the correct method is followed, in short that strategic issues are swallowed by operational problems, and operational by tactical, such that resolving the lower level solves the higher one. Such an approach is a cardinal fault in much military analysis especially among those who do not wish to address strategic issues. Secondly, there is the related focus on fulfilling the task irrespective of constraints.

Both of these assumptions can be queried, not least by adopting the counter-argument that it is best to frame strategic goals with reference to what can most readily be achieved, and with a high level of certainty. To do so entails concentrating on those areas in which there is a clear capability advantage, most obviously in the case of the West today, the maritime sphere and naval capability.

This point could be readily argued irrespective of the current emergency, but the latter gives it bite, and also underlines the degree to which scholarship has additional value if it can aid discussion of the present situation and help look toward the future. Put simply, we need to address failure, failure in the shape of acute fiscal crisis in Britain and the USA, Britiain's leading ally and ultimate security. Much of this fiscal crisis has nothing to do with military overstretch (even if that is a potential consequence), and, as a result, comparisons of modern America with say sixteenth-century Spain, in large part, are misleading, except (valuably) as aids to thought. Instead, a combination of unprecedentedly high levels of social welfare, poor fiscal management, and an inability to match planning to economic developments, have set much of the framework.

Yet, within that context, the wars in Iraq and Afghanistan have also been failures. Vast sums of money have been spent at a time when this has involved an increased indebtedness that has challenged national security more profoundly than terrorist activity. Moreover, instead of securing rapid outcomes, we have become involved in lengthy presences that have entailed not only significant human costs but also serious issues of commitment to particular force structures, doctrine and operational and tactical means. In short, we have allowed a particular expeditionary posture to challenge not only the overall capacity of the army to discharge other functions but also the balance between the services.[16] How far this situation can be related to the culture of war is unclear, but possibly the most profound link was that of the desire on the part of the Bush administration to do something big after the terrorist attacks of 2001 on New York and Washington, and the related preference for action. In short, bellicosity explains war.

This point adds a cultural element to the current issue of force structure. There is not only a danger, in both America and Britain, that crucial long-term naval capabilities will be sacrificed to the exigencies of the army in its current commitment, but also the risk of a focus on action in the shape of counter-insurgency operations rather than on the capacity for action in the form of naval strength. The latter, however, represents a far more potent form of power, not least because it is easier to choose whether to apply it and without that choice being dictated by opponents.

Yet, the nature of public discussion in Britain in 2009–10 has indicated a reluctance to engage with preparedness short of conflict,

---

[16] Jeremy Black, *Defence: Policy Issues For A New Government* (London: Social Affairs Unit, 2009).

a reluctance that reflects both the emotional character of much of the public discussion and the extent to which army advocates have found the media more receptive. Indeed, the symbolisation of individual military casualties, notably in terms of the public parade of hearses through the streets of Wotton Basset in front of crowds both grieving and respectful, as well as the Prime Minister reading the names of the dead in the House of Commons, and the focus of television and radio on individual casualties and on their families, has created a potent situation that has greatly affected the nature of the defence debate.

In part this is a feature of a wider failure in Western society, and maybe more so in (Western) Europe than in the USA to engage with the issue and implications of risk, a failure that reflects a more individualistic, hedonistic and atomistic society than heretofore, and also one that finds it easiest to respond to problems in an emotional fashion, with expertise and rational discussion both treated with suspicion. Thus, the defence debate in Britain in 2009–10 risked becoming restricted to the provision of more helicopters to support operations, with the misleading impression created that this step would somehow solve problems, instead, for example, at the tactical and operational level of the development of alternative lethalities by our opponents. In political terms, this media campaign provided an opportunity to dodge the question of strategic viability by focusing on a particular issue of procurement that could be afforded.

Yet, there was also a political failure to address the question of whether the policy of forward-action in South Asia could be sustained in the long-term; and also "should" in the sense of the danger to overall force structure and doctrine.[17] Thus, a key cultural problem, the failure to address strategic questions seriously, was repeated yet again. Possibly, this is one of the more important aspects of the cultural turn, in that analysis of military matters can be more aware of this dimension of military policy and its consequences for strategy.

There is, for example, a cultural as well as an intellectual challenge when discussing the Defence contribution to preparedness and indeed to operations short of war-fighting. As far as the public is concerned, this challenge owes something to the long-term difficulty of

---

[17] Strategic Trends Programme, Ministry of Defence, *Future Character of Conflict* (London: Ministry of Defence, 2010).

understanding deterrence as a concept; not only nuclear deterrence but the deterrence that naval and air power can offer.

This difficulty is mistaken for such deterrence is the basis of security. It involves trying to influence the attitudes of potential opponents and, as such, it is difficult to show a clear cost-benefit analysis of the type enjoined by financial controllers. It would not be misusing the cultural approach to note that this preference for cost-benefit analysis is a direct product not only of the dominance of bureaucratic procedural methods in Defence, but also of their particular character.

As a result, navalists are encouraged to emphasise more concrete factors than deterrence, notably the volume of trade moved by sea. These are indeed highly pertinent, and more so as they also direct attention to the vulnerability of other powers, notably China. Indeed, one of the key arguments for Western naval power is that, in so far as China, or any other state, is a potential threat,[18] then this threat can be lessened by the extent to which they are dependent on oceanic trade. Thus, for example, China is obtaining more oil from Atlantic sources, notably Equatorial Guinea, Nigeria, Angola, and Cameroon.

Yet, this focus on tangibles reflects, in part, a lack of willingness to engage with intangibles. These intangibles include the deterrent character of power and the extent to which it contributes to providing the presence necessary to maximise the political choice to prevent or calm incidents that might affect security.

Focusing on the present helps throw light on the misleading clarity that some discern when they look at the past because it clarifies the problems faced by policymakers confronting the risk of the future, and by analysts seeking to assess influence in decision-making. To look at the situation from the perspective of an individual service indicates the extent to which cultural assumptions are bound up in any discussion of its relevant value. The same point can be made about air forces, for which there is a considerable historical literature,[19] and about armies.

---

[18] James Kraska, "How the United States Lost the Naval War of 2015", *Orbis* 54 (2010), 35–45.

[19] Malcolm Smith, *British Air Strategy Between the Wars* (Oxford: Oxford University Press, 1984); Robert Wohl, *A Passion for Wings: Aviation and the Western Imagination* (New Haven, CT: Yale University Press, 1994); Carl H. Builder, *The Icarus Syndrome: The Role of Air Power Theory in the Evolution and Fate of the US Air Force* (New Brunswick, NJ: Transaction Publishers, 1994).

There is at present the fundamental choice for America and Britain between focusing on what we can do best or engaging in commitments that expose serious limitations. To follow the latter course and also, as a result, make poor choices about future capabilities is highly reckless.

MANSTEIN, THE BATTLE OF KHARKOV, AND THE LIMITS OF COMMAND

Robert M. Citino

I. *Introduction*

As I contemplate the scholarly career and impressive body of work of Dennis Showalter, I find myself thinking about the nature of history itself, of the relationship between personality and the impersonal phenomena that are said to determine how things unfold. No military historian has been as adept as Showalter at analyzing both sides of this equation. He knows his battles and leaders as well as anyone, and can "throw down," as our students say, on the details of battle, campaign, and strategy. At the same time, he is the best military sociologist around. No one can better trace the relationship of armies to the societies that spawn them and the matrix of factors that turns some forces into sharks and others into their bait.

In this, as in so many other things, Showalter has been anything but typical. Military history, by and large, is still wedded to the role of personality. Armies, doctrines, "ways of war," competing socio-economic systems and political ideologies: we all recognize that they have a role to play, of course, and often a very important one. As a collective, however, we continue to look to the individual—usually, of course "the man"—who at some crucial moment managed to bend an unruly battlefield situation to his will. It might involve a commander shifting a reserve division to a crucial spot on the battlefield; or identifying a critical enemy weakness that he is then able to exploit; or devising a bold stratagem that transforms a hopeless situation; or being aggressive enough to take advantage of fleeting opportunities when they offer themselves. Indeed, add those four items together—clever planning, skillful maneuver, the ability to take things in at a glance and see what must be done (Napoleon's famous *coup d'oeil*), and an innate sense of aggression, and you have a decent taxonomy of the term "genius," or at least what military historians usually mean when they employ the term.

No matter how sophisticated the analysis, therefore, we still tend to look to the man. We can take into account the differences in military systems between the Prussians and the Franco-Imperial Army in 1757, for example, parsing matters of soldierly motivation, variances in training, and the different societies out of which they sprung, as Showalter did so expertly in *The Wars of Frederick the Great*, but we still tend to say that Frederick the Great "won" the battle of Rossbach. And indeed, there is some truth to the claim. The steady calm when he realized the French were trying to slip around his left flank, the rapidity with which he had his army break camp and head to the east, the ease with which his well drilled cavalry outpaced their adversary, and then finally the culminating maneuver down onto the point of the Franco-Imperial column, literally "crossing their T" and riding over them before they were fully deployed: well, let's just say there was a reason his contemporaries decided to dub Frederick "the Great."

We can quibble with this particular *Rossbach-Bild*, of course. It was General Friedrich von Seydlitz who commanded the Prussian cavalry, not Frederick, and the *brio* of both the top-speed ride and the great charge itself may belong as much to the general as it did to the King. The Franco-Imperial army, with a dual-hatted leadership and a polyglot rank and file, was a command and control implosion waiting to happen. The French were tied to a logistics train a hundred miles long, burdened not just with the traditional military *impedimenta*, but with wigs and perfumes and cognac and silk stockings and every manner of creature comforts, and as a result any maneuver they tried to make was probably going to be too slow.[1] All these things are true. And yet, Rossbach seems destined forevermore to be one of the battles trotted out when historians want to discuss Frederick's greatness.

It is much the same with other alleged examples of battlefield genius: Robert E. Lee at Chancellorsville; Helmuth von Moltke (the Elder) at Königgrätz; Napoleon at Arcola or Ulm or Austerlitz or Friedland or any number of his other battles. Certainly we can say that there were systemic factors at work in all these decisive victories. Lee had a gifted subordinate commander, General Thomas "Stonewall" Jackson, whose

---

[1] The best analysis of the battle of Rossbach and the two armies who fought it is Dennis E. Showalter, *The Wars of Frederick the Great* (London: Longman, 1996), pp. 177–192. See also Robert M. Citino, *The German Way of War: From the Thirty Years' War to the Third Reich* (Lawrence, KS: University Press of Kansas, 2005), pp. 72–82.

intuition and aggressiveness matched his own, and he also had an army full of soldiers who had as yet no real reason to fear their Union adversaries.[2] Moltke possessed an imposing list of systemic advantages: a blizzard of firepower generated by the first production model breech-loading rifle, the Dreyse needle gun; hardy infantry drilled to fight in nimble company-sized columns; a flexible system of command, usually called *Auftragstaktik* (mission tactics), in which subordinate commanders received general directives but could choose the means and methods of achieving the mission themselves; and a group of highly aggressive attack-dogs masquerading as an officer corps.[3] Napoleon had something even better: the French Revolution and its attendant social transformation; an aroused populace fighting for its newly won liberties; not to mention the reformed army of the late Royal period, equally adept at fighting in line, column, or *ordre mixte*.[4]

And yet, the same military historical dynamic persists in all these cases. History recalls Lee, Moltke, and Napoleon as "geniuses," and their victories, we instinctively feel, are theirs alone. In the theater of our imagination, they are able to operate with impunity, to ignore the rules or to laugh at them, in the famous formulation of Clausewitz, for "what genius does is the best rule." Chancellorsville and Fredericksburg are inconceivable without Lee's presence, and military historians will always link Moltke and Königgrätz, with the latter serving as the main item entered into evidence to prove the genius of the former. As for Napoleon, it isn't just military historians who have canonized him. So, too, did many of those who knew him best, his adversaries, as in the Duke of Wellington's famous comment that "Napoleon's hat is worth 40,000 men," or even more vividly in the basic principle of the so-called "Trachenberg Plan," the Allied directive for the 1813 campaign. It actually stipulated that any Allied commander encountering a force led

---

[2] For Chancellorsville, there is still no rival to Stephen W. Sears, *Chancellorsville* (Boston: Houghton Mifflin, 1996).

[3] For the Königgrätz campaign, the two required volumes are Geoffrey Wawro, *The Austro-Prussian War: Austria's War with Prussia and Italy in 1866* (Cambridge: Cambridge University Press, 1996) and Dennis E. Showalter, *The Wars of German Unification* (London: Arnold, 2004). See also Citino, *German Way of War*, pp. 160–173.

[4] The literature on Napoleon is beyond voluminous. David G. Chandler, *The Campaigns of Napoleon* (New York: Macmillan, 1966) is still the appropriate starting point.

by Napoleon in person should do the sensible thing and retreat as soon as possible.[5]

This stress on the role of the individual—what professional historians refer to as "personalism"—is almost unique to military history. Social and economic historians have always, by definition, concentrated more on the great impersonal forces that they believe move history. Diplomatic historians have emerged from the archives to focus more and more on the interplay between domestic and foreign policies, between public opinion at home and what happens in the international diplomatic sphere. The historical profession at large today is obsessed with either more profound or more nebulous issues of culture and memory. And yet military historians continue to debate very traditional issues of generalship and genius. Indeed, this conservative methodological approach is one of the reasons that the broader profession mistrusts military history, insofar as that mistrust is not ideologically driven.

Military history soldiers on, however, especially operational military history, in a determined personalist quest to praise this commander and to criticize that one. Those who stray from that path, seeking to go beyond generalship as the primary criterion of success or failure to more sophisticated categories of analysis—historians like Showalter, for example—are all the more conspicuous by their rarity.

This is not to suggest a complete abandonment of the individual, or a complete reordering of military history's priorities, merely to mollify the rest of the profession. When the great scorer comes to write against all our names, military historians may well find themselves rewarded for refusing to chase the scholarly or historiographical flavor of the week. Modern military operations, however, are highly complex phenomena, influenced not only by a variety of interrelated factors like time, space, supply, weather, and terrain, but also by a number of imponderables. They are not merely "contingent"—i.e., with one thing leading to another—they are sometimes utterly unpredictable in their course. As a result, they are among the most complex of all subjects for historical inquiry, and the individual general, however convenient he may be as a symbol for all that goes right or wrong, has only limited

---

[5] The indispensable book on the 1813 campaign is Michael V. Leggiere, *Napoleon and Berlin: The Franco-Prussian War in North Germany* (Norman, OK: University of Oklahoma Press, 2002). See also Citino, *German Way of War*, pp. 132–141.

ability to influence the course of battle. It is precisely this factor—the limits on generalship in the modern era—that requires operational military historians to do more than cry "Ecce homo!", something Showalter recognized a long time ago.[6]

With that in mind, let us go back in time. It is 1943, a great war is raging, and—for the German Wehrmacht—all the signs have suddenly gone negative.

II. *Manstein and the Relief of Stalingrad*

Field Marshal Erich von Manstein certainly was a "genius," and he was happy to tell you so. Indeed, he spent much of the war doing just that, and afterwards he wrote memoirs in which his genius formed the principal theme, alongside denigrating judgments of just about every other officer in the army.[7] His personality could be acerbic, certainly, and his tongue was sharp. One of his operations officers, Colonel Theodor Busse, would look back on meeting him and recall, "During the first few weeks I hated his guts; I never left his presence without smarting."[8] But he could also deliver the goods. He understood both modern mobile operations and the traditional German way of war in which he had to operate. He could take in a highly complex situation with a single glance at the map, and once had had made a decision, he saw it through ruthlessly and single-mindedly. His fellow officers knew him as a highly skilled operator. General Wilhelm Keitel, chief of the wartime *Oberkommando der Wehrmacht* (OKW), a man with whom he had his share of scrapes, praised his "outstanding talents,"[9] Busse his "superior art of command, his bold power of decision, and his way of moving to the assigned goal despite interference from above or any

---

[6] For a discussion of the role of military history today within the broader field, see Robert M. Citino, "Military Histories Old and New: A Reintroduction," *American Historical Review* 112, no. 4 (October 2007), pp. 1070–90.

[7] See Erich von Manstein, *Verlorene Siege* (Bonn, Athenaeum Verlag, 1955). The English translation is *Lost Victories* (Novato, CA: Presidio, 1982). For his typically negative assessments of colleagues General Walther von Brauchitsch, chief of the OKH, and General Franz Halder, Chief of the General Staff, see *Verlorene Siege*, pp. 71–72 and 76.

[8] Quoted in Dana V. Sadarananda, *Beyond Stalingrad: Manstein and the Operations of Army Group Don* (Mechanicsburg, PA: Stackpole, 2009), p. 10.

[9] Field Marshal Lord Carver, "Manstein," in Correlli Barnett, ed., *Hitler's Generals: Authoritative Portraits of the Men Who Waged Hitler's War* (New York: Quill, 1989), p. 221.

local setbacks,"[10] and General Friedrich Wilhelm von Mellenthin his "studied discretion and recognizable shrewdness, his quick and sure grasp of the most complex situations," as well as the "absolute trust" he inspired in his subordinates.[11] Despite some muttering on their parts, they continued to support his memory into the postwar era. His 80th birthday, in 1967, was the occasion for a volume of encomia by his fellow officers, *Nie ausser Dienst*, in which the General Inspector of the Bundeswehr, General Ulrich de Maizière labeled Manstein "the most capable German general of the Second World War" ("der fähigste deutsche General des Zweiten Weltkriegs"), although he did qualify it by adding "in the realm of operational command" ("auf dem Felde der operativen Führung").[12]

Historians have generally agreed, as well. In his fine operational history of the 1942-43 winter campaign, Dana V. Sadarananda praises Manstein's "firm, decisive, inspiring, energetic, and... farsighted guidance to Army Group Don" in that most difficult time, and such rhetoric has been fairly common in the years since the war.[13] It would take the advent of a new, more critical historiography—one that emphasizes the crimes of the Wehrmacht as opposed to its military victories and defeats—to tarnish the Field Marshal, and both the primary documents and the secondary literature have now established beyond any reasonable doubt his deep involvement in the German *Vernichtungskrieg* (war of annihilation) in the East, his eager cooperation with the death squads working in 11th Army's zone of operations in the Crimea, for example.[14]

In a similar demythologizing vein, it is now possible to view Manstein as emblematic of the deep-seated problems in the German officer corps's view of war. He was relentlessly focused on the operational level, he was hopelessly naïve about the nature of the enemies Germany was facing, and he still had dreams—even after the Allied declaration

---

[10] Theodor Busse, "Der Winterfeldzug 1942/1943 in Südrussland," in *Nie ausser Dienst: Zum achtzigsten Geburtstag von Generfeldmarschall Erich von Manstein* (Köln: Markus Verlagsgesellschaft, 1967), p. 45.

[11] F. W. von Mellenthin, *German Generals of World War II as I Saw Them* (Norman, OK: University of Oklahoma Press, 1977), p. 19, 29.

[12] General Ulrich de Maizière, "Zum Geleit," in *Nie ausser Dienst*, p. 7.

[13] Sadarananda, *Beyond Stalingrad*, p. xi.

[14] For a representative sample of an anti-Manstein critique, see Marcel Stein, *Field Marshal von Manstein, a Portrait: The Janus Head* (Solihull, UK: Helion, 2007). A critical yet fair assessment is to be found in Mungo Melvin, *Manstein: Hitler's Greatest General* (London: Weidenfeld & Nicolson, 2010).

that the war would go on until the "unconditional surrender" of the Axis powers—that he might win some battlefield victory so dramatic that it would lead to a *Remis-Frieden*, a "stalemate," borrowing a term from chess.[15] Indeed, we might say that Manstein saw modern war as a kind of bloody chess game, which he could win simply by out-thinking his opponent, reacting more decisively, and planning several operational steps ahead.

In the 1942–43 winter campaign, he was going to need all of those skills and more. It had been a strange few months for him. A show of virtuosity as commander of 11th Army in the Crimea in the spring and early summer of 1942 had earned him a Field Marshal's baton, and his operations in the great encirclement battle of Kerch and the reduction of the Soviet fortress of Sevastopol are still worthy of study.[16] The start of Operation Blue, the make-or-break offensive in the southern sector of the Soviet Union, however, saw him far removed from the action. Originally tasked to cross over from the Crimea to the Taman peninsula to support the drive into the Caucasus, he and his army were instead transferred far to the north, preparing to assault Leningrad once conditions were ripe. They never were. The Soviets were by now deep in a cycle of relentless counterattacks to break the German ring around Leningrad, and Manstein found his command mired in tough positional fighting.[17] As a result, Manstein missed out entirely on Blue.

Perhaps that was just as well. Prussian-German armies had experienced the thrill of victory and the agony of defeat over the centuries, of course. Absolute debacles, however, had been pretty rare, and that is especially true of operational-level debacles, the level of war in which the German officer corps felt itself most at home. One would need to go back to Jena and Auerstädt in 1806 to find a disaster equivalent to what had just taken place at Stalingrad. Blue had been a German operation in the classic style of *Bewegungskrieg*, the war of movement, with large formations (divisions, corps, and armies) maneuvering

---

[15] See Manstein, *Verlorene Siege*, p. 398, where he speaks of the possibility of a "Remislösung." See also Andreas Hillgruber, "In der Sicht des kritischen Historikers," in *Nie ausser Dienst*, pp. 78–79.

[16] See Robert M. Citino, *Death of the Wehrmacht: The German Campaigns of 1942* (Lawrence, KS: University Press of Kansas, 2007), pp. 69–81.

[17] Manstein, *Verlorene Siege*, pp. 290–302. Manstein's eldest son, Gero, was killed in the fighting in this sector. He was a junior officer in the 51st Panzer Grenadier Regiment, 18th Infantry Division.

concentrically to encircle and smash their adversaries in a *Kesselschlacht*, a "cauldron battle," but more correctly a "battle of encirclement." The plan called for a carefully phased and sequenced set of army level maneuvers, designed to trap and destroy Soviet forces in the great bend of the Don river, somewhere around Millerovo. Instead, the Germans had moved a bit too slowly and the Soviets had managed to slip the noose with a helter-skelter retreat to the East. A second attempt to encircle them, at Rostov, had failed as well. The Wehrmacht had gone through its entire repertoire of maneuver, and eaten through much of its limited store of supplies, and all it could show for it were two "blows into the air" (*Luftstossen*). The end of the operation saw its best formations embedded in Stalingrad and in the Caucasus, just short of their strategic objectives, shorn of their ability to maneuver, and frankly, not long for this world.[18]

On November 19, the Soviets launched Operation Uranus, a breakthrough attempt north and south of Stalingrad. Targeting the weak Romanians armies holding the flanks, they easily overran them and linked up a few days later at Kalach on the Don. The 6th Army, Germany's principal and best equipped fighting formation in 1942, was now encircled inside Stalingrad. The Wehrmacht, in other words, had not simply been outnumbered and outproduced, two conditions that had obtained on the Eastern Front since the beginning of the German invasion, it had been outmaneuvered. The opening words of the situation report from 6th Army commander, General Friedrich Paulus, are chilling enough in any context, but seen through the historical lens of traditional German military operations take on even greater weight: "Armee eingeschlossen," he wrote: "The army is surrounded."[19] It was not just the end of a battle; it was the end of an era.

Such things are more obvious in retrospect, however, and there was still a war to be fought. On November 20, supreme commander Adolf Hitler and his Chief of the General Staff, General Kurt Zeitzler, responded to the emergency by activating a new formation called Army Group Don and appointing Manstein to command it. The news

---

[18] For the course of Operation Blue, see Citino, *Death of the Wehrmacht*, pp. 165–180.
[19] The dispatch is included in Manfred Kehrig, *Stalingrad: Analyse und Dokumentation einer Schlacht* (Stuttgart: Deutsche Verlags-Anstalt, 1974), p. 559–560.

reached him in Vitebsk, and he now set out by train for Novocherkassk. The weather had been too bad for flying, he would later claim, although he may well have preferred the longer travel time to study what was clearly a horrible, perhaps even hopeless, situation.

The principal formation tasked with carrying out the 1942 offensive had been Army Group South. In the course of the fighting, however, it had been split into two: Army Group A (commanded by Field Marshal Wilhelm List until his dismissal in September 1942, then by Hitler himself for a time, and finally by Field Marshal Ewald von Kleist) carried out the drive into the Caucasus; while Army Group B (General Maximilian von Weichs) had to take Stalingrad and guard the long operational flank along the Don river. The end of Operation Blue saw the Wehrmacht strung out into one of the most bizarre situation maps of the war: Army Group A was deep in the Caucasus facing more or less due south, its right wing anchored on the Black Sea and its left strung out along the Terek river just north of Grozny; Army Group B faced roughly northeast, following the course of the Don. Its extreme right wing consisted of the 6th Army, jammed into Stalingrad. Much of Army Group B consisted of non-German elements: the 3rd and 4th Romanian armies; the 2nd Hungarian Army, and the 8th Italian Army, holding an immensely long front along the Don. Liaison between the two army groups was virtually nil, with a single German division, the 16th Motorized, sitting on a very lonely perch at Elista on the Kalmyk Steppe.

It was an absurd arrangement, and the Soviet counteroffensive had exploited it in style. After smashing the Romanian armies on either flank of Stalingrad and encircling German 6th Army in the city, it had driven over the Don river to the Chir, the smaller river that flows into the Don at Nizhne Chirskaya. With Army Group B now fighting for its life and Army Group A sitting deep in the Caucasus chain to the South, a yawning void had opened between them. This was the operational space to be occupied by Army Group Don. Inserted between A and B, it had the dual task of re-opening a supply path to Stalingrad and of reconquering the territory lost to Operation Uranus.

Most of the operational analysis of Manstein's generalship emphasizes the first point: relieving 6th Army in Stalingrad. In fact, that was probably an impossible task. Besides encircling German 6th Army, and just as important from the standpoint of further operations, the Soviets had also destroyed two of the Wehrmacht's four satellite armies on the eastern front, prying open great operational-level gaps in the defensive position where 3rd and 4th Romanian Armies used to be.[20] The prospects of relieving 6th Army, as a result, were dim from the start. The Germans had exhausted themselves just getting to Stalingrad, and there were precious few reserves available to break the Soviet ring. While there was discussion of an immediate breakout, 6th Army was so deeply embedded in the city, and the army had shed so much of its operational mobility, that it would have been a great deal harder than most historians have been willing to admit. For Paulus, that left a strategy of sitting it out, being resupplied (sporadically) from the air, and waiting for a relief offensive from outside the pocket.

The hopes for the latter receded on an almost daily basis that December. Continued Soviet attacks on the northern wing pushed the Germans back across the Don to the Chir, and then across the Chir to the almost featureless plain leading to the Donets. All the Germans could throw in the path of these armor-heavy attacks were a series of *ad hoc* "Gruppen"–"groups" of various size thrown together hastily from the flotsam and jetsam of the defeated forces along the Don. Rather than divisions and corps, therefore, the situation maps from the period offer us "Gruppe Stumpffeld", "Gruppe Stahel," "Gruppe Abraham", "Gruppe Spang", and "Gruppe Pfeiffer."[21] While it is easy to romanticize them as a symbol of the Wehrmacht's supposedly miraculous improvisatory genius, the reality was something very different. All of them were formations of minimal fighting value, what the Germans called *Alarmeinheiten* (emergency units) consisting of rear area troops, remnants of destroyed formations, and the new Luftwaffe field divisions (a phenomenon that up to now has still not received the careful scholarly examination it deserves). One eyewitness describes the *Alarmeinheiten* as "construction battalions, railroad troops, rear echelons, Cossack bands, Luftwaffe ground personnel, all more or less thrown together."[22] Headquarters on all levels wound up commanding troops in their vicinity in a highly random manner, whether they were suited to command them or not. Thus, Gruppe Stumpffeld, under the

---

[20] The best book on military relations between Germany and its minor allies is Richard L. DiNardo, *Germany and the Axis Powers: From Coalition to Collapse* (Lawrence, KS: University Press of Kansas, 2005). Peter Gosztony, *Hitlers fremde Heere: Das Schicksal der nichtdeutschen Armeen im Ostfeldzug* (Düsseldorf: Econ Verlag, 1976), remains useful.

[21] Horst Scheibert, *Zwischen Don und Donez* (Neckargemünd: Kurt Vowinckel Verlag, 1961), pp. 25–29.

[22] *Ibid.*, p. 69. Scheibert was a company commander in the 6th Panzer Division.

commander of the 108th Artillery Regiment, consisted almost entirely of infantry, Gruppe Stahel was under the staff of the VIII *Fliegerkorps*, and Gruppe Abraham actually went into combat under the "IIa" (the chief personnel officer) of the 6th Army.[23] These diverse Gruppen would eventually coalesce into *"Armee-Abteilungen"* ("provisional armies"), multi-corps formations commanded by (and named for) whomever happened to be available, short of administrative personnel, heavy weapons, transport, and engineers. The current dire situation along the Chir saw virtually all of them handed rifles and ordered to comport themselves as infantry. The results were predictable. Some broke and ran on first contact. A few acquitted themselves respectably. At the very least, we can say that each got in the way of their Soviet attackers, and that was usually enough to slow them up. We are also now aware today of something that no one on the German side could have known at the time: all of those *Alarmeinheiten* benefited from a momentary ebb in the momentum of the Soviet offensives, as the Red Army command realized that the Stalingrad pocket was far larger than previously suspected, and therefore required more formations to man the perimeter along the encirclement.

At any rate, while the Soviets managed to grind their way across the Chir during the first two weeks of December, heading south, they never managed a clean breakthrough. What they did succeed in doing was keeping the Germans on the defensive and gradually pushing them back from Stalingrad, and thus reducing the chances of a relief effort towards into the pocket. One by one, German formations slated for Stalingrad found themselves sucked into the fighting along the Chir– the best example here being *Armee-Abteilung* Hollidt, another improvised group very hastily assembled from the reserve formations of Army Group B (essentially the XVII Corps, consisting of two regular German infantry divisions, along with the defeated remnants of the 3rd Romanian Army's I and II Corps). Tasked originally for the Stalingrad relief, it found itself instead fighting along the upper Chir all through December.[24]

When the relief attempt finally came, it was something of an anticlimax. Operation *Wintergewitter* ("Winter Storm") may well have been the most important operation of the war, but all that the Wehrmacht

---

[23] *Ibid.*, p. 26.
[24] *Ibid.*, p. 23.

could spare for it was a solitary corps, the LVII Panzer under General Friedrich Kirchner. It contained a brace of panzer divisions: the 23rd, detached from Army Group A and badly understrength after tough fighting in the Caucasus; and the 6th, under the command of the redoubtable General Erhard Raus, one of the great armor commanders of the war. It had just spent several months in France, resting, refitting, and receiving replacements of armor. Raus's division would by necessity have to do most of the heavy lifting in Winter Storm; 23rd Panzer Division had no more than thirty tanks to its name. While Winter Storm was originally intended as a multi-corps offensive, the dynamic of this phase of the fighting robbed it of one promised division after another: the 15th Luftwaffe Field Division was still assembling; 3rd Mountain Division had remained with Army Group Center to deal with various local emergencies; and the High Command had decided to deploy the 17th Panzer Division (also from Army Group Center) behind the right wing of the Italian 8th Army along the Don, as it was increasingly clear that the Soviets were massing forces for an attack in this sector. Finally, the reconstituted XXXXVIII Panzer Corps had all the trouble it could handle simply holding its own front along the lower Chir.[25]

As a result, Winter Storm was probably a forlorn hope from the beginning. Two mismatched divisions would have to travel more than ninety miles from their assembly point at Kotelnikovo to Stalingrad. The penetration would by definition be needle-thin. While a pair of Romanian corps would guard their flanks—VI Corps on the left (2nd and 18th Infantry Divisions) and VII Corps on the right (1st and 4th Infantry Divisions, along with Cavalry Group Popescu), no one was expecting them to keep up with the advance of LVII Corps's Panzers, nor to do much of anything save defend themselves. Altogether, we may characterize Winter Storm as too much mission and too little force. "A wretched balance," one German officer would later call it, and it is difficult to argue with that description.[26]

Nevertheless, the relief operation began on December 12th, and things went well enough at first. Lacking either surprise or any real possibility of maneuver, the two divisions drove northeast, almost

---

[25] For the tense armored battled along the Chir, see F. W. von Mellenthin, *Panzer Battles: A Study of the Employment of Armor in the Second World War* (New York: Ballantine, 1956), pp. 211–222.

[26] "Eine traurige Bilanz!" Scheibert, *Zwischen Don und Donez*, p. 30.

straight up the rail line out of Kotelnikovo on a nearly featureless plain, with 6th Panzer to the left of the line and 23rd to the right. The assault penetrated the initial Soviet defenses (302nd Rifle Division on the right and 126th on the left) and managed to breech the first river line (the Aksai) that evening. Soon, however, the Soviets peeled off a couple of mechanized corps from the Stalingrad encirclement (IV in the right and XIII on the left) and deployed them astride the German line of approach. High speed maneuver gave way to tough positional fighting, and finally to a locking of the front some 35 miles south of Stalingrad. That may seem like a pretty close shave, and most of the histories of the campaign speak of how close the Germans came, but with large Soviet mechanized probes lapping around both flanks of the narrow German penetration, LVII Panzer Corps was a lot farther away than it looked on the map, and the German high command called off the offensive on December 23rd.

Winter Storm had failed. 6th Army was probably doomed before it, but it was definitely doomed now. Inside Stalingrad, Paulus was supposed to have been preparing for a breakout to meet Winter Storm, and to initiate it upon receipt of the codeword "Thunder Clap" (*Donnerschlag*). Although there is dispute over this point, it appears that he never received it, and even if he had it is unlikely that he could have done much to affect the operational situation one way or another. He had very little maneuver capability by this point.[27]

Army Group Don, in other words, had failed in its first assignment. And yet, it is difficult to see what Manstein could have done one way or the other. He had an Army Group, yes, but it was filled with the wreckage of units smashed in the initial Soviet offensive at Stalingrad. Whatever he could bring to the table as a planner and commander, no matter how brilliant his operational genius, there wasn't much he could do about that. Hitler was already promising him a new armored corps made from freshly equipped SS divisions, but it was still a long way off in time and space, and Manstein knew it. A gaggle of ad-hoc formations

---

[27] Carl Wagener, *Heeresgruppe Süd: Der Kampf im Süden der Ostfront 1941–1945* (Bad Nauheim: Podzun, 1967), p. 193, makes the point that Paulus's instructions "den Ausbruch vorbereiten" ("to prepare the breakout") presented him with a scarcely soluble problem, in view of his low mobility. The best operational analysis of Winter Storm remains Horst Scheibert, *Entsatzversuch Stalingrad: Dokumentation einer Panzerschlacht in Wort und Bild: Das LVII. Panzerkorps im Dezember 1942* (Neckargmünd: Kurt Vowinckel Verlag, 1956).

like Gruppe Spang wasn't going to reopen a path to Stalingrad, nor were those clueless Luftwaffe divisions. He attempted to dignify all this in his memoirs, likening the 6th Army's sacrifice to that of the Spartans at Thermopylae, and praising it for diverting so much strength away from Army Group Don while he scrambled to rebuild the shattered front, but such arguments are difficult to take seriously.[28] A modern field army isn't a pawn to be sacrificed for position. As one German source put it, it isn't a machine gun nest or a bunker where individual soldiers may decide to die heroically for the sake of the whole. Losing one is a disaster—not a triumph to be celebrated or a tragedy to be memorialized.[29]

In the end, it was the Red Army that was responsible for Stalingrad. It's always good to remember the old nugget that "The enemy gets a vote," and in December 1942, the Red Army was definitely exercising its right. Fresh from smashing the Romanians in Uranus, the Soviets would launch a second great offensive in December. They now decided to reach further up the Don with a massive assault against the Italian 8th Army. It is possible to see the new Soviet doctrine of "consecutive operations" at work here, one that had emerged from the theoretical work of the interwar era. Its departure point was the idea that modern armies had grown so large, their recuperative powers so great, that it would rarely be possible to destroy them with one grand offensive. Rather, it was necessary to subject them to blow after blow, to smash and to keep smashing them, never letting up the pressure or allowing the defenders to recover their equilibrium. It is also possible to see a much older and much simpler notion here, one as old as warfare itself: the ruthless identification of an adversary's weak spot.

The original Soviet conception, Operation Saturn, aimed big. It included a concentric drive by the three armies of Southwestern Front (right to left, 1st Guards Army, 3rd Guards Army, and 5th Tank Army) against the 8th Italian Army along the Don, as well as against *Armee-Abteilung* Hollidt. Once the assault formations had pierced the Axis front and reached the Donets river crossing at Kamensk, Saturn would insert a second echelon (2nd Guards Army) for a drive to the south, seizing Rostov on the Don and choking off Army Group A,

---

[28] For Manstein, Stalingrad was a "tragedy" ("Tragödie"), the title of his chapter on the relief attempt. See Manstein, *Verlorene Siege*, pp. 319–96. See p. 319 for the Spartan funereal inscription.

[29] Points made well by Wagener, *Heeresgruppe Süd*, p. 188.

still at this point far down in the Caucasus. The entire German southern wing would be endangered, therefore, not simply the 6th Army in Stalingrad.

Unfortunately for that bold operational prospectus, the Soviets had to downsize. The incredible scale of the pocket in Stalingrad, estimated first at 90,000 men and then rapidly revised upward to over 200,000, forced the Soviet command into some hard choices. The second echelon now fell away, with 2nd Army committed to the reduction of the Stalingrad pocket, and Saturn became "Little Saturn," a much shallower envelopment of the Italian 8th Army and *Armee-Abteilung* Hollidt, with the assault formations concentrating on the destruction of their immediate operational targets, rather than preparing for a deeper drive south towards Rostov.[30]

The foreshortened operation opened on December 16th and remains one of the great operational-level successes of the war. No student of the conflict should be surprised that the Italian army failed to withstand a great armored onslaught. The same dynamic that had led to the demise of the Romanians was at work here: a largely non-motorized force attempting to hold an unfortified position along a meandering river bank against a highly mobile, heavily armored enemy. One of the army's four corps, in fact, consisted of *Alpini*, good mountain infantry now tasked to defend a battle-space as flat as a pancake.

All that being said, the speed and totality of the Italian collapse along the Don is still shocking and speaks of something different: a complete breakdown in morale and cohesion in the weeks leading up to the offensive. There was a general panic, and many units simply gave up without any fighting at all. The Soviet assault penetrated at will, linked up behind the lines, and surrounded and destroyed major portions of the Italian line one by one. The German XXIX Corps, holding the right flank of the army but consisting of Italian divisions, also found itself thrown into headlong flight, and would spend the next two weeks as a kind of "movable pocket," constantly threatened with encirclement by Soviet armored columns but heading steadily south. It would finally

---

[30] The indispensable work on all the Soviet winter offensives of 1942–43 (Little Saturn, the Ostrogozhk-Rossosh operation, Operation Gallop, and Operation Star) is David M. Glantz, *From the Don to the Dnepr: Soviet Offensive Operations, December 1942–August 1943* (London: Frank Cass, 1991). David M. Glantz and Jonathan House, *When Titans Clashed: How the Red Army Stopped Hitler* (Lawrence, KS: University Press of Kansas, 1995) continues to be useful as an operational précis.

reach the safety of friendly lines on December 28th, after what one German officer called "a true Odyssey," along with 5,000 of its original complement of nearly 40,000 men.[31]

Most worrisome to the Germans had been a series of deep penetrations by individual Soviet mobile formations. General V. M. Badanov's 24th Tank Corps, for example, had broken into the open, lunged 150 miles south to Tatsinskaia by Christmas Eve, and actually overran a Luftwaffe airfield there, always a signal achievement in this war. For hours, Badanov's T-34s drove back and forth across the runways, shooting up grounded aircraft, lightly armed Luftwaffe security formations, and supplies at will. Some sources describe over 300 German aircraft destroyed, an incredible and probably inflated figure, but with Tatsinskaya serving as one of the principal fields for the Stalingrad airlift, German losses were certainly high enough. Unfortunately, Badanov's great lunge had left him out of contact with supporting formations. He wound up surrounded by various German reserves and *Alarmeinheiten* and the subsequent fighting would see most his command destroyed.[32] Nevertheless, the episode had terrified the German command at all levels, raising the specter of waking up one morning to find Soviet tanks in Rostov.

Despite Badanov's misadventure, Little Saturn had been a disaster for the Germans. The destruction of the Italians had torn a huge gap in the German defensive position, Army Groups B and Don were no longer in contact with one another, and Soviet tank corps were roaming in open space between them. Moreover, by forcing Manstein to redeploy 6th Panzer Division to the west, Little Saturn had meant the end of Winter Storm. The year ended much as the last one had, with German forces on the run in the East. Manstein's operational skills notwithstanding, perhaps in some situations there is simply nothing to be done.

III. *The Backhand Blow*[33]

Nor did the New Year bring much relief. The same operational dynamic was at work through what was a very dark January for the Wehrmacht.

---

[31] Scheibert, *Zwischen Don und Donez*, pp. 36, 43.
[32] For a crisp description of Badanov's ride, see Glantz and House, *When Titans Clashed*, pp. 139–141.
[33] The primary source on Manstein's winter counteroffensive of 1943 is Chapter 13 of *Verlorene Siege*, "Der Winterfuldzug 1942/42 in Sudrüssland," pp. 397–472, although

The Soviets clearly held the initiative, what the Germans call the "Gesetz der Handelns." On January 13th, the Red Army struck a third time, this one still further up the Don, as Voronezh Front (General F. I. Golikov) launched the "Ostrogozhsk-Rossosh operation." Targeting Hungarian 2nd Army (General Gusztáv Jány), it managed to do the same thing to the under-gunned Hungarians that Uranus had done to the Romanians and Little Saturn to the Italians: erase it from the order of battle. Once again, there is no reason to see why it should have been otherwise. Jány's army consisted of nine light divisions, each containing only two regiments; they were holding impossibly long frontages, and they were very poorly equipped, especially with antitank weapons. One Hungarian historian describes 2nd Army's line on the Don as "merely a reinforced observation post on the river, not a sturdy defense at all."[34]

---

like the entire book, it needs to be read with caution. See also Friedrich Schulz, "Der Rückschlag im Süden der Ostfront 1942/43," Manuscript T-15 in the Foreign Military Studies series. The original is available in the U.S. Army Military History Institute/ Army Heritage and Education Center (MHI/AHEC) in Carlisle, PA. The author was a German general who ended the war as commander of Army Group South. The report is comprehensive—with its seven appendices, on matters as diverse as "The Conduct of Battle by XXXXIX Mountain Corps in the Caucasus Sector" (Appendix 3) and "The Italian Expeditionary Army" (Appendix 6), it comprises 343 pages, plus maps. The entire report is also available in English translation as "Reverses on the Southern Wing." There are two indispensable English-language works: Sadarananda, *Beyond Stalingrad* and Glantz, *From the Don to the Dnepr*. Equally important—the first book based on the archival records of Army Group Don/South—is Eberhard Schwarz, *Die Stabilisierung der Ostfront nach Stalingrad: Mansteins Gegenschlag zwischen Donez und Dnjepr im Frühjahr 1943* (Göttingen: Muster-Schmidt Verlag, 1985). Wagener, *Heeresgruppe Süd*, devotes a chapter to the "rettender Gegenangriff," pp. 211–220; he commanded XXXX Panzer Corps during the fighting. See also Wagener, "Der Gegenangriff des XXXX. Panzerkorps gegen den Durchbruch der Panzergruppe Popow im Donezbecken Februar 1943," *Wehrwissenschaftliche Rundschau* 7, 1957 (pp. 21–36). One of the first Soviet historians to analyze the campaign was Colonel V. P. Morozov, writing during the period of the Khrushchev thaw. See "Warum der Angriff im Frühjahr im Donezbecken nicht zu Ende geführt wurde," *Wehrwissenschaftliche Rundschau* 14, 1964 (pp. 414–430, 493–500). See also his monograph *Westlich von Voronezh: Kurzer militärhistorischer Abriss der Angriffsoperationen der sowjetischen Truppen in der Zeit von Januar bis Februar 1943* (Berlin [Ost]: Verlag des Ministeriums für Nationale Verteidigung, 1959). See also Busse, "Der Winterfeldzug 1942/1943 in Südrussland," in *Nie ausser Dienst*, and two works by the dean of modern German operational historians, Karl-Heinz Frieser: "Schlagen aus der Nachhand—Schlagen aus der Vorhand: Die Schlachten von Char'kow und Kursk 1943," in Roland G. Foerster, *Gezeitenwechsel im Zweiten Weltkrieg? Die Schlachten von Char'kov und Kursk im Frühjahr und Sommer 1943 in operativer Anlage, Verlauf und politischer Bedeutung* (Berlin: E. S. Mittler, 1996), and "Mansteins Gegenschlag am Donez: Operative Analyse des Gegenangriffs der Heeresgruppe Süd im February/März 1943," *Militärgeschichte* 9, 1999, pp. 12–18 (with Friedhelm Klein).

[34] Franz von Adonyi-Naredy, *Ungarns Armee im Zeiten Weltkrieg: Deutschlands letzter Verbündeter* (Neckargemünd: Kurt Vowinckel Verlag, 1971), p. 84.

Individual units here or there made a stand, but there were also mass surrenders and panic-stricken columns streaming westward in temperatures of -45 Celsius. Just two weeks later, on January 29th, Southwestern Front (General N. F. Vatutin) launched a fourth major blow across the Donets river and into the Donets basin (the *Donbas*) itself, code-named Operation Gallop.[35] Finally, on February 2nd, Voronezh Front launched Operation Star on the extreme right wing of the southern front. It smashed into German 2nd Army (General Hans von Salmuth), by now utterly threadbare due to the number of formations it had surrendered to the emergency to the south, with great force. Exceeding all expectations, Star drove back the defenders, not Italians or Romanians or Hungarians this time, but a core formation of the *Ostheer*, threatening 2nd Army with a Stalingrad-style encirclement, and reconquering the major cities of Kursk, Belgorod and Kharkov.[36] Indeed, Red Army expert David Glantz counts no fewer than "eight separate operations conducted simultaneously or consecutively by the Red Amy's Briansk, Voronezh, Southwestern, and Southern Fronts" from January to early March 1943. Soviet historians have labeled all of these operations collectively as a "strategic offensive,"[37] with the Red Army lunging forward some 350 miles and opening up a 300-mile wide gap between Army Group Center and the tattered remnants of Army Group B to its immediate south.[38]

Manstein's impact on all this had essentially been nil. He had successfully managed chaos, to be sure, shifting units hither and yon as emergencies arose, integrating the meager reinforcements coming up to the front, and attempting to talk some operational sense into the High Command—that is, Hitler—regarding the need to restore a degree of maneuver to the front. In this quest, however, he was aided immeasurably by the Chief of the General Staff, General Kurt Zeitzler, a true believer in educating the army along National Socialist lines, but also a man of undeniable operational acumen.[39]

---

[35] For a narrative of the offensive, as well as the pertinent archival sources, see David M. Glantz, "The Red Army's Donbas Offensive (February–March 1942) Revisited: A Documentary Essay," *Journal of Slavic Military Studies* 18, no. 3 (2005), pp. 369–503. The title is evidently a misprint. It should read "February–March 1943."

[36] Schwarz, *Stabilisierung der Ostfront*, p. 83, has 2nd Army "fighting for its life."

[37] Glantz, "The Red Army's Donbas Offensive," pp. 369–370.

[38] Wagener, *Heeresgruppe Süd*, p. 215.

[39] For Zeitzler's promotion of National Socialism within the army, see Geoffrey P. Megargee, *Inside Hitler's High Command* (Lawrence, KS: University Press of Kansas, 2000), pp. 181–183.

Zeitzler had his first success at the very end of 1942 when Hitler finally consented to a withdrawal of Army Group A from the Caucasus.[40] This was good news. The two constituent formations, 17th Army in the west (General Richard Ruoff) and 1st Panzer in the east (General Eberhard von Mackensen) would now be available for mobile operations against the onrushing Soviets. Zeitzler's sense of accomplishment diminished the next day when he received new orders: rather than evacuate the Caucasus altogether, Army Group A would withdraw to a so-called "Kuban bridgehead," perhaps with an eye to renewing the offensive into the Caucasus in 1943. In the course of the retreat, those orders would be changed again. Now only one of the armies, the 17th, would hold the Kuban, while 1st Panzer would leave the Caucasus to rejoin its sister formations in Ukraine.

With the retreat of 1st Panzer Army from the Caucasus at the end of January, what had been a swirling, even chaotic, campaign was beginning to sort itself out into more recognizable patterns. From our perspective today, it is possible to see signs that all these Soviet offensives were reaching what Clausewitz had called the "culmination point," the moment at which offensive power begins to wear down, friction reasserts itself, and the machine eventually stops.[41] Supplies of all sorts were running low, the tanks corps were losing their cutting edge, and machines and men were nearing exhaustion. It had been an amazing ride for the Red Army, one that had started on the Volga, reconquered the immense bend of the Don river, and was now hurtling across the Donets towards the Dnepr. Indeed, it had been one of the most successful military campaigns in modern history. But what David Glantz calls "the ravages of time and distance" were beginning to show, and actual fighting strength was probably half of what it had been at the start of the winter offensives.[42]

---

[40] See the pertinent chapter in Wagener, *Heeresgruppe Süd*, pp. 201–209. For the Soviet point of view, Andrei Grechko, *Battle for the Caucasus* (Moscow: Progress Publishers, 1971) is still useful. Grechko was an army commander in the Caucasus.

[41] The standard English translation is Carl von Clausewitz, *On War*, edited and translated by Michael Howard and Peter Paret (Princeton: Princeton University Press, 1984), with introductory essays by Paret, Howard, and Bernard Brodie. See book 7, chapter 4, "The Diminishing Force of the Attack," p. 527; chapter 5, "The Culminating Point of the Attack," p. 28, and Chapter 22, "The Culminating Point of Victory," pp. 566–573.

[42] Glantz, *From the Don to the Dnepr*, p. 146.

While the Soviets were wearing down, the German line was finally starting to solidify. The various *Armee-Abteilungen* may still have been short of manpower, heavy artillery and equipment, and administrative personnel, but they had at least been working together for months now, and familiarity had bred a sense of confidence. With *Armee-Abteilung* Hollidt in place of 6th Army, *Armee-Abteilung* Fretter-Pico where the Italian 8th Army used to be, and *Armee Abteilung* Lanz forming a new mobile command in the Kharkov region, the Germans had at least restored a semblance of a line. Adding to the fresh sense of well-being was the long-awaited arrival of the new II SS Panzer Corps under General Paul Hausser. Its three panzer divisions, 1st SS (*Leibstandarte Adolf Hitler*), 2nd SS (*Das Reich*), and 3rd (*Totenkopf*), were bursting with manpower, new equipment, and self-confidence.

That sense of swagger took a hit early on; the corps arrived piecemeal and was thrown into the path of Operation Star, the lunge westward by Voronezh Front. Fighting under *Armee-Abteilung* Lanz and ordered to hold Kharkov till the last man, SS commander General Paul Hausser took one look at the situation maps, with Soviet tanks corps about to bypass him north and south of the city, and decided to skedaddle. The SS officer's disobedience went unpunished. Someone had to pay for the loss of Kharkov, however, and Hitler decided to dismiss the regular army commander on the scene, General Hubert Lanz, on the grounds that he had sanctioned Hausser's withdrawal. The *Armee-Abteilung* now came under the command of General Werner Kempf (and received a new name, *Armee-Abteilung* Kempf).[43]

This combination of Soviet overstretch and a barely perceptible German revival led Manstein to devise a new operational conception. He was nothing if not operationally minded. First, since there were no more reinforcements coming out from the homeland, something would have to be done to free up troops within the theater itself. Manstein looked to the immense "balcony" occupied by *Armee-Abteilung* Hollidt, *Armee-Abteilung* Fretter-Pico, and 1st and 4th Panzer Armies, all currently deployed far into the eastern bend of the Donets and lower Don rivers. This entire position, including the eastern half of the "Donbas" itself, would have to be abandoned in favor of a much

---

[43] See Schwarz, *Stabilisierung der Ostfront*, pp. 118–121. Manstein, for one, took notice, remarking that, "If a general of the army had ordered the withdrawal," rather than an SS commander, "Hitler would have hauled him in front of a court martial" (*Verlorene Siege*, p. 453).

straighter, and thus shorter, line to the east, along the Mius river. It was not unfamiliar. In fact, it was same line the Wehrmacht had held during the winter of 1941–42. Holding a shorter line would free up troops for more mobile operations.

But where would those operations take place? Here, Manstein opted for a typically bold solution. He had always been a gambler and took a gambler's delight in a risky bet that paid off big. His plan for the 1940 campaign had been filled with dangerous gambits: the feint from the North by Army Group B, the risky drive by almost all of the Panzer formations through the Ardennes forest by Rundstedt's Army Group A, the bold lunge clear across the rear of the Allied armies further north in Belgium. That plan could have fallen apart on a multitude of occasions. His operational solution this time was no less daring. Borrowing again from the vocabulary of chess, Manstein envisioned a *Rochade*, a "castling maneuver," with the formations on the extreme right wing of the German position—the 1st and 4th Panzer Armies— now being shifted to the extreme left. Once they had arrived, they would launch a counteroffensive into the spent Soviet assault formations whose commanders were still driving them relentlessly to the west. It would be what Manstein liked to call a "Schlag aus der Nachhand," a "backhand blow" that was most effective once the enemy had committed himself and had exhausted his energy and supplies.[44]

After sending these proposals to Hitler and the High Command of the Army (OKH), Manstein received a summons to meet with the Führer on February 6th at the East Prussian headquarters in Rastenburg. Although Manstein painted the conference very much in epic terms in *Verlorene Siege*,[45] a battle of wills between two men dedicated to radically different visions of warfighting, there was, in fact, a synergy between the two men by this point in the war, between the "operator" and the advocate of a "Halte-Strategie."[46] Hitler, for all his irrationality

---

[44] For the *Rochade*, see Manstein, *Verlorene Siege*, p. 405. The term is translated, badly, as "leap-frogging" in the English translation (*Lost Victories*, 374). In similar clumsy fashion, Moltke's famous dictum that "Strategy is a system of expedients" ("Die Strategie ist ein System der Aushilfen") becomes "Strategy is a system of stop-gaps" (p. 367). Manstein actually introduces the term "backhand blow" a bit later in his memoirs, with reference to planning for the Kursk offensive (p. 477), but it is clear that he was employing the same concept in planning the winter counteroffensive.

[45] For the Rastenburg meeting, see Manstein, *Verlorene Siege*, pp. 437–444.

[46] Glantz is typically perceptive on this point: "Ironically, in a sense, he [Manstein] was assisted by the stubbornness of Hitler who demanded that all territory be held" (*From the Don to the Dnepr*, p. 148).

in other areas, had probably been right to demand a "no retreat" policy up till now. A retreat by immobile forces in the midst of winter made no sense and would almost certainly have resulted in higher German losses than the catastrophic ones already suffered. But Manstein was also right: the time had come to maneuver, to restore "operational mobility" ("bewegliche Operationsführung"), and to fight *Bewegungskrieg*, the kind of war in which German superiority in both leadership and troops could reassert itself.[47] Hitler knew it. Less than a week past 6th Army's final surrender at Stalingrad, the Führer was in the midst of what we might call a "teachable moment."

So there was no real struggle here. While Hitler did put up a fight to Manstein's suggestions, especially the need to abandon the eastern Donbas, it was essentially half-hearted. There was the by-now typical haggling over minutiae and statistics, and a desultory argument over the quality of the coal from the region. Hitler wanted to employ II SS Panzer Corps in a direct counterattack on Kharkov; Manstein preferred to let the Soviets come on and strike them when they were spent. Anyone who has read the stenographic minutes of the Führer conferences from this period will not see any of this as particularly obstructionist. Compared to what General Zeitzler and the rest had to endure on a daily basis, it was fairly small potatoes.[48] Even Manstein's incredible suggestion that he elbow Hitler aside and take over the day-to-day command of the war in the East failed to get much of a rise.

We must also recognize that Manstein himself wasn't particularly pleased with what he had to say. He was not happy about having to retreat, either. He really did consider his Soviet adversary to be hopelessly inept, especially in terms of generalship. "In my own case," he would later write, "it went right against the grain." Having to "goad Hitler into giving territory up," voluntarily surrendering a region that the army had conquered "at such heavy cost," was distasteful to him, as it would have been to virtually all German staff and field commanders. "I should have much preferred to be able to submit plans for successful

---

[47] Manstein, *Verlorene Siege*, p. 405.

[48] For evidence of how Hitler could string out a conversation to avoid having to follow his advisor's recommendations, see Helmut Heiber, ed., *Hitlers Lagebesprechungen: Die Protokollfragmente siner militärischen Konferenzen 1942–1945* (Stuttgart: Deutsche Verlags-Anstalt, 1962). He was expert at throwing out questions to derail strategic discussion: "How many tanks precisely does 17th Panzer have? (p. 81), "How much gasoline does a 3-ton truck use?" (p. 95), and "Why don't we organize special flamethrower detachments?" (p. 453, "That is a fearsome weapon," Hitler comments).

offensives," he remembered, rather than have to recommend the "now inevitable withdrawals."[49]

There was no choice, however, and both men agreed. Manstein came away from the Rastenburg meeting with what he wanted: Hitler's approval for the new operation. A *Rochade* it would be, although Manstein was concerned that by this point the decision had come too late. The principal threat now was Operation Gallop, the great Soviet operation in the Donbas. Southwestern Front—6th Army (General F. M. Kharitonov), 1st Guards Army (General D. D. Lelyushenko), and Mobile Group Popov, a prototype tank army under the command of General M. M. Popov and consisting of four tank corps and supporting formations—had leaped over the Donets and was now driving west and south at top speed. Juicy operational targets abounded. Reaching the coast of the Sea of Azov at Mariupol or Taganrog, for example, would cut off all German forces still deployed to the east, 1st and 4th Panzer Armies and *Armee-Abteilung* Hollidt. Even worse would result from Soviet forces crossing the Dnepr river. Seizing the crossings over the great river at Dnepropetrovsk, Zaporozhe, or Kremenchug would cut off supply to the entire German southern wing, turning an operational-level victory, potentially, into a strategic triumph—a "Super-Stalingrad," of sorts.[50] The two Panzer armies had to hurry, a problem made even worse by weather: they were motoring along the coast, areas where the thaw had already set in, and the mud along with it; Soviet forces to the north were still driving along frozen, hard roads.

There was, therefore, a certain frantic quality to German preparations, and indeed, so hurried was the planning that the operation never really received a name. There was, however, unity of command, with Manstein's Army Group Don renamed Army Group South and Army Groups A and B dissolved. Manstein now had something he had wanted since November: theater command. By mid-February, the pullback from the Don-Donets "balcony" had succeeded, and *Armee-Abteilung* Hollidt had retreated into the *Maulwurfstellung*, the "Mole position" behind the Mius. *Armee-Abteilung* Fretter-Pico, now reduced in status to XXX Corps, deployed to its left, defending along the middle Donets up to Slavyansk. Using this position as an operational shield,

---

[49] "Es ist gerade für mich meiner Wesenart nach besonders schwer gewesen…" (Manstein, *Verlorene Siege*, p. 440; *Lost Victories*, p. 410).
[50] Frieser and Klein, "Mansteins Gegenschlag am Donez," p. 12.

Mackensen's 1st Panzer Army, still weary from its long trek out of the Caucasus, came up into the line on the left. Unfortunately, with Soviet forces still hurtling southwards, it had to go into battle almost immediately, with predictable results. The III Panzer Corps, whose 3rd and 7th Panzer Divisions had probably forty tanks between them, drove north from Stalino, ran into heavy opposition and soon bogged down. The same happened to its left, where XXXX Panzer Corps (11th Panzer Division, 333rd Infantry Division, and elements of SS-Division Viking) went into the attack without a great deal of preparation and ran into hard driving Soviet armored columns coming down from Lissichansk and Slavyansk. Once again, there was a certain amount of panic within German command circle as Mobile Group Popov made a clean breakthrough into the operational depth of the German position.[51] Much as Badanov's experience in Little Saturn, however, Popov eventually found himself isolated at Krasnoarmeiskoe, and under concentric attack by virtually all of XXXX Panzer Corps.

By February 21st, 4th Panzer Army had arrived in the theater and fallen in on 1st Panzer Army's left, the final step in Manstein's *Rochade*. The entire array was facing almost due north, with the line along the Mius then falling off and forming a right angle to it. Hoth's men had moved hundreds of miles in four days (February 16th–19th), and they too were exhausted. Nevertheless, both German Panzer armies were in hand and concentrated for action, and the problem of supply had become much easier to solve now that the formations were not lying 400 miles to the east over two major rivers. Moreover, by this time, the operation had taken on an amazing shape, as strange, in its way, as Operation Blue in the previous fall. As Soviet forces faced more and more opposition on the road south, they had begun to slide to their right. Mobile Group Popov was already surrounded, to be sure, but the rest of Southwestern Front was motoring in open space in the 100-mile gap between Slavyansk and Kharkov, driving west and southwest and heading for the Dnepr: 6th Army on the right and 1st Gaurds army on the left. Two more tank corps, 25th and 1st Guards, were driving on Zaporozhe, the headquarters of both Army Group Don and 4th Air Fleet. With no major German formations between them and their targets, it must have seemed like a done deal. Meanwhile, sliding

---

[51] Wagener, "Gegenangriff der XXXX. Panzerkorps gegen der Durchbruch der Panzerguppe Popow," p. 27.

alongside the Soviets to the south, the Germans were desperately trying to extend their line to the left, or west. There was a race on, and the winner was still very much open to question.

In the end, the Germans would win the race, and it makes a certain sense: they were, after all, falling back on their supply bases while the Soviets were running away from theirs. Beyond that general notion, however, or the Clausewitzian idea of an inevitable "culmination point" to all offensive operations, there was another aspect of this campaign that was peculiar to the Soviet military experience. "Deep battle" held as many dangers as opportunities for the Red Army. "Deep" had become a buzzword to this generation of Soviet officers, and buzzwords can be deadly. Far from achieving some new breakthrough into a scientifically calculated "operational art," Soviet formations in this period tended to advance until they collapsed from losses, from lack of supply and replacements, and perhaps from a simple sense of exhaustion.[52]

Deep battle, in other words, implied a tendency to overreach, to underestimate enemy strength, and to overestimate the degree to which deep strikes would "paralyze the foe"—whatever that means. Joseph Stalin, General G. K. Zhukov, and the Stavka alike had overreached badly in 1941, they had reprised that mistake in the disaster in front of Kharkov in May 1942, and they were about to do it one more time. This would be the second winter in a row that the Soviet high command managed to conjure up a German enemy who was ripe for the picking, and the second year in a row that they would be shocked. Now that military history has finally begun to dispense with enthusiasm for any special "German genius for war," and to view the Wehrmacht's operations in a colder and more rational light, it would be a tragedy to substitute any special respect for Soviet warmaking. It was extraordinarily clumsy, wasteful of lives and manpower, and, in the end, highly dangerous to its own men, as its almost surreal casualty statistics would bear out for the rest of the war.[53]

---

[52] Even in the age of "new wars" and COIN, Soviet "operational art" continues to exert an almost magnetic pull on the educational establishments of the U.S. Army, especially the Command and General Staff College (CGSC) and the School of Advanced Military Studies (SAMS), both at Ft. Leavenworth, KS. For a representative sampling of essays circulated within the U.S. military, see Michael D. Krause and R. Cody Phillips, eds., *Historical Perspectives of the Operational Art* (Washington, DC: Center of Military History, 2007).

[53] The true strength of Glantz's work on the Soviet military is its complete lack of romanticism and its sober refusal to substitute a new enthusiasm for Soviet warmaking

As a result, there was never a really a moment in this operation that can legitimately be named a "turning point," one in which the momentum shifted and the Soviets suddenly realized to their horror that they were beaten. One moment 6th and 1st Guards Armies were driving west, riding high, and aiming for the Dnepr. On February 19th, Soviet armored columns seized the town of Sinelnikovo, cutting the main east-west railroad from Dnepropetrovsk to Stalino, halting all railroad traffic and placing the entire German southern wing out of supply. Hitler himself was visiting Manstein's headquarters in Zaporozhe on the east, unprotected side of the Dnepr at the time. The news that T-34s were only fifty kilometers away led to a hurried evacuation, with the Führer being trundled onto a plane and flown off for his own safety. The Soviets didn't know how close they had come to bagging the enemy *supremo*, of course, but they did know a number of other things. Intelligence was flowing into front and army headquarters alike of massive German troop movements to the west, which all levels of Soviet command from Vatutin on down interpreted as another sign of a wild and desperate German flight for the Dnepr crossings.[54] Army commanders urged their men on with redoubled urgency. The enemy was on the run, and on the ropes.

As it drove towards the Dnepr, the Red Army was riding high. And then, suddenly, it was crushed. On February 21st, Hoth's 4th Panzer Army launched its counterattack. Two convergent thrusts—one from the south spearheaded by LVII Corps on the left and XXXXVIII Panzer Corps on the right, and one from the region of Poltava in the northwest by II SS Panzer Corps—caught the spearheads of Soviet 6th and 1st Guards Armies completely by surprise, took them in front, flanks, and rear, and scattered them. Friendly casualties, at least for these few days, were minimal; Soviet casualties were nearly total in terms of materiel and high enough in men. And no wonder: formation after formation was, quite literally, running out of fuel just at the moment that the German counterattack struck. While in many ways a classic expression of the German way of war, *Bewegungskrieg* and "concentric operations," there was no real *Kesselschlacht*, no huge haul of prisoners. The Soviet

---

for one that has now been discredited, the German. For his criticism of the blind optimism of the Soviet high command, see "The Red Army's Donbas Offensive," p. 503, as well as *From the Don to the Dnepr*, p. 145.

[54] See Morozov, "Warum der Angriff im Frühjahr im Donezbecken nicht zu Ende geführt wurde," p. 429.

front simply exploded, and there were nowhere near enough German formations to draw any kind of ring around most of them.

Over the course of the next few weeks, the Germans kept up the momentum of their drive to the north. Mackensen's 1st Panzer Army ground forward to the Donets, although the Soviets managed to hold a few pesky bridgeheads south of the river. To his left, armored spearheads of the II SS and XXXVIII Panzer Corps, had the Soviets on the run, and there seemed for a brief moment to have been a breakdown in enemy command and control. Suddenly, it seemed as if it were 1941 again, or perhaps even 1940. There was even a recrudescence of the oldest Prussian-German tradition of all, the "independence of the subordinate commander." As SS General Paul Hausser drove his corps on Kharkov, he received explicit orders from Manstein to avoid anything that smacked of positional or street fighting in the city. Kharkov could be taken by a quick coup ("Handstreich") if the opportunity presented itself, but it was not to become a trap.[55] The ugly memory of Stalingrad was still too fresh, the wounds still open. Looping around to the north in an elegant little maneuver, II SS Panzer fought its way into Kharkov from the northeast and cleared the city after three days of gritty fighting (March 12th–14th). It wasn't a trap, but neither was it a coup, exactly. From there, it was another hop north to Belgorod, which the Germans took on March 23rd. By this point, the thaw had come, the mud had arrived, and no one was going anywhere. A planned coordinating strike by the neighboring 2nd Army (part of Army Group Center) never materialized, a sign of how badly that formation had suffered from Soviet attacks in Operation Star. The proposed target of 2nd Army, Kursk and the attendant salient in the line around it, remained in Soviet hands.

IV. *Conclusion: Manstein and the Limits of Genius*

We began this paper with a discussion of the role that personality plays, not only in modern military operations, but in our historical analysis of them. The Donets-Kharkov campaign of early 1943 would seem to be a testament to Manstein's genius, and that is almost always how it appears in the literature. Certainly, the Field Marshal had shown a deft touch, first in remaining calm when it looked like the

---

[55] See the discussion in Schwarz, *Stabilisierung der Ostfront*, pp. 196–97.

entire front was about to collapse, then in keeping ends and means clearly aligned, and finally in remembering that the campaign had to end with a maneuver-based counterattack and that it was senseless to slug it out toe-to-toe with an enemy who could vastly outproduce him. Above all, his timing had been perfect, a rare thing indeed on the operational level.

And yet, Manstein's genius is ultimately an unsatisfying explanation for what happened on the banks of the Donets in 1943. He was not a free agent, but a product of a long-standing tradition. In a brief analysis of the campaign by two soldier-scholars of the German *Bundeswehr*, Friedhelm Klein and Karl-Heinz Frieser, the authors argue that "the transformation of an apparently unavoidable catastrophe on the Donets in the winter of 1943 into a victory is due not least to the personality of the military commander: Field Marshall von Manstein. Like few others, he embodied the traditional thought of the German General Staff."[56] Notions of the "war of movement," or of war as a "free creative activity,"[57] or of the "independence of the commander"—these were concepts that were decades, perhaps even centuries, old. Frieser and Klein reproduce the entire operations plan for the February 21st counterattack, and it is a model of traditional Prussian-German brevity. It consists of a single sentence, which the officers on the spot would have to make internalize and apply as best they saw fit:

> Army Group South defends the *Maulwurfstellung* on the Mius and northwards to Slavyansk, strikes the enemy in the gap between 1st Panzer Army and Armee-Abteilung Lanz (Kempf) with 4th Panzer Army, and covers the deep flank and the attack of 4th Panzer Army in the Poltava-Achtyrka region with Armee Abteilung Lanz (Kempf).[58]

A simple order, yes, but it set into motion more than one million men.

Frieser and Klein are correct to set Manstein's achievement into context and perspective, of course, and no historian should object. As they point out, even the mechanics of the operation itself were hardly new. Since the 1880's, German staff officers had practiced the rapid shifting of armies to ward off threats that arose suddenly or surprisingly. Germany's strategic situation in the heart of Europe, ringed by enemies or potential ones, demanded it. The *Kaiserreich* even had its own

---

[56] Frieser and Klein, "Mansteins Gegenschlag am Donez," p. 17.
[57] The definition of war in paragraph 1 of the German manual *Truppenführung*.
[58] Frieser and Klein, "Mansteins Gegenschlag am Donez," p. 16.

exposed "balcony" against the Russians, East Prussia, a place where a mere passive defense would never suffice, where a vigorous counterblow was the only means of protecting the province. They had been practicing the *Rochade* and the "backhand blow" for decades, when Erich von Manstein was but a boy. In 1914, they had carried out an operation—the Tannenberg campaign—that bore more than a passing relation to Manstein's successful *retour offensive* on the Donets.[59]

Should we not go deeper here, however? If Manstein's strengths were actually those of the officer corps to which he belonged and the operational school that trained him, can we not say the same about his weaknesses? The simplistic equating of war with mobile operations, the absence of any sense of politics, the naïve belief that somehow—sometime, some way—these extraordinarily expensive and bloody military campaigns might add up to a strategic victory: were those, too, not the legacy of the German General Staff?

Finally, is it possible to see Manstein, like all the commanders on both sides in this campaign, as caught up in webs they could not even perceive? The victorious general in this campaign fought his traditional way of war to perfection, and in the process managed what had seemed impossible: he had reformed his front, torn open by the destruction of an entire field army at Stalingrad. No account of this campaign, no matter how brief it might be, omits the trope that Manstein had restored the front "to approximately where it had stood at the start of the 1942 campaign."[60] There was something approaching stupefaction even within the hard-boiled ranks of the General Staff. "One hesitates even now to believe it," one of them wrote at the time.[61] "We're in Kharkov again," exulted a headline in the glossy *Die Wehrmacht*,[62] and the same

---

[59] For a discussion of the difficulty of the retour offensive, Clausewitz's "blitzende Schwert der Vergeltung," see Wagener, "Gegenangriff der XXXX. Panzerkorps gegen der Durchbruch der Panzerguppe Popow," p. 21.

[60] See, among literally hundreds of references, Sadarananda, *Beyond Stalingrad*, p. 146: "Manstein's counterstroke had regained the initiative for the German aside and brought German forces back to the approximate line they held in the summer of 1942."

[61] Johann Adolf Graf von Kielmansegg, "Bemerkungen eines Zeitzeugen zu den Schlachten von Char'kov und Kursk aus der Sicht des damaligen Generalstabsoffiziers Ia in der Operationsabteilung der generalstabs des Heeres," in in Roland G. Foerster, *Gezeitenwechsel im Zweiten Weltkrieg? Die Schlachten von Char'kov und Kursk im Frühjahr und Sommer 1943 in operativer Anlage, Verlauf und politischer Bedeutung* (Berlin: E. S. Mittler, 1996), p. 142.

[62] "Wieder in Charkow," *Die Wehrmacht* 7, no. 7 (March 31, 1943), pp. 10–11.

magazine crowed that Manstein's blow represented a "turning point in the winter war."[63]

Give him his due. Mastering one crisis after another, and finally with Soviet tanks knocking on the door of the Dnepr river crossings, Manstein had engineered a dramatic revival, smashing the enemy he faced and thrusting forward all the way back to the Donets. In the process, however, he had driven his army up to a long, meandering river line that it could never hold in the coming year. He knew it, the high command knew it, and together they would try the rather desperate expedient of the Kursk offensive in the summer of 1943—just four months hence—in order to do something about it. *Bewegungskrieg*, in other words, led the Wehrmacht not to victory, but to the abyss.

As for the Soviets, they, too, had remained in character throughout this campaign, doggedly adhering to their new doctrine. They had driven on and on and on until they imploded. Their faith in "deep battle" had been disastrous, destroying Badanov's 24th Tank Corps, Mobile Group Popov, and eventually most of 6th and 1st Guards Armies alike.

The winter campaign of 1943, far from serving as a display of individual genius, offers us instead the unedifying spectacle of two armies trapped in their own doctrine.

---

[63] "Die Wende des Winterkrieges," *Die Wehrmacht* 7, no. 8 (April 14, 1943), pp. 4–5.

THE QUESTION OF MEDIEVAL MILITARY PROFESSIONALISM[1]

Kelly DeVries

As with all the other scholars in this collection, my debt to Dennis Showalter goes back many years, to when I was a young scholar, starting out rather bright-eyed and bushy-tailed, and filled with the desire to make a difference in military history, especially in my field of medieval military history. Such enthusiasm was likely to be quelled had I not been aided by the most generous of senior scholars, among them Dennis. My confidence grew especially after Dennis' article on medieval military history, "Caste, Skill, and Training: The Evolution of Cohesion in European Armies from the Middle Ages to the Sixteenth Century," which appeared in the *Journal of Military History* in 1993,[2] when he wrote and asked me to point out any errors that I may have found. There were but few, as the article was so good and complete (and it has stood the test of time to still be considered one of the finest articles on medieval military history); no doubt he knew this, but he also must have known what a feeling of importance it would give to a young scholar such as I to be asked to comment on the article's quality. One of the topics this article addressed was the professionalism of the medieval army. The following is but a brief answer to some of the questions Dennis asked.

By now there should be no question as to the high quality of medieval generalship. My own work on *Infantry Warfare in the Early Fourteenth Century* (1996) and *Joan of Arc* (1999)[3] built on that of J. F. Verbruggen, Philippe Contamine, John Gillingham, John France

---

[1] An earlier version of this paper was presented at the Society for Military History Meeting in Charleston, South Carolina on 27 February 2005.
[2] "Caste, Skill, and Training: The Evolution of Cohesion in European Armies from the Middle Ages to the Sixteenth Century," *Journal of Military History* 57 (1993), 407–30.
[3] *Infantry Warfare in the Early Fourteenth Century: Discipline, Tactics, and Technology* (Woodbridge: The Boydell Press, 1996) and *Joan of Arc: A Military Leader* (Stroud: Sutton Publishing, 1999).

and Bernard S. Bachrach,[4] while Clifford Rogers, Michael Prestwich, Matthew Bennett, Helen Nicholson, William Caferro, Donald Kagay, L. Andrew Villalon and Valerie Eads have added their own similar conclusions since I initially wrote.[5] And judging from the work of the

---

[4] J. F. Verbruggen, *The Art of Warfare in Western Europe During the Middle Ages from the Eighth Century to 1340*, 2nd ed., trans. S. Willard and R. W. Southern (Woodbridge: The Boydell Press, 1997), "L'armée et la stratégie de Charlemagne," in *Karl der Grosse: Lebenswerk und Nachleben*, band I: *Personlichkeit und Geschichte*, ed. H. Baumann et al (Dusseldorf: L. Schwann, 1965), pp. 420–36, and "Un plan de bataille du duc de Bourgogne (14 september 1417) et la tactique de l'époque," *Revue internationale d'histoire militaire* 20 (1959), 443–51; Philippe Contamine, Contamine, Philippe. *War in the Middle Ages*, trans. Michael Jones (Oxford: Basil Blackwell, 1984) and "L'art de la guerre selon Philippe de Clèves, seigneur de Ravenstein (1456–1528): innovation ou tradition?," *Bijdragen en mededelingen betreffende de geschiedenis der Nederlanden* 95 (1980), 363–76; John Gillingham, *Richard I* (New Haven: Yale University Press, 1999), "Richard I and the Science of War in the Middle Ages," in *War and Government in the Middle Ages: Essays in Honour of J. O. Prestwich*, ed. J. Gillingham and J. C. Holt (Cambridge: Cambridge University Press, 1984), pp. 78–91, and "William the Bastard at War," in *Studies in Medieval History Presented to R. Allen Brown*, ed. C. Harper-Bill et al. (Woodbridge: Boydell and Brewer, 1989), pp. 141–58; John France, *Victory in the East: A Military History of the First Crusade*. Cambridge: Cambridge University Press, 1994) and, later, *Western Warfare in the Age of the Crusades, 1000–1300* (Ithaca: Cornell University Press, 1999); and Bernard S. Bachrach, *Fulk Nerra, the Neo-Roman Consul, 987–1040: A Political Biography of the Angevin Count* (Berkeley and Los Angeles: University of California Press, 1993), "The Angevin Strategy of Castle Building in the Reign of Fulk Nerra, 987–1040," *American Historical Review* 88 (1983), 533–560, "The Practical Use of Vegetius' *De re militari* during the Early Middle Ages," *The Historian* 47 (1985), 239–55, and, later, *Early Carolingian Warfare: Prelude to Empire* (Philadelphia: University of Pennsylvania Press, 2001), "Dudo of St. Quentin and Norman Military Strategy, c. 1000," *Anglo-Norman Studies* 26 (2004), 21–36, and "Charlemagne and the Carolingian General Staff," *Journal of Military History* 66 (2002), 313–58.

[5] John D. Hosler, *Henry II: A Medieval Soldier at War, 1147–1189* (Leiden: Brill, 2007) and "Henry II's Military Campaigns in Wales, 1157 and 1165," *Journal of Medieval Military History* 2 (2004), 53–72; Nicolas Agráit, "Castilian Military Reform under the Reign of Alfonso XI (1312–50)," *Journal of Medieval Military History* 3 (2005), 88–126; "The Experience of War in Fourteenth-Century Spain: Alfonso XI and the Capture of Algeciras (1342–1344)," in *Crusaders, Condottieri, and Cannon: Medieval Warfare in Societies around the Mediterranean*, ed. L. J. Andrew Villalon, and Donald J. Kagay (Leiden: Brill, 2003), pp. 213–35, and "The Reconquest during the Reign of Alfonso XI (1312–1350)," in *On the Social Origins of Medieval Institutions: Essays in Honor of Joseph F. O'Callaghan*, ed. Donald J. Kagay and Theresa M. Vann (Leiden: E. J. Brill, 1998), pp. 149–65; David S. Bachrach, *Religion and the Conduct of War, c.300–c.1215* (Woodbridge: The Boydell Press, 2003), "Military Logistics during the Reign of Edward I of England (1272–1307)," *War in History* 13 (2006), 423–40, "The Organisation of Military Religion in the Armies of King Edward I of England (1272–1307)," *Journal of Medieval History* 29 (2003), 265–86, "Exercise of Royal Power in Early Medieval Europe: The Case of Otto the Great, 936–73," *Early Medieval History* 17 (2009), 389–419, and "The Military Organization of Ottonian Germany, c. 900–1018: The Views of Bishop Thietmar of Merseburg," *Journal of Military History* 72 (2008), 1061–88;

young talent, newly tenured professors, coming up in the field – John Hosler, Nicolas Agráit, David Bachrach and David Hay (all with books or substantial articles)[6] – there will be no turning back on this relatively recent belief. For it was as late as 1977 that Michael Howard wrote in his very popular *War in European History* that it was not until the sixteenth century that "cautious professional competence took the place of the quest for glory in the planning and conduct of campaigns."[7] Now, however, even modern military historians writing about medieval commanders are forced to agree with Michael Prestwich's comments written specifically about English leaders but able to be applied equally to other generals of the period:

> Successful generalship, in the middle ages as in other periods, demanded a range of qualities: strategic and tactical awareness, boldness in decision-making, persuasiveness, bravery and a measure of good fortune. The tools available to men such as Edward I or the Black Prince were limited. Communications were difficult, command structures were simple almost to a point of non-existence. Given the problems that they faced, the achievements of medieval commanders were remarkable.[8]

---

and David Hay, *The Military Leadership of Matilda of Canossa, 1046–1115* (Manchester: Manchester University Press, 2008).

[6] Clifford J. Rogers, *War Cruel and Sharp: English Strategy under Edward III, 1327–1360* (Woodbridge: The Boydell Press, 2000), "Edward III and the Dialectics of Strategy, 1327–1360," *Transactions of the Royal Historical Society*, 6th ser., 4 (1994), 83–102, "The Vegetian 'Science of Warfare' in the Middle Ages," *Journal of Medieval Military History* 1 (2002), 1–19, and "The Bergerac Campaign (1345) and the Generalship of Henry of Lancaster," *Journal of Medieval Military History* 2 (2004), 89–110; Michael Prestwich, *Armies and Warfare in the Middle Ages: The English Experience* (New Haven: Yale University Press, 1996) and *Edward I* (London: Guild Publishing, 1988); Matthew Bennett, "The Development of Battle Tactics in the Hundred Years War," in *Arms, Armies and Fortifications in the Hundred Years War*, ed. A. Curry and M. Hughes (Woodbridge: Boydell, 1994), pp. 1–20; Helen Nicholson, *Medieval Warfare: Theory and Practice of War in Europe, 300–1500* (Houndmills: Palgrave Macmillan, 2004); William Caferro, *John Hawkwood: An English Mercenary in Fourteenth-Century Italy* (Baltimore: Johns Hopkins University Press, 2006); Donald Kagay, "Jaime I of Aragon: Child and Master of the Spanish Reconquista," *Journal of Medieval Military History* 9 (2010), 609–108; L. J. Andrew Villalon, "'Cut Off Their Heads, or I'll Cut Off Yours': Castilian Strategy and Tactics in the War of the Two Pedros and the Supporting Evidence from Murcia," in *Hundred Years War (Part II): Different Vistas*, ed. L. J. Andrew Villalon and Donald J. Kagay (Leiden: Brill, 2008), pp. 153–84; and Valerie Eads, "The Geography of Power: Matilda of Tuscany and the Strategy of Active Defense," in *Crusaders, Condottieri, and Cannon: Medieval Warfare in Societies around the Mediterranean*, ed. L. J. Andrew Villalon and Donald J. Kagay (Leiden: Brill, 2003), pp. 355–88 and "Sichelgaita of Salerno: Amazon or Trophy Wife?" *Journal of Medieval Military History* 3 (2005), 72–87.

[7] Michael Howard, *War in European History* (Oxford: Oxford University Press, 1976), p. 27.

[8] Prestwich, *Armies and Warfare in the Middle Ages*, pp. 182–83.

But can we medieval military historians make the next leap in our military historical assessments: to describe medieval armies as "professional"? Such a task seems formidable, if not impossible, as here not only do we face the nay-saying of modern historians, such as the authors of one of the most popular textbooks of military history, *Men in Arms*,

> A feudal army in the field was an indescribably undisciplined force. Many tenants-in-chief would take orders only from their immediate overlord, the king; therefore an effective chain of command was impossible. There was a superabundance of courage, which tended to aggravate rather than to relieve the normal disorder. Long centuries of control of the art of war by one class, the exaggerated concentration upon cavalry warfare alone, and the absence of any provision for group training except in a restricted fashion in the reformed tournament meant that the study and practice of organized tactics had all but vanished . . . once the battle was joined, all semblance of order disappeared, and the struggle became nothing more than a confused melee of hundreds of individual encounters.[9]

but we must also face the judgments of our own medieval military historical predecessors. For example, at the turn of the twentieth century, Sir Charles Oman characterized medieval fighting skill as "when mere courage takes place of skill and experience, tactics and strategy alike disappear," adding that ". . . it was impossible to combine the movements of many small bodies when the troops were neither disciplined nor accustomed to act together."[10] Much closer to our own time, Philippe Contamine wrote:

> It should be agreed that medieval military history includes many battles which were nothing but hasty, instinctive and confused confrontations in which captains played the role of simple leaders of men, incorporated almost anonymously into the first line of battle, and where the warriors' chief concern was to find an adversary worthy of rank or valour, without any preoccupation for their companions in arms. They grappled on the battlefield with a sort of holy fury, free to flee precipitately as soon as things seemed to be going against them, and the individual search for booty and ransom was all-important.[11]

---

[9] Richard A. Preston, Alex Roland and Sydney F. Wise, *Men in Arms: A History of Warfare and Its Interrelationships With Western Society*, 5th ed (Fort Worth: Holt, Rinehart and Winston, Inc., 1991), pp. 69–70.

[10] Charles W. Oman, *The Art of War in the Middle Ages A.D. 378–1515*, rev. and ed. J. H. Beeler (Ithaca: Cornell University Press, 1953), pp. 58–59.

[11] Contamine, *War in the Middle Ages*, p. 229.

Clearly these statements, and there are several others that I could have used, suggest no professionalism whatsoever among those who participated in military conflicts between the fall of Rome in the fourth and fifth centuries and the conquest of Italy by French King Charles VIII in 1494, the traditional dates for the span of medieval military history. But has this attitude stood the test of time or fallen to later scholarship in a manner similar to the views on medieval generalship mentioned above? Recently an excellent collection of essays, entitled *The Chivalric Ethos and the Development of Military Professionalism*, edited by David J. B. Trim, has revisited the issue.[12] Admittedly from a perspective of the early modern period, several articles in this collection suggest that military professionalism could not have existed in the medieval world because the practice of chivalry precluded it. Michael Mallett, himself a great historian of Renaissance Italian military history, even writes in his essay, "Condottieri and Captains in Renaissance Italy," that the reason fourteenth- and fifteenth-century Italy became, in his words, a "breeding ground" of military professionalism was that it had an "absence of a strong chivalric tradition."[13]

Of course, the most immediate problem with this assessment is that chivalry as a medieval military practice only lasted for a short period of time, and even then it did not apply universally to all of Europe – as pointed out by Mallett above – nor to all of European military leadership. What of the rest of the Middle Ages and of the non-chivalric European military leaders? More importantly, how does this relate to medieval armies? Ultimately, can a medieval army ever be called professional?

From the very early years of the period, medieval armies, and what defines medieval military professionalism, depended on a system of military obligation. Military obligation was based mostly on what Philippe Contamine has termed "the feudo-vassalic system" wherein "Throughout the West, in tens of thousands, individuals, men and women, great and small, young and old, owed military service of various sorts to their lords for their fiefs."[14] However, it should be said that

---

[12] D. J. B. Trim, ed., *The Chivalric Ethos and the Development of Military Professionalism* (Leiden: Brill, 2003).
[13] Michael Mallett, "Condottieri and Captains in Renaissance Italy," in *The Chivalric Ethos and the Development of Military Professionalism*, ed. D. J. B. Trim (Leiden: Brill, 2003), pp. 67–88.
[14] Contamine, *War in the Middle Ages*, p. 77.

there was no uniformity in these obligations. Terms of feudo-vassalic responsibilities differed with nearly every contract made between lord and vassal. For example, in medieval Romania, service was given until the age of sixty, unless replaced by a suitable heir before then, four months of the year spent in castle duty, four months spent in the field, and four months at home; and in the Latin kingdom of Jerusalem, military service was for the entire year or until one died. Outside of these more embattled regions, however, feudo-vassalic military service was much shorter, usually being required only in defensive situations or when the lord who was owed the obligation desired to go on campaign. Under a particularly bellicose leader, this might mean a military service that could last much of the year for many years in a row; while under a weaker, more peaceful leader, there was a likelihood of never being required to perform military duties.[15]

When called up, the medieval soldier was required to bring himself and his retinue and to pay for almost all of the arms, armor, horses, and provisions needed to sustain them on their campaign or in their fortification. Ideally, this meant that no paid medieval army was needed. In reality, however, in order to fill out their numbers, most medieval military leaders were required to make promises of financial support or reimbursement for lost revenues or animals to those called into service. Or, they were forced to supplement their forces with mercenaries. Even this did not always work. For example, in 1300, when Edward I called his already fatigued feudal levy to military service, only forty knights and 366 sergeants responded.[16] Problems also arose over whom to call up. Peasants and urban militias were numerous, but they often lacked the skills or discipline to make them effective warriors; moreover, there was some hesitation to take soldiers from either the agricultural or tax-paying sectors of society.

Often during the Middle Ages, it became evident that the feudo-vassalic system was failing to call up sufficient troops to fight a major campaign or even to defend the borders of a state under attack. The result was an increased use of a "paid" military. At first this was simply the payment of service to the traditional feudo-vassalic leaders of forces. Taking as a model an earlier provision, called a "fief-rente" – monetary compensation as an annual payment to cover some of the

---

[15] Contamine, *War in the Middle Ages*, pp. 77–90.
[16] Contamine, *War in the Middle Ages*, p. 80.

costs of military service – that had been more and more frequently used during the Middle Ages, kings and princes began to institute a pension paid to the leaders of their armies. By the end of the fourteenth century, such pensions were in place everywhere throughout Europe, with most major military leaders paid well for their service.[17]

A second means of circumventing the traditional feudo-vassalic acquisition of military service was the war indenture. The war indenture was a slight variation on the pension, but was usually done on a smaller scale, a contract made between two minor military leaders (dukes, counts, earls, etc.) that one with his forces would assist the other if military service was needed. In return for the service of a certain number of cavalry, infantry, and missile troops, an annual payment would be made, as well as reimbursement for transport costs and any losses of warhorses. Booty and ransoms were to be divided between both parties. War indentures could also be sub-contracted out to leaders of smaller, often more specialized forces.[18]

Where does chivalry fit into these systems? It is difficult to know exactly when the practice of dubbing knights (*chevaliers* to make the definitional connection) began or where it originated. Simply put, no single document exists that indicates how or why the first knights were made. More than likely, medieval knights were the result of evolution rather than revolution, meaning that they came to exist as they were in the high and later Middle Ages not all at once, but over a long period of time. The reasons for the existence of a code of martial honor, medieval chivalry, are also not known.[19] Was it instituted by the Church at the time of the Crusades as a means of regulating the actions of the

---

[17] For example, the last English feudal levy was in 1385 for a campaign against Scotland. See N. B. Lewis, "The Last Medieval Summons of the English Feudal Levy, 13 June 1385," *English Historical Review* 73 (1958), 1–26 and J. J. N. Palmer, "The Last Summons of the Feudal Army in England (1385)," *English Historical Review* 83 (1968), 771–75. On "fief-rentes", see Contamine, *War in the Middle Ages*, pp. 92–94.

[18] Contamine, *War in the Middle Ages*, pp. 150–52. See also James Sherbourne, "Indentured Retinues and English Expeditions to France, 1369–1380," *English Historical Review* 79 (1964), 718–46 and Anthony Goodman, "The Military Subcontracts of Sir Hugh Hastings, 1380," *English Historical Review* 95 (1980), 114–20.

[19] There are some excellent studies on chivalry, although none are entirely convincing on its origins: Richard Barber, *The Knight and Chivalry*, 2nd ed. (Woodbridge: The Boydell Press, 1975); Maurice Keen, *Chivalry* (New Haven: Yale University Press, 1984); Richard W. Kaeuper, *Chivalry and Violence in Medieval Europe* (Oxford: Oxford University Press, 1999); and Richard W. Kaeuper, *Holy Warriors: The Religious Ideology of Chivalry* (Philadelphia: University of Pennsylvania Press, 2009).

warrior class? Or, was it something that came from within, from a class of knights who decided that they needed a set of virtuous qualities or a rule of conduct to offset their bellicose activities and reputation?

While the reasons for chivalry's existence may not be completely understood, the qualities that defined a chivalric knight are well known. John of Salisbury enumerated them in the twelfth century:

> [a knight's role is] to defend the Church, to assail infidelity, to venerate the priesthood, to protect the poor from injuries, to pacify the province, to pour out their blood for their brothers ... and, if need be, to lay down their lives.[20]

They were also to honor women, whose participation in this code was to allow for this esteem and to support their knights with love and, on many occasions, with symbols of their support–a garter or sash.

Medieval chivalry was sustained not only by the brotherhood of knights, but by numerous works of art and literature. There were an extremely large number of Tales of Arthur and his Knights of the Round Table written from the twelfth to the fifteenth century, reaching lands and languages that no comparable non-religious text or genre of text had before.[21] In an age before printing, such a feat must be considered remarkable. Chivalry was also sustained by frequent professional sporting events, tournaments, in which the knights often took part.

As so defined, the connection between the medieval army and chivalry can only be in the leadership and even then in not all of the leaders. Most medieval military leaders did not participate in chivalry. Generals and other top military leaders did not always participate, sometimes even during chivalry's most active period; additionally, fighting wars as frequently as they were fought, especially during the later Middle Ages, did not leave time for many of the chivalric displays mentioned above.[22] Most medieval military leaders were not tournament champions, and most tournament champions were not military leaders. The Ulrich von Liechtensteins and William Marshals of the thirteenth-century Holy Roman Empire and England respectively, were extraordinary jousters, the professional sportsmen of their day, but they saw few military

---

[20] From *Policraticus*, as quoted in *The Portable Medieval Reader*, ed. J. B. Ross and M. M. McLaughlin (Harmondsworth: Penguin, 1977), p. 90).

[21] See, for example, the numerous references to the various Arthurian tales in *The Arthurian Encyclopedia*, ed. N. J. Lacy (New York: Peter Bedrick Books, 1986).

[22] See Keen, pp. 219–37 for a discussion on the role of chivalry in medieval warfare.

engagements; Ulrich von Liechtestein did not fight in even one battle or siege.[23] On the other hand, such military leaders as Richard the Lionheart, Philip Augustus, Frederick Barbarossa, Henry the Lion, Edward I, and Edward III, may not have ever ridden in a tournament; although, often their younger brothers or sons did, as in the cases of John of Gaunt, son of Edward III, and Geoffrey, count of Brittany and brother of Richard the Lionheart, both of whom were reasonably good jousters – at least Geoffrey was until he was killed in a tournament – but terrible generals.[24]

Of course, military leaders sometimes sponsored tournaments, especially in an effort to celebrate diplomatic agreements, call crusades, or unite their nobility. Yet, these should be seen as displays of power rather than martial skills. An example of one of these tournaments took place in Lille in 1453. Called the feast of the Pheasant, it was sponsored by Philip the Good, duke of Burgundy, in order to announce his plans for a crusade against the Ottoman Turks. A joust preceded a large feast. Adolf of Cleves, one of Philip's lieutenants – Philip himself is not known to have participated in any jousts – was arrayed as the Swan Knight, who challenged all to cross lances. Following a few of these tilts was a flamboyant spectacle, with food, vows sworn on a pheasant (hence the name), the parading of an elephant (on which a weeping damsel rode, symbolizing the Holy Church), and a model of a child standing on a rock and urinating rose water. By the end of the exhibition, the original jousts had been forgotten, as had the reason for the feast, the crusading vows being abandoned not too long afterwards.

---

[23] On the life, writings and career of Ulrich von Liechtenstein see my "The Real Ulrich von Liechtenstein," *Medieval History Magazine* 1 (Sep 2003), 34–39, which also, with a few changes, serves as the introduction to the 2004 reissue of Ulrich von Liechtenstein, *The Service of Ladies*, trans. J. W. Thomas (Chapel Hill: University of North Carolina Press, 1969; rpt. Woodbridge: The Boydell Press, 2004). On William Marshal see the biographies by Sidney Painter, *William Marshal: Knight-Errant, Baron, and Regent of England* (Baltimore: The Johns Hopkins University Press, 1933; rpt. Toronto: University of Toronto Press, 1971); Georges Duby, *William Marshal: The Flower of Chivalry*, trans. Richard Howard (New York: Pantheon Books, 1984); and David Crouch, *William Marshal: Court, Career and Chivalry in the Angevin Empire, 1147–1219* (London: Longman, 1990).

[24] On John of Gaunt the biography of choice is now Anthony Goodman's *John of Gaunt: The Exercise of Princely Power in Fourteenth-Century Europe* (London: Longman, 1992). No good biography of Geoffrey, duke of Brittany, exists, but the story of his death can be found in Amy Kelly's *Eleanor of Aquitaine and the Four Kings* (Cambridge: Harvard University Press, 1950), p. 226, and Marion Meade, *Eleanor of Aquitaine: A Biography* (London: Penguin Books, 1991), pp. 293–94.

This was not a military endeavor, nor should it be linked to the lack of military professionalism.[25]

And, also of course, medieval military leaders patronized chivalric literary works feting the lives of Arthur, his Knights of the Round Table, and other chivalric heroes, as well as other works that educated a knight how to act. But these and other books, such as Geoffroi de Charny's mid-fourteenth century *Le livre de chevalerie* (the Book of Chivalry) and *Les demandes pour la joute, le tournoi, et la guerre* (Rules for the Joust, the Tournament, and War),[26] Honoré Bouvet's late fourteenth-century *L'arbre des batailles* (Tree of Battles),[27] or the fifteenth-century *Knyghthode and Bataile, Ritterspiegel*, by Jonathon Roth, *The Boke of Noblesse* of William Worcester, and *Le Jouvencel* of Jean de Bueil, to name just a few, were not manuals that taught the art of war.[28] Charny,

---

[25] Several recent works have been devoted to the Feast of the Pheasant: Agathe Lafortune-Martel, *Fête noble en Bourgogne au XVe siècle. Le* banquet du Faisan *(1454): Aspects politiques, sociaux et culturels* (Montreal: Bellarim,1984); Marie-Thérèse Caron, "17 février 1454: le Banquet du Voeu du Faisan, fête de cour et stratégies de pouvoir," *Revue du nord* 78 (1996), 269–88; Gail Orgelfinger, "The Vows of the Pheasant and Late Chivalric Ritual," in *The Study of Chivalry: Resources and Approaches*, ed. H. Chickering and T. H. Seiler (Kalamazoo: Medieval Institute Publications, 1988), pp. 611–44; and the numerous articles in Marie-Thérèse Caron and Denis Clauzel, ed, *Le Banquet du Faisan* (Arras: Artois Presses Université, 1997). I have also discussed this feast in relation to Philip the Good's vow to participate on a Crusade against the Ottoman Turks: "The Failure of Philip the Good to Fulfill his Crusade Promise," in *The Medieval Crusade*, ed. Susan J. Ridyard (Woodbridge: The Boydell Press, 2004), pp. 157–70.

[26] Geoffroi de Charny, *The Book of Chivalry of Geoffroi de Charney*, ed. and trans. Richard W. Kauper and Elspeth Kennedy (Philadelphia: University of Pennsylvania Press, 1996); Steven Muhlberger, *Jousts and Tournaments: Charney and the Rules for Chivalric Sport in Fourteenth Century France* (Union City: Chivalry Bookshelf, 2002). Discussions on the texts include: Kaeuper, *Chivalry and Violence*, pp. 284–88; Keen, pp. 11–15; Barber, pp. 138–39, 201; Colette Beaune, *The Birth of an Ideology: Myths and Symbols of Nation in Late-Medieval France*, trans. S. R. Huston, ed. F. L. Cheyette (Berkeley and Los Angeles: University of California Press, 1991), pp. 303–05; Elspeth Kennedy, "Geoffroi de Charny's Livre de Chevalerie and the Knights of the Round Table," in *Medieval Knighthood*, V, ed. S. Church and R. Harvey (Woodbridge: Boydell and Brewer, 1995), pp. 221–42; and Philippe Contamine, "Geoffroy de Charny (début de XIVe siècle-1356), 'Le plus prudhomme et le plus vaillant de tous les autres,'" in *Histoire et société: Mélanges Georges Duby, II, Le tenancier, le fidèle et le citoyen* (Aix-en-Provence: Publications de l'université de Provence, 1992), pp. 107–22. Tradition holds that Geoffroi de Charney was killed carrying the Oriflamme at the battle of Poitiers in 1356.

[27] Honoré Bouvet, *The Tree of Battles of Honoré Bonet*, ed. and trans. G. W. Coopland (Cambridge: Harvard University Press, 1949). See also N. A. R. Wright, "The Tree of Battles of Honoré Bouvet and the Laws of War," in *War, Literature and Politics in the Late Middle Ages: Essays in Honour of G. W. Coopland*, ed. C. T. Allmand (Liverpool: Liverpool University Press, 1975), pp. 12–31.

[28] See Keen, pp. 15–16; Beaune, pp. 303–05; Malcolm Vale, *War and Chivalry: Warfare and Aristocratic Culture in England, France and Burgundy at the End of the*

it is true, was an experienced medieval military leader – although one must wonder how effective he was, as he perished carrying the French Oriflamme during the battle of Poitiers in 1356 – but his rumored treatise on the art of war has never surfaced. Indeed, the most important medieval military manual of the late Middle Ages, *Le livre des fais d'armes et de chevalerie* (The Book of the Feats of Arms and Chivalry), was written by a woman, Christine de Pisan, who had never seen a battle or a siege.[29]

As medieval chivalry seems so distant from medieval warfare then, why has there been such a persistent desire to link the two and thereby deny any medieval military professionalism? Part of this is due to a modern mythological fascination with the "knight in shining armor;" part is due to a misunderstanding of what type of soldier the various methods of military recruitment in the Middle Ages produced – the feudo-vassalic system, pensions, and war indentures; and part of this is an insistence on defining military professionalism in modern terms and deriving that definition from modern studies. David Trim suggests as much in the introduction to his edited collection mentioned above when he identifies military professionalism with seven "markers":

1. a discrete occupational identity;
2. a formal hierarchy;
3. permanence;
4. a formal pay system;
5. a distinctive expertise and means of education therein;
6. an efficiency in execution of expertise; and
7. a distinctive self-conceptualization.[30]

Middle Ages (Athens: University of Georgia Press), pp. 14–32; Philippe Contamine, "The War Literature of the Later Middle Ages: The Treatises of Robert de Balsac and Béraud Stuart, Lord of Aubigny," in *War, Literature and Politics in the Late Middle Ages: Essays in Honour of G. W. Coopland*, ed. C. T. Allmand (Liverpool: Liverpool University Press, 1975), pp. 104–05; and Christopher Allmand, "France-Angleterre a la fin de la guerre de cent ans: Le 'Boke of Noblesse' de William Worcester," in *111e Congrès national des Sociétés savantes, Poitiers, 1986, Histoire médiévale, t. I: "La France anglaise,"* pp. 103–11. Manuscript numbers or editions of these works can be found in the bibliographies of Keen or Beaune.

[29] Christine de Pizan, *The Book of Deeds of Arms and of Chivalry*, ed. Charity Cannon Willard, trans. Sumner Willard (University Park: Pennsylvania State University Press, 1999).

[30] Trim, "Introduction," in *The Chivalric Ethos and the Development of Military Professionalism* (Leiden: Brill, 2003), pp. 6–7.

But do such "markers" really exclude medieval armies from military professionalism? Let me answer that in the negative by recalling one of the most famous engagements of the Middle Ages, the battle of Hastings on 14 October 1066. The history of this battle is well-known, but let me just recount the details and, in doing so, match each of the above markers to the soldiers who fought in it.

At Hastings, after a brief and small archery exchange, the Norman cavalry, led by William the Conqueror, charged numerous times up a fairly large hill into solid infantry lines formed by Anglo-Saxon *huscarls and fyrd*, under the leadership of Harold Godwinson. Eventually after a very lengthy battle – indeed, what Stephen Morillo has rightly called "an unusual battle" because of its extraordinary length – the fatigued infantry defenders were drawn from their protective formation by a masterfully performed feigned retreat. Rushing disordered down the hill after the "retreating" Normans, they were easy prey for the lances and swords used against them once the cavalry wheeled and returned to the battlefield. The small number of Anglo-Saxons who were able to regroup around their king were defeated a short time later and their leader killed.[31]

How many of Trim's markers do the soldiers in this battle fulfill? Neither force was very large, with probably no more than 5,000 on either side and perhaps much less; and neither was raised out of a strictly feudo-vassalic obligation.[32] The Normans had more of these,

---

[31] So many modern studies of the battle of Hastings exist that it would be impossible to recount them all. However, anyone seeking to understand the battle must begin with Stephen Morillo's seminal essay, "Hastings: An Unusual Battle," *Haskins Society Journal* 2 (1990), 96–103, which has been reprinted many times, most recently in *Medieval Warfare, 1000–1300*, ed. John France (Aldershot: Ashgate, 2006), pp. 313–22. Recent longer studies include: Jim Bradbury, *The Battle of Hastings* (Stroud: Sutton Publishing, 1998); Matthew Bennett, *Campaigns of the Norman Conquest* (London: Osprey, 2001); and M. K. Lawson, *The Battle of Hastings, 1066* (Stroud: Tempus, 2002). All of the original sources on the battle can be found in Stephen Morillo, ed., *The Battle of Hastings: Sources and Interpretations* (Woodbridge: The Boydell Press, 1996), although several newer translations of the original sources have been published in the Oxford Medieval Text series.

[32] Numbers in medieval battles are never secure, and the numbers at Hastings are disputed by every historian who has written on the battle. A discussion of those appearing in histories before 1966 can be found in Charles H. Lemmon, "The Campaign of 1066," in Dorothy Whitelock, David C. Douglas, Charles H. Lemmon, and Frank Barlow, *The Norman Conquest: Its Setting and Impact* (London: Eyre and Spottiswoode, 1966), pp. 85–87. These often put the number at much higher than 5,000. Modern historians of the battle decidedly put the number at lower than 5,000, but often do

with almost all of William's nobles participating in his campaign out of an obligation to him, although several – including Flemings and Bolognese[33] – also served for the promise of lands, booty, favor, and adventure, while the Anglo-Saxons, who did not have the same obligatory feudo-vassalic system as the continental realms, were a mixture of paid soldiers, the *huscarls* and militia, the *fyrd*. All soldiers, on both sides, had an "occupational identity," with the Norman cavalry and Anglo-Saxon *huscarls*, having no other occupation, thus indicating a "permanence" as well. The Anglo-Saxon *fyrd*, both infantry and archery troops, performed a yearly military duty, the same soldiers every year; in wartime, this service could be extended for the length of the campaign, while, in peacetime, their service was spent in garrisons and public works, such as bridge construction and maintenance. Such service also must be described as an "occupational identity" and a "permanence."[34] Less is known about the Norman infantry, except it seems more and more likely, based on research at the same time and later, that they, too, were permanently employed as soldiers[35] – one need not be a member of the cavalry or a knight to have the occupation of soldier in the Middle Ages.

A "formal hierarchy" was also present on both sides. Names of several of William's commanders are known, especially as almost all held noble titles and later inherited large amounts of land in the newly conquered kingdom, thus appearing in the famous *Domesday Book*; there was even a Bishop who fought alongside them, Odo, Bishop of Bayeux,

---

not speculate on any further clarification. See, especially, Morillo's introduction to *The Battle of Hastings* and "Hastings: an Unusual Battle;" R. Allen Brown, "The Battle of Hastings," *Proceedings of the Battle Conference on Anglo-Norman Studies* 3 (1980), 1–21 (reprinted in several other works); and Bradbury, p. 97.

[33] On these troops see Robert H. George, "The Contribution of Flanders to the Conquest of England, 1065–1086," *Revue Belge de philologie et d'histoire* 5 (1926), 81–99 and Heather J. Tanner, "The Expansion of the Power and Influence of the Counts of Boulogne under Eustace II," *Anglo-Norman Studies* 14 (1991), 251–86.

[34] The best work on the Anglo-Saxon military is Richard Abels, *Lordship and Military Obligation in Anglo-Saxon England* (Los Angeles and Berkeley: University of California Press, 1988), which corrects most of the errors of C. Warren Hollister, *Anglo-Saxon Military Institutions on the Eve of the Norman Conquest* (Oxford: Clarendon Press, 1962), which still has some influence on the scholarship of the period. I also discuss the Anglo-Saxon military in *The Norwegian Invasion of England in 1066* (Woodbridge: The Boydell Press, 1999), pp. 210–29.

[35] See C. Warren Hollister, *The Military Organization of Norman England* (Oxford: Oxford University Press, 1962) and Stephen Morillo, *Warfare under the Anglo-Norman Kings, 1066–1135* (Woodbridge: The Boydell Press, 1994).

the half-brother of the Conqueror.[36] Fewer names of commanders are known on the Anglo-Saxon side, although two of Harold's brothers, Gyrth and Leofwine, are identified as holding subordinate command among the army. Although no lesser unit commanders are named in the sources, it can be assumed that they were present, based if nothing else on the fact that the feudo-vassalic and militia systems were established on quite small obligatory musters. There also should be no question about a "distinctive self-conceptualization," as these all were members of a class that even then was being distinguished as "those who fight," the least populated of any medieval socio-economic class. The *fyrd*, too, held this self-conception; although perhaps not of the same class as the *huscarls*, their ability to perform militia duty distinguished them among other "peasants," especially in consideration of work, as the rest of the villagers from whom they were drawn would support them and their families during this service, and of wealth, should they participate in any victorious military adventure resulting in booty.

Additionally, there should be no question of "efficiency in execution." The Norman cavalry's impressive charges were repeated time after time; they were delivered in an ordered, disciplined line, despite the distance of charge and the steepness of the hill. When these charges did not break their enemy's infantry formation, William called for a feigned retreat. This was in 1066 a well known tactic, spoken of by Vegetius in his handbook, *De re militari*, the most popular manual of military techniques (the proper translation of its name) in the Middle Ages. For a feigned retreat to succeed, it not only required the horsemen to perform an impressive manoeuver, but a general who also knew when to call for it, as it could only be tried once (or perhaps twice – the sources seem confused about the number of feigned retreats at Hastings), and should it fail, generally meant morale collapse for those performing it.[37]

---

[36] David R. Bates, "The Character and Career of Odo, Bishop of Bayeux (1049/50–1097)," *Speculum* 50 (1975), 1–20.

[37] While at one time there was some scholarly doubt as to whether William performed the feigned retreat at Hastings – as in John Marshall Carter, "The Feigned Flight at Hastings: Birth, Propagation, and the Death of a Myth," *San Jose Studies* (Feb 1978), 95–106 and "Une réévaluation des interprétations de la fuite simulée d'Hastings," *Annales de Normandie* 45 (1995), 27–34 – there is less uncertainty now – see Bernard S. Bachrach, "The Feigned Retreat at Hastings," *Mediaeval Studies* 33 (1971), 344–47.

In breaking their formation and rushing down the hill after the "fleeing" Norman cavalry, the Anglo-Saxons fell for the feigned retreat, guaranteeing its success. But this result should not condemn them as somehow being "inefficient in the execution" or "unprofessional" in their own tactical manoeuvers. Instead, the picture these infantry paint on the day of Hastings is also one of discipline and order. Forming a shield wall, infantry standing side-by-side close enough to overlap their shields with their neighbors, thus forming a sort of field fortification, on its whole was not a difficult tactic to perform. However, it was extremely difficult to sustain, especially in the face of the numerous Norman cavalry charges and for the length of battle that Hastings became. Although not seen in the contemporary sources, most of which were written from the Norman perspective and not from the Anglo-Saxon, similar lengthy battles saw severe thirst and fatigue hit quite early an infantry line continually stressed by constant warfare.[38] Medieval battles did not often last long, most with sustained fighting of less than an hour. Hastings lasted much longer, and eventually such a length meant that troops on both sides became anxious to see a result, and such anxiety in this battle led the Anglo-Saxons to drop their caution and, in seeming victorious rejoicing, chase after those withdrawing from the fight. But could one think of this as a lack of professionalism? After all, in the month prior to the battle of Hastings these soldiers had journeyed from the southern coast of England to York and back in forced marches, fighting and winning a decisive battle against the Norwegian invasion of King Háraldr Harðráði (Harald Hardrada in most English translations) in between. They had then stood strongly against the Normans for several hours. They had lost, but they were not unprofessional in doing so.

Such military discipline and the ability to make such maneuvers in battle should also denote "a distinctive expertise and education." Although there was no military academy *per se*, most of the soldiers who took part in the fighting at Hastings since their childhoods had been trained in martial skills, and those whose nobility was likely to lead to generalship would also be trained in the art of military strategy

---

[38] Other lengthy battles show a similar fatigue, as, for example, the Battle of Mons-en-Pévèle in 1304 (Kelly DeVries, *Infantry Warfare in the Early Fourteenth Century: Discipline, Tactics, and Technology* [Woodbridge: The Boydell Press, 1996], pp. 32–48).

and tactics.[39] As such, they were educated for a far longer period than any early modern or modern counterpart. Moreover, throughout almost the entire Middle Ages, there was a continuous military activity that brought further training and the development of fighting and leadership skills. All of the soldiers at Hastings had seen previous combat: the Normans with William throughout the entirety of his career – a small part of which is seen in the *Bayeux Tapestry*[40] – as he fought to gain legitimacy, power, and lands, and the Anglo-Saxons had fought in Wales in 1063 and, as mentioned, against the Norwegians earlier in the year.[41]

One needs also to note that William the Conqueror's campaign was very efficient and quite professional. Not being able to count on the decisive battle that Hastings became, he had built a series of five motte-and-bailey castles in order to form a foothold on the English island.[42] This would allow him to acquire piecemeal the land he claimed was his, serving also as a landing spot for further reinforcements from Normandy. Although it would not ultimately be needed as such, the practice of building castles as a means of subjecting the Anglo-Saxons would become the pattern of William's campaign, and it would eventually lead to his occupation of England, the last successful conquest of this land.

The only one of Trim's markers not so far commented on in the example of Hastings is the "formal pay system." Without further discussion on the obvious modern concept of this point, with wages alone considered military economic compensation, those who fought for William the Conqueror and survived the battle were recompensed

---

[39] Contamine, pp. 208–18.

[40] The most authoritative edition of the *Bayeux Tapestry* remains Frank M. Stenton, ed., *The Bayeux Tapestry: A Comprehensive Survey*, 2nd ed. (London: Phaidon, 1957), although David M. Wilson's *The Bayeux Tapestry* (London: Thames and Hudson, 1985) is a good updating.

[41] On Harold Godwinson's Welsh campaign see my "Harold Godwinson in Wales: Military Legitimacy in Late Anglo-Saxon England," in *The Normans and their Adversaries at War: Essays in Memory of C. Warren Hollister*, ed. Richard P. Abels and Bernard S. Bachrach (Woodbridge: The Boydell Press, 2001), pp. 65–85, and on Háraldr Hárðraði's (Harald Hardrada) invasion of England in 1066 see my *The Norwegian Invasion of England in 1066* (Woodbridge: The Boydell Press, 1999).

[42] R. Allen Brown, "The Castles of the Conquest," in *Castles, Conquest and Charters: Collected Studies* (Woodbridge: Boydell and Brewer, 1989), pp. 65–74 is a good introduction to these castles, but see Robin Higham and Philip Barker, *Timber Castles* (Mechanicsburg: Stackpole Books, 1995) as a more complete study of motte-and-bailey castles in England.

very well indeed according to the *Domesday Book*.[43] The Anglo-Saxon survivors appear not to have been paid, but this would not be considered unusual for a defeated force at any time in history. Payments for service before this battle are not accounted for in contemporary sources, but this absence of evidence should not be seen as proof of non-existence.

A similar description could be made of almost any medieval battle. I also had initially intended to describe the battle of Agincourt, fought in 1415 between the English and the French during the Hundred Years War, and the Battle of Courtrai, fought in 1302 between the Flemish urban militias and the French army. Suffice it to note that at Agincourt even the English archers were professional troops. By this time, and certainly also due to the large amount of warfare then being fought, English longbowmen fulfilled the same markers defining professionalism as those who fought at Hastings, or any other medieval, ancient, early modern, or modern soldier.[44] At Courtrai, the urban militias too could be said to fit the definition of military professionals, and have been so considered in numerous studies by the great Belgian military historian, J. F. Verbruggen.[45]

There is also no space to discuss the frequent use of mercenaries during the Middle Ages and the aspects of professionalism that came to characterize them, whether Brabantese or Flemish pikemen, Genoese Crossbowmen, Swiss halbardiers, or any of the numerous soldiers of varying nationalities or wielding various weapons who fought up and down the Italian peninsula during the fourteenth or fifteenth

---

[43] As seen in George. A translation of the complete *Domesday Book* is now available: *Domesday Book: A Complete Translation* (London: Penguin Books, 2002).

[44] This battle has recently received three scholarly studies, all of which make several good arguments: Michael K. Jones, *Agincourt 1415: Battlefield Guide* (Barnsley: Pen and Sword, 2005); Juliet Barker, *Agincourt: The King, The Campaign, The Battle* (London: Little, Brown, 2005); and Anne Curry, *Agincourt: A New History* (Stroud: Tempus, 2005). Anne Curry also has assembled and translated all the original sources in *The Battle of Agincourt: Sources and Interpretations* (Woodbridge: The Boydell Press, 2000).

[45] The best study of this battle remains J. F. Verbruggen, *The Battle of the Golden Spurs: Courtrai, 11 July 1302*, ed. Kelly DeVries, trans. David Richard Ferguson (Woodbridge: The Boydell Press, 2002) (original: *De slag der guldensporen: Bijdrage tot de geschiedenis van Vlaanderens vrijheidsoorlog, 1297–1305* [Antwerp: N. V. Standaard Boekhandel, 1952]), but see also his *1302 in Vlaanderen: De guldensporenslag* (Brussels: Musée Royal de l'Armée, 1977) and (with Rolf Falter) *1302 opstand in Vlaanderen* (Tielt: Lannoo, 2002).

centuries.[46] Then there are the late medieval gunpowder artillery operators, who in but a very short period gained an ability to be paid on the scale of the knights of their time.[47] Without a more complete discussion of the roles of these soldiers in medieval warfare, or an analysis of different types of military engagements, the argument in favor of medieval military professionalism cannot be conclusive. So let this be but an introduction to the subject.

---

[46] A recent work on medieval mercenaries is John France, ed., *Mercenaries and Paid Men: The Mercenary Identity in the Middle Ages* (Leiden: Brill, 2008). But for more specific studies on mercenaries fighting in Italy see Michael Mallett, *Mercenaries and their Masters: Warfare in Renaissance Italy* (Totowa: Rowman and Littlefield, 1974) and Geoffrey Trease, *The Condottieri: Soldiers of Fortune* (New York: Holt, Rinehart and Winston, 1971).

[47] See in particular my and Robert Douglas Smith's *The Artillery of the Dukes of Burgundy, 1363–1477* (Woodbridge: The Boydell Press, 2005).

MODERN SOLDIER IN A BUSBY:
AUGUST VON MACKENSEN, 1914-1916

Richard L. DiNardo

Winston Churchill once described the war on the eastern front in World War I as "the unknown war." Certainly in terms of commanders, this has remained true, at least for the English speaking audience. Despite the best efforts of Holger Herwig, Norman Stone, Hew Strachan and others, coverage of the war has remained largely Anglo-centric and oriented towards the western front.[1] Consequently this has skewed the amount of attention paid to both commanders and developments during the war.

Nowhere has this western bias been felt more than in the coverage given to the major commanders and battles. Bookshelves fairly groan with works on Douglas Haig, Helmuth von Moltke and Erich Ludendorff, or on operations such as the Somme or the British 1917 campaign in Flanders.[2] Lately the French Army and some of its major personalities have been the subjects of scholarly monographs.[3]

Major commanders and staff officers who made their names on the eastern front on both sides of the conflict remain relatively unknown.

---

[1] Winston Churchill, *The Unknown War: The Eastern Front* (New York: Charles Scribner's Sons, 1931), Holger H. Herwig, *The First World War: Germany and Austria-Hungary 1914–1918*, (London: Arnold, 1997), Norman Stone, *The Eastern Front 1914–1917* (New York: Charles Scribner's Sons, 1975) and Hew Strachan, *The First World War* Vol. I: *To Arms* (New York: Oxford University Press, 2001).

[2] Just a sampling of the literature includes Denis Winter, *Haig's Command: A Reassessment* New York: Viking, 1991), Andrew A. Wiest, *Haig: The Evolution of a Commander* (Washington, DC: Potomac Books, 2005), Robin Prior and Trevor Wilson, *Command on the Western Front* (Oxford: Blackwell, 1992), Anika Mombauer, *Helmuth von Moltke and the Origins of the First World War* (Cambridge: Cambridge University Press, 2001), Roger Parkinson, *Tormented Warrior: Ludendorff and the Supreme Command* (New York: Stein and Day, 1979), Tim Travers, *The Killing Ground: The British Army, the Western Front and the Emergence of Modern Warfare, 1900–1918* (London: Routledge, 1987), Prior and Wilson, *Passchendaele: The Untold Story* (New Haven: Yale University Press, 1996), Ian Passingham, *Pillars of Fire: The Battle of Messines Ridge June 1917* (Stroud: Sutton Publishing, 1998) and Peter Hart, *The Somme: The Darkest Hour on the Western Front* (New York: Pegasus Books, 2008).

[3] Robert A. Doughty, *Pyrrhic Victory: French Strategy and Operations in the Great War* (Cambridge: Harvard University Press, 2005) and Michael S. Neiberg, *Foch: Supreme Allied Commander in the Great War* (Washington, DC: Brassey's, 2003).

Recent scholarship on the imperial Russian Army has greatly improved our understanding of that institution.[4] Nonetheless, recent scholarly studies of the major Russian figures the war, such as Grand Duke Nicholas, Alexei Brusilov, Vladimir Sukhomlinov and Mikhail Alexeev, to name but a few, are still lacking. Likewise on the Austro-Hungarian side, only Franz Conrad von Hötzendorf has been the subject of a recent study in English.[5]

In terms of operations on the eastern front, Dennis Showalter broke new ground with his work on Tannenberg. Still, coverage of the major operations between Tannenberg and the Russian Revolution has been scant until recently. Graydon Tunstall has outlined in vivid detail the horrors of the Carpathian front during the winter of 1914-15, and major studies of the Gorlice-Tarnow offensive and the ensuing conquest of Poland and the Brusilov offensive have also appeared. The German operation against the Baltic Islands in October 1917 has garnered both article and book length studies.[6] Finally, the subject of occupation policy, both in the west and east, has attracted attention that has brought forth several interesting works.[7]

---

[4] See for example William C. Fuller, Jr., *The Foe Within: Fantasies of Treason and the End of Imperial Russia*, (Ithaca: Cornell University Press, 2006), David Schimmelpennick van der Oye and BruceW. Menning, eds., *Reforming the Tsar's Army* (Cambridge: Cambridge University Press, 2004) and Bruce W. Menning, *Bayonets before Bullets: The Imperial Russian Army, 1861-1914* (Bloomington: Indiana University Press, 1992).

[5] Lawrence Sondhaus, *Franz Conrad von Hötzendorf: Architect of the Apocalypse* (Boston: Humanities Press, 2000). A classic study of the Austro-Hungarian Army is Gunther E. Rotherberg, *The Army of Francis Joseph* (West Lafayette, IN: Purdue University Press, 1976).

[6] Dennis E. Showalter, *Tannenberg: Clash of Empires, 1914* (Reprinted Edition) (Dulles, VA: Brassey's, 2004), Graydon A. Tunstall, Jr. *Blood on the Snow: The Carpathian Winter War of 1915* (Lawrence: University Press of Kansas, 2010), Richard L. DiNardo, *Breakthrough: The Gorlice-Tarnow Campaign 1915* (Westport, CT: Praeger, 2010) and Timothy C. Dowling, *The Brusilov Offensive* (Bloomington: Indiana University Press, 2008). For Operation ALBION, see Richard L. DiNardo, "Huns With Web-Feet: Operation Albion, 1917" *War in History* Vol. 12, Nr. 4 (November 2005): pp. 396-417 and Michael B. Barrett, *Operation Albion: The German Conquest of the Baltic Islands* (Bloomington: Indiana University Press, 2008).

[7] Larry Zuckerman, *The Rape of Belgium: The Untold Story of World War I* (New York: NYU Press, 2004), Mark von Hagen, *War in a European Borderland: Occupations and Occupation Plans in Galicia and Ukraine, 1914-1918* (Seattle: University of Washington Press, 2007), Vejas Gabriel Liulevicius, *War Land on the Eastern Front: Culture, National Identity and German Occupation in World War I* (Cambridge: Cambridge University Press, 2000) and Jonathan E. Gumz, *The Resurrection and Collapse of Empire in Habsburg Serbia, 1914-1918* (Cambridge: Cambridge University Press, 2009).

German commanders and staff planners such as Max Hoffman, Otto von Below, Remus von Woyrsch and Hermann von François remain relatively obscure figures. Hans von Seeckt, who filled a number of critical staff positions for important operations, is better known for his post-war activities as head of the *Truppenamt*.[8] Although such notable personalities as Ludendorff, Erich von Falkenhayn and August von Mackensen have been the subjects of biographies in German, only Holger Afflerbach's work on Falkenhayn, Robert Foley's study of the early part of Falkenhayn's tenure as head of the German High Command (*Oberste Heeres Leitung* or OHL) and Franz Uhle-Wettler's book on Ludendorff really fills the bill as military studies. Theo Schwarzmüller's biography was far more concerned with Mackensen's social attitudes than with his military exploits.[9] This article will try to fill that gap and deal with August von Mackensen's career as a military commander, which essentially covered the years 1914–16.

During this thirty month period, Mackensen went from a *General der Kavallerie* commanding an infantry corps to a *Generalfeldmarschall* commanding a force that contained troops from every member of the Central Powers.[10] In terms of the art of war, Mackensen was able to make the transition from a corps commander having to command troops for the first time in combat under the uncertain conditions of 1914, to an army group commander whose final campaigns in Romania included the proper use of air power, overcoming a well-fortified enemy and mastering the intricacies of coalition warfare.

Mackensen's early life can be quickly described. Born on 6 December 1849 to a prosperous, non-noble Saxon family, he entered the Army on 1 October 1869 as a one-year volunteer in the 2nd Life Hussars. Mackensen served in the Franco-Prussian War with distinction,

---

[8] James S. Corum, *The Roots of Blitzkrieg: Hans von Seeckt and German Military Reform* (Lawrence: University Press of Kansas, 1992). Since the Great General Staff was abolished by the treaty of Versailles, the *Truppenamt* was created to serve the same purpose.

[9] Franz Uhle-Wettler, *Erich Ludendorff in Seiner Zeit: Soldat – Stratege – Revolutionär: Eine Neubewertung* (Augsburg: Kurt Vowinckel Verlag, 1995), Holger Afflerbach, *Falkenhayn: Politisches Denken und Handeln im Kaiserreich* (Munich: Oldenbourg, 1996), Robert T. Foley, *German Strategy and the Path to Verdun: Erich von Falkenhayn and the Development of Attrition; 1870–1916* (Cambridge: Cambridge University Press, 2005) and Theo Schwarzmüller, *Zwischen Kaiser und Führer. Generalfeldmarschall August von Mackensen: Eine politische Biographie* (Paderborn: Ferdinand Schöningh, 1995).

[10] *General der Kavallerie* is equivalent to Lieutenant General in the United States Army.

receiving the Iron Cross and obtaining a commission as reserve lieutenant. After the war, Mackensen entered the University of Halle. In 1873 Mackensen decided to abandon academia and moved from the reserve into the regular army. Over the next four decades Mackensen made his way through the army, marked clearly as an officer worthy of high advancement.[11]

During his career as a company and field grade officer, Mackensen filled a variety of command and staff positions. Perhaps the most important one personally for him was a stint as commander of the 2nd Life Hussars. Owing to the peculiarities of the Imperial German Army, when he became a general officer, Mackensen was able to choose the uniform of the 2nd Life Hussars, with its distinctive Death's Head busby, as his normal uniform. He also wrote a history of the regiment. Service with the Life Hussars also brought him into close contact with Wilhelm II, who was the proprietary colonel of all Life Hussar regiments. While Mackensen served as commander of the Life Hussar Brigade from 1901–03, the Crown Prince was assigned to the brigade as commander of the 1st Life Hussars, a high mark of imperial favor.[12]

Like most of the Germany Army's officers who attained the rank of general before 1914, Mackensen did not attend the *Kriegsakademie*. As a young officer, Mackensen's record and reputation led to a stint on the Great General Staff from 1881–83, where he worked in the section of the staff that dealt with Austria- Hungary, Russia and the Balkans, precisely the area where he spent his time in World War I.[13]

Another critical appointment for Mackensen was his selection as Wilhelm II's adjutant in 1891, allowing him to win the favors of the *Kaiser*, including an ennoblement and selection to command the XVII

---

[11] For details, see Schwarzmüller, *Generalfeldmarschall August von Mackensen*, pp. 17–91 and Wolfgang Foerster, ed., *Mackensen: Briefe und Aufzeichnungen des Generalfeldmarschalls aus Krieg und Frieden* (Leipzig: Bibliographisches Institut, 1938), pp. 11–25. A short chronology can also be found in Karsten Brandt, *Mackensen: Leben, Wesen und Wirken des deutschen Feldherrn* (Leipzig: Gustav Schloessmanns Verlag, 1916), p. 27. See also Holger H. Herwig and Neil M. Heyman, *Biographical Dictionary of World War I* (Westport, CT: Greenwood Press, 1982), pp. 235–236.

[12] Schwarzmüller, *Generalfeldmarschall August von Mackensen*, p. 82 and Short Biographical Chronology of August von Mackensen, File MSg 109/10865, Bundesarchiv-Militärarchiv, Freiburg-im-Breisgau, Germany (Hereafter cited as BA-MA MSg 109/10865). Like all European monarchs of that day, Wilhelm had a number of honorary military appointments. Showalter, *Tannenberg*, p. 177.

[13] Daniel J. Hughes, *The King's Finest: A Social and Bureaucratic Profile of Prussia's General Officers, 1871–1914* (Westport, CT: Praeger, 1987), p. 85 and Schwarzmüller, *Generalfeldmarschall August von Mackensen*, p. 48.

corps, a rare posting for a cavalry general. Equally critical was that his time at the Hohenzollern court made him aware of – and sensitive to – the importance of matters such as protocol.[14]

In 1908, Mackensen's appointment to the command of the XVII Corps, located in West Prussia, seemed an excellent way to bring a fine military career to a close. Although an unusual posting for a *General der Kavallerie*, it was a safe assumption that, all things remaining the same, it would be Mackensen's last assignment before his retirement. All things stopped being the same, however, on 1 August 1914.

Over the next two and a half years, Mackensen was involved in nearly every major German campaign in the east. One would not have suspected that in early August 1914, as his debut as a commander in combat was not a success. A combination of bad intelligence, poor aerial reconnaissance and sheer inexperience resulted in a botched attack at Gumbinnen.[15] Mackensen, however, recovered quickly from this setback. He led the XVII Corps south to play an important role in the first major German victory of the war, Tannenberg.

Assigned the mission of getting into the rear of General Alexander Samsonov's Russian 2nd Army, Mackensen led his corps with verve. Telling his soldiers that the outcome of events in the east now depended on the marching ability of the XVII Corps, Mackensen put that capability to the test. On 25 August 1914 the XVII Corps covered some thirty miles.[16] After several more days of fighting, interspersed with marches and countermarches owing to a rapidly changing situation, by 29 August the XVII Corps had attained positions that effectively blocked the Russian 2nd Army's escape route to the east. Over the next two days, Mackensen's men held off attempts by fleeing Russians to breakout of encirclement. By 1 September 1914 the XVII Corps had taken some 25,000 prisoners, the largest share of the total haul of 90,000 taken by the Eighth Army.[17]

---

[14] Showalter, *Tannenberg*, p. 177 and Schwarzmüller, *Generalfeldmarschall August von Mackensen*, p. 78.

[15] Many of the place names mentioned in this article have undergone numerous changes over the past half century. Therefore, for the sake of simplicity, the places names used in this article will be those that were employed during World War I.

[16] Foerster, ed., *Mackensen: Briefe und Aufzeichnungen*, p. 48 and Germany, Reichsarchiv, *Der Weltkrieg 1914 bis 1918* (Berlin: E. S. Mittler und Sohn, 1925), Vol. 2, p. 169. Not surprisingly, Mackensen's wartime hagiographers glide over Mackensen's Gumbinnen fiasco. Otto Kolshorn, *Unser Mackensen: Ein Lebens und Charakterbild* (Berlin: E. S. Mittler und Sohn, 1916), p. 89.

[17] Foerster, ed., *Mackensen: Briefe und Aufzeichnungen*, pp. 55–59 and Showalter, *Tannenberg*, pp. 290–291.

After Tannenberg another German Army, the Ninth, was formed in the course of late September 1914 in upper Silesia. Extending the left flank of the Austro-Hungarian armies fighting in Galicia, the Ninth Army, commanded by Hindenburg, would launch an attack on the Russian fortress of Ivangorod and eventually Warsaw, the capital of Russian Poland. To accomplish the capture of Warsaw Mackensen, still commanding his own XVII Corps, was also given control of an *ad hoc* organization called Corps Frommel (8th Cavalry, 35th Reserve and 18th *Landwehr* Divisions) and later the XX Corps, essentially a substantial portion of the German Ninth Army.[18]

Starting on 9 October 1914, Mackensen's attack enjoyed some initial success but then, like the rest of Hindenburg's offensive, was brought to a halt. Hindenburg's offensive coincided with a Russian attempt, based on a rebuilt 2nd Army supported by further reinforcements around Warsaw, to regain the initiative in the east against the Central Powers. The cleverly planned attack aimed at the Ninth Army's left flank, compromising the German position in Poland.[19]

By 15 October the Ninth Army's offensive had ground to a halt, due to a combination of poor weather and poorer roads. Worse yet, the Russians ably evaded the Ninth Army's thrust, falling back on Ivangorod while completing the assembly of the 2nd Army at Warsaw. Accurate German aerial reconnaissance provided Hindenburg and Mackensen with clear evidence of the Russian build up, and a fortuitous document capture confirmed the details of the impending Russian counterattack. This timely intelligence allowed the Ninth Army to avoid the Russian counterstroke with a well-conducted retreat, although the Russian offensive did give Mackensen some anxious moments. The retreat, although successfully conducted, made it abundantly clear that taking Warsaw was now a dead letter, at least for the time being.[20]

---

[18] Foerster, ed., *Mackensen: Briefe und Aufzeichnungen*, pp. 71–72, Germany, Reichsarchiv, *Der Weltkrieg 1914 bis 1918*, Vol. 5, p. 438, Franz Baron Conrad von Hötzendorf, *Aus Meiner Dienstzeit 1906–18* (6th Edition) (Vienna: Rikola Verlag, 1925), Vol. 5, p. 21 and Erich Ludendorff, *Meine Kriegserrinerungen 1914–1918* (Berlin: E. S. Mittler und Sohn, 1919), p. 66.

[19] Paul von Hindenburg, *Aus meinem Leben* (Leipzig: Verlag von S. Hirzel, 1920) pp. 107–108 and Germany, Reichsarchiv, *Der Weltkrieg 1914 bis 1918*, Vol. 5, pp. 443–444.

[20] Foerster, ed., *Mackensen: Briefe und Aufzeichnungen*, p. 79, Germany, Reichsarchiv, *Der Weltkrieg 1914 bis 1918*, Vol. 5, p. 444, Yuri Danilov, *Russland im Weltkriege 1914–1915* (Jena: Frommannsche Buchhandlung, 1925), p. 321, Herwig, *The First World War*, p. 107, Stone, *The Eastern Front 1914–1917*, pp. 99–100 and Boris Khavin,

On 1 November 1914 Hindenburg was placed in command of all German forces in the east (*OberOst*), effectively institutionalizing the command arrangements that had existed informally since September. When Hindenburg and Ludendorff took over *OberOst*, the duo recommended that Mackensen take over command of the Ninth Army, a proposal that was accepted by OHL.[21] During the late fall of 1914 the peripatetic hussar, after a railroad facilitated deployment through Silesia to the area between Posen and Thorn, launched another offensive into Poland on 11 November 1914 with the Ninth Army. The target this time was Lodz, an important communications node for the Russians and the center of the textile industry in Russian Poland. The possession of Lodz would also provide good billeting areas for the troops in the face of the rapidly oncoming winter. The campaign turned into a month-long duel, marked by some of the most interesting cut-and-thrust moves made by both sides in the war. After a Russian counterattack forced Mackensen's army back to the Bzura River, reinforcements from the western front arrived, allowing Mackensen to regain the initiative. By 6 December 1914 Lodz was in German hands for good. Mackensen had won his first major campaign as well as a place in the German pantheon of heroes, right behind the massive (in every sense) figure of Hindenburg.[22]

In January 1915 the Ninth Army launched an attack towards Warsaw. The attack was designed to provide some distant support to Austro-Hungarian Chief of the General Staff Franz Baron Conrad von Hötzendorf, then engaged in launching his first offensive to relieve the besieged fortress of Przemysl. It would also serve to draw Russian forces away from the German Eighth and Tenth Armies, then preparing

---

"Russland gegen Deutschland. Die Ostfront des Ersten Weltkrieges in den Jahren 1914 bis 1915," *Die vergessene Front. Der Osten 1914/15* (Gerhard P. Gross, ed.) (Paderborn: Ferdinand Schöningh, 2006), p. 73.

[21] Ludendorff, *Meine Kriegserinnerungen*, p. 75, Schwarzmüller, *Generalfeldmarschall August von Mackensen*, p. 97, Short Biographical Chronology, BA-MA MSg 109/10865 and DiNardo, *Breakthough*, pp. 13–14.

[22] C.R.M.F. Cruttwell, *A History of the Great War 1914–1918* (Oxford: Oxford University Press, 1934), p. 87, Herwig, *The First World War*, p. 109, Stone, *The Eastern Front 1914–1917*, pp. 104–107, Schwarzmüller, *Generalfeldmarschall August von Mackensen*, p. 99, Kolshorn, *Unser Mackensen*, p. 112, Hindenburg, *Aus meinem Leben*, p. 115 and John W. Wheeler-Bennett, *Wooden Titan: Hindenburg in Twenty Years of German History 1914–1934* (New York: William Morrow and Company, 1936), p. 46. Max Hoffmann, one of Hindenburg's top staff officers, was rather critical of Mackensen. Major General Max Hoffmann, *War Diaries and Other Papers* (Eric Sutton trans.) (London: Martin Secker, 1929), Vol. I, p. 51.

for another attack in the Masurian Lakes region. The Ninth Army's attack was also noteworthy for the size of its artillery support (518 guns) and the fact that the Germans would use poison gas (xylyl bromide, a choking agent), in both of which Mackensen placed great hope.[23]

The Ninth Army's attack was planned to begin on 27 January 1915, but delays pushed the start of the artillery bombardment back to 30 January, with the infantry assault to begin the next day. Although the attack was designed as a limited operation, it was regarded as operationally unsuccessful. Freezing weather severely limited the effects of the gas. The artillery did, however, take its toll on the Russians. In three days the Russians suffered some 40,000 casualties. Tactically Mackensen's attack was designed as a limited effort, and made only limited territorial gains.[24]

Mackensen, now a *Generaloberst*, was now chosen for a much more prominent role for operations in 1915.[25] With the major focus of effort being in the east, Mackensen was given command of another new German army, the Eleventh. It would spearhead the attack on the Russians in the Gorlice-Tarnow area. The goal of the attack, agreed to by German Chief of the General Staff Erich von Falkenhayn and Conrad, was to drive the Russians back out of western Galicia and compromise the right flank of the Russian forces facing the Austro-Hungarians in the Carpathian Mountains, perilously close to the Hungarian plain. Aside from keeping Austria-Hungary in the war, the German and Austro-Hungarian high commands also hoped that a successful operation would dissuade both Italy and Romania from entering the war on the Allied side. Recovering Austrian Galicia would also regain control of Austria-Hungary's oil producing area, a matter of importance to the Austro-Hungarian Navy, and to a lesser extent, the German Navy.[26]

---

[23] Foerster, ed., *Mackensen: Briefe und Aufzeichnungen*, p. 125 and Herwig, *The First World War*, p. 135.

[24] Germany, Reichsarchiv, *Der Weltkrieg 1914 bis 1918*, Vol. 7, p. 166, Manfred Rauchensteiner, *Der Tod des Doppeladlers: Österreich-Ungarn und der Erste Weltkrieg* (Vienna: Verlag Styria, 1993), p. 203, Foerster, ed., *Mackensen: Briefe und Aufzeichnungen*, p. 125, Archivist von Gontard, "Ninth Army From 1 January to 5 February 1915," c. 1927, p. 60, BA-MA W 10/51443 and Herwig, *The First World War*, p. 135.

[25] *Generaloberst* is equivalent to the rank of General in the United States Army.

[26] Austria, Bundesministerium, *Österreich-Ungarns Letzter Krieg 1914–1918* (Vienna: Verlag der Militärwissenschaftliche Mitteilungen, 1932), Vol. 2, p. 298 and Alison Fleig Frank, *Oil Empire: Visions of Prosperity in Austrian Galicia* (Cambridge: Harvard University Press, 2005), pp. 183–184.

Mackensen's instrument for the attack, the German Eleventh Army, would be composed of units dispatched from the western front, including the Guard Corps, XXXXI Reserve Corps, the Austro-Hungarian VI Corps and the newly created Bavarian 11th Infantry Division, plus the 119th Infantry Division. Later on the X Corps (19th and 20th Infantry Divisions) was added to Mackensen's force.[27] In addition, Mackensen was also given operational command of a portion of the Austro-Hungarian Fourth Army, to cover his left flank. Mackensen took directives from either OHL or from Austro-Hungarian headquarters (*Armee Ober Kommando*, or AOK), although Conrad agreed not to issue orders to Mackensen without prior agreement from Falkenhayn.[28]

The attack entrusted to Mackensen and his chief of staff, Hans von Seeckt, was again marked once again by a large concentration of artillery, up to 1,000 guns if one includes the whole of the Austro-Hungarian Fourth Army. The artillery brought to Galicia incorporated some of the heaviest guns in the German and Austro-Hungarian arsenals, including 210mm and 305mm howitzers.[29]

Launched on 2 May 1915, it produced Germany's best success up to that point. Facing a short but violent bombardment with a large concentration of heavy guns, plus field artillery accompanying the German infantry, the forward positions of General R. D. Radko-Dmitriev's Russian 3rd Army were overrun on the first day. The Eleventh Army then systematically widened and deepened its penetration, although hard fighting was required in some sectors. By 5 May it was clear that Mackensen's force had torn a huge hole in the line of the Russian 3rd

---

[27] Oskar Tile von Kalm, *Schlachten des Weltkrieges. Gorlice* (Berlin: Oldenbourg, 1930), pp. 196–198 and Bavarian 11th Infantry Division, Order of the Day, 5 April 1915, File 11/52/2, Bayerisches Hauptstaatsarchiv – Kriegsarchiv, Munich, Germany. (Hereafter cited as BH-KA.)

[28] Colonel August von Cramon to General Erich von Falkenhayn, 6 April 1915, BA-MA W 10/51388, Gerhard Tappen Diary, 14 April 1915, BA-MA W 10/50661, Afflerbach, *Falkenhayn*, p. 291, Germany, Reichsarchiv, *Der Weltkrieg 1914 bis 1918*, Vol. 7, p. 362 and Austria, Bundesministerium, *Österreich-Ungarns Letzter Krieg 1914–1918*, Vol. 2, p. 306.

[29] General Alfred Ziethen, "Aus grosser Zeit vor zwanzig Jahren. Die Durchbruchsschlacht von Gorlice," *Militär Wochenblatt* Vol. 119, Nr. 41 (4 May 1935): p. 1628, Eric Dorn Brose, *The Kaiser's Army: The Politics of Military Technology in Germany during the Machine Age, 1870–1918* (New York: Oxford University Press, 2001), p. 228, Herbert Jäger, *German Artillery of World War One* (Ramsbury: The Crowood Press, 2001), p. 34 and Austria, Bundesministerium, *Österreich-Ungarns Letzter Krieg 1914–1918*, Vol. 2, p. 318.

Army, chewing up not only the front line units, but Radko-Dmitriev's reserves as well.[30]

Unlike so many other World War I offensives that only achieved a break-in against a defensive system, Mackensen turned this one into a major breakthrough. Pressing forward as relentlessly as possible, by 15 May 1915 the penetration had widened from almost 25 miles to nearly 187 miles. On that front, the Germans and Austro-Hungarians had advanced to a depth of over 60 miles from their assault positions (up to 90 miles from its railheads), crossing the Wisloka, Wislok and Jasiolka Rivers. The seizure of Zmigrod and its immediate environs gave Mackensen control of the roads leading north from the Carpathians. The right flank of the Russian forces in the Carpathians was thus fatally compromised. The only course of action open to elements of Radko-Dmitriev's 3rd Army and Brusilov's 8th Army was to retreat east. The Russians were pressed by the Austro- Hungarian Third Army, which succeeded in surrounding and destroying the Russian 48th Infantry Division. The threat to Hungary, which had loomed so large early in the spring, was now eliminated.[31]

Having punched the huge hole, Mackensen sought some guidance from Falkenhayn as to the next objective of the campaign. Falkenhayn and Conrad agreed that the next objective should be the fortress of Przemysl and the creation of bridgeheads on the San River.[32] The parlous nature of the Eleventh Army's artillery ammunition situation required that the operation be conducted in short phases. The initial intermediate objectives were Jaroslau and Radymno, the seizure of

---

[30] Tappen Diary, 3 May 1915, BA-MA W 10/50661, German Eleventh Army Order, 4 May 1915, *Nachlass* Hans von Seeckt, BA-MA N 247/24, August von Cramon, *Unser Österreich-Ungarische Bundesgenosse im Weltkriege* (Berlin: E. S. Mittler und Sohn, 1920), p. 15, DiNardo, *Breakthrough*, p. 67 and Foerster, ed., *Mackensen: Briefe und Aufzeichnugen*, p. 152.

[31] General Erich von Falkenhayn, *The German General Staff and Its Decisions, 1914–1916* (New York: Dodd, Mead and Company, 1920), pp. 117–119, Germany, Reichsarchiv, *Der Weltkrieg 1914 bis 1918*, Vol. 7, p. 428, Austria, Bundesministerium, *Österreich-Ungarns Letzter Krieg 1914–1918*, Vol. 2, p. 337 and Danilov, *Russland im Weltkriege 1914–1915*, pp. 492–493.

[32] Falkenhayn to Conrad, 6 May 1915 and Conrad to Falkanhayn, 9 May 1915, AOK Operations Bureau, Conrad – Falkenhayn Correspondence, Russia, File 512, Österreichisches Staatsarchiv – Kriegsarchiv, Vienna , Austria (Hereafter cited as ÖSA-KA R512), Tappen Diary, 12 May 1915, BA-MA W 10/50661, Hans von Plessen Diary, 12 May 1915, BA-MA W 10/50656, Germany, Reichsarchiv, *Der Weltkrieg 1914 bis 1918*, Vol. 7, p. 426, Hans Meier-Welcker, *Seeckt* (Frankfurt-am-Main: Bernard und Graefe für Wehrwesen, 19670, p. 53 and Foerster, ed., *Mackensen: Briefe und Aufzeichnungen*, p. 158.

which would sever Russian rail communications north of Przemysl, while also positioning the German Eleventh and Austro-Hungarian Fourth Armies to create bridgeheads over the San River.[33]

From 13–18 May 1915 the Eleventh Army made a series of short advances, as the army shifted the main weight of its attack from the right flank to the left. Once assault positions west of Jaroslau and Radymno had been reached, another operational pause of five days ensued, allowing logistics to catch up, and build up artillery ammunition stocks. In addition bridgeheads across the San needed to be expanded, as Mackensen and Seeckt explained to Falkenhayn, in order to gain maneuver space to the east to allow the Eleventh Army to pivot to the southeast and operate against Przemysl if necessary.[34]

Once launched on 24 May 1915, both Jaroslau and Radymno were eventually taken by hard fighting, and bridgeheads over the San were established. With the Austro-Hungarian Third Army making only slow progress towards Przemysl from the west and south, the Eleventh Army shifted its weight yet again, this time back to the right as the Army's rightmost corps wheeled to the east and southeast against Przemysl. By the end of May the XXXXI Reserve Corps was in position to act against Przemysl's eastward communications, while the Bavarian 11th Infantry Division and elements of the Prussian Guard Corps, supported by heavy artillery, was ready to assault Przemysl's ring of fortifications from the north.

The siege itself took a little less than four days. Przemysl's forts, as Seeckt had expected, proved no match for German and Austro-Hungarian heavy artillery, aided by good ground observation and aerial reconnaissance.[35] After some of the outer forts fell to the Bavarians and Prussian guardsmen, the Russian garrison made a serious counterattack early on 2 June. With its repulse, the defense of the fortress collapsed. Much of the remaining garrison evacuated the fortress,

---

[33] German Eleventh Army, Special Orders Nr. 28, 15 May 1915, BH-KA File 11/43/4, Germany, Reichsarchiv, *Der Weltkrieg 1914 bis 1918*, Vol. 7, p. 426, Hans von Seeckt, *Aus meinem Leben 1866–1917* (Leipzig: von Hase und Koehler Verlag, 1938), p. 131 and Foerster, ed., *Mackensen: Briefe und Aufzeichnungen*, p. 158.

[34] Falkenhayn to Eleventh Army, 18 May 1915, Eleventh Army to OHL, 18 May 1915, Falkenhayn to Eleventh Army, 18 May 1915, Eleventh Army to Falkenhayn, 18 May 1915 and Eleventh Army to Falkenhayn, 19 May 1915, BA-MA W 10/51388.

[35] German Eleventh Army, Report on the Fall of Przemysl, June 1915, *Nachlass* Seeckt, BA-MA N 247/24, François, *Gorlice 1915*, p. 155 and Seeckt, *Aus meinem Leben 1866–1917*, p. 142.

blowing up the bridge over the San.[36] Przemysl was now back in the hands of the Central Powers.

Mackensen's offensive had produced a major victory, although some writers after the war regarded it as an incomplete victory, largely because there was no encirclement associated with it. Nevertheless, the haul of booty surpassed even Tannenberg. Falkenhayn calculated in a 17 May a letter to Conrad that Mackensen's forces had rounded up as many as 170,000 prisoners, plus 100 guns and 300 machine guns. Total losses for the Russian Southwest Front in May 1915 alone ran to more than 400,000. German casualties were about 28,000, including about 5,500 killed. While not light, by the standards of World War I these casualties were not excessive.[37]

With Przemysl retaken and bridgeheads over the San in hand, Falkenhayn and Conrad agreed to play their hand against the Russians for all it was worth. Falkenhayn and Conrad ultimately decided to unleash Mackensen on a broad front to the east, with the objective being the capital city of Austrian Galicia, Lemberg. Mackensen and Seeckt regarded this operation as a logical extension to the offensive that had started the month before, and had communicated this to OHL.[38] As usual, the command arrangements proved to be the real bone of contention. This time Falkenhayn was able to have Mackensen exercise direct operational control over the Austro-Hungarian Fourth and Second Armies that were operating on the German Eleventh Army's flanks. The German Eleventh Army would also be reinforced with several more divisions from both the western front and *OberOst*.[39]

---

[36] German Eleventh Army, Report on the Fall of Przemysl, June 1915, *Nachlass* Seeckt, BA-MA N 247/24, Paul Fleck to *OHL* Operations Section, Pless, 2 June 1915, BA-MA W 10/51388 (Fleck was the German assistant liaison officer at *AOK*.) and Franz *Freiherr* von Stengel, *Das K. B. 3. Infanterie-Regiment Prinz Karl von Bayern 1914–1918* (Munich: Verlag Bayerisches Kriegsarchiv, 1924), p. 23.

[37] Falkenhayn to Conrad, 17 May 1915, BA-MA W 10/50683, Austria, Bundesministerium, *Österreich-Ungarns Letzter Krieg 1914–1918*, Vol. 2, p. 451 Germany, Reichsarchiv, *Der Weltkrieg 1914 bis 1918*, Vol. 7, p. 428, Seeckt to Wife, 12 May 1915, *Nachlass* Seeckt, BA-MA N 247/57, Foerster, ed., *Mackensen: Briefe und Aufzeichnungen*, p. 166 and Leonhard *Graf* von Rothkirch *Freiherr* von Trach, *Gorlice-Tarnow* (Oldenbourg: Verlag vom Gerhard Stalling, 1918), p. 86.

[38] Seeckt, *Aus meinem Leben 1866–1917*, p. 145. Foerster, ed., *Mackensen: Briefe und Aufzeichnungen*, p. 171, Tappen Diary, 30 May 1915, BA-MA W 10/50661, German Eleventh Army to OHL, 3 June 1915, BA-MA W 10/51388 and Rudolf Kundmann Diary, 4 June 1915, Conrad Archive, ÖSA-KA B/13.

[39] Falkenhayn to Conrad, 2 June 1915, AOK Operations Bureau, Conrad – Falkenhayn Correspondence, Russia, ÖSA-KA R512, Falkenhayn to Eleventh Army,

Having obtained replacements, rebuilt his ammunition stocks, and conducted aerial reconnaissance of the new Russian defensive positions, Army Group Mackensen resumed the offensive on 13 June 1915, after another short but violent artillery bombardment.[40] The offensive quickly crashed through the Russian defenses and Mackensen's troops advanced to the east and northeast. Some 35,000 prisoners were taken, a number that was regarded as paltry by some in the Kaiser's retinue, given earlier numbers.[41] By 18 June the Germans and Austro-Hungarians were closing in on the Grodek position, a hastily constructed defense line based on a chain of lakes and rivers west and southwest of Lemberg. This represented the last attempt by the Russian Southwest Front to hang on to what was left of the gains that had been won in the opening battles of 1914.[42]

Mackensen and Seeckt had no doubt that the Grodek position could be penetrated easily. That expectation held true on the Russian side as well.[43] Aided by aerial reconnaissance, Mackensen and Seeckt decided to break the position north of Grodek. The objective chosen for the attack was Rava Ruska, a critical communications center north of Lemberg. The seizure of Rava Ruska and its rail line would isolate Lemberg from the north and sever communication between the Russian Northwest and Southwest Fronts. Launched on 19 June, Mackensen's main effort, the Prussian Guard Corps and the 119th Infantry Division, made good progress. The importance of the Guard's

---

3 June 1915 and AOK to All Armies, 4 June 1915, BA-MA W 10/51388, Meier-Welcker, *Seeckt*, p. 54 and Foerster, ed., *Mackensen: Briefe und Aufzeichnungen*, p. 171.

[40] Max Eder, *Das Preussische Reserve-Infanterie-Regiment 269* (Zeulenroda: Berhard Sporn Verlag, 1937), p. 68, Thilo von Bose, *Das Kaiser Alexander Garde-Grenadier-Regiment Nr. 1 im Weltkriege 1914–1918* (Zeulenroda: Bernhard Sporn, 1932), p. 187, Oskar von Rosenberg-Lipinsky, *Das Königin Elisabeth Garde-Grenadier-Regiment Nr. 3 im Weltkriege 1914–1918* (Zeulenroda: Verlag Bernhard Sporn, 1935), p. 183, German Eleventh Army, Special Orders Nr. 53, 10 June 1915, BH-KA File 11/43/4, German Eleventh Army, Order For Aerial Reconnaissance, 6 June 1915, BH-KA File 8R/11/1 and François, *Gorlice 1915*, p. 195.

[41] Foerster, ed., *Mackensen: Briefe und Aufzeichnungen*, p. 175 and Plessen Diary, 15 June 1915, BA-MA W 10/50656.

[42] Douglas Wilson Johnson, *Topography and Strategy in the War* (New York: Henry Holt and Company, 1917), p. 103 and François, *Gorlice 1915*, p. 220.

[43] Falkenhayn to Conrad, 13 June 1915 and Conrad to Falkenhayn, 14 June 1915, AOK Operations Bureau, Conrad – Falkenhayn Correspondence, Russia, ÖSA-KA R512, German Eleventh Army, Estimate of the Situation as of Noon, 15 June 1915, BA-MA W 10/51388, Seeckt, *Aus meinem Leben 1866–1917*, p. 150, Foerster, ed., *Mackensen: Briefe und Aufzeichnungen*, pp. 174–175 and Stone, *The Eastern Front 1914–1917*, p. 142.

attack was highlighted by the presence of the Kaiser, Falkenhayn and their respective retinues near the front to observe the proceedings.[44]

On 22 June elements of the Austro-Hungarian Second Army entered Lemberg. Recapturing the capital city of Galicia provided a major boost to Austro-Hungarian morale. Celebrations were held in Vienna, Teschen and Pless. Lemberg's capture also won Mackensen a promotion to *Generalfeldmarschall*.[45]

With Galicia back in Austro-Hungarian hands and the Russian Southwest Front disposed of, Mackensen's chief of staff, the brilliant Hans von Seeckt, proposed a change of direction for the advance to the north. Seeckt saw the situation as now offering an opportunity to destroy the Russian Northwest Front, and perhaps open up the possibility of forcing Russia to abandon the war in a separate peace. Mackensen fully backed Seeckt's concept, which also resonated with the mood at OHL. On 19 June Seeckt informally briefed the idea to Falkenhayn when the Kaiser and the OHL entourage visited Mackensen's headquarters at Jaroslau.[46]

After some preliminary discussions by Falkenhayn and Conrad regarding this idea, Seeckt formally briefed the concept to them after delivering a situation report at Jaroslau on 24 June 1915.[47] Mackensen's force would move north, entering Russian Poland from the south. This

---

[44] Austria, Bundesministerium, *Österreich-Ungarns Letzter Krieg 1914–1918*, Vol. 2, p. 491, Germany, Reichsarchiv, *Der Weltkrieg 1914 bis 1918*, Vol. 8, p. 231, Bose, *Das Kaiser Alexander Garde-Grenadier-Regiment Nr. 1 im Weltkriege 1914–1918*, p. 193, Prince Freidrich of Prussia, *Das Erste Garderegiment zu Fuss im Weltkrieg 1914–1918* (Berlin: Junker und Dünnhaupt, 1934), p. 106, Plessen Diary, 19 June 1915, BA-MA W 10/50656, Tappen Diary, 20 June 1915, BA-MA W 10/50661, Seeckt, *Aus meinem Leben*, p. 153, Foerster, ed., *Mackensen: Briefe und Aufzeichnungen*, p. 176 and DiNardo, *Breakthrough*, pp. 95–96.

[45] Herwig, *The First World War*, p. 144, Germany, Reichsarchiv, *Der Weltkrieg 1914 bis 1918*, Vol. 8, p. 234, Cramon to OHL, 22 June 1915, BA-MA W 10/51388, Kundmann Diary, 22 June 1915, Conrad Archive, ÖSA-KA B/13, Walter Görlitz, ed., *The Kaiser and His Court: The Diaries, Note Books and Letters of Admiral Georg Alexander von Müller, Chief of the Naval Cabinet 1914–1918* (New York: Harcourt, Brace and World, Inc., 1959), p. 86. Foerster, ed., *Mackensen: Briefe und Aufzeichnungen*, p. 178, Cramon, *Unser Österreich-Ungarischer Bundesgenosse im Weltkriege*, p. 16 and Manfred Rauchensteiner, *Der Tod des Doppeladlers: Österreich-Ungarn und der Erste Weltkrieg* (Vienna: Verlag Styria, 1993), p. 283.

[46] German Eleventh Army, Estimate of the Situation as of Noon, 15 June 1915, BA-MA W 10/51388, Seeckt, *Aus meinem Leben 1866–1917*, p. 153 and Foerster, ed., *Mackensen: Briefe und Aufzeichnungen*, pp. 183–184.

[47] Tappen Diary, 20 June 1915, BA-MA W 10/50661, Kundmann Diary, 20 June 1915, Conrad Archive, ÖSA-KA B/13, Meier-Welcker, *Seeckt*, p. 57 and DiNardo, *Breakthrough*, p. 107.

thrust would be supported by an attack by *OberOst*, although specifics were to be determined later. If completely successful, the Russian Northwest Front would be trapped in Russian Poland west of the Bug River. Falkenhayn agreed and gained the Kaiser's support by 28 June. Although Hindenburg and Ludendorff opposed Falkenhayn's choice of objectives for *OberOst*'s projected part in the operation, their opposition was overridden by OHL and the Kaiser, who officially approved the offensive on 2 July 1915 at a conference between OHL and *OberOst* at Posen.[48]

After a brief period of preparation, the offensive began in mid July, moving to the north and northeast. Mackensen's "phalanx" rolled on relentlessly. Aided by a subsidiary thrust from *OberOst*'s armies, by late August 1915 the Russians had been driven from Poland. The offensive resulted in the capture of Brest Litovsk on 26 August and Grodno on 2 September. One last offensive spurt brought the German advance into western Russia and Lithuania. The Russian Northwest Front, however, had managed to elude the encirclement hoped for by the Germans. Also unfulfilled was Falkenhayn's hope that Russia might be willing to conclude a separate peace. Diplomatically, the results were mixed. Mackensen's victories could not prevent Italy from declaring war against Austria-Hungary, something that had become apparent to the both Germany and Austria-Hungary by mid-May 1915. Italy did indeed declare war against Austria-Hungary on 23 May 1915. Events in Galicia, however, did make a substantial enough impression on the Romanian government that it declined to enter the war, Russian promises of Austro-Hungarian territory notwithstanding.[49]

Nonetheless, Mackensen and Seeckt had scored one of the great victories of the war. The Russians had suffered immense losses in

---

[48] Plessen Diary, 28 June 1915, BA-MA W 10/50656, Meier-Welcker, *Seeckt*, p. 57, Gerhard Granier, ed., *Adolf Wild von Hohenborn: Briefe und Tagebuchaufzeichnungen des preussischen Generals als Kriegsminister und Truppenführer im Ersten Weltkrieg* (Boppard-am-Rhein: Harald Boldt Verlag, 1986), p. 77, Tappen Diary, 2 July 1915, BA-MA W 10/50661, Lamar Cecil, *Wilhelm II* Volume II: *Emperor and Exile, 1900–1941* (Chapel Hill: The University of North Carolina Press, 1996), p. 227, Hoffman, *War Diaries and Other Papers*, Vol. I, p. 62 and Foerster, ed., *Mackensen: Briefe und Aufzeichnungen*, p. 186.

[49] Conrad to Falkenhayn, 18 May 1915 and Falkenhayn to Conrad, 19 May 1915, BA-MA W 10/50683, Tappen Diary, 19 May 1915, BA-MA W 10/50661, Richard F. Hamilton and Holger H. Herwig, *Decisions for War, 1914–17* (New York: Cambridge University Press, 2004), p. 176 and Danilov, *Russland im Weltkriege 1914–1915*, p. 510.

manpower and equipment that even dwarfed Tannenberg, and the Russian Army had been effectively eliminated as a military factor for the immediate future. In summing up the campaign for the Kaiser, the always historically minded Mackensen wrote that "what began on the day of Gross Görschen ended on the day of the Katzbach."[50]

Falkenhayn wanted to pursue a campaign against Serbia much earlier in 1915, but events in the Carpathians had precluded such an operation. With the Russian threat to Hungary disposed of and Russian Poland now in German hands, Falkenhayn now saw that both time and resources were available to square accounts with Serbia, thus opening a land route to Turkey. Although Conrad was more concerned with his most recent obsession, Italy, Falkenhayn had made it abundantly clear to Conrad that once operations against Russia were concluded, Serbia would be the next target of the Central Powers.[51]

A military convention with Bulgaria was signed on 6 September 1915, with Germany and Austria-Hungary promising to send material assistance to Bulgaria, while each power pledged to deploy some six divisions for offensive operations against Serbia. Four reinforced Bulgarian divisions would be committed to the invasion of Serbia. Although Conrad wanted an Austro-Hungarian general to be in charge of the offensive, Falkenhayn successfully demanded that the operation be entrusted to a German commander. The German commander in question would be Mackensen, as reflected in the military convention with Bulgaria. Thus Mackensen, who was then on leave for the first time since the war started, once again got the call. In point of fact, Mackensen was probably the only viable choice for the position.[52]

---

[50] Stone, *The Eastern Front 1914–1917*, pp. 179–180, Herwig, *The First World War*, p. 145, Foley, *German Strategy and the Path to Verdun*, p. 147 and Foerster, ed., *Mackensen: Briefe und Aufzeichnungen*, p. 206. The events Mackensen referred to were two battles from the 1813 campaign against Napoleon.

[51] General Hermann von Kuhl, *Der Weltkrieg 1914–1918* (Berlin: Verlag Tradition Wilhelm Kolk, 1929), Vol. I, p. 119, Notes of General von Falkenhayn on the Results of the Conference at Teschen, 18 May 1915, BA-MA W 10/50683, Falkenhayn to Conrad, 13 June 1915, AOK Operations Bureau, Conrad – Falkenhayn Correspondence, Russia, ÖSA-KA R512 and Kundmann Diary, 17 June 1915, Conrad Archive, ÖSA-KA B/13. Conrad's obsession with Italy is well laid out in his letters to Artur Baron von Bolfras, Chief of Francis Joseph's Military Chancery. See for example Conrad to Bolfras, 19 May 1915 and Conrad to Bolfras, 21 May 1915, Military Chancery of His Majesty (MKSM), ÖSA-KA MKSM 78 and Manfred Rauchensteiner, *Der Tod des Doppeladlers*, p. 215.

[52] Kundmann Diary, 3 September 1915, Conrad Archive, ÖSA-KA B/13, Richard C. Hall, *Bulgaria's Road to the First World War* (Boulder, CO: East European Monographs,

Although the Austro-Hungarian forces posted along the Serbian border had been in a defensive posture, as early as 1 June 1915 the Austro-Hungarian commander in the area, *General der Infanterie* Josef Tersztyansky, had been ordered to prepare for eventual offensive operations against Serbia.[53] These forces would now be augmented by the small Austro-Hungarian Third Army, commanded by *General der Infanterie* Hermann Baron Kövess von Kövesshaza. Kövess had at his disposal the Austro-Hungarian VIII and XIX Corps, a total of four divisions. Kövess' force would be increased by the addition of the German XXII Reserve Corps. The German Eleventh Army, now commanded by *Generaloberst* Max von Gallwitz, was composed of the German III, IV Reserve and X Reserve Corps. Mackensen's force was rounded out by the Bulgarian First Army, four divisions commanded by *Generalleutnant* Kliment Bojadjev. Given the fact that two major rivers had to be crossed, Mackensen's forces contained a large number of engineers. In addition nine Austro-Hungarian Navy monitors and ten air detachments were at Mackensen's disposal.[54]

The Serbian Army in 1915 consisted of eleven infantry divisions and one cavalry division, plus numerous small independent battalions, totaling about 250,000 men, supported by about 780 guns, including 240 heavy pieces, and a smattering of French aircraft. Although the Serbians were incapable of offensive action into Austro-Hungarian territory, overrunning Serbia was another matter. The tough Serbians had brought two Austro-Hungarian invasions in 1914 to grief. The Serbians enjoyed the protection of three wide and powerful rivers, the Save, Danube and Morava, with mountainous terrain beyond.[55]

1996), p. 305, Afflerbach, *Falkenhayn*, p. 339, Rauchensteiner, *Der Tod des Doppeladlers*, p. 298, Austria, Bundesministerium, *Österreich-Ungarns Letzter Krieg 1914–1918*, Vol. 3, p. 11, Foerster, ed., *Mackensen: Briefe und Aufzeichnungen*, p. 208 and General der Artillerie Richard von Berendt, "Aud grossen Zeit vor zwanzig Jahren. Der Feldzug in Serbien," *Militär Wochenblatt* Vol 120, Nr. 13 (4 October 1935): p. 523.

[53] Conrad to Bolfras, 31 May 1915, ÖSA-KA MKSM 78 and Austria, Bundesministerium, *Österreich-Ungarns Letzter Krieg 1914–1918*, Vol 3, p. 188.

[54] C. E. J. Fryer, *The Destruction of Serbia in 1915* (New York: Columbia University Press, 1997), p. 65, Austria, Bundesministerium, *Österreich-Ungarns Letzter Krieg 1914–1918*, Vol. 3, p. 227, Foerster, ed., *Mackensen: Briefe und Aufzeichnungen*, p. 213 and Meier-Welcker, *Seeckt*, pp. 65–66.

[55] Germany, Reichsarchiv, *Der Weltkrieg 1914 bis 1918*, Vol. 9, p. 197, Foerster, ed., *Mackensen: Briefe und Aufzeichnungen*, p. 217, Rauchensteiner, *Der Tod des Doppeladlers*, p. 300 and Johnson, *Topography and Strategy in the Great War*, pp. 153–154.

After a careful reconnaissance in late September by Colonel Richard Hentsch, who had been posted by OHL to Mackensen's headquarters, plus extensive aerial reconnaissance, detailed planning began. The staffs at OHL and AOK put together a general plan, which was then handed off to Mackensen and his staff.[56] Although he had about 500,000 men, Mackensen would once again rely on his trump card, the heavy artillery among the 1,400 guns at his disposal. The Austro-Hungarian Third and German Eleventh Armies would attack simultaneously, crossing the Save and Danube Rivers. Five days later the Bulgarian First Army would commence its operations further south against the already overstretched Serbian forces. The Bulgarian Second Army would also conduct offensive operations into Serbia, but would not be under Mackensen's control.[57]

As German divisions arrived at their assembly areas, division and regiment commanders conducted tactical reconnaissance. In keeping with established practice, officers reconnoitered their crossing points in the most inconspicuous clothing they could wear. Meanwhile Mackensen spent his time visiting with his principal subordinate commanders, especially those he did not know well, such as Bojadjev, the commander of the Bulgarian First Army. The attack was originally set for 10 October, but was moved up to 6 October 1915. The timing of the attack also probably served to provide Mackensen's force with the element of surprise, as the weather in the area, marked by the powerful storm known as the *Kossava*, could be expected to hinder the conduct of offensive operations.[58]

Speed would have to be essential, and not only for reasons of climate. The French government, both seeking to pursue strategic alternatives as well as anticipating an attempt by the Central Powers to overrun Serbia, decided to dispatch an expeditionary force to Salonika in Greece, from where direct support to Serbia could be provided, and Turkey's isolation maintained. Mackensen noted that German intelligence reports indicated that in case of an attack on Serbia, some sort of

---

[56] Austria, Bundesministerium, *Österreich-Ungarns Letzter Krieg 1914–1918*, Vol. 3, pp. 189–190 and Foerster, ed., *Mackensen: Briefe und Aufzeichnungen*, p. 213.

[57] Rudolf Dammert, *Der Serbische Feldzug: Erlebnisse Deutscher Truppen* (Leipzig: Verlag von Bernhard Tauchnitz, 1916), p. 18, Germany, Reichsarchiv, *Der Weltkrieg 1914 bis 1918*, Vol. 9, p. 201, Austria, Bundesministerium, *Österreich-Ungarns Letzter Krieg 1914–1918*, Vol. 3, p. 188 and Meier-Welcker, *Seeckt*, p. 65.

[58] Dammert, *Der Serbische Feldzug*, p. 20 and Foerster, ed., *Mackensen: Briefe und Aufzeichnungen*, pp. 219–220.

Franco-British intervention, with perhaps as many as 150,000 French and British troops, had to be expected. The news of the Salonika landing, which reached Mackensen and Seeckt almost immediately, probably forced the acceleration of the date for the attack up to 6 October. Mackensen issued the final orders for the attack on 4 October.[59]

Artillery preparation began on 5 October, and the offensive was launched the next day. With Serbian manpower stretched and the Serbian Army's defenses vulnerable to heavy artillery, Mackensen's force quickly beat down the Serbian positions with firepower. The Austro-Hungarian Third Army, including the German XXII Reserve Corps, crossed the Save on both sides of Belgrade. Meanwhile Gallwitz's German Eleventh Army crossed the Danube with the III Corps at Semendria, while the X Corps established a bridgehead across the river at Ram. The crossings were considerable feats in themselves, considering that the average width of the Danube was about 1,000 yards, while the lower Save's width was 300–500 yards, and both had strong currents. Although hard fighting was required in some instances, the Serbian defenses at the respective crossing points were quickly overcome. German and Austro- Hungarian forces entered a nearly depopulated Belgrade on 11 October. Meanwhile attempts by the Serbians to bring reinforcements against the German bridgehead at Semendria failed.[60]

With Belgrade in the hands of the Central Powers, Mackensen sought to trap and destroy the Serbian Army, while trying to prevent any effective intervention by Entente forces at Salonika. Thus the next major objective for Mackensen's forces was Kragujevac, a key communications center and the location of Serbia's armaments industry.[61]

Mackensen's attempt to envelop and destroy the Serbian Army failed. Serbian forces continued to resist stoutly, and there were instances

---

[59] Doughty, *Pyrrhic Victory*, pp. 214–216, Foerster, ed., *Mackensen: Briefe und Aufzeichnungen*, p. 221, Meier-Welcker, *Seeckt*, p. 66, Max von Gallwitz, *Meine Führertätigkeit im Weltkriege 1914/1916* (Berlin: E. S. Mittler und Sohn, 1929), p. 385 and Austria, Bundesministerium, *Österreich-Ungarns Letzter Krieg 1914–1918*, Vol. 3, p. 200.

[60] Kuhl, *Der Weltkrieg 1914–1918*, Vol. 1, p. 281 and Berendt, "Der Feldzug in Serbien," p. 524. The III Corps' bridge over the Danube used over 100 pontoons. Major General Otto Tiemann, "Ausstattung neuzeitlichen heere mit Gerät für den Kampf um Flüsse," *Militärwissenschaftliche Rundschau* Vol. 2, No. 6 (December 1937): p. 781 and Rauchensteiner, *Der Tod des Doppeladlers*, p. 300. Belgrade's prewar population was about 92,000. At the time of its occupation, only 10,000 remained. Dammert, *Der Serbische Feldzug*, p. 52.

[61] Fryer, *The Destruction of Serbia in 1915*, p. 68.

where German troops had to contend with sniping by Serbian civilians in villages. In addition the *Kossava* put in an appearance, producing 9–12 foot waves that wrought havoc on the German bridges over the Save and the Danube. Even when the bridges were put back in operation, poor roads and worsening weather made the movement of heavy guns and equipment difficult. Finally, the Bulgarian declaration of war and simultaneous offensive started a day late due to logistical difficulties. Once it did start, Bulgarian progress was slow.[62]

Nonetheless, Mackensen tried to quicken the pace as much as he could. Critical to the success of the offensive was bringing the railroad forward and getting the railroad bridges over the rivers rebuilt, a time-consuming process. On 24 October 1915 a train arrived at Orsova, on the border between Serbia and Austria-Hungary, the first since the onset of the war. The Bulgarians had also severed the rail line between Nish and Salonika, thus cutting off Serbia from allied assistance. By the end of October 1915 rail bridges over the Danube were open to traffic. Mackensen and Seeckt decided that the time was right to resume the offensive, hoping to defeat the Serbian Army decisively at Kragujevac, while the Bulgarians continued their subsidiary thrust on Nish. Mackensen also urged the Bulgarian high command to devote as many resources as possible to the Bulgarian Second Army, to make sure that no effective Franco-British intervention could be mounted from Salonika.[63]

Launched on 31 October 1915, Mackensen's attack broke Serbian resistance. Although the anticipated encirclement did not come about, Kragujevac was seized with little fighting by the III Corps on 1 November. Four days later the Bulgarian First Army took the rail junction of Nish. The Austro-Hungarian Third and German Eleventh Armies brought in over 15,000 prisoners, with the Bulgarian First Army taking 6,000 more. Around 100 guns were captured, and Mackensen noted that large amounts of material were captured in

---

[62] Gallwitz, *Meine Führertätigkeit im Weltkrieg 1914/1916*, p. 397, Germany, Reichsarchiv, *Der Weltkrieg 1914 bis 1918*, Vol. 9, p. 222, Dammert, *Der Serbische Feldzug*, p. 34, Seeckt, *Aus meinem Leben 1866–1917*, p. 238 and Berendt, "Der Feldzug in Serbien," p. 526.

[63] Dammert, *Der Serbische Feldzug*, p. 38, Foerster, ed., *Mackensen: Briefe und Aufzeichnungen*, p. 231, Seeckt, *Aus meinem Leben 1866–1917*, p. 253, Rauchensteiner, *Der Tod des Doppeladlers*, p. 301 and Gallwitz, *Meine Führertätigkeit im Weltkriege 1914/1916*, pp. 422–423.

Kragujevac. A good deal of ammunition was also blown up by the retreating Serbs.[64]

By 6 November 1915 Mackensen and Seeckt were convinced that Serbian resistance was broken. Mackensen noted the war weariness of the Serbian population. That day, a tense meeting at Pless between Falkenhayn and Conrad produced agreement only in regard to the fact that military operations against the Serbian Army should continue. Kövess and Gallwitz would continue their advance from the north, while the Bulgarians would continue an advance from the west, while also securing the flank of Mackensen's forces from any attack from the Entente forces at Salonika.[65]

With his new mission in hand, Mackensen set the next objective as Pristina, again trying to destroy the Serbian Army. He noted the difficulties however, given the increasingly mountainous terrain. By the third week of November, it was clear that the Serbian Army, now in full flight, was going to escape. The pursuit was hampered by logistics, as the Austrian Third Army was now operating nearly 81 miles from its railhead. Weather also steadily worsened, with heavy snow falling on 17 November.[66]

By 21 November 1915 both Mackensen and Seeckt were convinced that the campaign was over and that German forces could be withdrawn for other fronts. The campaign was, by the standards of World War I, a major success bought at a fairly cheap price. Mackensen's forces had inflicted about 95,000 casualties on the Serbian Army, and taken 150,000 prisoners, no doubt including vast numbers of Serbian wounded. The entire Serbian artillery park fell into the hands of the Central Powers. Total losses for the Central Powers were 67,000, including 12,000 German casualties. The losses also included some 7,000 Bulgarian casualties incurred in fending off a half-hearted French offensive from Salonika. The beaten remnants of the Serbian Army fled

---

[64] Foerster, ed., *Mackensen: Briefe und Aufzeichnungen*, p. 233, Gallwitz, *Meine Führertätigkeit im Weltkrieg 1914/1916*, p. 427, Germany, Reichsarchiv, *Der Weltkrieg 1914 bis 1918*, Vol. 9, p. 244, Austria, Bundesministerium, *Österreich-Ungarns Letzter Krieg 1914–1918*, Vol. 3, p. 263, Meier-Welcker, *Seeckt*, p. 68 and Fryer, *The Destruction of Serbia in 1915*, p. 73.

[65] Foerster, ed., *Mackensen: Briefe und Aufzeichnungen*, pp. 234–235 and Rauchensteiner, *Der Tod des Doppeladlers*, pp. 303–304.

[66] Germany, Reichsarchiv, *Der Weltkrieg 1914 bis 1918*, Vol. 9, p. 264, Seeckt to Wife, 19 November 1915, *Nachlass* Seeckt, BA-MA N 247/58 and Kuhl, *Der Weltkrieg 1914–1918*, Vol. 1, p. 284.

over the mountains into Albania and its Adriatic ports. From there, the Serbian soldiers who had survived the rigors of the retreat were taken by ship to Corfu and then later to Salonika and the Allied forces there.[67]

With the Serbian campaign concluded, Mackensen turned his attention to other matters. These included taking control of the railroads in Serbia in order to open up land communications to Turkey. His efforts were aided by the German capture of a considerable amount of Serbian rolling stock, including 42 locomotives. The matter of military occupation would be left to the Austro-Hungarian Army, which began setting up the Military General Government of Serbia in Belgrade.[68]

With Serbia crushed, Mackensen's next mission moved him even further into the realm of coalition warfare and controversy. Conrad had opposed Mackensen's appointment before the offensive against Serbia. His anger was exacerbated further when Mackensen received orders directly from OHL, something Conrad regarded as a breach of the command arrangements agreed upon before the Serbian campaign. Matters worsened as Conrad and Falkenhayn had a series of acrimonious meetings over the course of November. By late 1915 the two men were barely on speaking terms.[69]

Mackensen's position was both clarified and complicated by the resolution of the dispute between Falkenhayn and Conrad. Conrad sent Kövess' Austro-Hungarian Third Army off to invade Montenegro. Falkenhayn withdrew most of the German divisions from Mackensen's army group and transferred them to other theaters. The reorganized Army Group Mackensen now consisted of the German Eleventh Army and the Bulgarian First and Second Armies. With the majority of German divisions removed from the theater, Gallwitz's Eleventh Army was now composed of two German, one Austro-Hungarian and three

---

[67] Falkenhayn, *The German General Staff and Its Decisions, 1914–1916*, pp. 180–181, Austria, Bundesministerium, *Österreich-Ungarns Letzter Krieg 1914–1918*, Vol. 3, p. 310, Fryer, *The Destruction of Serbia in 1915*, pp. 91–104, Doughty, *Pyrrhic Victory*, pp. 225–227, Germany, Reichsarchiv, *Der Weltkrieg 1914 bis 1918*, Vol. 9, p. 276 and Kuhl, *Der Weltkrieg 1914–1918*, Vol. 1, p. 285.

[68] Army Group von Mackensen, Order of the Day Nr. 22, 6 December 1915, BA-MA PH 5I/77, Dammert, *Der Serbische Feldzug*, p. 105 and Gumz, *The Resurrection and Collapse of Empire in Habsburg Serbia, 1914–1918*, p. 5.

[69] Gunther E. Rothenberg, *The Army of Francis Joseph* (West Lafayette, IN: Purdue University Press, 1976), p. 191, Afflerbach, *Falkenhayn*, pp. 341–342 and Sondhaus, *Franz Conrad von Hötzendorf*, p. 182.

Bulgarian divisions. Mackensen's next mission was to drive the Entente forces from Salonika.[70]

This new mission brought with it a variety of new and familiar challenges. The most familiar was having to amass a sufficient amount of heavy artillery and ammunition to give any attack the best chance of success. Mackensen noted that the Entente forces at Salonika numbered about 160,000, but were strongly entrenched and well equipped with heavy artillery. Equally well known were the diplomatic elements of the position held by Mackensen and the demands they made on both Mackensen and Seeckt. As early as 28 October 1915 Seeckt noted in a letter to his wife that the changing circumstances in the Balkans had turned Mackensen's chief of staff into something of a cross between a "diplomat and travel agent." Finally, the fact that Mackensen now commanded far more Bulgarian troops than German troops presented a new problem, namely that of finding a sufficient number of interpreters, either Germans who could speak Bulgarian or Bulgarians who could read, write and speak German.[71]

The idea of attacking Salonika, however, quickly faded. Although Falkenhayn desired an attack on Salonika immediately, difficulties in amassing sufficient artillery ammunition. Undoubtedly, Mackensen would have preferred to have German troops to execute the attack, but with Verdun about to start, Falkenhayn did not have either the men or the guns to spare. February 1916 was marked by a series of postponements of the attack on Salonika. As spring turned to summer, the best Mackensen could do was to get his forces positioned on a line that, provided he had sufficient heavy artillery, would render any Entente attack from Salonika difficult if not impossible. By the end of June 1916 Falkenhayn essentially confirmed that an offensive aimed at Salonika was out of the question, owing to the German Army's needs in the west.[72]

While Mackensen and Falkenhayn were considering the various courses of action open to them in regard to the Salonika front, Falkenhayn sought to upgrade Mackensen's status. Command of all

---

[70] Gallwitz, *Meine Führertätigkeit im Weltkriege 1914/1916*, p. 465.
[71] Foerster, ed., *Mackensen: Briefe und Ayfzeichnungen*, p. 251, Seeckt to Wife, 28 October 1915, *Nachlass* Seeckt, BA-MA N 247/58 and Army Group von Mackensen, Army Order of the Day Nr. 21, 3 December 1915, BA-MA PH 5I/77.
[72] Foerster, ed., *Mackensen: Briefe und Aufzeichnungen*, pp. 258–259, Schwarzmüller, *Generalfeldmarschall August von Mackensen*, p. 128, Mackensen to Falkenhayn, 19 June 1916 and Falkenhayn to Mackensen, 27 June 1916, BA-MA W 10/50696.

forces north of the Pripet Marshes lay with Hindenburg and Ludendorff at *OberOst*. A combination of German and Austro-Hungarian forces operated south of the Pripet Marshes, but without any overarching command structure. Falkenhayn sought to have all German and Austro-Hungarian forces south of the marshes placed under Mackensen. Unfortunately for Falkenhayn, his attempt was opposed by Conrad, and Falkenhayn could not accept what he regarded as a second-best alternative of giving Mackensen a force composed of the Austro-Hungarian Seventh and German Süd Armies.[73]

As Romania's entry into the war against the Central Powers evolved from a possibility to a fact, Mackensen launched a limited offensive against the Entente forces at Salonika in late August 1916. While Mackensen was well aware that Salonika could not be taken, he sought to shorten the front of the Bulgarian forces there so that troops could be freed up for operations against Romania.[74]

Operationally Mackensen had to be at his best, however, when Romania, emboldened by French success at Verdun and Brusilov's shattering offensive against the Austrians, declared war on the Central Powers in August 1916. In accordance with an agreement reached in July 1916 between OHL and the Bulgarian General Staff, the Bulgarian Third Army was quickly placed under Mackensen's orders, as his Army Group headquarters was shifted from Macedonia to Dobrudja. Meanwhile the Chief of the Bulgarian General Staff, General Nikolaus Jekov, took over command of the defenses of Macedonia, in effect trading places with Mackensen.[75]

Mackensen obtained detailed intelligence about the Romanian forces opposing him. About five Romanian divisions were concentrated on the south bank of the Danube, most notably the two most important crossing points, the fortresses of Tutrakan and Silistria. These could be reinforced by as many eight more divisions. In addition, the appearance of Russian reinforcements was expected.[76]

Mackensen quickly recognized that the best chance to thwart the Romanian offensive was by gaining the Danube crossing points. His

---

[73] Afflerbach, *Falkenhayn*, p. 414, Schwarzmüller, *Generalfeldmarschall August von Mackensen*, p. 133 and Falkenhayn to Mackensen, 14 June 1915, BA-MA W 10/50696.

[74] Foerster, ed., *Mackensen: Briefe und Aufzeichnungen*, pp. 278–279.

[75] Germany, Reichsarchiv, *Der Weltkrieg 1914 bis 1918*, Vol. 11, pp. 193–194 and Army Group von Mackensen, Order For Bulgarian Third Army, 28 August 1916, BA-MA PH 5I/59.

[76] Foerster, ed., *Mackensen: Briefe und Aufzeichnungen*, p. 284.

efforts would be aided by reinforcements from every one of the Central Powers. Austria-Hungary sent heavy artillery, Bulgarian units were sent to the Third Army from the Macedonian front, and Ottoman Turkey sent the VI Corps. Later the German 217th Infantry Division was placed at Mackensen's disposal. In addition, German and Austro-Hungarian air units were sent as well.[77]

The quick counterattack mounted by the Bulgarian Third Army in early September 1916 caught the Romanian Third Army flat footed. Tutrakan was stormed on 6 September 1916, with heavy losses inflicted on the Romanians. This event made a strong impression on the Romanian government in Bucharest.[78] That sense was deepened a few days later when Silistria was taken three days later. Thus by mid-September 1916, as Mackensen's initial attack ground to a halt, any momentum the Romanians might have had in Dobrudja had been completely dissipated.

With his assortment of Germans, Austro-Hungarians, Bulgarians and Turks together by mid-October 1916, Mackensen now sought to complete the conquest of Dobrudja. As before, Mackensen put his trust in the combination of German infantry and heavy artillery. This was supplemented by an active campaign employing aircraft to isolate the Romanian forces in Dobrudja from both Romanian reinforcements from the other side of the Danube and Russian aid coming via the Black Sea.[79]

Judiciously employing his assets, Mackensen and his new chief of staff, Gerhard Tappen, thinned the front along the Danube in order to build up an assault force. The principal German attack would be made along the Black Sea coast, spearheaded by two reinforced German divisions.[80] Launched on 19 October, the attack quickly broke Romanian

---

[77] KTB/Army Group Mackensen, 30 August 1916, BA-MA PH 5I/59 and Germany, Reichsarchiv, *Der Weltkrieg 1914 bis 1918*, Vol. 11, p. 208.

[78] KTB/Army Group Mackensen, 6 September 1916, BA-MA PH 5I/59, Germany, Reichsarchiv, *Der Weltkrieg 1914 bis 1918*, Vol. 11, p. 205, Tappen Diary, 6 September 1916, BA-MA RH 61–986 and Foerster, *Mackensen: Briefe und Aufzeichnungen*, p. 287.

[79] General Ernest von Hoeppner, *Germany's War in the Air: The Development and Operations of German Military Aviation in the World War* (Reprinted Edition) (Nashville: The Battery Press, 1994), p. 92, Army Group von Mackensen, "The Dobrudja Campaign," Part II, c. December 1916, BA-MA PH 5I/18 and KTB/Army Group Mackensen, 9 October 1916, BA-MA PH 5I/59.

[80] KTB/Army Group Mackensen, 12 October 1916, BA-MA PH 5I/17.

resistance in Dobrudja. Constanta fell on 22 October and Cernavoda two days later.[81]

With Dobrudja secure, Mackensen's forces now turned north towards Bucharest. He would be operating in concert with Falkenhayn, who after being deposed as head of OHL had taken command of the German Ninth Army on the northern end of the Romanian front. By late November 1916 the Romanian Army was in a state of near disintegration. After crossing the Danube at Sistovo and Belene in late November, the united forces of Mackensen and Falkenhayn defeated the last major organized Romanian field force. Mackensen rode into Bucharest on 6 December 1916.[82]

With Bucharest secure, Mackensen's forces spent the remainder of 1916 moving up to the Sereth River, taking control of more Romanian territory. This operation effectively marked the end of Mackensen's time as a combat commander. For the rest of the war he spent the majority of his time in Bucharest as the German military governor of Romania, if not the "uncrowned king" of the country. Mackensen also played a role in the negotiations that ultimately resulted in the Treaty of Bucharest, signed on 7 May 1918.[83]

In this incredible spurt of activity, Mackensen distinguished himself in several ways. First, Mackensen was not simply the front man for his chief of staff, who did all of Mackensen's thinking for him. Second, he was able to make the jump from the tactical level of command to the operational fairly smoothly. Third, he was able to incorporate the emerging technologies of improving artillery and aircraft into his campaigns. Finally, he proved himself a master at the art of command in coalition operations, a tricky and even exasperating business for even the most experienced general officers. Each of these will now be considered in turn.

One of the most pernicious notions in World War I scholarship has been to depict senior German commanders such as Paul von Hindenburg and Crown Prince Rupprecht of Bavaria as mere ciphers,

---

[81] Foerster, ed., *Mackensen: Briefe und Aufzeichnungen*, p. 295 and Army Group Mackensen, Army Order, 25 October 1916, BA-MA PH 5I/17.

[82] Herwig, *The First World War*, pp. 221–222 and Foerster, ed., *Mackensen: Briefe und Aufzeichnungen*, 312.

[83] Gerhard Ritter, *The Sword and the Scepter: The Problem of Militarism in Germany* (Coral Gables: University of Miami Press, 1973), Vol. 4, pp. 174–175 and Schwarzmüller, *Generalfeldmarschall August von Mackensen*, p 160.

totally dominated by their brilliant chiefs of staff. If one looks at John Wheeler-Bennett's biography of Hindenburg, or even more recent popular books, Hindenburg is depicted as nothing more than an ambulating anesthetic, someone who only had to be woken up only when needed to soothe the strained nervous system of Erich Ludendorff. In Mackensen's case, the thinking for Gorlice was supposedly done by the exceptional intellect of his chief of staff, Hans von Seeckt, described by British historian B. H. Liddell Hart as "Mackensen's guiding brain." This perception of Mackensen was probably exacerbated by his appearance. Wearing the uniform of the 2nd Life Hussars, with its distinctive fur busby with the death's head insignia, Mackensen gave the appearance of a soldier who looked like something out of the Napoleonic Wars.[84]

Such a depiction is grossly unfair, if not insulting, to Hindenburg and Mackensen. Both men had spent long careers in the Army, and both had served in positions that required them to use their brains. Indeed, one post-war military analyst argued that the improvement in communications technology before the war, while reducing the physical demands on a commander, increased the mental demands "immensely."[85] Mackensen certainly showed himself able to meet those demands. Seeckt noted in his memoirs that Mackensen possessed a wide range of both theoretical and practical knowledge. During the summer of 1916 Mackensen was in direct contact with OHL, keeping Falkenhayn apprised of developments regarding the situation in Macedonia. During the Romanian campaign, Mackensen had to act on his own, as at times he did not have steady contact with OHL.[86] All of these tasks required a high degree of intelligence. The relationship between Mackensen and Seeckt, as well as Seeckt's successors Richard

---

[84] Wheeler-Bennett, *Wooden Titan*, p. 17, John Lee, *The Warlords: Hindenburg and Ludendorff* (London: Weidenfeld and Nicholson, 2005), p. 54, Uhle-Wettler, *Ludendorff in seiner Zeit*, p. 177, Herwig and Heyman, *Biographical Dictionary of World War I*, p. 236 and B. H. Liddell Hart, *History of the First World War* (Reprinted Edition) (London: Cassell, 1970), p. 197.

[85] Wolfgang Foerster, "Das Bild des modernen Feldherrn," Deutschen Gesellschaft für Wehrpolitik und Wehrwissenschaften, *Heerführer des Weltkrieges* (Berlin: E. S. Mittler und Sohn, 1939), p. 10.

[86] Seeckt, *Aus meinem Leben 1866–1917*, p. 116, Falkenhayn to Mackensen, 27 June 1916 and Mackensen to Falkenhayn, 28 June 1916, BA-MA W 10/50696 and Gerhard Tappen to Wolfgang Foerster, 22 October 1935, *Nachlass* Tappen, BA-MA N 56/5.

Hentsch and Gerhard Tappen, should be seen as other examples of the military marriage of a commander and his chief of staff, in the best tradition of Prusso-German military practice.[87] The Imperial German Army, like any other competent military establishment, did not give colonels lobotomies when they reached the rank of general officer.

Mackensen's staff at the XVII Corps remembered their boss as the quintessential hard-driving cavalry officer. He spent hours in the saddle every day, either out on military exercises or hunting, if the Corps was in garrison. He tried to be as forward as possible as a corps commander, both at Gumbinnen and then Tannenberg.[88] The circumstances of high-level operational command in World War I, once the implications of technological developments over the period 1890–1914 became at least partially clear, changed drastically.[89] Mackensen captured this in a 14 November 1914 letter from his Hohensalza headquarters during the Lodz campaign. It is worth quoting here at length:

> It seems quite strange to me, that I sit here at my desk and map table, while my troops fight between the Warthe and the Vistula. But such is the conduct of modern warfare. The distances of the march routes and the battlefield, the extent of the latter and the whole technical apparatus of the modern army brings it out so. Hohensalza is very good in this respect. It is valuable for the conducting of business when a headquarters remains in the same place for a longer time and becomes a traffic center. Units report by telephone and wireless radio and receive their orders by the same means. One is far from particular staffs and still speaks constantly with them and is constantly in contact with the battle front. The business area of my headquarters is here in a Gymnasium. All of my sections make demands on my time. I work in the room with the directors. It is regrettable that the days are so short that it limits tactical success and the day's accomplishments.[90]

---

[87] Robert M. Citino, *The German Way of War: From the Thirty Years' War to the Third Reich* (Lawrence: University Press of Kansas, 2005), p. 150 and Gunther E. Rothenberg, "Moltke, Schlieffen and the Doctrine of Strategic Envelopment," *Makers of Modern Strategy From Machiavelli to the Nuclear Age* (Peter Paret, ed.) (Princeton: Princeton University Press, 1986), p. 301.

[88] Germany, Reichsarchiv, *Der Weltkrieg 1914–1918*, Vol. 2, p. 90 and Foerster, ed., *Mackensen: Briefe und Aufzeichnungen*, pp. 29 and 67.

[89] Foerster, "Das Bild des modernen Feldherrn," Deutschen Gesellschaft für Wehrpolitik und Wehrwissenschaften, *Heerführer des Weltkrieges* (Berlin: E. S. Mittler und Sohn, 1939), p. 2 and Antulio J. Echevarria II, *After Clausewitz: German Military Thinkers Before the Great War* (Lawrence: University Press of Kansas, 2000), p. 65.

[90] Foerster, ed., *Mackensen: Briefe und Aufzeichnungen*, pp. 93–94.

Two days later, as his soldiers were taking Kutno, Mackensen wrote that "I followed them on the map and in my thoughts." He also noted the importance of the staff in the Ninth Army's success.[91]

Although Mackensen understood the limits imposed on army commanders by the available technology and tactical dispersion, he never let himself become desk bound. When the situation warranted, he went in person to the critical sectors of an operation. Mackensen did so at various stages of the offensives in Galicia and Romania; in the Serbian campaign, he personally observed the crossing of Gallwitz's Eleventh Army at Ram, the most important piece of his plan for overcoming the Serbian defenses on the Danube.[92]

As a field commander, Mackensen proved most adept at being able to exercise command over large units in complex tactical and operational situations, as both the Serbian and especially Romanian campaigns showed. This was a leap any number of his contemporaries tried to make and failed. World War I and the three decades that preceded it, was a period in which the conduct of war veritably seethed with technological change. This was particularly true in regard to artillery and aircraft. Mackensen had begun his military career at the very apex of the "Prusso-German Revolution in Military Affairs," epitomized by the Wars of German Unification and culminating in the Franco-Prussian War. His initial use of artillery at Gumbinnen was rather poor, attempting to deploy artillery within range of lethal Russian small arms fire.[93]

Mackensen was able to absorb the lessons afforded by four months of hard combat in 1914 in regard to artillery. This clearly showed in his conduct of a limited attack on the Russians in late January 1915. To beat down the Russian defenses, Mackensen amassed some 518 heavy and light artillery pieces. In the attack, wrote Mackensen, "the artillery should do the main work." Also employing gas shells, the attack was launched on 31 January 1915, and renewed briefly on 3 February 1915. As expected, some limited gains were made.[94]

---

[91] Ibid., p. 96.
[92] Fryer, *The Destruction of Serbia in 1915*, p. 49, Germany, Reichsarchiv, *Der Weltkrieg 1914 bis 1918*, Vol. p, p. 214 and Gallwitz, *Meine Führertätigkeit im Weltkriege 1914/1916*, p. 389.
[93] Germany, Reichsarchiv, *Der Weltkrieg 1914–1918*, Vol. 2, p. 92 and Showalter, *Tannenberg*, p. 185.
[94] Foerster, ed., *Mackensen: Briefe und Aufzeichnungen*, p. 125.

Nonetheless, Mackensen was now clearly convinced that the key to overcoming a well-posted enemy defense was a proper amount of artillery, especially heavy guns.

The old hussar's newfound respect for artillery was highlighted in all of his later campaigns. For Gorlice, with the his own Eleventh Army, the Austro-Hungarian Fourth Army and part of Austro-Hungarian Third Army for the attack (the Austro-Hungarian Fourth Army was under his orders), Mackensen massed 733 light, medium and heavy guns for the attack, as well as 70 trench mortars. In the Eleventh Army's sector alone, 506 light and heavy pieces were concentrated, along with most of the mortars. Just before the onset of the operation, Mackensen made a trip to examine the artillery preparations for the attack along with his artillery commander, General Alfred Ziethen.[95] Although aided by a mistaken Russian decision to devote attention and resources to the wrong place and at the wrong time, Mackensen's artillery concentration would have been sufficient to crush even a stouter Russian defense.[96] Likewise for the key attack against Serbia, Mackensen again massed 40 of the Eleventh Army's 124 batteries against the Serbian defenses at Ram, the most important crossing point on the Danube for the Germans. It too succeeded in bashing down the Serbian defenses.[97]

The importance of artillery, especially heavy guns for a successful defense was also clearly understood by the old hussar. This was particularly true when he was entrusted with the defense of the Vardar River valley, the route of advance any Entente offensive from Salonika would have to follow. In his defense of Dobrudja against the Romanians in the late summer and fall of 1916, Mackensen regarded the arrival of

---

[95] Obtaining an accurate figure for the number of guns used in the attack is difficult, as sources differ. In addition, the Austro-Hungarians and the Germans each had their own definition for what was a light, medium or heavy gun. Ziethen, "Die Durchbruchsschlacht von Gorlice," *Militär Wochenblatt* Vol. 119, No. 41, (4 May 1935): pp. 1627–1628, Austria, Bundesministerium, *Österreich-Ungarns Letzter Krieg 1914–1918*, Vol. 2, p. 318, Foerster, ed., *Mackensen: Briefe und Aufzeichnungen*, p. 141 and Stone, *The Eastern Front 1914–1917*, p. 131.

[96] François, *Gorlice 1915*, pp. 47–48, Foerster, ed., *Mackensen: Briefe und Aufzeichnungen*, p. 147, General Alexei A. Brussilov, *A Soldier's Notebook, 1914–1918* (Reprinted Edition) (Westport, Ct.: Greenwood Press, 1970), pp. 128–129 and Herwig, *The First World War*, pp. 141–142.

[97] Fryer, *The Destruction of Serbia 1915*, p. 45, Foerster, ed., *Mackensen: Briefe und Aufzeichnungen*, p. 213 and Austria, Bundesministerium, *Österreich-Ungarns Letzter Krieg 1914–1918*, Vol. 3, p. 200.

both a German infantry division as well as a proper amount of heavy artillery as critical to both a successful defense and the possibility of transitioning to the attack.[98]

Mackensen also realized early on the need for the coordination of infantry and artillery. This was clearly the case in the Gorlice offensive, where the German infantry was able to quickly advance and overrun the initial Russian positions in most cases while the Russians were still stunned from the effects of the preceding four-hour hurricane bombardment. Equally critical was the fact that the Germans had built up a stockpile of shells sufficient for the creation of a "mobile ammunition reserve." In addition batteries or individual guns were detailed to follow the first waves of infantry. The added firepower, made feasible by the weak response of the Russian artillery, proved invaluable in dealing with Russian machine gun nests and strong points.[99] For the attack against the Romanians in Dobrudja in October 1916, troops were instructed to approach as closely as possible to the Romanian positions while the artillery barrage was in progress. As soon as the barrage lifted, they were to storm into the positions before the Romanians could recover. Once the forward trenches had been taken, units were to move as rapidly as possible into the rear areas to knock out the Romanian artillery.[100]

The other major technological advance embraced by Mackensen was aircraft. In 1914 each German army and in many cases individual corps had an organic aircraft detachment for the purposes of reconnaissance. In the Tannenberg campaign, however, aerial reconnaissance often brought back no information, or in some cases false information. This played a part in the disaster that befell Mackensen's first attack at Gumbinnen.[101] Rather than let this poison his view towards the fledgling air arm, Mackensen took it in stride. Aerial reconnaissance, along with an important document capture, informed

---

[98] Mackensen to Falkenhayn, 19 June 1916, BA-MA W 10/50696 and Foerster, ed., *Mackensen: Briefe und Aufzeichnungen*, p. 289.

[99] François, *Gorlice 1915*, p. 52, Foerster, ed., *Mackensen: Briefe und Aufzeichnungen*, p. 147, Ziethen, "Die Durchbruchsschlacht von Gorlice," p. 1630 and Max Eder, *Das Preussische Reserve-Infanterie-Regiment 269* (Zeulenroda: Bernhard Sporn Verlag, 1937), p. 38.

[100] KTB/Army Group von Mackensen, 16 October 1916, BA-MA PH 5I/17 and Army Group von Mackensen, "The Dobrudja Campaign," Part II, c. December 1916, BA-MA PH 5I/18.

[101] Showalter, *Tannenberg*, p. 181 and Hindenburg, *Aus meinem Leben*, p. 88.

Mackensen of the size of the Russian force that awaited him in Warsaw during the abortive Polish campaign in 1914. During the Serbian campaign, Mackensen made excellent use of aerial photography to explain to OHL why it was no longer feasible to continue the pursuit of the beaten Serbian Army over the increasingly rugged terrain. Once the campaign had concluded and the Central Powers forces had taken a defensive posture against the Entente troops at Salonika, Mackensen again noted the importance of aerial reconnaissance. The ability to maintain watch over the area in daylight forced the enemy to confine any kind of moves preparatory to an offensive to be conducted at night.[102]

The other major use of aircraft was for artillery observation. This was particularly critical for Mackensen in that his campaigns were often conducted on logistical shoestrings compared to the much better resourced campaigns on the western front. With heavy artillery ammunition a valuable commodity during the siege of Przemysl, Mackensen's headquarters issued orders to the effect that the fall of every heavy artillery shell fired had to be observed.[103]

For the Romanian campaign, numerous reconnaissance missions made possible an extensive bombing campaign. Bucharest was subject to raids, and strikes were launched against Romanian troop deployments and munitions dumps. To isolate the battlefield from potential Russian intervention, numerous attacks were devoted to troop and vehicle traffic using the bridge over the Danube at Cernavoda, as well as the port facilities at Constanta, Romania's major Black Sea port. In addition, Mackensen also called on the services of the Austro-Hungarian Danube Flotilla. All this, combined with an imaginatively conducted thrust by the German Ninth Army, commanded by the now deposed Falkenhayn, managed to quickly overrun Romania, while also fending off Russian attempts to mount an effective intervention.[104]

---

[102] Germany, Reichsarchiv, *Der Weltkrieg 1914–1918*, Vol. 8, p. 264, Mackensen to Falkenhayn, 19 June 1916, BA-MA W 10/50696, Foerster, ed., *Mackensen: Briefe und Aufzeichnungen*, p. 240 and Fryer, *The Destruction of Serbia 1915*, p. 85.

[103] German Eleventh Army, Special Orders Nr. 28, 15 May 1915, BH-KA File 11/43/4 Lieutenant Colonel Schirmer, "Schwere Artillerie," *Die militärischen Lehren des Grossen Krieges* (M. Schwarte, ed.) (Berlin: E. S. Mittler und Sohn, 1920), p. 118.

[104] *KTB*/Army Group von Mackensen, 9 October 1916, BA-MA PH 5I/59, Army Group von Mackensen, "The Dobrudja Campaign", Part II, c. December 1916, BA-MA PH 5I/18, J. Breckinridge Bayne, *Bugs and Bullets* (New York: Richard R. Smith, 1944), p. 47, Austria, Bundesministerium, *Österreich-Ungarns Letzter Krieg 1914–1918*, Vol. 5, pp. 245 and 626–627, Afflerbach, *Falkenhayn*, pp. 465–468 and Herwig, *The First World War*, pp. 219–222.

For an officer who had spent much of his career serving in the cavalry, Mackensen understood that the time of mounted soldiers playing a major role on the battlefield had passed. In none of his campaigns did cavalry play a really critical role. To be sure, the ad hoc cavalry corps commanded by *Generalleutnant* Ernst von Heydebreck did exert some influence in Mackensen's offensive into southern Poland by its advance on Kovel. In the Serbian campaign, the link up of the German Eleventh Army and the Bulgarian First Army was accomplished by cavalry patrols from both armies. These actions, however, were subsidiary to the main operation.[105]

To some degree, the absence of cavalry was in any case unavoidable, since few such units were available anyway. In addition, much of the German cavalry on the eastern front was deployed in *OberOst*'s area of operations. The Germans also discovered that the Russian practice of employing large numbers of Cossacks to screen retreats tended to reduce German cavalry operations to sheer futility. Thus a combination of lack of numbers and bitter experience, compounded by the logistical realities of the eastern front, led Mackensen to avoid the wasteful practice of piling up cavalry formations behind the front for the chimera of the post-breakthrough exploitation.[106]

What made Mackensen almost unique among German commanders during World War I was his ability to excel in the realm of coalition warfare.[107] Mackensen's first real experience in coalition warfare was in the Gorlice-Tarnow campaign in 1915, when Falkenhayn was able to have his way and make sure that Mackensen was in overall charge of the operation, and could thus exercise command over the Austro-Hungarian Fourth Army as well as his own Eleventh Army.[108]

As the commander designated to conduct the Gorlice operation, Mackensen was stepping into a most delicate situation. Personal relations between Mackensen's two superiors, Falkenhayn and Conrad, were strained to say the least. Marked by differences over strategy,

---

[105] Stone, *The Eastern Front 1914–1917* and Dammert, *Der Serbische Feldzug*, p. 47.
[106] Captain von Ammon, "Kavallarie," *Die militärischen Lehren des Grossen Krieges*, p. 71 and Bavarian 8th Reserve Infantry Division, Excerpt From Campaign Experiences of the German Eastern Army, June 1915, BH-KA File 8R/11/1. The British still continued this practice, even though it was becoming plainly evident that the cavalry's day had passed. Hart, *The Somme*, p. 407.
[107] Mackensen's closest rival in this would be Colmar von der Goltz, who was able to work with the Turks very successfully before his death in 1916.
[108] Afflerbach, *Falkenhayn*, p. 291.

personal snubs, sarcastic remarks and very different styles of conducting business, relations between the two men were deteriorating rapidly by the late spring of 1915.[109] Mackensen thus had to be careful not only in conducting the attack, but also in dealing with both Austrian and German headquarters.

In the end, however, Mackensen pulled it off superbly. His time as an adjutant at the Hohenzollern court served him well in this capacity. He understood the importance of protocol, and the critical need to establish personal relationships with his Austrian counterparts. Still handsome at age 66, his "elegant appearance and courtly charm," made a great impression on the Habsburg court, most notably on Mackensen's first visit to the aged Francis Joseph in September 1915. He was aided in this effort by Seeckt, whose air of quiet confidence also reassured the Austrians.[110] In addition, Mackensen went out of his way to get to know his Austrian colleagues personally. On 26 April 1915, for example, Mackensen and Seeckt went to Brzesko to visit the principal Austrian commander, Archduke Josef Ferdinand, and his chief of staff to discuss the upcoming attack. Aside from making sure there was broad agreement on the conduct of the impending offensive, Mackensen thought that the making of a close acquaintance in the Archduke made the trip worth taking. This was in stark contrast to Falkenhayn, who thought personal meetings too time consuming and preferred telephone, and Ludendorff, whose antipathy to the Austrians was made clear both publicly and privately.[111]

In the actual conduct of the campaign, Mackensen generally showed a deft touch in handling the Austrians. Although German troops took Przemsyl, a deed that Mackensen, in a surprisingly tactless move,

---

[109] Austria, Bundesministerium, *Österreich-Ungarns Letzter Krieg 1914–1918*, Vol. 1, p. 494, Count Josef von Stürgkh, *Im deutschen Grossen Hauptquartier*, (Leipzig: Paul List Verlag, 1921), p. 103, Afflerbach, *Falkenhayn*, pp. 256–257 and Sondhaus, *Franz Conrad von Hötzendorf*, p. 169.

[110] Schwarzmüller, *Generalfeldmarschall August von Mackensen*, p. 122, Foerster, ed., *Mackensen: Briefe und Aufzeichnungen*, p. 212 and Cramon, *Unser Österreich-Ungarischer Bundesgenosse im Weltkrieg*, pp. 14–15.

[111] Afflerbach, *Falkenhayn*, pp. 256–257, Foerster, ed., *Mackensen: Briefe und Aufzeichnungen*, pp. 146 and 220, Erich Ludendorff to Helmuth von Moltke, 1 April 1915, *Nachlass* Ludendorff, BA-MA N 77/2 and Erich Ludendorff, *Meine Kriegserinnerungen 1914–1918* (Berlin: E. S. Mittler und Sohn, 1919), pp. 69–70. Some interesting commentary also in August von Cramon and Paul Fleck, *Deutschlands Schicksalsbund mit Österreich-Ungarn: Von Conrad von Hötzendorf zu Kaiser Carl* (Berlin: Verlag für Kulturpolitik, 1932), p. 102.

announced with fanfare, he was able to arrange for Austro-Hungarian forces to take Lemberg. The capture of the capital city of Galicia was a major boost to Austrian morale, and Mackensen's attention to Austrian sensibilities earned him a good many plaudits in Vienna, and more importantly, the trust of his Austrian allies. In his own writings, Mackensen was gracious enough to credit both Conrad and Falkenhayn for the concept of this most successful attack.[112]

This approach to command served Mackensen well for the rest of his active wartime service. In the case of the Serbian and Romanian campaigns, Mackensen again made the time to visit subordinate allied commanders personally. Such endeavors, as well as the successful outcomes of his campaigns, particularly in Serbia where Austria-Hungary's most implacable enemy was laid low, won Mackensen much trust and respect in the capitals of the Central Powers, and in the case of Vienna, the personal esteem and affection of Emperor Francis Joseph.[113]

In an environment rife with personal rivalries and poisonous relationships, Mackensen had the happy facility of being able to remain on good terms personally with everybody. Ludendorff, not known for being complimentary, described Mackensen as a "generous and noble man and a brilliant soldier." Mackensen's two long-serving chiefs of staff, Hans von Seeckt and Gerhard Tappen, were both devoted to the old hussar, and Gallwitz was delighted to be working for such an "amiable old gentleman." The Kaiser's affection was well known. Even Hans von Plessen, the person at imperial headquarters who was perhaps the most critical of Mackensen as a military leader, still thought him "a splendid man," even if he was "a mediocre commander."[114]

Perhaps the most remarkable aspect of these campaigns is the casualties, which for the Central Powers turned out to be rather light.

---

[112] Kundmann Diary, 3 June 1915, Conrad Archive, ÖSA-KA B/13, Herwig, *The First World War*, pp. 142–144 and Foerster, ed., *Mackensen: Briefe und Aufzeichnungen*, p. 153. Both Conrad and Falkenhayn claimed authorship of the plan. Field Marshal Franz Conrad von Hötzendorf, *Aus Meiner Dienstzeit 1906–1918* (Sixth Edition) (Vienna: Rikola Verlag, 1925), Vol. 5, p. 791 and Falkenhayn, *The German Gteneral Staff and Its Decisions, 1914–1916*, pp. 88–91. See also DiNardo, *Breakthrough*, pp. 30–31.

[113] For such visits Mackensen usually brought with him his chief of staff, Seeckt, and his aide, Major Fedor von Bock. Foerster, ed., *Mackensen: Briefe und Aufzeichnungen*, pp. 146, 212 and 220 and Arthur J. May, *The Passing of the Habsburg Monarchy 1914–1918* (Philadelphia: University of Pennsylvania Press, 1966), Vol. I, p. 427.

[114] Ludendorff, *Meine Kriegserinnerungen*, p. 109, Gallwitz, *Meine Führertätigkeit 1914/1916*, p. 379 and Plessen Diary, 2 June 1915, BA-MA W 10/50656..

While the Gorlice operation and the subsequent conquest of Poland was a glittering but costly success, the overrunning of Serbia cost the combined German, Austrian and Bulgarian forces about 67,000 casualties, including 12,000 German and 18,000 Austro-Hungarian losses.[115] Such losses were trifling compared to the bloodletting that was occurring in places such as Verdun and the Somme.

Mackensen also had the ability, rare in the faction-ridden atmosphere of Imperial Germany, to steer clear of political infighting. His only allegiance was to his friend and sovereign, Wilhelm II. After the capture of Lemberg, Mackensen and Seeckt were given precisely the same promotions that Hindenburg and Ludendorff were given after Tannenberg. Seeckt wrote to his wife that he and Mackensen were being set up as a counterweight to the Hindenburg – Ludendorff duumvirate.[116]

The old hussar, however, never let himself become embroiled in the contentious power struggle between Falkenhayn and the Hindenburg – Ludendorff duo at *OberOst*. Mackensen was surprised when Falkenhayn was dismissed as head of OHL in August 1916. During the war, Mackensen was able to remain on excellent terms with Hindenburg, Ludendorff and Falkenhayn.[117]

How then, can we sum up Mackensen's service in this brief study? Mackensen's biographer, Theo Schwarzmüller, described the old hussar as the "Pyrrhus of the Central Powers," a description that strikes me as somewhat facile. Mackensen's best campaigns, namely Serbia and Romania, generated relatively small casualties for his forces and were strategically critical in propping up the faltering Austro-Hungarian Empire. Operationally, one of the best descriptions of Mackensen comes from one of the great students of the war in the inter-war period, Charles Cruttwell. He said of Mackensen "his name is specially associated with enterprises demanding surprise and speed, like those against Serbia and Romania." Mackensen's chief of staff for the Romanian campaign, Gerhard Tappen, considered him the "greatest and most successful field commander of the World War." To be sure, Mackensen was indeed fortunate that his service in the war was spent on the eastern

---

[115] Germany, Reichsarchiv, *Der Weltkrieg 1914–1918*, Vol. 9, p. 276 and Austria, Bundesministerium, *Österreich-Ungarns Letzter Krieg 1914–1918*, Vol. 3, p. 336.

[116] Seeckt to Wife, 28 June 1915, *Nachlass* Seeckt, BA-MA N 247/57.

[117] Foerster, ed., *Mackensen: Briefe und Aufzeichnungen*, p. 282 and Schwarzmüller, *Generalfeldmarschall August von Mackensen*, p. 142.

front, a place where breakthroughs still could be achieved and mobility could still matter.[118]

For his advanced age, however, Mackensen proved to be an old dog who could still learn any number of new tricks. Confronted with the stark realities of an unfolding military revolution marked by unprecedented changes in technology and scale, Mackensen was able to make those critical adjustments needed to allow commanders to succeed. For all of his rather anachronistic appearance, marked by his trademark hussar's busby, he was indeed a twentieth century soldier.

---

[118] Schwarzmüller, *Generalfeldmarschall August von Mackensen*, p. 143, Cruttwell, *A History of the Great War 1914–1918*, p. 173, Tappen to Foerster, 22 October 1935, *Nachlass* Tappen, BA-MA N 56/5 and Showalter, *Tannenberg*, p. 342.

WINNING AND LOSING: FRANCE ON THE MARNE AND ON THE MEUSE

Robert A. Doughty

The 1914 battle of the Marne and the 1940 battle of the Meuse are two of the most famous battles of the twentieth century. In 1914 France lost the battle of the frontiers and won the "miracle of the Marne." The victory on the Marne brought elation and celebration; the French had parried the Germans' knockout blow and driven them back from the outskirts of Paris. Victory in the war, however, came only after four more years of huge battles and terrible casualties. In 1940 France suffered a crushing defeat after the Germans broke through French defenses along the Meuse near Sedan. Although the French remained in the fight for another month, the armistice on June 22, 1940, brought immediate pain and shame and swept France from the first rank of world powers. Rarely has a world power been defeated so quickly and so decisively. Except for a common enemy, Germany, and a common ally, Great Britain, the battles are more different than they are similar. Among the differences, the French suffered three to four times as many killed-in-action in the victory of August–September 1914 than in the defeat of May–June 1940. Other differences appear in the French preparation for and conduct of the two battles. An analysis of these differences suggests France had the capability and opportunity to respond to Germany's actions in 1914 but had neither the capability nor the opportunity to respond in 1940.

In 1914 the battle of the Marne was the culmination of a month-long campaign that ranged across the entire northeastern and northern frontier of France. When the war began, the first clash between the Germans and French occurred when the Germans sent a cavalry raid on August 2 across the Franco-German frontier. The first large operation began on August 7, when General Joseph Joffre pushed a corps forward into Alsace. Although thousands of cheering Alsatians lined the route of advance, things went badly almost immediately. One regimental commander sitting astride a handsome white horse was severely wounded as he tried to lead his regiment forward. Soldiers in his regiment also suffered heavily when they fixed bayonets and charged the Germans. The second large operation began on August 14 when Joffre, thinking the main German forces would drive into France at points no deeper than Sedan or Montmédey, launched an attack into Lorraine. While the first attack into Alsace sought to reinforce public confidence, the second, a much larger operation, aimed to inflict serious damage on the enemy and aid Russia's offensive into Germany. Joffre held back, however, the main mass of his forces west of Luxembourg (Third and Fourth armies) and awaited the right moment for unleashing them into what he thought was the weakened center of German forces in eastern Belgium. Much to his surprise, this attack into eastern Belgium on August 21 also failed. The unsuccessful operations in the battle of the frontiers demonstrated clearly the inadequacy of French operational and tactical preparation and unveiled the main German attack through central Belgium toward Paris across Liège, Namur, and Maubeuge.

After the disasters in Alsace and Lorraine, the French shifted their focus and effort to their left wing. The highly efficient French railway system could move an entire corps from Joffre's right to his left in five or six days. Joffre first tried to envelop the German flank near Amiens but, when this failed, he began pulling French forces farther back. From August 30 to September 5, soldiers in the Fifth Army withdrew some 140 kilometers. On September 1 French and British aviation reported German columns moving east of Paris. Two days later Joffre, relying on additional aviation reports and on intercepted German radio traffic, learned that the entire German First Army, on the enemy's far right, was moving east of Paris. Yet, Joseph Gallieni's much-celebrated strike from Paris (including the famous "taxis of the Marne") into the vulnerable flank of the Germans as they passed east of Paris did not halt the enemy's advance. The battle of the Marne itself occurred between September 5 and 12. After the Germans passed east of Paris and drove farther south, the French halted them along the Marne and counterattacked. Meanwhile, Gallieni's attack caused German leaders to bring forces back from their forward-most point of advance and open a hole in German lines. As other French forces returned to the offensive, General Sir John French's British Expeditionary Force and General Louis Franchet d'Espèrey's Fifth Army advanced cautiously through the unexpected opening and forced the Germans to withdraw. In the aftermath, the sobriquet "miracle of the Marne" seemed eminently appropriate, for the French had snatched victory from the jaws of defeat.

The French proceeded much more cautiously in 1940 than they had in 1914. To assist Poland, they made a feeble effort in September 1939 to advance to the edge of the Siegfried Line but they did little else thereafter, thus giving birth to what became known as the *drôle de guerre* or the phoney war. While holding forces along the Belgian, Luxembourg, and German frontiers, General Maurice Gamelin refused to make the mistake Joffre had made by throwing his forces forward in futile offensives. Instead, he held them in their positions and prepared to rush a significant portion of them forward into western and central Belgium once the Germans violated Belgian territory. He wanted to fight this war on another country's soil, not France's, and he expected to meet the main German attack as it moved through the Gembloux Gap and marched *à la 1914* toward Paris. At the same time he placed some of his most mobile forces on his left flank and prepared to send them toward Breda in The Netherlands. He apparently expected the highly mobile force at Breda to fall onto the rear of the advancing German forces.

During the phoney war, German intelligence learned of Gamelin's plan to send significant forces into central and western Belgium and German commanders abandoned their plans to march through central Belgium. They prepared instead to drive through the Belgian Ardennes and the French center. After changing the date of the German offensive twenty-nine times, Adolf Hitler finally unleashed the attack on May 10, the leading edge of which consisted of Panzer Group von Kleist with two panzer and one motorized infantry corps moving through the Ardennes. As soon as the Germans entered Luxembourg and Belgium, Gamelin sent his forces forward into western and central Belgium and sent screening forces into the Belgian Ardennes to make sure the Germans were not driving through eastern Belgium. These screening forces did little to delay the large number of German forces actually moving through Luxembourg and eastern Belgium and, even worse, failed to identify the size of the dangerous enemy thrust moving through the Ardennes.

When the Germans reached and then crossed the Meuse River, General Ewald von Kleist's panzer group struck the right of the French Ninth Army and the left of the Second Army, neither of which fared well. In an especially important action around Sedan, an action in which the role of the German infantry was far more important than sometimes thought, General Heinz Guderian's XIXth Panzer Corps fought its way across the Meuse River against the French Xth Corps and 55th Division. The 55th Division, which had performed well in the battle of the Marne in 1914, crumbled in the face of German infantry. The French rushed reinforcements forward and attempted several counterattacks, but none of their efforts succeeded. To make matters worse, the French expected the Germans to drive south of Sedan or turn east behind the Maginot Line, but much to their surprise the XIXth Panzer Corps pivoted west. By the morning of May 16, little or nothing lay between the Germans and the English Channel. Three days later Guderian's panzer corps reached Abbeville and cut off the left wing of French and British forces. Only later did Marc Bloch's *Strange Defeat* capture the sense of helplessness and frustration associated with the campaign.

The speed of the German advance in 1940 proved devastating to the French. In 1914 the German drive across Belgium and France began when German forces moved westward out of Aachen into Belgium on August 2. After advancing some 450 kilometers, the Germans reached their farthest point near Mondement, France, on September 9, or 39 days later. In 1940, the campaign began on May 10, when German elements entered Luxembourg. Nine days later leading elements of the German XIXth Panzer Corps reached Abbeville; they had traveled about 375 kilometers in nine days. The two battles thus differ dramatically in their tempo and in the time France had to make adjustments. Had the advance of the main German forces through central Belgium been faster in 1914, the outcome of that battle may have been dramatically different. Similarly, slowing the Germans only one more day around Sedan in 1940 could have given the French enough time to make critical adjustments and slow or stop the German advance. In 1914 Joffre had the time to make adjustments; in 1940 Gamelin did not.

The amount of resources given the military does not explain the different performances in 1914 and 1940. Though some critics have said France devoted too little of its resources before 1940 to the military, it had in fact devoted considerable sums. As a percentage of national revenue, military expenditures in 1938 were double those of 1913 (8.6% versus 4.2%) Between 1918 and 1935 the French spent a greater percentage of their national revenue on defense than any other great power. Only between 1936 and 1940 did Germany spend a greater percentage than France. The Germans began rearming after Hitler came to power in 1933, and as part of this rearmament program, they had the sometimes under-appreciated advantage of starting from scratch as they rebuilt and modernized their forces. Since Germany had lost so much war matériel as a consequence of the Treaty of Versailles, it could design its forces without the constraints imposed by existing weapons and old ideas. Until the 1930s, France spent most of its funds on building the Maginot Line and making incremental changes in its arsenal. In 1934–35 it took its first steps toward rearmament and in 1936–37 accelerated its efforts. Many of these steps sought to build on what France already had, not to begin something completely new. While the French military could have used more funding, especially in pay for personnel, a shortage of funding did not compel military leaders to field a poorly equipped, inadequately supported force. What mattered most was how the money was spent, not how much was spent.

Failures in strategic intelligence also do not adequately explain the differences in 1914 and 1940, for the French failed in both campaigns to discern initially the main outline of the Germans' strategy and the location of their main attack. In 1914, the French did not expect the Germans to make their main attack in central Belgium; they expected the Germans to concentrate in eastern Belgium. Not until after the failure of the French offensives into Alsace and Lorraine did Joffre recognize what the Germans were doing. In 1940, the French had some intelligence reports suggesting that the Germans were advancing through eastern Belgium and the Ardennes, but they focused on reports of the Germans moving through central Belgium. The Germans took advantage of the French experience in 1914 by making diversionary attacks in Belgium, thereby leading the French to conclude the Germans were once again coming through central Belgium. Not until the morning of May 13, the day Guderian's corps crossed the Meuse at Sedan, did the French understand that the Germans were making their main attack through eastern Belgium and the Ardennes. In both cases the French paid closest attention to intelligence reports that confirmed their preconceived ideas, not to those that suggested the Germans were doing the unexpected. French intelligence performed better after the initial battles of 1914, but the French did not have the luxury of making improvements after the fighting began in 1940.

An important difference between the 1914 and 1940 campaigns, however, concerns signals intelligence. As the French fell back on their lines of communication, Joffre used telephone and telegraph lines to communicate with his subordinates and did not have to use easily intercepted wireless radiograms. On the other side of the hill General Helmuth von Moltke remained in contact via telephone and telegraph with his center and left field armies even though the Germans found the wires for most land lines cut in Belgium and France as they advanced. For the more rapidly moving First and Second armies on his right, however, he had contact only via a single wireless radio set which was often jammed by French radio transmitters. The French had the advantage of having created before the war a network of intercept stations–primarily located in the great fortresses of Maubeuge, Verdun, Toul, Épinal, and Belfort but also in the Eiffel Tower–that intercepted many of the radiograms transmitted by the Germans. Adding to their strengths, the French had a cryptologic section that worked tirelessly on deciphering German messages. The best intelligence, however, came from radiograms transmitted in the clear by the Germans and intercepted by French listening stations. After the failure of Joffre's Alsace and Lorraine offensives, these intercepts gave him a much better understanding of what the Germans were doing.

By October 1, after the Marne victory, the French had reconstructed the transposition key used to encrypt German messages, and despite subsequent changes in the key they maintained an edge over the Germans for the remainder of the war. That edge enabled them at the end of the war to decipher the famous *radiogramme de la victoire* and halt the final German offensive. Building on this success, however, proved difficult. In 1931 the French acquired information from a German agent about the German Enigma machine, a portable cipher machine with rotor-based scramblers, but they received no information on the rotor wiring or the keys used to encrypt and decrypt messages. After consulting with the British and agreeing that they lacked sufficient information about Enigma to decipher German messages, the French provided the information to the Poles, who built a replica of the Enigma machine. After a German agent, for considerable sums of money, sold the French expired keys for the Enigma machine, the French provided copies to the Poles, who proceeded to reconstruct other keys and then to decipher German radio transmissions. In July 1939, the Poles informed the French and British of their success. When the Germans and Soviets invaded Poland in September 1939, Polish cipher experts fled and some of them eventually made their way to France. A month later they were deciphering German messages in France, and things seemed in place for the French to have a significant advantage over the Germans. Shortly before May 10, 1940, however, the Germans changed procedures for enciphering messages and temporarily kept the Allies from deciphering their transmissions. Unfortunately for the French, they did not succeed in deciphering messages again until May 20, a day after Guderian's panzer corps reached Abbeville. While Joffre had a fairly clear picture of German forces' location and objectives at the crucial moment of the campaign, Gamelin did not. That clearer understanding proved vital to French success on the Marne.

Another important difference between 1914 and 1940 pertains to the strategic role played by Russia. In 1914 the French expected and got great assistance from the Russians. French strategy rested on the assumption of powerful offensives by France and Russia into Germany, thereby forcing the enemy to fight on two fronts. Germany recognized this threat and based its strategy on leaving minimum forces in East Prussia, concentrating against and defeating France quickly, and then rushing troops to eastern Europe. In the early phase of the fighting, the Germans appeared to be doing well in France and Belgium and poorly in East Prussia, and Moltke responded on August 25 and 26 by moving two corps from the French to the Russian theater. The momentum of the fighting in East Prussia, however, switched decisively in favor on the Germans on August 27 and 28, prior to the arrival of reinforcements from France. Although the Germans had won the battle of Tannenburg by August 30, the Russians had done enough to convince the Germans to weaken their offensive into France, and they had provided the French a better chance of succeeding with their counterattack on September 5. The German-Soviet Nonaggression Pact of August 1939, however, left the French without any hope of assistance from the Russians in 1940. Great Britain stood by France's side in 1914 and 1940, but the absence of Russia in 1940 left Germany free to concentrate its power in the West. That concentration gave Gamelin little or no leeway for errors.

Other important differences between 1914 and 1940 concern preparation in peacetime for war, for the battles on the Marne and Meuse followed periods of great technological advances and institutional changes. Between 1910 and 1914 the French devoted serious efforts to considering technological advances and integrating them into their planning and preparation. These advances permitted the introduction of rapid-fire artillery, breech-loading rifles, and machine guns; they also provided new means of aerial warfare. Heated debates occurred over the role of machine guns, the relationship between infantry and artillery, the mix of heavy and light artillery, and the potential of aviation. Autumn maneuvers tested not only the new technologies but also new operational and tactical ideas. New technologies, the French recognized, had increased the breadth and depth of the battlefield and had enhanced the operational mobility and lethality of tactical units. They spent a great deal of time trying (but only partially succeeding) to increase the size of maneuver areas so large units such as the division and corps could practice the integration of fire and maneuver.

Improved communications from the wireless telegraph and the telephone also had significant effects. Though the telegraph had played an important role in previous wars, commanders in 1914 had much more reliable and capable means of communicating rapidly with subordinates and superiors than in previous decades. And political and military leaders had better communications with allies. After working diligently to establish redundant means of wireless communications with Russia, French leaders planned on using these communications to coordinate simultaneous offensives on Germany's eastern and western frontiers.

Additionally, railways and motor vehicles revolutionized the transportation of troops and supplies in 1914. For military and commercial purposes, France expanded its railway network in the pre-war period until it resembled a wagon wheel with its hub on Paris and its spokes extending from Paris to the various frontiers. Subsequent improvements connected the spokes so trains could move from one spoke to another without having to pass through the hub, thus enabling trains to run from eastern France to northern France without passing directly through Paris. After the introduction of the "horseless carriage," the French also improved their road network and added motor vehicles to their inventory. At the beginning of the war the French field armies had about 6,500 motor vehicles. Though horse-drawn wagons remained extremely important, automobiles and trucks provided transportation for commanders, units, and supplies. In 1914, however, it was the rapid shifting by railway of forces from eastern to northern France, as well as the "taxis of the Marne," that revealed the potential of the ongoing revolution in transportation.

As the French debated the effects of these important advances before 1914, most theorists foresaw highly mobile battles in which the offensive reigned supreme. Between 1918 and 1940 critics often chastised pre-1914 military writers and thinkers for focusing excessively on Napoleonic warfare and not paying sufficient attention to more recent wars. Some of these accusations are well-aimed because important military writers before 1914 did frequently publish articles and books on the Napoleonic era. Instructors at the army's schools preached the importance of maneuver and the offensive and often praised leaders in the Napoleonic period whose actions demonstrated aspects of maneuver and offensives favored by the instructors. Other theorists and historians, however, analyzed more recent wars such as the Boer War, the Russo-Japanese War of 1904–05, and various Balkan wars. Important journals such as *Revue d'infanterie* had only a small percentage of their articles in the decade before the war focusing on the Napoleonic era. Military journals published many more articles on the Franco-Prussian War of 1870–71 and on the Russo-Japanese War of 1905 than on the Napoleonic wars. In fact, they achieved much better balance than journals before 1940 which tended to focus primarily on World War I.

Other debates before 1914 occurred over the relationship between active and reserve forces and the means of obtaining the best possible performance from young conscripts and older reservists. The French had suffered an embarrassing defeat in 1870–71 against better-organized and more effective Prussian/German forces, and they took numerous steps between 1871 and 1914 to mobilize and employ the nation's citizens in a total war to annihilate the enemy. Politically, France was split between those who believed in the republican theory of the nation in arms (that is, all able-bodied males should serve in uniform long-enough to be trained and then be mobilized in an hour of need to defend their country) and those who believed France required a larger standing army (meaning longer service by conscripts) to defend against an *attaque brusquée* and provide a resilient structure around which the reserves could be mobilized. The debate became particularly heated in the wake of the Agadir crisis in 1911 and the Germans' expansion of the size of their standing army in 1912 and 1913. Joffre argued for three years' service; he believed an increase to three years would provide more experienced and capable small-unit leaders, ensure better training and cohesion, and increase readiness for the demands of first battles. Despite unrest in the barracks from young conscripts who faced another year of service, the French adopted three years' service for conscripts in July-August 1913 and thereby increased the size of the active army to 700,000 soldiers. Longer service thus ensured Joffre had a more capable force, able to execute the aggressive strategy and operations he foresaw. Careful planning also ensured mobilization in July 1914 went far more smoothly than the chaotic attempt of 1870.

The French army in 1914, nevertheless, had some severe shortcomings. Most notable among these was preparation for a long war.

Even though planners arranged a highly effective mobilization of personnel, they paid little attention to industrial mobilization or to economic requirements in something other than a short war. And their prewar assumptions about the consumption of munitions and material proved completely inadequate for the actual demands of trench warfare. Another especially severe shortcoming pertained to insufficient heavy artillery. Although the French increased the number of heavy artillery pieces slightly on the eve of the war, they entered the war with 120 75-mm cannon in a corps, while a German corps had 108 77-mm, 36 105mm, and 16 150-mm pieces. In essence, the French favored mobility over firepower. They had some heavy artillery they could concentrate along threatened portions of the front, but the Germans had a significant advantage in the range and destructive capability of their front-line artillery. As for casualties, the French recognized the new weapons could cause horrific casualties. They assured themselves losses would be less in a short war with a series of bloody battles than in a long drawn-out war, and they steeled themselves and their soldiers for heavy losses in a short, decisive war.

After a great deal of reflection and analysis, France prepared to fight mobile battles in August 1914. While such battles bore little resemblance to the static warfare that characterized most of the fighting during the next four years, preparation for bloody, mobile battles enabled the French army to respond successfully to the demands of the Marne campaign. Despite an excessive emphasis on the offensive, the French army fielded a surprisingly flexible and responsive force. They were prepared for and capable of doing far more in August–September 1914 than fixing bayonets and charging forward.

A period of great technological and institutional change also preceded the 1940 battle. Important advances in weaponry, mobility, and communications rivaled those of the pre-1914 era. As before 1914, the French studied these changes carefully and made changes in their weapons, doctrine, and strategy. Unlike 1914 they had recent combat experience in a victorious but costly war, and they had confidence in the technology and methods, as well as the weapons remaining in their arsenal, that had enabled them to gain that victory. They also remembered the costly failures of the recent war, especially those of 1914, and resolved not to repeat them. Even though the French expected a future war to be even more deadly than the recent one, the memory and remaining weapons of World War I shaped their preparation for a future war.

The terrible experience of 1914–18 had demonstrated that France had to mobilize all its people and resources if it were to defend itself successfully against as large and powerful a state as Germany. The length of service for conscripts again became an enormously important issue in the post-war period and the reductions from forty-one, to thirty-two, and then to twenty active divisions corresponded to reductions in terms of service to two years, eighteen months, and one year in 1921, 1923, and 1928. The government adopted a series of laws in 1927–28 that not only required one-year's service but also shaped the organization, mobilization, and deployment of the army in a crisis or in wartime. The laws established a complicated mobilization system that, in the event of a war, essentially dismantled the active army and re-assembled a new army of mixed active and reserve forces. As mobilization of the nation occurred in the opening days a war, France could not risk a limited engagement or launch an immediate offensive that would upset its complete mobilization. In reality, France had only a total war capability and no graduated deterrent. Even though the French returned to two years of service in March 1935, the system cost them dearly in the 1936 remilitarization of the Rhineland when Gamelin refused to send forces into the Rhineland without a complete mobilization. Charles de Gaulle was one of those who emerged as a critic of this system when he called for the formation of a professional armored force capable of an immediate offensive. The bulk of French political and military leaders nonetheless remained confident in their "army of reservists."

As in the years before 1914, the French devoted considerable resources and time to field the latest weapons and develop the best doctrine and strategy. These efforts consisted of much study of the methods and experiences of World War I, numerous field tests, and spirited debates in a talented, intelligent officer corps. The French also spent enormous sums building the Maginot Line. After the disaster of 1940, the Maginot Line became the symbol of the French failure to prepare adequately for war. Critics often forget, however, that the Maginot Line, though expensive, worked. They also forget that, had the line not been built, the money spent on fortifications probably would not have been spent on other national defense needs, such as increasing mobility or adding armored formations. The Maginot Line protected France's valuable resources and population in northeastern France and encouraged the Germans to go around the fortifications. What did not work was what the French attempted to do when the Germans went around the Maginot Line.

In organizing their forces and formulating their doctrine, the French valued firepower more than maneuver and expected newly mobilized soldiers to be "very excitable reservists." The 1936 field service regulations emphasized that firepower would be the "preponderant factor of combat," and the regulations repeated a sentence that had appeared in the 1921 edition: "The attack is the fire that advances, the defense is the fire that halts [the enemy]." Amassing and coordinating the necessary firepower, the French believed, could only be done through the *bataille conduite*, or the methodical or directed battle. Consequently, they sought a tightly controlled, step-by-step battle in which units and weapons were carefully marshaled and then employed in combat. Such methods did not place excessive demands on incompletely trained soldiers and represented an intensification of the methods of World War I.

To paint the French as blindly trying to fight World War I again, however, distorts what they tried to do from 1919-39 and what they did in 1940. The French experience with tanks illustrates their effort to field a modern force. Even though the French had some 4,000 tanks remaining from World War I, they conducted a series of special studies immediately after the war to ensure they were heading in the right direction with the tank. A special commission in 1921 examined the role of the tank, and another one in 1925 completed another analysis. Two new manuals on tank units appeared in 1929. In the early 1930s the French reassessed their tank program and conducted several field tests and special studies. From these came the B-1 tank, as well as the R-35, H-35, and F.C.M.-36 tanks, all of which replaced World War I tanks. Sharp debate and further study brought additional changes, including new manuals and the R-39 and H-39 tanks, to the overall tank program in the late 1930s. Beginning in 1932 the French considered constituting division-size armored forces, but they did not form their first armored division until January 1940 after they had enough modern tanks on hand to form a division and after the Germans had demonstrated in Poland the potential of such formations.

Meanwhile, the French made much greater progress in the development of tanks and mechanized formations for the cavalry. In the early 1930s, under the aggressive leadership of General Maxime Weygand, the French began development of the SOMUA S-35, probably the best tank on the battlefield in 1940. They also formed the first "light mechanized division" long before sufficient S-35 tanks were available to fill one. The light mechanized divisions, which were essentially mechanized cavalry divisions, escaped the constraints placed on armored divisions because they were designed to operate as a covering force in front of French forces advancing into Belgium; they had to be highly mobile and capable of operating independently. In the crucible of 1940 the light mechanized divisions proved more flexible, responsive, and capable than the armored divisions, but too few of them existed to affect the outcome of the 1940 campaign.

Despite energetic efforts before 1940 to analyze the employment and potential of tanks, the French made only modest progress toward the development of mobile, armored forces. By May 1940 the French had considerable experience with their separate tank battalions and light mechanized divisions but much less experience with their armored divisions. The newly-formed armored divisions proved unable to operate rapidly, powerfully, and effectively. Instead of organizing highly mobile reserves that could launch violent strikes against an unexpected enemy penetration or gain, the French emphasized *colmater*, or the assembling of forces around an enemy penetration and the slowing of the enemy's advance. The French had studied carefully the possibility of the Germans advancing through the Belgian Ardennes, and they had concluded they could concentrate additional forces in a threatened sector faster than the Germans could advance. This method may have worked in 1918, but it failed completely in May–June 1940. The Germans established the tempo of battle in 1940, not the French.

As in 1914 the French army in 1940 had some severe shortcomings. In essence, the French tied the tank and other technological advances (in areas such as aviation and communications) to their overall doctrine and resisted advances that could alter their doctrine or strategy. The newly-formed armored divisions were restrained by the doctrine of the methodical battle and incapable of fighting under more dynamic, unpredictable circumstances. And as they allocated their resources, the French provided few resources for equipment, such as radios, needed on a more mobile battlefield. The French spent only 0.15% of their defense budget between 1923 and 1939 on communications. Since many of these funds were spent on ensuring contact with the Maginot Line, there was relatively little spent on wireless radios for armored formations. Very few tanks had radios, and large units relied primarily on methods of communication (telephones, signal flags, liaison officers, etc.) that had been used in World War I. The French also did not value improvisation. Under the constraints of French doctrine, there was little room for creative thinking or responding to unexpected events. Tactical units were expected to adhere to timetables and move from phase line to phase line, not race ahead and risk upsetting the intricate actions of the methodical battle. After much reflection and analysis, the French were prepared to fight carefully controlled battles that bore little resemblance to the mobile warfare that characterized the 1940 campaign. Once again the French army had prepared for and tried to fight a different type of war than the one it encountered. This time, however, leaders did not have the mental flexibility and units did not have the adaptability to adjust to unexpected demands.

Despite significant advances in technology and capability, French aviation also failed to meet the German challenge in 1940. Still in its infancy in August 1914, the French had 140 aircraft organized into squadrons of five or six planes. These aircraft proved useful in the gathering of intelligence but not as useful in attacking targets. From the beginning Joffre sent aircraft and dirigibles into Belgium to ascertain what the Germans were doing. Reports from aerial observers on August 19 reinforced Joffre's erroneous belief that the Germans' main force was passing in front of his Third and Fourth armies and vulnerable to an attack in their rear. Reports from French and British aerial observers on September 1 proved more valuable; they revealed the Germans' turning east around Paris. Additional reports on subsequent days, especially from British aviators, suggested the Germans had left one corps east of Paris and moved three corps toward Château-Thierry on the Marne River. This information, along with intelligence gleaned from German radio traffic transmitted in the clear, proved vital in Joffre's shaping of the Marne battle.

Between 1914 and 1940 numerous advances occurred in aerial warfare, thereby enabling aircraft to play a much more active role in the 1940 campaign. During the Great War, France manufactured more than 52,000 aircraft, a number significantly higher than Germany's 48,000 and Great Britain's 43,000. At the end of the war France had 247 air squadrons with 3,222 aircraft. The wartime experience and production, however, did not give France an advantage in 1940. In the late 1930s, especially during the Munich crisis of 1938, France became very concerned about the adequacy of its air force. After spending huge sums, the French made some improvements in their air fleet, but in 1940 the Germans had advantages in numbers and performance. More importantly, the Germans concentrated their aircraft in 1940 at critical times and places while the French spread their aerial resources across the entire frontier.

At the beginning of the campaign, Gamelin sent few bombers into German air space because he was fearful of German reprisals against French cities near the Franco-German border. As in 1914, he sent aircraft into Belgium to determine what the enemy was doing, but the intelligence gathered through aerial flights did not prove as important as it did in 1914. An opportunity to change the entire campaign occurred when a French plane circled above Germans from the XIXth Panzer Corps gathering at Martelange, Belgium, on the first day of the attack. After shooting down a German plane circling above the troops, the French pilot circled but did not see any tanks. His subsequent report reinforced the idea in French headquarters that the Germans were sending light troops through the Ardennes, not a powerful armored force. When the Germans reached the Meuse and began their river crossing on May 13, the Luftwaffe played a key role in weakening French defenses and encountered little opposition from French aircraft or air defense weapons. Only one anti-aircraft battalion was in the Sedan region, and it reported shooting down one German plane. Even though the continuous attacks by German planes from around 1000 to 1700 hours on May 13 did not seriously damage French forces, the attacks significantly eroded the soldiers' will-to-fight and contributed to the later panic of the 55th Division. The French initially held a substantial number of their best aircraft out of the battle around Sedan and concentrated them too late to make a difference. On the morning of May 14, French and British bombers belatedly concentrated over Sedan but failed to destroy German bridges across the Meuse. Despite this desperate effort, Allied air forces did not significantly delay or disrupt the Germans' crossing of the Meuse.

An explanation for the poor performance of French and allied aviation around Sedan can be found in superior German aircraft, but a better explanation comes from French failures in perception and execution. Much like the French pilot circling over German armored forces punching through the Ardennes on May 10, the French did not recognize what was happening in May 1940 until it was too late. To the soldiers along the Meuse, the Germans seemed to have almost complete control of the airspace over their heads, and the small number of French aircraft challenging the Germans seemed to suggest how little the High Command cared about them. The Germans did not give French air force leaders the luxury of leisurely collecting their assets from across the Franco-German frontier and employing them in the Sedan region. In essence, the Germans used airpower far more effectively than the French.

Joffre and Gamelin bear much of the responsibility for the poor preparation of French forces for the 1914 and 1940 campaigns. More so than any other individual, including Louis Loyzeaux de Grandmaison, Joffre was responsible for the failures in 1914. After he became Chief of the General Staff in 1911, he opened the way for the *offensive à outrance* to dominate the thought and actions of the army, failed to demand more heavy artillery, and favored preparation for a short, rather than long, war. He also made egregious mistakes in the first battles by ignoring intelligence reports suggesting the Germans were doing something other than what he expected. His ill-fated and costly attacks into Alsace and Lorraine drained the French army of many of its finest soldiers and brought France to the edge of defeat.

Gamelin also did not distinguish himself. From 1931 to 1935 he served as the vice president of the Superior Council of War (and thus the designated generalissimo of the French army), and from 1935 until the war he held this position plus that of Chief of the General Staff. Even though he served longer than Joffre as the head of the French army, he exerted less influence over the formulation of doctrine and the shaping of the French army than Joffre. At the Riom Trials after the defeat of France, the Vichy government blamed Gamelin for many of the army's matériel and operational shortcomings. He scribbled on his copy of the formal charges brought against him, "The title is one thing. The power is another." In the post-1940 era of finger-pointing, he energetically defended his role and accomplishments before the war and placed much of the blame for the defeat on the ideas of Marshal Philippe Pétain, particularly those placing emphasis on the defensive. Yet, he did little himself before 1940 to bring emphasis on the offensive to the forefront of the army. By his very nature he was one who sought compromise, not confrontation; he had a knack for telling his listeners whatever they wanted to hear. His efforts emphasized the role of the commander, not the offensive, and his view of the commander as the director of a tightly controlled operation fit perfectly with the methodical battle. Though he supported mechanization more than most French officers, he offered only lukewarm support, and he never attempted a transformation of the French army, such as that attempted by Joffre. Unlike Joffre, his failures were errors of omission, not commission.

Joffre proved himself more capable than Gamelin of rising to the challenge of commanding an army in battle. Unlike Moltke, who eventually broke under the strain, Joffre maintained his composure under the direst circumstances. Even the failure of his offensives and the recognition of the actual German maneuver did not crush his spirit. Additionally, he was one of the few officers who had worked with and understood railway units, and his being the commander of French forces in August–September 1914 ensured the French took advantage of the spiderweb-like transportation network and were able to shift large numbers of troops from the French right to the left. Joffre also learned from his mistakes. After misinterpreting intelligence in the first battles, he believed reports of the Germans' having moved east of Paris and responded appropriately. Ironically, the highly mobile forces that Joffre had developed and pushed forward in bloody but useless attacks in Alsace and Lorraine proved ideal for transporting over great distances at a crucial moment in the 1914 campaign.

Joffre also maintained contact with his subordinate commanders and never lost control of them. An engineer by training, he had the temperament and confidence that only the best commanders have. As French forces fell back on their lines of communication, he made excellent use of personal visits and the telephone and telegraph. While blaming the failures on everyone but himself, Joffre accelerated the relief and replacement of key commanders and thereby molded his subordinates into a much more cohesive and effective group. One of his key changes involved the movement of General Ferdinand Foch from commander of XX Corps to command of a hastily assembled "detachment," soon to be renamed the Ninth Army, with the mission of closing the gap between Fourth and Fifth armies. Foch played an extremely important role in halting the German advance and returning the French to the offensive. He performed superbly even though he suffered the loss of his son and his son-in-law in the August fighting. Another important change concerned Franchet d'Espèrey who advanced from the command of a corps, which had performed superbly on the Sambre River, to command of Fifth Army. At a key moment in the Marne campaign, Franchet d'Espèrey not only revived the fighting spirit of Fifth Army but also arranged for British participation in the resumption of the offensive. Joffre paid him the highest praise when he said, "It is he who made the battle of the Marne possible." By September 9, Joffre had shaped his subordinate commanders into a highly responsive and capable group, and by September 12 he had demonstrated that his generalship was superior to that of Moltke.

In 1940 Gamelin had neither the capability nor the opportunity that Joffre had. The quintessential staff officer who seemed more comfortable offering advice than giving orders, he was more intelligent than Joffre, but he lacked his resolve and composure. He also lacked the firm grip Joffre kept on the throats of his subordinate commanders. In December 1939 Gamelin split his headquarters into three components, one being his personal headquarters at the Château de Vincennes, another being his larger headquarters at La Ferté-sous-Jouarre, and the third being the headquarters of General Alphonse Georges who commanded the northeastern front. Along with the splitting of headquarters came confusion about the splitting of responsibility for planning and conducting operations, and staff officers found themselves constantly on the road to confer with their counterparts at one of the other headquarters. At his personal headquarters Gamelin relied on telephone, telegraph, and messengers for information, not personal visits. Much like Moltke in 1914, he was cocooned in his personal headquarters and shielded from the desperation that flooded and overwhelmed French units in May 1940. Unlike Joffre's famous meeting with Sir John French or his notorious relief of General Charles Lanrezac, commander of Fifth Army, Gamelin had few opportunities—once the German attack began—to exercise his power and personal influence over his subordinates, and he evinced no fiery spirit such as that showed occasionally by Joffre. Even though Joffre lacked charisma, the contrast in command styles is decidedly in his favor.

Like Joffre, Gamelin erred in his initial operational efforts. A onetime executive officer for Joffre and supposed heir, Gamelin apparently attempted to replicate aspects of the battle of Marne by rushing his mobile reserves toward Breda in The Netherlands in an attempt to fall on the German rear. The "Breda Variant," however, proved futile since the Germans sent their main forces through the Belgian Ardennes, not through Liège, Namur, and Maubeuge. More importantly, the Breda maneuver squandered France's reserves and left Gamelin with too few forces to halt the German breakthrough on the Meuse. Unlike Joffre, Gamelin did not have the time to correct his mistakes. French political leaders replaced him on May 20 with the charismatic but eventually unsuccessful General Maxime Weygand.

Other French leaders also made significant mistakes in 1940. General Charles Huntziger, who commanded Second Army in the Sedan area, refused to acknowledge inadequate preparation along the Meuse River and dismissed calls for improvement. He also foresaw a German attack, if it came, hitting his right at Carignan and Mouzon, not at Sedan, where Guderian's XIXth Panzer Corps struck. Before the battle Huntziger had a fine reputation and reputedly had the potential to rise to the top of the French army. Below him, General Charles Grandsard, who commanded Xth Corps, demonstrated little energy and proved unwilling to move forward and reestablish control over the rapidly deteriorating situation along the Meuse River. Even worse, General Henri-Jean Lafontaine failed to prepare the 55th Division for the fluid battle of 1940 and, at a crucial moment in the campaign, was overwhelmed by events. Lafontaine's failures deserve special emphasis because they contributed so much to the French collapse. In particular, his mindless rotating of individual companies into and out of different defensive positions along the Meuse in the months before the battle resulted in the soldiers not knowing the units on their flanks and rear and in their having little confidence in their commanders.

The French had an opportunity to change the tempo, if not the success, of the German XIXth Panzer Corps south of Sedan, but poor leadership and the friction of war prevented them from doing so. On the night of May 13–14, when the Germans were still fighting to establish a bridgehead across the Meuse, the French ordered the XXIst Corps under General Jean Flavigny to move to the heights of Mont Dieu-Stonne and then counterattack toward Sedan. The XXIst Corps included the newly formed 3rd Armored Division, the 3rd Motorized Infantry Division, and the 5th Light Cavalry Division. With approximately 280 modern tanks the corps had the opportunity to strike Guderian's corps on the 14th or 15th when it was attempting to pivot west. Success seemed possible because the corps was commanded by the hard-nosed, chain-smoking Flavigny, France's Guderian or Patton. As the main proponent of a mechanized cavalry division and an important contributor to the design of the SOMUA S-35, Flavigny had commanded the first light mechanized division and knew as much or more about armored operations than anyone else in France. Yet, because of inexperienced subordinate commanders, poorly trained troops, and inadequate logistical support, he failed to make the counterattack. Instead of leading from the front, as did Guderian, he remained in the rear and placed the counterattack and the armored division under the command of the motorized division commander. The counterattack degenerated into a series of bloody fights along the heights of Mont

Dieu-Stonne. In the litany of missed opportunities, none was more important than this failure.

The different qualities of leaders on the Marne and the Meuse rivers stem from the contrasting doctrines of 1914 and 1940. In 1914 French officers were steeped in the ideas of the *offensive à outrance*. Ironically, the operational and tactical ideas that yielded such bloody results in 1914 also yielded an officer corps capable of meeting the demands inherent in the Marne victory. The commission that wrote the October 1913 version of the regulations on the operations of large units (corps, army, and army group) observed, "The French army, returning to its traditions, accepts no law in the conduct of operations other than the offensive." The regulations emphasized, "Only the offensive yields positive results." Battles were viewed as moral contests, not clashes of matériel. The regulations stated, "Defeat is inevitable when hope for victory ceases. Success will come, not to the one who has suffered the least losses, but to the one whose will is the steadiest and whose morale is the most highly tempered." A regulation on the operations of smaller units (regiment, brigade, and division) preached, "Once begun, combat is pushed to the end; success depends more on the vigor and the tenacity of execution than on the skill of combined actions. All units thus are employed with the most extreme energy." The practical effect of this was to produce an officer corps steeled to expect losses and press on under the worst circumstances. In the initial battles of 1914, commanders often led their troops into combat and died in front of them. Casualties among junior officers were especially heavy, since many of them refused to seek cover when they came under fire. All too often they wasted the lives and limbs of their soldiers with romantic but senseless charges against strong enemy defenses. They refused, however, to acknowledge defeat.

As the French offensives on August 14 and 21 ground to a halt and were thrown back, Joffre and his subordinate commanders realized that throwing dense masses of troops in attacks without adequate artillery support did not work against defensive positions anchored on machine guns and artillery. As the focus of operations shifted to Joffre's left flank and as the German main attack drove toward Guise, St. Quentin, Amiens, and Paris, the French made some adjustments, but local offensives and counter-offensives continued. Soldiers rushed into battle by taxis from Paris suffered heavily, much as those who had fought in Alsace and Lorraine. By September 9, German bullets and artillery had removed much of the sharp edge of the French army, but the officer corps as a whole continued to value initiative and aggressiveness above all other qualities. Foch's famous comment that he supposedly uttered during the campaign aptly demonstrates this attitude: "My center is giving way, my right is withdrawing. Situation excellent, I attack." It would take bloody battles in places such as Notre-Dame de Lorette, Verdun, and the Chemin des Dames to bring caution and centralized control to the forefront.

In 1940 the French remembered the heavy losses and excesses of 1914, and they placed the greatest emphasis on massing and coordinating firepower on the modern battlefield. Instead of mobility, they favored "curtains" of fire coordinated and delivered through commanders maintaining tight control over the battle. They considered mobility primarily in terms of applying firepower, and they rejected the aggressiveness, as well as the foolhardiness, of the methods of 1914. French doctrine and training in 1940 encouraged commanders to remain in their command posts, be constantly updated on events in the ongoing battle, and make decisions about the movement and commitment of units and supplies. By keeping their hands on the "handle of a fan," rather than on a rifle stock, and by managing units and resources, commanders could ensure the entire operation proceeded smoothly and efficiently.

Such an approach discouraged commanders from leaving their command posts and making personal assessments of combat actions or going forward to inspire soldiers to do more. On the evening of May 13, Lafontaine, commander of the 55th Division at Sedan, was fulfilling this role completely until soldiers began fleeing past his headquarters toward the rear. Lafontaine initially blocked the road with two trucks and, with a pistol in his hand, tried to turn back the fleeing soldiers. Not long thereafter, however, he moved his headquarters to the southwest, thereby contributing further to soldiers' believing they were being abandoned. To make matters worse, soldiers in Lafontaine's headquarters misunderstood the reason for his moving the command post and, fearing the Germans were about to arrive, destroyed communications equipment and code books. This destruction crippled Lafontaine's communication with and control over his division. At the new location of his headquarters, Lafontaine stood dejectedly in the road and encouraged units to move faster toward the south. Rarely has the absence of inspirational leadership been so apparent.

The disintegration of the 55th Division, as well as others, convinced many observers and historians that the *poilus* of 1940 did not have the courage, fortitude, and discipline that their fathers had evinced in 1914. After all, some have argued, many of the young men in 1940 had been raised without their fathers and without constant reminders of the loss of Alsace-Lorraine and the importance of *revanche*. Instead, they had been immersed in self-pity and remorse for the losses suffered in 1914–18 and dreaded the prospect of another bloody war. This immersion, critics have argued, did not enhance the cohesion and effectiveness of units along the Meuse.

While such an argument has some merit, one cannot overlook the poor training received by French soldiers in 1940. Many of the soldiers around Sedan had served in the navy or air force during their active duty and knew little about their soldierly duties. Others had served their time in the army years before and were barely familiar with their basic weapons such as rifles, machine guns and grenades. Even though the French had from September 1939 until May 1940 to prepare, units along the Meuse spent far more time building bunkers, stretching barbed wire, and digging entrenchments than in conducting tough, realistic training. To make matters worse, many of the men who occupied defensive positions along the Meuse entered their bunkers on May 10, the day the Germans unleashed their offensive and began marching across Luxembourg and Belgium. For the next several days, the nervous, green soldiers remained in their bunkers, often without seeing their commanders and receiving little information about events. Not until May 12, when the Germans reached the Meuse, did they know what was happening. As they watched bedraggled, disorganized French troops returning from the Ardennes and crossing over the Meuse, their will to fight melted away. Beginning on the afternoon of May 13, amidst much aerial bombardment, some soldiers from the 55th Division around Sedan began fleeing, and a wholesale panic occurred around 1800 hours. While one could blame this failure on the low expectations the French had of soldiers within the framework of the methodical battle, the failure also come from poor leadership. The soldiers of 1940 may have lacked the same spirit of sacrifice as those of 1914, but they also lacked combative, inspirational, competent leaders.

Despite these failures, some units and soldiers acquitted themselves quite well in 1940, especially after the shock of the first contact with the Germans. Most notably, the 3rd Spahis Brigade, which was composed of Moroccan and Algerian regiments and had performed poorly in the Ardennes, performed superbly at La Horgne. More than half of the brigade's soldiers who fought at La Horgne died there, including twelve of the thirty-seven officers and the commander of one of the regiments and his successor. Similar fighting occurred at Chagny, south of La Horgne. Here a hodgepodge of units threw back the tanks of the 1st Panzer Division. Without reinforcements or depth, however, the valorous resistance eventually succumbed to attacks, and the route west to Abbeville was opened for the Germans. The *Strange Defeat* approached.

In comparison to 1940, the soldiers of 1914 seem a well-disciplined force. There nonetheless were some problems. Some units broke down after suffering heavy losses in the bloody attacks in Alsace and Lorraine. As the French withdrew in the face of German pressure, a few soldiers pillaged villages and terrified civilians. Most French soldiers nonetheless maintained their discipline and most units kept their cohesion. They did this even though they had suffered heavy losses, remained under constant bombardment and pursuit, and marched and countermarched over great distances. Some of this resilience came from soldiers' hearing rumors of the Germans having slaughtered defenseless civilians and burned villages. And some of it came from soldiers' seeing for themselves the misery unleashed by the German invasion. The increase in service from two to three years on the eve of the war also may have reinforced discipline and cohesion. Whatever the reason, French soldiers as a whole did not panic or desert in 1914; instead, they did an about-face and attacked. In many ways, this was the greatest miracle of the entire campaign.

The French placed the National Monument to the First Battle of the Marne at Mondement, one hundred kilometers east of Paris near Sézanne. Some of the bitterest fighting of the battle occurred here where infantry under Foch's hastily cobbled-together Ninth Army held in the face of strong German pressure. Though the monument was completed in 1938, the outbreak of another world war interrupted its dedication in September 1939, and the formal dedication did not occur until September 1951. The unusual monument resembles a Breton menhir, a large upright standing stone akin to those of Stonehenge, suggesting the important role played at Mondement by the Breton 77th Infantry Regiment. The monument is 35.5 meters high and is composed of pink concrete reinforced by an internal metal frame. At its top Winged Victory flies west to east through lightning bolts and storms. At its base the monument has bas-relief images of Joffre and the seven general officers, including Sir John French, who commanded field armies during the battle. In the center, larger than the other images,

Joffre stands with his left arm around the shoulder of a French *poilu*. The message, of course, is that the field army commanders played important roles, but Joffre and the individual French soldier played the most important roles.

The monuments and memorials around Sedan differ dramatically from the one at Mondement. In the village of Stonne, which is south of Sedan and the scene of heavy fighting in late May 1940, the French have a memorial that consists primarily of a B-1 BIS tank and an anti-tank gun. Veterans' associations have placed numerous plaques and memorials along the road to the west, where the French 3rd Armored and 3rd Motorized Infantry divisions fought tenaciously to keep the Germans from driving south. At the time of the fighting, the French did not realize they were playing into the hands of the Germans by attempting to hold this line of hills instead of attacking into the vulnerable flank of the German XIXth Panzer Corps. A more extensive memorialization occurred in 1990 on the occasion of the 50th anniversary of the battle. In this case the French chose to hold their ceremony at La Horgne, where the 3rd Spahis Brigade fought one of the most valiant engagements of the entire campaign. Without any knowledge of their purpose, one could view the monuments at Mondement and near Sedan and recognize that one celebrates victory and the other emphasizes sacrifice.

Neither the victory nor the sacrifice was pre-ordained, nor were they the product of bad luck or German invincibility. The French organized their forces, developed their doctrine, and formulated their strategy based on their visions of the future battles. And then they fought the battles within the constraints of pre-war preparation and opportunities (or the lack of opportunities) inherent in the actual flow of events. In both cases, French pre-war expectations and preparation proved wrong or faulty. Yet, in 1914 the diversion of German troops to East Prussia and Joffre's ability to "see" the actions and locations of German forces as they turned to the east of Paris gave the French a better chance of success. In contrast to the Meuse campaign, the French could adjust in 1914 to the unexpected, units could react quickly despite heavy losses, and Joffre was able to seize the opportunity when it appeared. Gamelin had no similar opportunity since the Germans maintained the initiative and French forces had precious little flexibility. In the end, sacrifice in 1940 could not compensate for numerous mistakes or failures prior to and during the battle. The French could respond to the unexpected in 1914; they could not in 1940.

THE FORGOTTEN CAMPAIGN: ALSACE-LORRAINE AUGUST 1914[1]

Holger H. Herwig

"Nine days after completing its concentration and after continuous victorious battles, the German army in the West has penetrated French territory from Cambrai to the South Vosges. The enemy has been defeated everywhere and is in full retreat."[2] This communiqué of 27 August 1914 accurately summarized the view of the Army Supreme Command (Oberste Heeres-Leitung, or OHL) at Koblenz. But it stood in stark contrast to the events on the German left wing during the Battle of the Frontiers, officially ended three days earlier. A series of brutal engagements in Alsace and Lorraine, planned by neither side before the war, had left both armies severely battered. What had led to this development on a flank that had no pride of place in either side's deployment plan?

In July 1911 Joseph Joffre was appointed Chief of the French General Staff. Six months later, he and his closest advisers, Édouard de Castelnau and Yvon Dubail—ironically, the commanders of the two French armies in Alsace-Lorraine in August 1914—had arrived at the basic design for a future war with Germany. They unveiled that design at a critical meeting of the Conseil Supérieur de la Défense Nationale on 9 January 1912. While it lacked specifics, the concept nevertheless was forthright in its thrust: "to seize the offensive and to take the war into enemy territory."[3] President Raymond Poincaré was delighted. Joffre had expertly abandoned past "defensive" contingency war planning, which had always constituted an "admission of inferiority," in favor of

---

[1] I first presented this research at a session of the Society for Military History's annual convention at Ogden, Utah, in April 2008, and profited much by Dennis Showalter's commentary.

[2] Germany, Reichsarchiv, *Der Weltkrieg-1914–1918. Die militärischen Operationen zu Lande* (Berlin: E. S. Mittler, 1925–56), vol. 4, p. 508. Hereafter cited as WK.

[3] Note de présentation, 9 January 1912. Conseil Supérieur de la Défense Nationale, 2N1, VI/36, Service Historique de la Défense (hereafter SHD), Vincennes, France. I am indebted to Dr. Stephanie Cousineau for research she conducted for me at Vincennes.

a "resolute offensive." The latter was more in tune "with the character of our soldiers," Poincaré crowed, and was designed "to bring us victory."[4]

More specifically with regard to this presentation, one month later Joffre advised Poincaré and other senior members of the Cabinet that he favored operations against the Germans in Luxembourg and Belgium, and that Alsace and Lorraine could only remain "theaters for secondary and limited operations."[5] The great German fortress belt Molsheim-Straβburg (Strasbourg)[6] barred a rapid advance through Alsace, while another massive enemy fortress system at Metz-Diedenhofen (Thionville) likewise made a quick march through Lorraine and into the heart of Germany unlikely. "Neither in Alsace nor in Lorraine," Joffre informed the ministers at a secret meeting at the Foreign Ministry on 21 February 1912, "will we find terrain suitable for a decisive offensive."[7] But Poincaré adamantly refused to have France be first in violating Belgian neutrality.

Joffre, Castelnau and Dubail thereafter fine-tuned their operational planning. The final product, the *Plan de renseignements* of 1914, popularly called Plan XVII, placed the bulk of French forces along a line Paris-Metz, from where five armies were to advance northeast against the Germans.[8] Joffre firmly believed that the enemy would simply "hold" (*durer*) in Alsace-Lorraine while its main forces would wheel through central Belgium (and perhaps the Netherlands). Thus, he planned two powerful attacks, one north of the line Verdun-Metz, and the other between Metz and the Vosges Mountains. General Dubail's First Army was to advance north from Baccarat toward Saarburg (Sarrebourg), and General de Castelnau's Second Army northeast from Nancy toward Saarbrücken. Their objective was to tie down German defenders and to prevent the adversary from shunting them to the decisive right wing in Belgium. Hence, when Dubail later requested

---

[4] Procès-verbal, 9 January 1912. Ibid., 2N1, VI/38.
[5] Description sommaire du théatre du Nord-Est de part et d'autre des frontiers. Ibid., 7N1784.
[6] All place names in Alsace and German Lorraine are given according to their 1914 designations, with the French equivalents in parentheses on first mention.
[7] Minute, Conférence tenue au Ministère des Affaires Étrangèr, 21 February 1912. SHD, 2N1, VI/39.
[8] For Plan XVII, see *Les armées françaises dans la grande guerre* (Paris: Imprimerie nationale 1922–37), vol. 1, pp. 53ff, 77ff; and vol. 1–1, pp. 21–35. Hereafter cited as AFGG. Also, Robert Doughty, "French Strategy in 1914: Joffre's Own," *Journal of Military History* 67 (April 2003): 427–54.

additional forces for a major offensive in Alsace, Joffre curtly cut him off: "That's your plan, not mine."[9]

Alfred von Schlieffen similarly had planned merely to tie down French forces in Alsace-Lorraine and to prevent them from being removed to the critical front in Belgium. Two weak armies of five corps, or 15 percent of the invading force, along with the promised Italian Third Army (two cavalry divisions at Straßburg and three army corps south of there along the Rhine River), were to anchor the German left wing on the Upper Rhine and west to Verdun. Depending on the pace of the fighting in the South, Schlieffen was prepared to detach two army corps from Lorraine and to rush them north to reinforce the right wing (which would then constitute 91 percent of German forces).[10] But his successor, Helmuth von Moltke, the Younger, grew concerned about concentrating seven-eighths of the army on the right wing: the renewed "offensive spirit" of the French army ruled out a purely defensive posture in Alsace-Lorraine, and the vital industries of the Saar could not be left unprotected. Accordingly, in one of his first Deployment Plans (*Aufmarsch 1908/09*), Moltke assigned an entire army corps to protect Upper Alsace. In the *Aufmarsch 1913/14* he increased the left flank, apart from Italian Third Army, to seven corps: Seventh Army was to secure Alsace and the Rhine, and Sixth Army was to hold southern Lorraine.[11] The relative strength of the German right wing in Belgium and Luxembourg now shifted from Schlieffen's 7:1 to a mere 3:1. The Younger Moltke would have done well to remember his Great Uncle's sage counsel that "a single error in the original assembly of the armies can hardly ever be rectified during the entire course of the campaign."[12]

Crown Prince Rupprecht of Bavaria and his chief of staff, Major-General Konrad Krafft von Dellmensingen, received specific orders for the deployment in the West (*Westaufmarsch*) from Moltke on 2 August 1914. They were clear. "*The main forces of the German army* are to advance via Belgium and Luxembourg into France. Their advance ... is

---

[9] Charles Lanrezac, *Le plan de campagne français et le premier mois de la guerre (2 août-3 septembre 1914)* (Paris: Payot, 1921), pp. 60–61.
[10] See *Aufmarsch 1905/06* in *Der Schlieffenplan. Analysen und Dokumente* ed. Hans Ehlert, Michael Epkenhans and Gerhard P. Groß (Paderborn: Fredinand Schöningh, 2006), pp. 394–99.
[11] Plans in ibid., pp. 430, 474, and WK, vol. 1, p. 62.
[12] "Taktische Aufsätze aus den Jahren 1857 bis 1871," in *Moltke's Militärische Werke*, ed. Großer Generalstab (Berlin: E. S. Mittler, 1900), vol. 2/2, p. 291.

to be seen as a wheeling movement with its pivot point anchored securely by Fifth Army at Diedenhofen-Metz." Sixth Army and Seventh Army southeast of Metz "are to protect the left flank of the army's main forces." Just to make sure that the Bavarians understood their role in the upcoming campaign, Moltke and his staff underlined the section of the document outlining Rupprecht's specific orders for Sixth and Seventh armies:

> It is the task of the common supreme commander to advance against the Mosel below Frouard and [against] the Meurthe—while storming Fort Manonviller—in order to tie down the combined French forces there and to prevent their transport to the French army's left wing.[13]

Krafft von Dellmensingen fully understood his assignment. He at once committed his operational design for Sixth and Seventh armies to paper—and to Moltke. In light of the bitter controversy that would later rage as to who was responsible for the campaign on the left flank of the German army, it is worth citing at some length:

> We must under all circumstances keep in mind that the group [of armies] in [Alsace-Lorraine] charged with protecting the army's flank have been given the duty at all cost to accord the decisive [right] wing the time (a[nd] the opportunity to deliver its blows). ... All other considerations must be subordinated to this purpose. Under no circumstances can the Army Group allow itself to be defeated; it is the shield that the O.H.L. holds up to protect its left flank.[14]

To put it simply, Sixth and Seventh armies were to stand on the defensive in the South and to engage enemy forces only sufficiently aggressively to keep them in theater.

With the possible exception of the Palatinate, no area of the historic wars between France and Germany so agitated the public as Alsace and Lorraine. Under Louis XIV, in the words of the Elder Helmuth von Moltke, they "were severed like a sound limb from the living body of Germany."[15] That same Moltke brought the "old Reichsland" back into Germany in 1871. But in the bickering leading up to the Treaty of Frankfurt (1871), the Germans committed two errors that were to

---

[13] Armee Ober-Kommando (hereafter AOK) 6, 369. Bayerisches Hauptstaatsarchiv, IV, Kriegsarchiv (hereafter BHStA-KA), Munich, Germany. Italics in the original.
[14] Beurteilung der Lage u. Aufgaben über die ersten Operationen der 6. und 7. Armee. Nachlaß Krafft von Dellmensingen 145, BHStA-KA.
[15] Cited in Otto Pflanze, *Bismarck and the Development of Germany* (Princeton: Princeton University Press, 1990), vol. 1, p. 487.

impact the course of events in 1914: Belfort remained with France (in exchange for a German victory parade through Paris), and the new border was drawn along the crest of the Vosges rather than further west at the eastern edge of the Lorraine plateau. Belfort in 1914 anchored the French extreme right flank; the Vosges crests secured the passes through the mountains.

The Younger Moltke's deployment orders for his left wing of 2 August 1914 were a dead letter before the Bavarians ever arrived in Alsace. Friction and interaction dominated the opening moves of the battle. The French were first out of the gate. Joffre hoped to arouse the nation by an early *coup de théâtre*. At 5 a.m. on 7 August Général de division Louis Bonneau led VII Corps (14th and 41st Divisions) out of the Belfort Gap against Altkirch and Thann in the Sundgau region of Alsace. The infantry was conspicuous in their bright blue jackets, shining red trousers and képi, led by officers in white gloves clutching drawn swords. Louis Aubier's flanking 8th Cavalry Division was resplendent in dark blue jackets, red breeches with blue seams, and brass helmets streaming long back plumes.[16] Cadets from the Saint-Cyr Military Academy deployed in full dress uniforms with white plumed capes. In a spirited bayonet charge, they drove the small German garrison out of Altkirch. Bonneau sent news of the victory to Paris, where it evoked wild celebrations. Joffre, displeased by Bonneau's theatrics and the slow pace of his follow-up advance, ordered VII Corps to move at once against Mülhausen (Mulhouse). The city fell virtually unopposed the next day. Joffre hailed the soldiers of VII Corps as "pioneers in the great work of revenge."[17]

How would the enemy react? Generaloberst Josias von Heeringen, commanding Seventh Army (125,000 soldiers), at once spied a chance at a "small Cannae."[18] He halted his army's deployment between Metz and Straßburg, and, with the blessing of the OHL, ordered Ernst von Hoiningen-Huene's XIV Corps and Bertold von Deimling's XV Corps

---

[16] Anthony Clayton, *Paths of Glory: The French Army 1914-18* (London: Cassell, 2003), p. 20.

[17] Cited in Michael S. Neiberg, *Fighting the Great War: A Global History* (Cambridge, MA: Harvard University Press, 2005), p. 22, and see also Joseph Joffre, *Mémoires du maréchal Joffre (1910-1917)* (Paris: Plon, 1932), vol. 1, pp. 247-48.

[18] In 216 BC Carthaginian forces under Hannibal encircled a superior Roman army near the town of Cannae in Apulia in one of the greatest tactical feats in military history. It was Schlieffen's model for the planned encirclement of French forces in a future war.

to head south into the Sundgau, and there to sweep around the left wing of Bonneau's VII Corps and to encircle and crush it at Mülhausen. The advance, on foot for XV Corps, disintegrated into a series of bloody frontal assaults under a blazing 40-degree Celsius sun.[19] The fighting in heavily wooded and vineyard studded terrain was bitter and often at close quarters. Heat, exhaustion and thirst took their toll. Men dropped off in roadside ditches. Others had to be carried forward on trucks and carts. Field kitchens fell behind. By nightfall, vicious street fighting ensued in the small Alsatian villages. Confusion reigned at battalion and regimental levels; orders were ignored or not received.

Heeringen's extra tour was a failure. Seventh Army had taken a mere 300 prisoners and captured but three heavy guns. It had failed to score its "small Cannae." Enemy forces, with their left flank hard up against the protective slopes of the Vosges Mountains, could not be enveloped. French VII Corps, now commanded by Frédéric Vautier, retreated to Belfort. The detour cost Seventh Army a week in which it had to recuperate, reorganize and resume its original deployment plan. Dynastic bitterness for the first, but certainly not the last, time raised its ugly head in the Reichsland: Heeringen gave a "cold shoulder" to Rupprecht's entreaties for Seventh Army to hasten its reorganization and to link forces with Sixth Army; the proud Prussian was not about to bow to the wishes of a commander twenty years his junior, and a Bavarian to boot.[20]

Ominously, numerous commanders reported that their men had been fired on by civilians. The nightmarish specter of 1870 had raised its ugly head: *francs-tireurs*! Reaction was swift. A General Corps Order of 11 August stated: "Soldiers or civilians offering even the least resistance are to be shot at once." At Baldersheim, *francs-tireurs* operating out of houses flying the Red Cross flag were hanged.[21] At Didenheim and Niedermorschweier (Niedermorschwihr), Germans took mayors and priests hostage.[22] *Franktireure* were "to be killed at once, naturally in self-defense." Residents of the Reichsland who operated as

---

[19] WK, vol. 1, pp. 159–68.

[20] Diary entry, 11 August 1914. Major Rudolf von Xylander, staff of Sixth Army, at Heeringen's headquarters. Rudolf von Xylander, *Deutsche Führung in Lothringen 1914. Wahrheit und Kriegsgeschichte* (Berlin: Junker und Dünnhaupt, 1935), p. 34.

[21] Entry for 12 August, 1914. 456 F43 KTB des Inf. Regt. 170, Nr. 345. Generallandesarchiv (hereafter GLA), Karlsruhe, Germany.

[22] Entries for 11 and 12 August 1914. 456 F43 KTB des Inf. Regt. 170, Nr. 317; ibid.

francs-tireurs were to be summarily executed; those merely suspected of such actions handed over to courts-martial.[23] The war in the West turned ugly in its first week.

The Battle of Mülhausen had been fought for the wrong reason and at the wrong place. Joffre's General Instruction No. 1 of 8 August had made clear that he just wanted to "jab" in Alsace, to "fix" the German left wing, and if possible to draw enemy units to the South while he delivered the main blow against the German center via a two-pronged offensive on each side of the Metz-Diedenhofen defenses.[24] His German counterpart, Moltke, likewise had instructed the commanders on his left flank to "attract and to tie down" as many French forces "as possible" in the area between the Upper Moselle and Meurthe rivers to prevent the French from transporting them to their left wing, where the main German attack would be delivered. Beyond that, they were to secure Alsace and Baden against invasion.[25]

But, as Carl von Clausewitz had made clear in *Vom Kriege*, "war is the realm of uncertainty." A host of "intangibles" such as interaction, friction, moral factors, and the "fog of uncertainty" at all times interacted with what he called "primordial violence" or "slaughter" and the "passions of the people" to prolong war, to escalate conflict, and to bedevil the best laid plans of staff officers.[26] Thus it was with regard to Alsace and Lorraine in 1914.

Crown Prince Rupprecht's Sixth Army—220,000 men organized into 183 infantry battalions, 28 cavalry squadrons and eighty-one artillery batteries—constituted the *Schwerpunkt* (center of gravity) of the German operation in the South. It set up headquarters in Saint-Avold on 9 August, and the following day Rupprecht assumed command of Seventh Army as well. His first task was reconnaissance. Unfortunately, Bavarian cavalry failed to penetrate the French border screen and aircraft had trouble sighting well-concealed enemy forces. Still, Rupprecht and Krafft von Dellmensingen were chomping at the bit to go on the offensive. They feared that the purely defensive role assigned to them by the OHL would have negative effects on the morale of their troops.

---

[23] Entry for 31 August 1914. 456 F58 Brigadebefehle, Nr. 27; ibid.
[24] AFGG, vol. 1–1, p. 21, also Joffre, *Mémoires*, vol. 1, p. 252.
[25] AOK 6, 369, BHStA-KA; Wenninger to War Ministry, 15 August 1914, Nachlaß Krafft von Dellmensingen 187, BHStA-KA.
[26] Carl von Clausewitz, *On War* ed. Michael Howard and Peter Paret (Princeton: Princeton University Press, 1976).

Any form of withdrawal, of course, would be disastrous. "An offensive solution of our task," Rupprecht noted in his diary, "seems desirable to me in order for us to seize the initiative."[27] They began to toy with options. Krafft von Dellmensingen's first plan was to advance to the line of the Upper Moselle and Meurthe rivers and thereby to threaten the flank of the French center. But the OHL, in its first formal directive to Sixth Army, counseled Rupprecht that it was not "interested" in a joint advance by Sixth and Seventh armies "*across*" the Upper Moselle and Meurthe.[28] This seemed a veiled order to remain on the defensive.

Frustrated in their offensive design, Rupprecht and Krafft von Dellmensingen turned to a second option: if they had to remain on the defensive, then why not entice the French into advancing into an artificially created "sack" somewhere between Metz and Straßburg? That is, show the French that the Bavarians were withdrawing in the face of superior forces, lure them into the "sack," and then cut them to pieces with Fifth Army from the West, Sixth Army from the East, and Seventh Army from the South.[29] The "small Cannae" that had eluded Heeringen at Mülhausen might thus still be achieved. A secret report from the German military attaché at Bern, Switzerland, suggested that the French had deployed perhaps half of their entire army—12 to 15 army corps—in Alsace-Lorraine.[30] The campaign in the West just might be decided on the south flank.

As the Germans deliberated, Joffre acted. On 14 August he sent First Army (260,000 men) and Second Army (180,000 men) as well as a newly constituted Army of Alsace under General Paul Pau—in all, roughly 400 battalions and 1,600 guns, almost one-third of his effective strength—into Lorraine between Toul and Épinal with bands playing the *Marseillaise*.[31] They were to "retain and draw toward them an

---

[27] Diary entry for 12 August 1914. Nachlaß Kronprinz Rupprecht 699, Bayerisches Hauptstaatsarchiv, Geheimes Hausarchiv (hereafter BHStA-GH), Munich, Germany.

[28] AOK 6, folder 369, 48, BHStA-KA.

[29] Nachlaß Krafft von Dellmensingen 145, BHStA-KA, also Thomas Müller, *Konrad Krafft von Dellmensingen (1862–1953). Porträt eines bayerischen Offiziers* (Munich: Kommission für Bayerische Landesgeschichte, 2002), p. 328.

[30] Diary entry, 14 August 1914. Nachlaß Krafft von Dellmensingen 145, BHStA-KA.

[31] The German official history lists Sixth Army at 183 battalions of infantry and 1,068 guns; Seventh Army at 145 battalions and 698 guns. French forces ranged against them were set at 218 battalions of infantry and 864 guns for Second Army; 202 battalions and 734 guns for First Army. WK, vol. 1, p. 646.

important part of the opposing forces," while the main French blow would be delivered in eastern Belgium and Luxembourg.[32] Joffre restricted their advance to about five kilometers a day, afraid that he just might be putting his head into a German "noose" between Metz and Straßburg. For four days, the *poilus* advanced methodically. The Germans relied mainly on long-range artillery fire and brief but violent actions by their rearguards to slow the French advance. The first rain of the campaign soaked the fields and turned the Lorraine clay into beige-gray ooze. Moltke rushed his iron reserve, the six Ersatz Divisions assigned by Schlieffen to the right wing for mop-up and siege operations in Belgium, to Alsace and Lorraine.

The French advance continued the next two days in dreary cloud and rain. German Sixth Army continued to retreat, leaving behind guns, wagons, field kitchens, knapsacks, and rifles as well as its dead and wounded. It also left behind a burning Saarburg, having doused its stores of ammunition and supplies with gasoline and set them on fire. As an interesting footnote in history, the war diary of 2nd Battalion, Baden 112th Infantry Regiment, recorded on 18 August: "Lt. Goering 8C brings in 3 prisoners of [French] IR 85."[33] The twenty-one-year-old Hermann Göring of 8th Company later received the Iron Cross, Second Class, for his service in Lorraine.[34]

At their new headquarters at Hellimer, Rupprecht and Krafft von Dellmensingen returned their thoughts to mounting a counterattack.[35] When they relayed their decision to the OHL, Koblenz reacted with what the Bavarians sarcastically called "a most oracle-like" directive: stick to the original *Aufmarschplan*![36] To clarify matters, Moltke dispatched Lieutenant-Colonel Wilhelm von Dommes, head of the General Staff's Political Section, to Hellimer on 17 August. Dommes was the first in a series of envoys sent by Moltke to Rupprecht's headquarters, in part to overcome the abysmal state of communications between the OHL and its field commanders. The OHL, Dommes allowed, had now dropped the idea of luring the French into the

---

[32] Particular Instruction No. 18 and Telephone Message, 21 August 1914. AFGG, vol. 1–1, pp. 693, 604.
[33] 456 F41 KTB des Inf. Regt. 112, Nr. 171, GLA. Göring served with 8th Company at Mülhausen, Saarburg-Mörchingen and Nancy-Épinal.
[34] 456 D Kriegsrangliste Bad. Inf. Regt. Prinz Wilhelm Nr. 112; ibid.
[35] Tagebuch Krafft, 17 August 1914. Nachlaß Krafft von Dellmensingen 145, BHStA-KA.
[36] Ibid.

vaunted "sack" between the Saar and Nied rivers. Sixth and Seventh armies were to stand on the defensive between Metz and the Lower Nied River in order to check any French attempt to turn the flank of German Fifth Army between Metz and Verdun.

Neither Rupprecht nor Krafft von Dellmensingen was willing to accept a prolonged passive stance by the Bavarian army on the Nied as this would "damage" its "offensive spirit" and "erode" the soldiers' confidence in their leaders. The two Bavarian commanders pressed their case for the offensive on Dommes. Rupprecht backed the OHL's representative against the wall: "One either lets me do as I want or one gives me concrete orders."[37] Dommes possessed no formal orders. The next day, Rupprecht and Krafft confirmed their decision to attack by telephone with Quartermaster-General Hermann von Stein. Moltke's deputy raised no objections. "Do whatever you want to do."[38]

The morning of 20 August broke gray and foggy, prohibiting aerial reconnaissance by either side. Then a blood-red sun appeared through the mist. For a sixth day, Joffre's armies in Lorraine renewed the attack. On this day, however, they were met by a withering hail of artillery shells from Crown Prince Rupprecht's armies—and by a spirited counterattack.[39] The two forces, quite unaware of the fact, had each mounted separate attacks that morning and crashed head-on along a 100-kilometer-wide front. It was the first major battle of the war.

The clash immediately disintegrated into a series of isolated and uncoordinated engagements. Clumps of soldiers rushed wildly across the hills and valleys of the Vosges, through the fences and hedges of its quaint villages. Ferdinand Foch's XX Corps, composed of men from Nancy, made progress at Mörchingen (Morhange),[40] but he had undertaken this deep penetration of enemy lines against Castelnau's express orders and in the process had exposed the left flank of Second Army's two center corps. German Sixth Army counterattacked the exposed flank of Joseph de Castelli's French VIII Corps with wave after wave of infantry supported by heavy artillery. Enfilading machine-gun fire from Ludwig von Gebsattel's III Bavarian Corps caused what Foch called

---

[37] Entry for 17 August 1914; ibid, also Nachlaß Kronprinz Rupprecht 699, BHStA-GH, and Müller, *Krafft von Dellmensingen*, pp. 330–31.
[38] Entry for 18 August 1914. Nachlaß Kronprinz Rupprecht 699, BHStA-GH.
[39] Joffre, *Mémoires*, vol. 1, pp. 280–81.
[40] See Maréchal Foch, *Mémoires pour server a l'histoire de la guerre de 1914–1918* (Paris: Plon, 1931), vol. 1, pp. 61–62, 65.

"gruesome" losses among his XX Corps. In the heated melee, it was often difficult to distinguish friend from foe. Near Bisping, 1st Bavarian Infantry Brigade was nearly annihilated by a withering barrage of artillery shells from 9th Bavarian Field Artillery Regiment.[41]

A disaster ensued for the French—despite the fact that they had captured the war diary of a fallen German officer detailing Rupprecht's plan of attack. By late afternoon, as the broiling heat of the first two weeks of the campaign returned, Castelnau had lost much of his field artillery. Louis Espinasse's XV Corps and Louis Taverna's XVI Corps were in full retreat. Foch's XX Corps had taken a bad knock. Castelnau had no choice but to call a retreat to the original starting line of the offensive on 14 August—the Meurthe River and the Grand Couronné de Nancy. Believing the situation to be "very grave," and his army desperately in need of at least forty-eight hours' rest, he entertained thoughts of further withdrawals behind the Upper Moselle and perhaps as far as Toul and Épinal. Joffre refused to consider the suggestion. "Speak no more of retiring beyond the Moselle."[42] Instead, he rushed 64th and 74th Reserve Infantry Divisions to buttress Second Army and halted the shunting of Gilbert Defforges' IX Corps to the North, already in progress.

Castelnau's retreat also sealed the fate of Dubail's advance. Initially, and without contact to Castelnau, the fiery Dubail was determined to continue the attack. Louis de Maud'huy's 16th Division was engaged in bitter house-to-house fighting in Saarburg. A relief attempt by Léon Bajolle's 15th Division was repulsed with heavy losses by Oskar von Xylander's Bavarian I Corps. De Maud'huy had no choice but to abandon Saarburg. He did so with a defiant last gesture: amidst a storm of shrapnel, he and his staff stood at attention at the southern end of the city while 16th Division's massed bands played the *Marche Lorraine* as the troops marched out of Saarburg.[43] It was heroic, but it was not war. Late in the day, Joffre apprised Dubail that Second Army's retreat threatened to turn into a rout. Dubail was left no option but to withdraw VIII and XIII Corps to cover Castelnau's exposed flanks. Pau's Army of Alsace was nowhere in sight.

---

[41] Crown Prince Rupprecht of Bavaria, *Mein Kriegstagebuch* ed. Eugen von Frauenholz (Munich: Deutscher National Verlag, 1929), vol. 1, p. 25.
[42] AFGG, vol. 1-1, p. 263, also Joffre, *Mémoires*, vol. 1, pp. 284–86.
[43] Sewell Tyng, *The Campaign of the Marne 1914* (New York and Toronto: Longmans, Green, 1935), p. 70.

The Great Retreat in the South was in full swing by the evening of 20 August. The French army admitted 5,000 casualties; historians have set that figure at 10,000. Friedrich von Graevenitz, Württemberg's Plenipotentiary to the OHL, reported "total victory" against "at least nine active corps," and the capture of 14,000 prisoners of war and thirteen artillery batteries.[44] Kaiser Wilhelm II celebrated "the greatest victory in the history of warfare."[45]

At daybreak on 21 August the Bavarians showered Castelnau's shaken army with another withering artillery barrage. As the early morning mists evaporated, Foch's 39th Division was hurled back north of Château-Salins and his 11th Division likewise was forced to retreat. Rupprecht's Bavarians began a sweep around Castelnau's Second Army and the previously shattered XV Corps and XVI Corps disintegrated. By 10 a.m., Castelnau, the little "monk in boots," ordered the first general retreat of the day. The relentless German pursuit continued. Castelnau's men, morally and physically shaken, abandoned carts and wagons, guns and horses. At 6 p.m. the commander ordered another retreat under cover of darkness. Dubail's First Army, with its western flank left in the air by Castelnau's precipitous retreat, was forced to fall back to the line of the Meurthe River as well. He never forgave Castelnau.

The violent engagement around Saarburg shocked even its victor in terms of the human toll.[46] Annual staff rides and field maneuvers had not prepared commanders for the true "face" of modern, industrial war. On 21 August Rupprecht inspected the previous days' battlefields as he rode toward his new headquarters at Duß (Dieuze). In the region around Château-Bréhain, he noted, the enemy had "left behind masses of dead and wounded." At Conthil, the fields were studded with mass graves, for both men and horses. Houses were burned out, shot to pieces by the artillery. Cows not milked for days, their udders nearly bursting, roamed about "bellowing in pain." At Mörchingen, artillery

---

[44] Graevenitz to War Minister Otto von Marchtaler, 22 August 1914. M 1/2 Berichte des Militärbevollmächtigten beim Grossen Hauptquartier und des stellv. Militärbevollmächtigten in Berlin 5. August 1914, vol. 54; Hauptstaatsarchiv Stuttgart, Germany.

[45] General Karl von Wenninger, diary entry for 20 August 1914. Cited in Bernd Schulte, "Neue Dokumente zu Kriegsausbruch und Kriegsverlauf 1914," *Militärgeschichtliche Mitteilungen* 25 (1979): 153.

[46] Diary entries for 21 and 22 August 1914. Nachlaß Kronprinz Rupprecht 699, BHStA-GH.

shells had hit the gas works and fires still ravaged the city. On a nearby hillside, where a French unit had been caught in the flank, the dead, recognizable by their red pants, "lay in rows and looked like a field of poppies." It was an eerie sight. "They lie man to man. Some still hold their rifles at the ready. Due to the intense heat, most of the men's faces have already turned a bluish black." Rupprecht estimated French losses at 30,000 dead and wounded.[47] Yet again, he witnessed the effects of "friendly fire" as the Bavarian artillery had mistakenly fired on its own advancing infantry.

Ominously, reports once more began to filter in to Sixth Army headquarters that the fighting had not been restricted to regular forces. Numerous commanders stated that French civilians had shot at their troops as they entered a town. Reprisals were swift. At Nomeny, just north of Nancy, 3rd Battalion, Bavarian 8th Regiment, burned much of the village; fifty-five residents died, and of those, forty-six had been shot.[48] At Gerbéviller, southeast of Nancy, the Bavarians pillaged and burned the city; sixty civilians died.[49] And at Lunéville, on the Meurthe, Bavarian 5th Reserve Infantry Division and 6th Infantry Division shot wildly into homes and shops, at anything that moved. As darkness fell, seventy homes had been burned and nineteen civilians killed. Major Rudolf von Xylander of Rupprecht's staff wrote in his war diary: "In Lunéville, murder and slaughter, fires. Panic among our rearguard formations."[50]

Fritz Nieser, the Grand Duchy of Baden's Acting Plenipotentiary at Munich, reported that the capital was decked with flags to celebrate Rupprecht's victory in the Battle of the Saar, and that King Ludwig III had received enthusiastic public ovations. The French Army "obviously had been totally defeated in the West."[51]

The Battle of the Saar (for the French, Sarrebourg-Morhange) had not fulfilled Rupprecht's dream of a great flanking movement.

---

[47] Rupprecht, *Mein Kriegstagebuch*, vol. 1, p. 36.
[48] John Horne and Alan Kramer, *German Atrocities, 1914: A History of Denial* (New Haven and London: Yale University Press, 2001), pp. 63–65, but see also Karl Deuringer, *Die Schlacht in Lothringen und in den Vogesen. Die Feuertaufe der bayerischen Armee* (Munich: M. Schick, 1929), vol. 1, p. 185, for a much different version.
[49] Horne and Kramer, *German Atrocities*, pp. 65–66.
[50] Cited in *Keiner fühlt sich hier mehr als Mensch ... Erlebnis und Wirkung des Ersten Weltkriegs* ed. Gerhard Hirschfeld and Gerd Krumeich (Essen: Klartext, 1993), pp. 90–91. Entry for 25 August 1914.
[51] Dated 22 and 26 August 1914. 233 Politische Berichte des Großherzogl. Gesandten in Berlin und München über den Kriegsausbruch 34816; GLA.

The "real war" had proved much more difficult than prewar maneuvers had suggested. Unlike the French, the Germans had neither specially trained Alpine troops nor high-angle-fire mountain artillery. The going was nearly impossible. Dense fog not only inhibited accurate fire but turned the battlefields into an eerie semi-darkness. Combat was usually up close, in most cases ending with blood-curdling bayonet charges. The small creeks of the Vosges at times ran red. The woods rang with the screams of wounded soldiers rolling on the forest floor. Drums and bugles sounded advance and retreat, alternately. Men accidentally shot their own. And even in the mountains, there was little relief from the broiling heat.

Adolf Hartner, a German trooper, noted that the artillery reduced the trees of the Vosges to matchsticks and enemy soldiers to grotesque heaps of body parts. "Here a torn off foot, there an arm, a leg, then another body torn apart to the point of non-recognition; one was missing half his face & both hands; truly horrible." At one point, Hartner almost became sick at the sight of a pitiful French corporal.

> A grenade had ripped open his body & and he now attempted to push back into it the intestines that had spilled out of it—until death took mercy on him. Thus he lay there with distorted eyes & a snarl on his teeth. I believe that none of us could resist a mild shudder.[52]

A German officer, Karl Gruber, wrote in his war diary that the war enthusiasm of the first days of August quickly wilted in the heat and savagery of mountain warfare. More and more, his Baden soldiers badgered him with questions such as: "Lieutenant, will we be in Paris soon?"; and "Lieutenant, won't the murdering soon stop?"[53]

Karl Deuringer, the Bavarian semi-official historian of the war, reproduced the travails of two battalions of 15th Reserve Infantry Regiment in the area around Markirch (Sainte-Marie-aux-Mines) in Upper Alsace. What today is a charming Vosges resort known for its Munster cheese and Riesling wine, in 1914 was a tough textile town of 12,000. The countryside was studded with open mine pits and slag heaps from earlier days of silver, copper and lead mining. Bavarian infantry ran up against a natural fortress. "Everywhere, felled trees, barricades made with branches, barbed-wire entanglements, and

---

[52] Letter of 20–21 August 1914. S Kriegsbriefe und Kriegstagebücher 53; GLA.
[53] Entries dated 23–24 August 1914. Msg 2/3112, Aufzeichnungen von Karl Gruber über die ersten Kriegstage 1914, 22; Bundesarchiv-Militärarchiv, Freiburg, Germany.

tripwires impeded progress." Enemy sharpshooters hid behind "bushes, boulders, rock walls," in "holes and trenches," as well as in tree tops.[54] At Brifosse, the advance of 5th Reserve Infantry Regiment over a bridge crossing the Robinot stream was halted by French machine gunners. Panic ensued.

> The troops, seized by fear, run for their lives down the southern hillside ... to seek safety in Brifosse. The horses, hit by the bullets, roll on the ground and wildly flay their legs into the harnesses. The wagons, wheels inter-locked, crash into one another; are pulled to the side; then pushed over the edge. Dead and wounded men and horses lie about everywhere. There was neither any going "forward" nor any going "backward."[55]

Nor were conditions much better on the Plain of Alsace. There, the heat was abominable, the roads dry and dusty, and the still unripe fruit fuel for intestinal disorders. In the region near Sennheim (Cernay), where almost two millennia before Julius Caesar had clashed with the German chieftain Ariovistus, French and German troops engaged one another in fierce combat.[56] By and large without artillery, they resorted to savage bayonet charges. The steep, terraced vineyards of the eastern slopes of the Vosges around Colmar, Türkheim (Turckheim), Kaysersberg, and Reichenweiher (Riquewihr) were easily turned into miniature fortresses by interweaving felled trees with chest-high grape vines and barbed wire. German Seventh Army's losses in August 1914 were greater than those of their forefathers in the entire Franco-Prussian War.[57]

Kaiser Wilhelm II was "simply ecstatic" over the battlefield success of a fellow royal, and on 27 August bestowed the Iron Cross, First and Second Class, on Crown Prince Rupprecht. Moltke, in the words of a Bavarian staff officer, had been "moved to tears" by the good news. But their Prussian paladins were less charitable. Rupprecht's failure to dispatch his "tired" cavalry to cut the defeated French Second Army to pieces after the Battle of the Saar, War Minister Erich von Falkenhayn testily noted, meant that the Bavarians had missed a "golden moment" to decide the war on the southern flank. Prussian cavalry, unlike its

---

[54] Deuringer, *Die Schlacht in Lothringen*, vol. 1, pp. 354–55.
[55] Ibid., vol. 1, pp. 531–32.
[56] Ibid., vol. 1, pp. 366–67.
[57] From Konrad Krafft von Dellmensingen, *Das Bayernbuch vom Weltkriege 1914–1918. Ein Volksbuch* (Stuttgart: Chr. Belser, 1930), vol. 2, pp. 11–23.

Bavarian counterpart, he savagely noted, was never "too tired" to pursue a beaten foe![58]

The Battle of the Frontiers was over by 24 August.[59] For nearly two weeks, the opposing armies had been locked in murderous combat in a campaign that had not been planned by either side before 1914. It had simply taken on a life of its own, absorbing almost one-third of the forces on either side. By the end of August, there existed near numerical parity on the two German wings: 331,597 men with Sixth and Seventh armies in Alsace-Lorraine, and 372,240 with First and Second armies in Belgium.[60] There existed command chaos at the OHL, now sited at Luxembourg.

What role to assign the 332,000 battle-tested soldiers on the southern flank? There was never any thought of winding down the campaign in Lorraine after the Battle of the Saar and moving the men to the right flank to wheel around Paris, Lieutenant-Colonel Gerhard Tappen, Moltke's chief of operations, later acknowledged. The railroads heading north from Metz and Straßburg went only as far as Aachen, and from there the already exhausted troops would have had extremely long marches to reach the rapidly advancing First and Second armies.[61] Still, the soldiers in Lorraine had to be tasked. For the time being, they were ordered to pursue what was taken to be a defeated foe toward the South. In reality, the men dug in to seek shelter from the lethal fire of the French 75mm flat-trajectory guns—and from the blistering heat.

Once somewhat recovered from the battles of the past three weeks, Bavarian Sixth Army advanced cautiously toward the Moselle. Its objective was to drive between the two great French fortress towns of Toul and Épinal in the general direction of Neufchâteau. From 24 to 28 August, as heat turned to rain and fog, Rupprecht's soldiers engaged the men of Castelnau's Second Army in the so-called Battle of the Trouée des Charmes. Joffre needed to tie down as many German forces as possible in the South as the great German sweep through Belgium approached the Marne River. Yet again, the fighting was desperate and

---

[58] Wenninger diary entry, 6 September 1914. Cited in Schulte, "Neue Dokumente," pp. 167–68.

[59] For a glowing account of German tactics, see Terence Zuber, *The Battle of the Frontiers, Ardennes 1914* (Stroud, UK: Tempus, 2007).

[60] *Sanitätsbericht über das Deutsche Heer im Weltkriege 1914/1918* (Berlin: E. S. Mittler, 1934–35), vol. 3, p. 36.

[61] WK, vol. 1, p. 569.

bloody. Yet again, it brought no decision. Yet again, the OHL laid the blame at the feet of Rupprecht and Krafft von Dellmensingen.

Moltke for the first time took a personal active role in the campaign in the South. On 30 August, the day that Joffre transported the first infantry contingents from Second Army to his threatened left wing near Paris,[62] he dispatched his artillery expert, Major Max Bauer, to Hellimer to deal with the Bavarians. Bauer laid out a bold plan, one that he (incorrectly) informed Rupprecht had been devised by the OHL. If the Bavarians could push across the Moselle, drive through the Charmes Gap toward Neufchâteau, and then point north to link up with Crown Prince Wilhelm's Fifth Army near Verdun, what Moltke termed a "Cannae in grand style," one beyond even Schlieffen's wildest dreams, could be accomplished. There was only one problem, Bauer averred: the so-called "*position de Nancy*." In fact, the major was referring to the 300-meter-high Grand Couronné, a massive defensive works extending some three kilometers east of Nancy, and bristling with forts, artillery, machine guns, and barbed wire. Ironically, many of the defenses had been constructed by Foch, the arch advocate of the offensive, after August 1913, when he had assumed command of XX Corps at Nancy.

No sooner had Krafft von Dellmensingen drafted orders for the assault on the Grand Couronné—as the first step toward the break through the Charmes Gap—than command chaos set in again. Rupprecht's staff officer, Major von Xylander, happened to be in Luxembourg and "purely by coincidence" heard Chief of Operations Tappen announce that the OHL had no interest whatsoever in taking the "*position de Nancy*." Quite the contrary, Tappen returned to the original concept of 2 August: Sixth Army was "at all cost to tie down" French forces in the South.[63] Already startled by this news, Xylander was further astonished when Moltke's deputy, Quartermaster-General von Stein, revised Tappen's concept within minutes, and demanded that Sixth Army again storm what he called the "Bayon bridgehead" on the Moselle, that is, the Charmes Gap![64] And when an utterly befuddled Krafft von Dellmensingen visited Luxembourg on 2 September to seek clarity, he was told that the attack on the "Bayon bridgehead" was off, that the campaign on the right wing was going splendidly,

---

[62] AFGG, vol. 2, pp. 380, 382, 388.
[63] Xylander, *Deutsche Führung*, p. 153.
[64] WK, vol. 3, p. 287.

and that German troops were conducting a merry "promenade through France."[65] Joffre quietly took two army corps out of the line Toul-Épinal and moved them to Paris by rail.

In the early morning fog of 4 September the assault on "*la position de Nancy*"—the right angle formed by the Moselle and Meurthe rivers from Pont-à-Mousson in the North to Baccarat in the South—began with the first great artillery barrage of the war. General Otto Kreppel, chief of Bavarian Foot Artillery, had concentrated 272 heavy guns (including 30.5cm and 42cm howitzers) in 66 batteries for the assault, and he had seconded twenty-six ammunition trains for Nancy.[66] Infantry followed the artillery barrage in waves—only to be mowed down by deadly artillery and machine-gun fire. In some of the most murderous fighting of the war, the Bavarians battled over every inch of territory east of Nancy. To no avail. Joffre kept Castelnau and his Second Army in place and refused all suggestions by the commander of Second Army to withdraw behind the Moselle.

At Luxembourg, Moltke was besieged by wild rumors: British reinforcements had arrived in France; Hindus had landed in southern France; and a Siberian army corps had disembarked in Britain, bound for the Western Front. Rather than close down the bloody assault on Nancy, Moltke ordered General Ludwig von Sieger, Prussian chief of Munitions, to starve Sixth Army of 13cm and 15cm shells for the heavy guns and howitzers. And when he diverted several trainloads of heavy artillery shells from the Bavarian to the Prussian Crown Prince to assault the French forts between Verdun and Toul, the rift in the German chain of command was complete. On 9 September, at the very moment that the Battle of the Marne reached its climax, Crown Prince Rupprecht ordered a halt to the assault on the Grand Couronné. Beginning the next day, Sixth Army withdrew from land it had won at horrendous cost in blood and treasure, and, under a fitting burst of cloud and rain, began the long trek that eventually would bring them to Flanders. Therewith, in the words of historian Dieter Storz, "the first great breakthrough battle of the world war ended."[67]

---

[65] Diary entry for 2 September 1914. Tagebuch Krafft, Nachlaß Krafft 145, BHStA-KA.

[66] Deuringer, *Die Schlacht in Lothringen*, vol. 2, p. 749.

[67] Dieter Storz, "'Dieser Stellungs- und Festungskrieg ist scheußlich!' Zu den Kämpfen in Lothringen und in den Vogesen im Sommer 1914," *Der Schlieffenplan*, p. 197.

Not surprisingly, recriminations set in almost at once. Moltke and his staff accused the Bavarians of having pursued purely dynastic ambitions in launching their offensives, of having willfully overestimated the size of the French forces ranged against them, and of having lacked the will to advance under heavy fire. As "punishment" for this "incompetence," Prussian War Minister von Falkenhayn demanded that Sixth Army "be disbanded."[68] General Karl von Wenninger, Bavaria's Military Plenipotentiary to the OHL, in reply stuck a dagger in the heart of the German federal army when he spoke of the unfortunate "anti-Bavarian *Kollegium*" that dictated operations: Gerhard Tappen (Operations) was a Prussian, Richard Hentsch (Intelligence) was a Saxon, and Wilhelm Groener (Railways) was a Württemberger.[69]

What conclusions can be drawn from the campaign in Alsace-Lorraine? First, the German army's prewar neglect of electronic communications and the need to assign royal heirs to command field armies combined against efficient coordination between Koblenz and Hellimer. Moltke and Tappen relied on a host of "special emissaries" (Wilhelm Dommes, Max Bauer, Ludwig von Sieger, Erich von Redern)—well before Lieutenant-Colonel Richard Hentsch's famous tour of the front in September[70]—to raise general "talking" points, but never to issue orders to Rupprecht and Krafft von Dellmensingen. Moltke, upon arriving at his first headquarters at Koblenz, had made clear to his staff that his field commanders were much better positioned "to assess the enemy's situation" than he was, well behind the front.[71] Kaiser Wilhelm II, for his part, was so sensitive about issuing orders to a fellow royal, Rupprecht, that he had instructed Lieutenant-Colonel von Dommes "to avoid anything embarrassing that might give his planned 'suggestions' the impression of an 'order.'"[72] Joffre had no such concerns or qualms. The war in Alsace-Lorraine had revealed both the limits and the dangers of the vaunted Prussian *Auftragstaktik*.[73]

---

[68] Wenninger diary entry, 10 September 1914. Tagebuch Wenninger, HS 2546, BHStA-KA.

[69] Wenninger diary entry, 7 September 1914. Ibid., p. 170.

[70] See Holger H. Herwig, *The Marne, 1914: The Opening of World War I and the Battle That Changed the World* (New York: Random House, 2009), pp. 266ff.

[71] WK, vol. 1, p. 258. Testimony by Chief of Operations Tappen for 1914.

[72] Hermann Mertz von Quirnheim, *Der Führerwille in Entstehung und Durchführung* (Oldenburg: G. Stalling, 1932), p. 70.

[73] Thus Storz, "Zu den Kämpfen in Lothringen und in den Vogesen," p. 199. The term is usually loosely translated as "leading from the front."

Second, much has been said about the Younger Moltke "watering down" Schlieffen's recipe for victory in the West. This begs the question whether an extra two or three army corps could, in fact, have made a difference in the grand "sweep" around Fortress Paris—especially given the state of German communications and logistics in 1914. As well, it skirts the issue of how the General Staff was going to deal with two armies of more than 300,000 *poilus* set to break across the Lorraine plateau into central Germany, at a time when seven-eighths of its armies were quick stepping through Belgium. Rupprecht's Sixth and Seventh armies simply had no choice but to fight where they had been deployed in Moltke's *Westaufmarsch*. The campaigns conducted by both sides in the South reinforced the Elder Helmuth von Moltke's admonition that no operations plan "survives with certainty beyond the first encounter with the enemy's major forces."[74]

Third, the nature of the fighting in Alsace-Lorraine presaged much of what was to come further north, and which has made its way into most histories of the Great War. Sometime after the Battle of the Saar, the war of maneuver planners had envisioned before 1914 broke down amidst a storm of steel rained down on the soldiers by heavy artillery guns, massive howitzers, trench mortars, and machine-gun fire. Bavarian infantry, long before it was tasked to storm the Grand Couronné, had taken to ground, literally, and dug trenches to seek shelter from the seemingly never-ending artillery barrages of the French *soixante-quinzes*. This had not escaped notice by its senior officers. Chief of Staff Krafft von Dellmensingen had deplored how modern maneuver warfare had degenerated in less than a month: "This trench- and siege war is horrible."[75] It had reminded Crown Prince Rupprecht of another conflict—the Russo-Japanese War of 1904–05.

Fourth, the term "battles of material" (*Materialschlachten*) that the historian Hans Delbrück coined for the dreadful slaughter at Verdun and the Somme in 1916 could (and should) have been applied already to the campaign in Alsace-Lorraine. There, French First and Second armies had battled tenaciously with German Sixth and Seventh armies along a relatively short front from Markirch to Baccarat for a month. There, one side had deployed 272 heavy guns and howitzers

---

[74] "Taktisch-strategische Aufsätze aus den Jahren 1857 bis 1871," in *Moltkes Militärische Werke*, vol. 2/2, p. 291.
[75] Entry dated 7 September 1914. Tagebuch Krafft, Nachlaß Krafft von Dellmensingen 145, BHStA-KA.

in a "murderous cannonade" to reduce a single salient—the Grand Couronné—in a week. A decade earlier, the Imperial Japanese Army had assaulted Port Arthur with "only" 192 heavy pieces of artillery in what was then regarded as the greatest artillery siege of modern times.

Fifth, I suggest that the campaign on the southern flank of the German campaign in the West offers the historian a magnificent chance to study the development of strategy, operations, and tactics in World War I in microcosm. Unlike the Prussian case, where most of its records (from General Staff to Division commands) were destroyed by Allied air raids on the Reichsarchiv at Potsdam in 1944 and 1945, in the Bavarian case we have the full record of its campaign at the Kriegsarchiv in Munich; and in the Baden case we also have the documentary record at the Generallandesarchiv at Karlsruhe. These two sources alone allow the historian to reconstruct the campaign in Alsace and Lorraine with some confidence.

Finally, as always, the price for the debacle in the Vosges was paid by the troops. While there never was a precise official calculation of Sixth Army's losses, Deuringer, the semi-official historian of the Bavarian army, has "guesstimated" total casualties for the infantry at 60 percent, and total killed at between 20 and 25 percent. Just in the region of the heaviest fighting between Pont-à-Mousson and Markirch, Deuringer has tabulated the deployment of 50 infantry brigades of slightly more than 300,000 men. Using his rule-of-thumb method for calculating losses, this translates into 180,000 casualties, with 60,000 to 75,000 paying the ultimate price.[76] The German army's official ten-day medical reports (*Sanitätsberichte*) roughly bear out Deuringer's findings for Sixth Army—63,555 casualties (including 18,163 killed) for August and September 1914.[77] To this should be added Seventh Army's losses for the same two months in Alsace Lorraine—63,941 casualties, including 20,712 killed.[78] It is highly unlikely, given the ferocity of the battles, that French casualty rates would have been markedly different. In that case, both sides suffered somewhere between 350,000 and 400,000 casualties during the Battle of the Frontiers south of Metz in August and September 1914. It is a campaign that deserves not to be forgotten.

---

[76] Deuringer, *Die Schlacht in Lothringen*, vol. 2, p. 848.
[77] *Der Sanitätsdienst im Gefechts- und Schlachtenverlauf im Weltkriege 1914/1918* (Berlin: E. S. Mittler, 1938), vol. 2, pp. 342–43, 365.
[78] Ibid., vol. 1, pp. 438–39.

"TOTAL WAR, TOTAL NONSENSE" OR "THE MILITARY HISTORIAN'S FETISH"[1]

Eugenia C. Kiesling

The two world wars of the twentieth century left in their wake not only crumbled empires and shattered lives, memories of the death camps and the prospect of future nuclear annihilation, but an addition to the military lexicon. "Total war" seemed not only an appropriate label for the recent cataclysms but a useful description of a general phenomenon.[2] Historians seized upon the concept, proffering definitions and arguing over which conflicts deserved the title.[3] A few people invested heavily in the process; most simply accepted its utility without question. Especially after the unsatisfactory outcomes of less than "total" wars in Korea and Vietnam, the phrase began to take on positive connotations, as if "total wars" were more desirable than other wars. By the

---

[1] It is a pleasure to offer this essay in homage to Dennis Showalter because it is the offshoot of an article originally written for submission to the journal *War in History*, which Denny co-edits with Hew Strachan. In writing the piece I happily indulged in polemic in the hope that Denny would find the tone amusing.

Denny's forthright speech stands in marked contrast to his unwillingness to give offense. He follows up outrageous remarks with effusive concern lest anyone might have taken them personally. Denny is, quite simply, as nice and generous a man as one will find in the historical profession. He is also, of course, so broadly expert that there is almost no aspect of the field in which one would safely choose to compete with him. There is a pleasing irony in saluting Denny with a rare example of an essay he could not himself have written only because he would never have risked offending quite so many people.

Though much of it was written in 2008–09, the roots of this essay lie in my experiences during the period 1995–2001. Since then, things have changed enough that young instructors arriving at the Academy during the past two years find some of my observations unrecognizable. For that I am glad, but I am not convinced that my fundamental objections to the use of "total war" in the West Point curriculum have been understood, let alone addressed.

Reversing the usual order of events, I will begin by insisting that I am wholly responsible for any objectionable elements of this essay; that said, I owe enormous debts to the many colleagues at West Point and elsewhere who offered valuable criticism of a series of drafts.

[2] In traditional philosophical language, they ascribed to "total war" sense or intrinsic meaning as well as having the quality of referring to the world wars of 1914 to 1945.

[3] For an early example of the claim to totality, see John B. Walters, "General William Tecumseh Sherman and Total War," *Journal of Southern History* 14 (1948): 447–80.

end of the century, "total war" had been adopted by my own institution, the Department of History of the United States Military Academy at West Point, not only as a fundamental concept in the military history survey course but as a desirable way to fight.

This essay argues that there is nothing to gain, and indeed much to lose, in treating total war as a thing in itself rather than as a loose label for the conduct of the First and Second World Wars. Like "hoplite warfare" or "linear war," total war adumbrates general attributes of a specific military epoch, in this case the period 1914-45. The first of this essay's five parts urges the rejection of the phrase "total war" as meaningless, while the second adds, more urgently, that employing such a concept does serious moral harm. The third part argues for intellectual damage. The dangers of the concept of "total war" are illuminated by the solecisms it engenders in otherwise admirable works of historical analysis. The fourth part reinforces the third by rebutting conventional defenses of the concept. The final section suggests some reasons why historians (and soldiers) cling to an intellectually and morally bankrupt idea.

Part I: Meaningless

Calling a war "total" says nothing about it. Were people (friendly or hostile) conscripted either to fight or work? Did those conscripts include children or geriatrics? Were prisoners taken, and how were they treated? Were deaths among enemy civilians regretted or desired? Were the inhabitants of conquered lands ignored, absorbed, taxed, enslaved, or butchered? What methods of fighting, if any, were rejected as inhumane? Was the ultimate objective to change the enemy's behavior, to replace its government, or to eradicate its population? There seems no reason for historians to apply a label offering the reader no concrete information. Indeed U.S. Department of Defense has rejected the term with a succinct "Not to be used."[4]

---

[4] Joint Chiefs of Staff, *Department of Defense Dictionary of Military and Associated Terms* (Washington, DC: U.S. Government Printing Office, 1987), 374. The power of total war apparently obscures this point at USMA even to cadets and faculty reading Mark E. Neely, Jr., "Was the Civil War a Total War?" *Civil War History* 37 (1991), 434–458. The DOD's prohibition may stem less from philosophical concerns than awareness of the gap between Army and Air Force use of the term, a subject beyond the scope of this paper.

Part II: Morally Pernicious

The essay could end there with the observation that total does not impart one whit of information. But some undefinable ideas are useful. Arguments over the nature of the "art of war" do not break down over definitions of art even though the label "art" reveals as little about an artifact as "total" does about a conflict. A darker comparison, and the necessary, as opposed to sufficient, reason to repudiate the language of total war is that, just as our society allows under the rubric "art" behavior that might otherwise be proscribed, calling a war "total" trumps morality and law.

Taking total war to its literal extreme, West Point cadets blithely write on examination papers that because the Civil War was a total war, Sherman's army marched through Georgia killing all the men, raping all the women, and destroying all the property.[5] Or, as this author recently learned from a fellow passenger on a commercial airline, the total wars fought during the twentieth-century were competitions to kill the greatest number of civilians. It is not stupid to believe that "total" means total, but these claims about the Union Army in the Civil War and American bomber doctrine in World War II are not simply errors of fact, rendered possible by the essential meaningless of "total war." They are shocking demonstrations of moral blindness.

By inventing a category of total war, historians have rendered their readers comfortable with the idea that the United States has fought repeated wars of extermination. Should we expect Americans to be disturbed by Abu Ghraib after facilitating the belief that Union soldiers raped the female population of Georgia?

The phrase "total war" obfuscates even legal writing. What is the layman to think when the distinguished American military jurist W. Hays Parks refers in an essay on strategic bombing in World War II to "the limits of the law in total war?"[6] Parks, whose essay is predicated on the existence of law, uses "total war" as shorthand for the obstacles to legal interpretation under the novel conditions produced by World War II.

---

[5] One wonders how cadets imbued with this definition of total war would understand the events described in Jeffrey W. Legro, *Cooperation under Fire: Anglo-German Restraint during World War II* (Ithaca and London: Cornell University Press, 1995).

[6] W. Hays Parks, "Air War and the Laws of War," in Horst Boog, ed., *The Conduct of Air War in the Second World War: An International Comparison* (New York and Oxford: Berg Publishers, 1992), 310. "Air War and the Laws of War," W. Hays Parks, at that time the Chief of the International Law Branch in the U.S. Army J.A.G. Office

His uncertainty about the legality of the Allied bombing campaign against German cities stems from the complexity rather than the irrelevance of law.[7] Readers, accustomed to assume that total wars allow total destruction, may have different assumptions. Indeed soldiers alarmed to learn that total war renders law obscure even to legal experts and wary of growing international enthusiasm for war crimes trials, have reason to embrace an imaginary notion of total war as a legal free-fire zone.

The pernicious idea that total war justifies switching off one's moral calculus finds unintentional support from prominent just war theorist James Turner Johnson, who defines total war as one in which "there *must* be disregard of restraints imposed by customs, law, and morality on the prosecution of war."[8] Johnson's "must" is merely descriptive, but the reader can reasonably take it as prescriptively denying that morality is possible in total war. Martin Kutz surely understates the case in observing that the use of the phrase "total war" in Germany in the 1930s "strengthened a general tendency towards loosening the hold of traditional ethical standards on thinking and action...."[9] Surely language that contributes to the dissolution of legal and ethical norms—and serves no useful purpose—ought to be discouraged.

Part III: Inherent Solecism

Meaninglessness is a sufficient reason—and moral hazard an imperative one—to relegate total war to its proper place as a contemporary description of specific twentieth-century conflicts. Discussing wars in terms of a meaningless notion of totality naturally leads to an appallingly low standard of intellectual discourse as military historians struggle to defend the concept or, best of all, earn the sobriquet for their own favorite conflicts. Anyone concerned to defend the rigor of military history against its academic critics should be delighted not to be encumbered by debates about total war.

---

[7] Parks, 355.

[8] My italics. James Turner Johnson, *The Just War Tradition and the Restraints of War* (Princeton: Princeton University Press, 1981), 229.

[9] Martin Kutz, "Fantasy, Reality, and Modes of Perception in Ludendorff's and Goebbel's Concepts of "Total War,"" in Roger Chickering, *et al. A World at Total War: Global Conflict and the Politics of Destruction, 1937–1945* (Washington, DC and Cambridge: German Historical Institute and Cambridge University Press, 2005), 205.

This section will offer a number of examples of illogical or meaningless uses of "total war" in otherwise admirable historical work. Readers of earlier drafts of this essay have asked whether the concept of "total war" is useless because some people have used it clumsily, but solecism is so inherent in the concept that one cannot use it well. The examples below were chosen from many possibilities not with any desire to castigate particular scholars but because their authors' historical credentials are above reproach and their popularity allows them to influence a broad reading public. My quarrel is less with people who offer bad arguments than with a community that leaves them unchallenged. Critical faculties topple before the onslaught of total war.

For the unreflecting embrace of total war, one need only look at West Point's survey military history course, which uses the distinction between "limited" and "total" as an organizing theme and ought, therefore, to provide a thoughtful definition.[10] As late as 2001, however, the course glossary defined "total war" as "a war conducted by a belligerent in which the objective is more total and in which few restraints are placed on the means… used to achieve that objective. Phrases like "few restraints," and "generally has a significant impact" are vague, and drawing my cadets' attention to the circularity of "a total war is relatively more total" did not please the course director.[11]

The problematic definition of "total" war as "more total" survived in part because few cadets or instructors turn to the glossary when dealing with such an obvious concept as "total war." Taking total war for granted, the course contrasted it with a new, "limited" war invented as much for purposes of conceptual comparison as because it matches any historical reality. While limited war is a *bona fide* feature of the military theory of the second half of the twentieth century, it is a problematic description of the eighteenth century. This essay will later discuss the implications of West Point's treatment of total as better war; the immediate concern is with the intellectual gymnastics undertaken

---

[10] The structure and language of the textbook adopted in 1996 tacitly communicates that the trend towards total war since the Napoleonic Wars constituted progress while limited war is a regrettable "resort" (preface), v, Robert A. Doughty and Ira Gruber, et al., *Warfare in the Western World*. 2 vols. (Lexington MA and Toronto; D. C. Heath and Company, 1996.

[11] Definitions from the 2001 Course Notebook. Since this essay was written, I have been appointed to a three-year term as Course Director of the History of the Military Art and have revised the syllabus to eliminate "total war" as an organizing theme. It will be interesting to see whether that change, combined with increasing cadet interest in the course on unconventional warfare, will affect the discourse at the Academy.

by instructors in an effort to sustain an intellectually viable distinction between total and limited war.

The standard approach is that, while few, if any, wars are precisely limited or total, each somehow can be placed somewhere on a spectrum" ranging from peace through limited war to total war.[12] The analysis gains a semblance of rigor by distinguishing three discrete aspects of war: objectives, resources, and methods. Thus, a total war aims at the complete subjugation of the enemy state rather than at a limited political objective; it mobilizes all of the belligerents' resources, while limited wars do not; it is fought without restraint while limited wars are, *a priori*, limited. Differentiating objectives, resources, and methods makes individual wars more comprehensible but forces a three-dimensional analysis onto a one-dimensional spectrum. And three dimensions hardly suffice since a war's character may change across time and space. Debating where to put the American Revolution on the "limited-total spectrum" relative to the Seven Years War fills time in the classroom but hardly explains either conflict.

As with ruminations about angels cavorting on pinheads, such discussions are alleged to stimulate critical thinking. In fact, the exercise imbues future soldiers with the scholastic practice of drawing conclusions from labels unsupported by events in the real world. Thus, because we call the War of the Spanish Succession "limited," cadets deem the war slight in objectives, degree of mobilization, and quantities of violence without being required to offer any details about what Louis XVI and his adversaries actually did. Conversely, since the Thirty Years War was "total," how could a cadet be criticized for contending that Gustav Adolph intended to subjugate the Habsburg Empire?

West Point does not intend to teach that any kind of war takes place outside the constraints of law, but cadets naturally draw parallels between an allegedly lawless and total Thirty Years War and a legal vacuum in any future total war. The reasons for West Point's elevation of total over limited war will be discussed below; it suffices to note here that an institution dedicated to producing honorable soldiers fails to note the moral consequences of disparaging limits to war.

But discussions of total war seem exempt from normal intellectual standards. Anyone curious about total war might reasonably seek

---

[12] Though problematic, limited war differs from total war in having a clear history, some analytical utility, and no inherent tendency to undermine rational thought about war.

illumination in a book called *Total War: What it is, How it Got that Way*. The work, by Thomas Powers and Ruthven Tremain, turns out to be a compilation of quotations, nary a one mentioning total war, though the introduction offers a fatuous description of World War II as a total war in which "all was permitted and all was possible."[13] A reader might feel aggrieved, but the authors and publisher surely feared no repercussions. It is not as if Power's *Heisenberg's War* failed to talk about Werner Heisenberg. That would be fraud, while appending the words "total war" to a book about something else is merely marketing. Does the appeal of a book whose spine advertises only *Total War* evaporate after potential readers see the full title: *Total War and Twentieth-Century Higher Learning: Universities of the Western World in the First and Second World Wars*?[14]

But these are inconsequential books. That anything goes as long as the topic is total war finds more alarming demonstration in works likely to have far greater influence. Examples abound, and the two books discussed below are chosen largely for their impact on the reading community.

After 450 pages of compelling description of military operations in Sicily and Italy in his highly acclaimed *Day of Battle*, Rick Atkinson, with characteristic economy of force, employs three efficient pages to remind the reader of the disparity between the American and German war production as their armies faced off in Italy in 1943. What he is describing is "industrial war," the role of the "American war machine" in turning out war materiél so rapidly that it did not matter how many tons were stolen in transit on the road from Algiers through Naples to the battle front.[15]

Though descriptive, "industrial war" is hardly sexy, and Atkinson switches to "total war," which he calls "largely a German concept, conceived by General Erich Ludendorff as an alternative to the grinding stalemate of World War I."[16] Ludendorff did publish a book entitled

---

[13] Thomas Powers and Ruthven Tremain, *Total War: What It Is, How It Got That Way* (New York: William Morrow, 1988). 11.

[14] Willis Rudy, *Total War and Twentieth-Century Higher Learning: Universities of the Western World in the First and Second World Wars* (London and Toronto: Associated University Presses, 1991)

[15] Richard Atkinson, *The Day of Battle: The War in Sicily and Italy, 1943–1944* (New York: Henry Hold, 2007), 450–52; On the other hand, Atkinson's suggestion that the casualties in the Italian campaign represented combat on "an industrial scale" offers shades of meaning obliterated by the all-encompassing "total war," 573.

[16] Atkinson, 451.

Der totale Krieg in 1935, but that book's status as a foundational document for a useful concept of total war survives among military historians only because few bother to read obscure Germans texts printed in *fraktur*. Efforts to derive total war from the English translation published in 1938 are suspect because it bears the title *The Nation at War*, and "*totale*" is translated throughout as "totalitarian."[17] Had Atkinson read *Der totale Kriege*, he would have denied any relationship between Ludendorff and U.S. actions in World War II. For Ludendorff's explanation of total war as "born, not only through a change of policy in which the striving for power of the Jewish people and the Roman Church was made clear and their desire sharply revealed to exsanguinate the nations resisting them…" is a fair sample of the level of argument.[18]

Readers who ought to resist the alleged connection between American policies and Ludendorff's ravings are so comfortable in sharing in a German notion of total war that they fail to wonder whether the label is even compatible with Atkinson's campaign narrative. If total war is the use of superior matériel to avoid attrition, the thoroughly attritional Italian campaign is a poor advertisement of the idea. On a more practical note, why did a nation engaged in total war refrain from solving the massive pilfering problem mentioned above through mass executions?

At the risk of falling into the trap of arguing about what total war would be like, it is difficult to justify Atkinson's claim that Italy suffered "invasion, occupation, civil strife, and total war" without "total war" exposing the vacuousness of the phrase.[19] Atkinson's narrative places Italy's experience of total war mostly after the country's *negotiated* surrender. Even before the surrender, the Italians and the Allies fought one another with less than total ferocity, and many Italians welcomed the invaders. Allied forces were guilty of pillage, but they also assigned officers as "Venus Fixers" to identify cultural artifacts worthy of protection and to repair damage where possible. Instead of indulging in wholesale rape, Allied soldiers generally paid for sex and occasionally

---

[17] General Ludendorff, *The Nation at War*. Trans. A. S. Rappoport (London and Melbourne: Hutchinson & CO., 1938).

[18] Ludendorff, *Der totale Kriege* (Munich, 1936), 5. The looseness of the translation reflects the difficulty of translating lunacy.

[19] Atkinson, 580.

executed rapists.[20] If the Allied treatment of the defeated Italians was "total war," what does one call the far more savage behavior of the Germans against their erstwhile allies? But even the Germans showed signs of moderation, as when Hitler rejected the scorched earth policy recommended by his commander in Italy, Field Marshal Albert Kesselring.[21]

Atkinson's introduction of total war into an otherwise sensible book is illustrative of the seductive power of the phrase on authors who use it carelessly and readers who willingly collaborate. Because it contributes nothing substantial to his argument, it creates no problems not readily solved by a few strategic deletions. More dramatic pruning would have a salutary effect on David A. Bell's *The First Total War*, a book whose moments of originality and insight are overwhelmed by the analytical problems introduced by the phrase "total war."

Bell offers a fascinating discussion of rhetorical violence endemic to the French Revolution, but his insistence on linking this violence to a general phenomenon of total war illustrates the effectiveness of concept as a damper on intellectual processes of author and receptive readers alike.[22] The book's full title, *The First Total War: Napoleon's Europe and the Birth of Warfare as We Know It* invites the reader to place him or herself among cognoscenti of modern "total war." This tactical ploy to bring the reader into his camp is intellectually democratic and, because total war is something we all "know," Bell sees no need to justify his cursory dismissal of the definitions of total war previously offered by "many" (unnamed) historians.[23] Although many of the specialist reviews were highly critical of Bell's methodology, the general reception is exemplified by the *New Yorker* essay in which Adam Gopnick intelligently challenges Bell's claims while correcting his take on "total war." Apparently the meaning of total war is sufficiently clear

---

[20] However exploitative, these were transactions, not manifestations of untrammeled violence.

[21] Atkinson, 568.

[22] David A. Bell, *The First Total War: Napoleon's Europe and the Birth of Warfare as we Know It* (Boston and New York: Houghton Mifflin, 2007).

[23] That Bell himself is a specialist on the French Revolution rather than Revolutionary or Napoleonic military operations is obvious from his descriptions of Napoleon's *battalion carré* and Wellington's tactics, Bell, 238, 254, 7. One wonders how he would have treated Lawrence Keeley's arguments for very early total war in *War Before Civilization* (Oxford: Oxford University Press, 1996).

a priori that two men trained in the history of art can understand it even if they disagree on the details.[24]

Bell explains total war as what was envisioned by the French politicians who declared war on Austria in 1792, a "war of extermination" aimed at "total victory or total defeat."[25] The idea then drove action; having proclaimed a total war, the French had no choice but to fight one. Napoleon, though, "no conscious advocate of total war" was its "product, master, and victim." Whether the "master" of total war has any agency in the matter remains unaddressed.[26]

The idea that total war somehow took charge of Europe, subordinating all human choices to internecine hatred, begs fundamental questions of causality, especially since the seven major wars from 1792 to 1815 all ended with negotiated treaties. Bell's insistence that war at sea did not contribute to the evolution of total war makes one wonder why the passionate desire for extermination ended at the water's edge. While the "logic of total war" did not affect operations at sea, however, it somehow compelled Napoleon to invade Russia.[27]

Bell's regular reiterations of the verb "foreshadow" serve to finesse the relationship between Revolutionary or Napoleonic total war and "war as we know it." Nothing, exactly, causes anything else, but prewar speeches "foreshadowed, and arguably helped to invent…the new culture."[28] But it is not obvious how the rather conventional Valmy campaign foreshadowed "the total war to come."[29] The claim that Napoleon's defeat of Prussia "eerily foreshadowed the total wars of the twentieth century" is further obscured by the suggestion of a preternatural connection. The suggestion that Napoleon's visit to Frederick II's tomb, which "eerily foreshadowed" Hitler's visit to Napoleon's, meant that "1806 was a blitzkrieg," represents a failure of both logic and

---

[24] See, for example, Daniel Moran, A review of: David A Bell, *The First Total War: Napoleon's Europe and the Birth of Warfare as we Know It*. Boston and New York: Houghton Mifflin, 2007. http://www.ccc.nps.navy.mil/si/2008/Apr/moranApr08.asp. Bell's response is at http://www.h-france.net/forum/forumvol2/Bell1Response.html. Adam Gopnik, "Slaughterhouse: The Idealistic Origins of Total War," *The New Yorker* 12 February 2007, 82–85.

[25] Bell, 8.

[26] Bell, 8.

[27] "Nothing illustrates the implacable logic of total war more than Napoleon's decision to attack Russia," 256.

[28] Bell, 114.

[29] Bell, 131, especially since Bell allows that it ended in "good, aristocratic, Old Regime style," 135–6.

understanding. Blitzkrieg is meaningless in reference to 1806; if it means anything at all in 1940, it was an effort by Germany to avoid fighting an attritional war. To say that Clausewitz's 1812 writings "foreshadow" *On War* simply avoids making comparisons.[30] Calling the Spanish insurgency against Napoleon both "eerily" and "uncannily" similar to the current Iraqi insurgency undermines the argument for a natural connection between Napoleonic war and "war as we know it."[31] If Bell means to imply that insurgent action in Iraq renders that conflict total war, the phrase surely means whatever one wants it to. What is "uncanny" is the power of war to demolish logic and language, a point familiar to any reader of Elaine Scarry or Thucydides.[32]

It is instructive to watch Bell fall prey to the kind of fantastic language he rightly attributes to his subjects. Yes, the Revolutionary leaders embraced a "classical republican fantasy" connecting citizenship and war, and saw "the looming conflict almost entirely through the prism of classical fantasy."[33] Indeed, "the Girondins were falling in love with war—or at least, with the idea of war."[34] But Bell is falling in love with his own fantastic vision of wars of extermination.

Bell's embrace of the rhetoric of the Girondins contrasts with his more measured assessment that the French nation was utterly unprepared for war in terms of military manpower, planning, logistics, and training. "Fight a war of extermination" is not a war plan; France needed an army and that army needed a set of operational objectives.[35] Bell correctly rejects the myth that the *levée en masse* of 23 August 1793 instantly transformed France into an armed camp inhabited by

---

[30] Bell, 240, 241. Blitzkrieg resembles total war only in that "everyone" knows what each word means.

[31] Bell, 270, 284. He also, albeit improbably (or perhaps only prematurely), sees the two conflicts as equally destructive. Why "sneak attacks on small detachments" constitute total war is baffling. Napoleon's understanding of the nature of war is also "preternatural;" Bell seems to romance "total war," 190.

[32] See Thucydides' brilliant description of war's perversion of language, 3.82; cf., Elaine Scarry, *The Body in Pain: The Making and Unmaking of the World* (Oxford and New York: Oxford University Press, 1985).

[33] Bell, 113; cf. 145. 161.

[34] Bell, 79, 117.

[35] Bell notes that France began the war by invading "a perennial target of French territorial ambitions," Belgium, without considering that "total war" thereby took the same form as its *ancien régime* precursors, 126. Nor does he offer evidence that French armies did anything to demonstrate that "the absolute destruction of the enemy became a moral imperative," 126. For a nice observation about Girondin lack of planning, see 150.

lint-picking children or even instituted regular military conscription.[36] The actual process by which France manned and supplied her massive new armies cannot be explained simply as a manifestation of implacable hatred.[37]

Mostly, however, the text demonstrates total war's devastation of logical processes. The total war launched by the National Assembly against Austria and Prussia in 1792 only became "fact" during the civil war in the Vendée, but the Vendée conflict resulted from "demands of total war abroad sparking what would soon turn into total war at home."[38] When Bell insists that the French armies from 1794 to 1799 had fought "not simply to defeat France's enemies but also to destroy them," one seeks in vain for a real, opposed to rhetorical, example.[39] The hard bargains that France drove with Prussia, Russia, and Austria were entirely in the spirit of Louis XIV and Frederick II.[40]

Bell compellingly explains French brutality in the Vendée in terms of poor logistics, incompetent leadership, and dehumanizing propaganda in a world in which failure could mean the guillotine.[41] Nevertheless, Bell's insistence on the "logic of total war" renders inexplicable the behavior of those professional soldiers who resisted its allegedly inexorable pressure.[42] Individual temperament determined which Republican commanders would respond to fraught circumstances with atrocity; the revolutionary situation, not the abstract "logic of total war," attracted the services of so many sadistic incompetents.

Solecism abounds. If the *Grande Armée* was the perfect vehicle for the implementation of total war," why did it do best in the early campaigns against Prussia and Austria? The closer events got to Bell's notion of "totality," that is in Spain and Russia, and the more time the Allies had to adapt to the new conditions, the less evident is the *Grande*

---

[36] Bell, 147–149.
[37] Bell explicitly denies mobilization to be a necessary constituent of "total war," 7, 17.
[38] Bell, 161, 163.
[39] Bell, 190–91.
[40] Bell notes that the Treaty of Campo Formio "fulfilled the long frustrated dreams of the monarchy," 194, without justifying his claim that doing so required "total war." That the treaty compensated Austria with territory in Italy reinforces the familiar eighteenth-century feel of the negotiations.
[41] Bell, 166, 168, 172, 179–180. Surely it is no coincidence that "a disastrous combination of savagery and incompetence" in Bavarian efforts to put down insurrection in 1809 only fueled the insurgency, Bell, 275.
[42] Bell, 177.

Armée's perfection.[43] And what about the Allies? How did Napoleon's adversaries "learn to play the game of total war" without reaping the bloody consequences of insurrection and repression?[44] Indeed, Bell's notion of total war allows for a remarkable degree of asymmetry. Especially before 1799, there is no suggestion that France's enemies were equally compelled by a need to defend against "total war."

Ignoring Bell's book as rather poor military history might validate Bell's complaint that certain military historians' critiques of his book "reek unpleasantly of condescension."[45] More to the point, the work deserves attention because it demonstrates how thoroughly the true "logic of total war" leads intelligent readers to abandon all critical faculties.[46] Why they do so is a matter for later discussion, but Bell hints at the answer in a tantalizing reference to "a quasi-erotic celebration of violence."[47]

A more reasoned study fails more prosaically to bring coherence to the idea of "total war." Holger Herwig's "Total Rhetoric, Limited War: Germany's U-Boat Campaign 1917–1918" exemplifies a consciously disciplined approach to subject—"No romanticism. No adventure."[48] Herwig investigates how close an unrestricted submarine campaign came to "total war," defined as the application of all available resources "without respite until the enemy succumbed."[49] Germany failed to achieve "total war," he concludes, because the naval experts miscalculated British resources and resolve.[50] Moreover, Germany's campaign was effectively "restricted" by lack of submarines. Herwig's total war is "war by slide rule," a matter of computing battle casualties and calorie consumption, but logic fails even here. Because he determines a war's "totality" in terms of its results, Herwig implies that the loser, who lacks

---

[43] Bell, 234.
[44] Bell, 227. For the logic of insurgency, see 215–216.
[45] to http://www.h-france.net/forum/forumvol2/Bell1Response.html
[46] Moreover, any discussion of total war tacitly implies some utility for this pernicious concept.
[47] Bell, 247. His insistence on the relevance of Napoleon's love life seems rather more forced, 205.
[48] These significant words appear in the version published in *Journal of Military and Strategic Studies* 1(1998) http://www.jmss.org/1998/article2.html), but not in the conference paper Holger H. Herwig, "Total Rhetoric, Limited War: Germany's U-Boat Campaign 1917–1918, in Roger Chickering and Stig Foerster, eds., *Great War, Total War* Washington, DC and Cambridge: German Historical Institute and Cambridge University Press, 2005), where they would be in the final paragraph of page 206.
[49] Herwig, in Chickering and Foerster, 190.
[50] Herwig, 200–203.

the resources to achieve a total victory, can never fight a total war; one cannot, therefore, know which side fought total war until the conflict ends.[51]

Herwig's version could not be more different than Bell's description of German total war as "…a fantasy of creative violence, of total engagement that would end either in glorious victory or in equally glorious self-immolation."[52] Total war is what one wants it to be.

Part IV: Defending Total War

And "want" is the operative word, for many people are strongly invested in the idea. Its defenders tend to offer four standard lines of argument—after one has broken through an initial barrier of complete incredulity. For, like the atheist's denials of the existence of God, a rejection of total war merely reinforces believers' faith that there is something there to be arguing over. In a thought process reminiscent of Saint Anselm's ontological argument for the existence of God, some "total warriors" assume that total war must exist because an actual total war comes closer than a notional one to the ideal of "totality." That sort of thinking tends to divert discussions of the legitimacy of the concept into futile rehashing of definitions and redistributions of wars between the "limited" and "total" categories. The longer such debates go on, the more legitimacy they appear to imbue to the concepts.

This essay will explore four common defenses of total war. The phrase has a pedigree in serious military thought; two total wars have actually happened; total war is the necessary antithesis of "limited" war; debating the notion of total war is a valuable line of historical inquiry whether the outcome be fruitful or not. None of these arguments bears much investigation, and their survival is further testament to the impact of total war on rigorous thought.

Section 1: Intellectual Pedigree

As implied earlier, it is ironic that anyone would treat Erich von Ludendorff as the father of "total war." Were the concept brought to trial, the prosecution could ask for no more damning evidence than

---

[51] Herwig, 206.
[52] Bell, 300. It is repulsive to think of the signal event of twentieth-century "total war," the Holocaust, as "creative violence."

the contents of *Der totale Krieg*. The passage quoted above, in which Ludendorff announces a Jewish and Catholic threat to European nations, is not a bizarre tangent but central to Ludendorff's concept. The work as a whole offers more warnings about Jews than recommendations about national mobilization. This is not a work of policy but of insane metaphysics. Thus, the argument of the second chapter, "*Seeliche Geschlosseheit des Volkes: Die Grundlage des totalen Kreiges*" (Consolidating the German Soul: The Foundation of Total War) is that total war involves replacing a soul-destroying Christianity with a new religion based on the organic requirements of the German race.[53] Even the chapter on economic preparation exhorts that "Spirit creates victory."[54] The tract concludes with a plea for Germany to find a *Führer* worthy of her people.

But historians of total war act as if the appearance of the phrase alone transforms Ludendorff's lunatic ravings into military theory. Ignoring the racial polemic and the complete lack of economic detail, Martin Kutz observes of *Der totale Kriege*, "the most remarkable feature of this picture was that Ludendorff believed that total war would be short."[55] More remarkable is that any historian could, as Roger Chickering claims to do, find in this tedious and nauseating work a "systematic theory of war and society." By attributing to *Der totale Kriege* the principal role in popularizing the term total war but dismissing its author as "by no means an original thinker," Chickering simultaneously captures a famous German general as a source of intellectual credibility for total war while deflecting discussion of details.[56] Lack of originality is the least of Ludendorff's felonies, but the charge conceals the irrelevance of this allegedly seminal text (or rather "tract").[57]

Ludendorff is an ancestor even a bastard child should repudiate with disgust, but no one can blame the "total warriors" for co-opting Carl

---

[53] Ludendorff, 11, 17.
[54] Ludendorff, 57.
[55] Kutz, 192.
[56] Roger Chickering, "Total War: The Use and Abuse of a Concept," in Manfred F. Boemeke, Roger Chickering, Stig Foerster, eds., *Anticipating Total War: The German and American Experiences, 1871–1914* (Cambridge: G.H.I and Cambridge University Press, 1999), 16–17; Roger Chickering and Stig Foester, "Are We There Yet? World War II and the Theory of Total War," in Roger Chickering and Stig Foester, and Bernd Greiner *A World at Total War: Global Conflict and the Politics of Destruction, 1937–1945* (Cambridge: G.H.I and Cambridge University Press, 1999), 9.
[57] Kutz accurately offers this label, though without pursuing its implications, in Chickering, *et al.*, *A World at Total War*, 191.

von Clausewitz into the concept's intellectual family tree by equating his "absolute" war with their own total variety.[58] Clausewitz's ambiguous treatment of absolute war is worth an essay in itself, but even a brief investigation suggests that his theory is mostly useful, like Ludendorff's work, for the prosecution's case

In his opening chapter, Clausewitz introduces "absolute" war as a theoretical ideal encompassing three logical "extremes" so as to achieve a logical state of pure violence.[59] He is clear, however, that absolute war is "logical fantasy," an abstraction useful for heuristic purposes but not to be found in the real world.[60] On this point, he never changes his mind; Book Eight reiterates the difference between *absoluter* and *wirklicher Krieg*, between "theoretical concept" and actual war. He then appears to contradict himself with the claim that Napoleon Bonaparte actually achieved "absolute war."[61] By bringing the Platonic "absolute" down to Napoleon's earth, Clausewitz opened the way for twentieth-century commentators to equate his "absolute war" with their "total war."[62]

By describing war under Napoleon as "its absolute state," Clausewitz reveals that his imagination does not encompass violence at magnitudes beyond his own experience.[63] On the one hand, he enthuses over "the God of War," operating "untrammeled by any conventional restraints."[64] "There seemed no end to the resources mobilized; all limitations disappeared in the vigor and enthusiasm shown by governments and their subjects." On the other hand, Clausewitz is not troubled that unrestrained violence produces relatively restrained outcomes. "The sole aim of the war was to overthrow the opponent" is revealed to be hyperbole (or, more accurately, "overthrow" to resemble a wrestling fall) when the consequence of the enemy's prostration turns out to have

---

[58] Incidentally, a more useful interwar analysis of total war can be found in Giovanni Fioravanzo's two-volume *la Guerra sul mare e la Guerra integrale* (1930).

[59] Clausewitz, On War 77.

[60] *On War*, 78. "Fantasy" is an illuminating choice of word, but it may be helpful to describe Clausewitz's "absolute" war as something logically, but not physically, possible. See below for Jon T. Sumida's different treatment of Clausewitz's absolute war.

[61] *On* War, 579–580.

[62] There are actually two versions of the cooption of Clausewitz for total war. One insists that twentieth-century total war reified Clausewitz's "absolute war;" the other retains "absolute war" as a philosophical concept, but insists upon total war as its closest real world manifestation.

[63] A limitation generally shared by most enthusiasts for maximizing violence in war, most notably those people who envision nuclear war as a practical strategy.

[64] *On War*, 583, 593.

been "to pause and try to reconcile the opposing interests."[65] Napoleon had a fairly extravagant notion of his own interests, but Clausewitz sees no need to explain why his victorious "absolute" wars ended as had those of the *ancien régime*, with negotiated treaties and even a dynastic marriage. Defeated, the man who had aroused the absolute enmity of Europe was allowed, twice, to retire.

Clausewitz's excitement over the Napoleonic wars led him to hyperbole, but he never moved Napoleon into a world of exterminatory violence. If war under the *ancien régime* was like dining at an elegant restaurant where one paid extravagantly for small, elaborately presented portions, Napoleon took advantage of the all-you-can-eat buffet. But in spite of apparently unlimited temptations and however much the appetite grew in the eating, he, not an impersonal "logic of total war," chose what he wanted. Napoleon's wars lacked the internal escalatory dynamic of the World Wars, which Vilfredo Pareto labels "hyperbolic," a phrase usefully describing the behavior of warring twentieth-century states without implying that the trajectory of violence necessarily reaches a state of "totality."[66] To continue the dining analogy, hyperbolic war might resemble an all-you-can-eat buffet populated by West Point cadets engaged in an eating competition. Things may get ugly, but internal dynamics ultimately bring the fighting to an end. The inconceivable total war would require some extraordinary external intervention, the appearance for example of John Cleese's waiter from *Monty Python's The Meaning of Life*.

Students of Clausewitz normally analyze his understanding of absolute war without introducing anachronistic notions of total war. The theorist Raymond Aron even wrote a book on Clausewitz that does not mention "total war" and one on "total war" without referring to Clausewitz.[67] Jon Sumida treats Clausewitz's absolute war as a real thing rather than a philosophical idea but admits that even "real absolute war" would be constrained by such realities as policy.[68] Thus his "absolute

---

[65] *On War*, 593.

[66] Raymond Aron, *The Century of Total War* (Boston: Beacon Press, 1955), 19–22. Aron's preference for "hyperbolic" over total war in a book apparently about "total war" is compelling evidence for the analytical vacuity of "total war."

[67] Raymond Aron, *Clausewitz: Philosopher of War*, trans. Christine Booker and Norman Stone (Englewood Cliffs, NY: Prentice-Hall, 1985).

[68] Jon Tetsuro Sumida, *Decoding Clausewitz: A New Approach to On War* (Kansas, 2008), 123–5.

war" reflects the all-you-can-eat restaurant offering an unlimited menu but the freedom to desist when appetite has been satisfied.

The wars Clausewitz called "absolute" were not even hyperbolic, among other reasons because the opposing coalitions sought to dampen the escalatory impetus provided by French actions. They were simply the biggest wars of which he could conceive. In the limits of his imagination, in his moderate expectations of actual "absolute war," Clausewitz is very like the individuals who spoke in the twentieth century of planning for "total war."

Section 2: Real Total War

The second defense of total war is that it happened. Indeed, I have no quarrel with Gordon Wright's decision to call his superb study of World War II *The Ordeal of Total War*, for he uses the label to refer to war as perceived by the people who experienced it. In the twentieth century phrases *"la guerre totale," "la guerre intégrale," "la guerra integrale," "der totale krieg,"* and "total war" referred to actual policies based on contemporary conditions, not to universal theories. A quick survey of the two "total wars" of the twentieth century suggests that total war was not a theoretical concept or even an ideal type but a general label referring to a variety of specific responses to national circumstances.

"Total war" entered use, though not yet in English, only well into the Great War, when the newly appointed French Premier Georges Clemenceau called upon the French parliament in his Ministerial Deposition of 20 November 1917 to fight *"la guerre intégrale"* against the Germans. The phrase, which would appear in French newspapers and later in histories of the French war effort, did not represent a particular doctrine but a call for further sacrifices for the war effort. The language is eloquent, but Clemenceau's specific total war policies, flour rationing and an increase in the national debt, seem rather moderate after almost three years of carnage.

In the 1920s, the French Army spoke of total war in demanding the creation of mechanisms for comprehensive economic mobilization in time of war.[69] Uneasy about their national security, French leaders

---

[69] Eugenia C. Kiesling, *A Staff College for the Nation in Arms:* The *Collège des Hautes Etudes de la Défense Nationale* (Unpublished PhD dissertation: Stanford University, 1988). The ideas are sketched in Kiesling, *Arming against Hitler: France and the Limits of Military Planning* (Lawrence, Kansas: University of Kansas Press, 1996). Talbot Imlay provides more detailed analysis in "Preparing for Total War: The *Conseil*

identified the tradition of the *nation armée* as an inherent wartime advantage over the less motivated Germans. However comforting the rhetoric of total war, it did not compel effective efforts at peacetime mobilization. Offered a serious national mobilization proposal in 1927, French politicians rebelled against such obvious components of a total national effort as mandatory war work for women or the nationalization of essential defense industries. Ultimately, the moderate blueprint for national mobilization passed in 1938 suggests that total war was simply a name for the level of effort that the French government was willing to demand and the people were willing to make. As the prospect of a German invasion loomed in the spring of 1940, French political and military leaders backed away from total war and sought new war plans aimed at achieving a rapid victory.[70]

The mainstream historiography places Germany behind France in acknowledging the "totality" of twentieth-century war. Hitler's uncertainty about the level of popular support for war led Germany to embark upon the campaign for world domination without even a rhetorical commitment to full national mobilization. Because "blitzkrieg," another popular and unedifying term, sought rapid victories without devoting the entire economy to military production, it represented an effort to avoid rather than prosecute total war.[71] Only in desperate response to Allied successes in North Africa and Stalingrad, did Joseph Goebbels declare at the *Sportpalast* on 18 February 1943 a German commitment to "*totale Krieg*." Defeat, he warned, would bring the "Bolshevization of the Reich" and the ensuing "liquidation of our entire intelligentsia and leadership, and the descent of our workers into Bolshevist-Jewish slavery." Against the Soviets who employed "men, women, and even children…not only in armaments factories, but in the war itself," Germany required a commensurate response. "Total war is the demand of the hour."[72] Bars, night clubs, and luxury restaurants were to be shut down and women to leave their homes for war

---

Supérieur de la Défense Nationale and France's Industrial and Economic Preparations for War after 1918 *War in History* 15 (2008): 43–71. Though the essay's title helped to spark this essay, it demonstrates a valid use of the phrase "total war."

[70] See Imlay, *Facing the Second World War*, 70–75.

[71] For an introduction to the historiography of blitzkrieg and the argument that blitzkrieg could be a means of avoiding national mobilization, see Karl-Heinz Frieser, *The Blitzkrieg Legend: The 1940 Campaign in the West* (Annapolis, Maryland: The Naval Institute Press, 2005), 4–9.

[72] http://www.calvin.edu/academic/cas/gpa/goeb36.htm.

work. People were urged to work more and travel less. Goebbels denounced the sale of fashionable clothing and deemed beauty salons, however "wonderful in peacetime," a "waste" during "total war."

Following the applause of the party faithful came a counter-attack by the hairdressing profession. In the struggle over the use of valuable chemicals in producing permanent waves, Herr Goebbels surrendered unconditionally. "During total war," he explained, "war must not be conducted against women. Never yet has such a war been won by any government."[73]

Although no one has yet proved the consolidation of the beauty parlor into Hitler's war machine, the picture of a German state unable to mobilize because of ideological constraints or the sheer incompetence of a "gangster state," has recently suffered a potentially lethal blow in the writings of economic historian Adam Tooze. Tooze's brilliant *Wages of Destruction* offers a compelling argument for National Socialist success in mobilizing a second-rate economy against the combined military and industrial power of Britain, the United States, and the Soviet Union.[74]

It is of no consequence for the purpose of this essay whether Germany was a militarized productive juggernaut rivaling the Soviet Union in its degree of mobilization, an uneven economy stalemated by internal ideological frictions, or a floundering gangster state. What is important is that all of these variations have been called "total war," which turns out to be whatever happened during World War Two.[75]

Whatever the actual policies of the National Socialist government, the emotional content of "totalitarianism" and the SS State reinforce an image of German total war. Dunkirk, the Beveridge Report, stiff upper lips, and royal morale-building promenades through London lack the same impact even though Great Britain's population mobilized more openly. Hitler lacked the confidence to offer his people the grim prospect of fighting in their own fields, streets, and hills, as Sir Winston Churchill did in his address speech to Parliament on 4 June 1940. Less famous is Churchill's suggestion to Canada's parliament on 30 December

---

[73] Irene Gunther, *Nazi Chic? Fashioning Women in the Third Reich* (Berg; New York and London, 2004), 250.

[74] Adam Tooze, *Wages of Destruction: The Making and Breaking of the Nazi Economy* (New York: Penguin, 2006), 660–668. In arguing for the comprehensiveness of German economic mobilization Tooze eschews the label "total war."

[75] The holocaust gets little attention in military histories of German "total war" because this most total of measures does not fit the worldview of the "total warriors."

1941 that the "the total and final extirpation of the Hitler tyranny, the Japanese frenzy, and the Mussolini flop" demanded total mobilization.[76] Churchill was quicker than Hitler to evoke the language of national sacrifice and total war. "In this strange, terrible world war there is a place for everyone, man and woman, old and young, hale and halt; service in a thousand forms is open... The enemies ranged against us, coalesced and combined against us, have asked for total war. Let us make sure they get it."[77]

The Soviet Union fought total war without talking about it. In spite of communist visions of worldwide class struggle, militaristic "Five-Year Plans," totalitarian institutions, and the propensity to load its military manuals with jargon, the interwar Soviet armed forces did not adopt the language of total war even as they grimly mobilized men, women, and children. Whether defined in terms of objectives, resource mobilization, or suffering inflicted or endured, it is difficult to imagine a more bitter struggle for survival than that waged by Soviet Union against Germany from 1941 to 1945.[78]

The United States talked "total war," as demonstrated in President Franklin D. Roosevelt's budget message to Congress of January 1943:

> We wage total war because our existence is threatened. ... Total war in a democracy is a violent conflict in which everyone must anticipate that both lives and possessions will be assigned to their most effective use in the common effort—the effort for community survival—National survival. ... Total war requires nothing less than organizing all the human and material resources of the Nation.[79]

Rhetoric aside, the American war was total only in the generic sense applied to the Second World War as a whole. As Atkinson argues, the American war was industrial war, victory through production. It was a war of complete mobilization of persons for "their most effective use in

---

[76] But "extirpation" did not mean extirpation. "For ourselves we want nothing of Germany, of the German. We do not desire their destruction, we do not grudge them their prosperity, we do not want to make them the helots that they have made of millions, or to make of their land the desert that they have made of a quarter of Europe. We want them to be peaceful and happy members of a peaceful and happy Europe," Oliver Stanley, the Sec. State for War, 3 Feb 1940, quoted in Stephen King-Hall, *Total Victory* (London: Faber and Faber Limited, 1941), 124.

[77] Churchill, *Unrelenting Struggle*, p. 367

[78] Which is not to say that the Soviet Union sought the utter destruction of the Axis states.

[79] Roosevelt, Budget Message to Congress, 11 January 1943, quoted in Hobbs, 61–2.

the common effort" only if one has a very narrow view of the possible roles of women, married men, and, for example, tobacco farmers. In a newspaper column called "Total War" of 28 December 1944, by which time much of Europe lay in ruins, Eleanor Roosevelt offers the honest appraisal that, "civilians at home have so far been annoyed by the war, but still on the whole we are comfortable at home." http://www.gwu.edu/~erpapers/myday/displaydoc.cfm?_y=1944&_f=md056985 - New Footnote! #80

Americans thought of their war as total mostly because it aimed at the complete defeat of an evil enemy. Moral justification made it "the good war," but the title of Studs Terkel's oral history conveys the irony that the war was a time of relative national prosperity. Production may have won the war, but it also made Americans better off. Surely no Soviet citizen would share the American Red Cross worker's memory of a war that was "fun." "I'm not talking about the poor souls who lost sons or daughters," he explains, "but for the rest of us, the war was a hell of a good time."[80] Only an American could express the hope that the war would last long enough for her to pay off the debt on her refrigerator.[81]

In short, total war refers to the wide range of experiences people had during the two salient conflicts of the twentieth century. Only by acknowledging that total war lacks intrinsic meaning can we understand how Rick Atkinson can describe as a total war one in which Italian civilians scrounged for food in American Army garbage pails while Americans back home were exhorted to consume the country's excess eggs.[82] Moreover, American garbage would have seemed a feast to the besieged citizens of Leningrad, who ate their pets and sometimes the bodies of their dead.

Section 3: To Abandon Total war is to Embrace Limited War.

The argument that we need a notion of total war to avoid having to fight limited ones seems particularly common at West Point. It stems from the particular historical circumstances of the US Army in the aftermath of the Vietnam War and is reflected in the textbook

---

[80] Studs Terkel, *"The Good War: An Oral History of World War II* (New York: Ballantine, 1984). 8. Life became a series of weekend dates," 114; it was an absolute [financial] miracle, 105; "There was a feeling of optimism," 145; "It was fun, being young, with all that excitement," 307.

[81] Terkel, 109. It is fair to note that a bystander responded to the remark by whacking her with his umbrella.

[82] Atkinson, 577.

specifically written for the United States Military Academy. In contrast to the Second World War, the wars in Korea and Vietnam were discouraging experiences for the U.S. Army—apparently because they were "limited." Thus, as George Herring writes in his chapter on Vietnam, "the one thing on which most Americans could agree was that Vietnam had discredited the limited-war doctrines so much in vogue in the 1950s and 1960s." Following this attack on a specific version of limited war is the more general statement that "Politicians and military thinkers, liberals and conservatives, all generally concurred in the aftermath of America's failure in Vietnam that limited war was unworkable, even immoral."[83]

To reject the limited war theory of the post-1945 period need not imply embracing total war as its antithesis, but a central theme of West Point's "History of the Military Art" has for the past fifteen years been evolution from the unsatisfactory "limited" wars of the eighteenth century through the increasingly "total" Napoleonic and the Civil Wars to reach twentieth-century "total war." Imposing on earlier periods a concept developed in the 1950s to deal with the existence of nuclear weapons, cadets are taught that limited war, whether fought by the Duke of Marlborough, Louis XIV, Frederick the Great, or George McClellan, never achieved "decisive" aims. Constrained as they were by their political, social, and military institutions, Marlborough, Louis, and Frederick were not at fault. Rather than condemning their methods as "unworkable and immoral," the course sympathizes with their frustrated efforts to overcome the contemporary constraints on war. If only, West Point instructors used to sigh, Frederick II had been blessed with the social conditions available to Napoleon, then he too could have escaped the chains of limited war.[84]

The rebranding of conventional or "general war" as total war was a natural product of the post-Vietnam army's desire to resurrect itself as an organization for fighting large-scale conventional war against the Soviet Union in Central Europe. The entirely unnecessary decision to dub large-scale conventional wars "total," with all the baggage contained in the phrase, stems from a desire to fight "good" wars, not wars

---

[83] George Herring, "The Vietnam War, 1961–1975: Revolutionary and Conventional Warfare in an Age of Limited War," in Robert Doughty and Ira Gruber, et al *Warfare in the Western World* v. 2 (Lexington, Massachusetts and Toronto: D. C. Heath and Co., 1966), 933.

[84] General McClellan gets less sympathy.

of annihilation. Frustration with "limited" war must have been enhanced by the apotheosis of the veterans of total war as "the Greatest Generation."

It is ironic but necessarily the subject of another paper that West Point embraces total war even as it teaches cadets that war is a political tool rather than a manifestation of sheer violence and uses the notion of military professionalism as a means of inculcating ethical behavior in future officers. The same cadets who should be learning that the essence of military professionalism is the restrained use of power have been taught for the past couple of decades to yearn for "total war."[85]

A tendency to prefer total over "limited" war is common among American civilians as well as solders. The attitude reflects not a national craving for carnage but resentment at apparently artificial restrictions on our ability to accomplish our objectives. Winning is so important in American culture that total war might be defined as "doing whatever you have to do to win." The unspoken problem here, of course, is that people tend to give inadequate thought to what would constitute "winning."

Facilitating the U.S. embrace of total war is the comfortable assumption that the United States tends to behave morally, that its version of total war would not resemble that of Genghis Khan—unless the enemy deserved it. It is probably more significant, however, that the U.S. view of total war encompasses only American actions, not enemy responses. Americans complacently prefer total to "limited" war because they do not expect themselves, their homes, and their families to suffer annihilation. Europeans, who experienced both sides of the total wars of the twentieth century, have fewer illusions about the prospect.[86]

Section 4: Valuable Mental Gymnastics

Over the past fifteen years, dozens of historians have participated in a series of five international conferences convened for the express

---

[85] This claim may seem a bit odd, as one tends to think of effectiveness as more crucial than restraint, but the concept of professionalism serves to educate officers of the armed forces of the United States to understand their place in civil-military relations as well as to increase their efficiency in combat.

[86] See James J. Sheehan, *Where Have All the Soldiers Gone? The Transformation of Modern Europe* (Boston and New York: Houghton Mifflin Company, 2008) for the argument that two twentieth-century total wars led to the civilianization of Europe.

purpose of elucidating the concept of "total war." Can one publish over 100 papers analyzing aspects of a vacuous concept? Apparently one can, producing some excellent scholarship in the process. The papers offer valuable explorations of modern warfare while reaffirming the points of this essay, many of them made by Roger Chickering.

In introducing the first volume, Chickering describes total war as "the master narrative of modern military history," but warns trenchantly of its tendency to inspire "bombast, confusion, misinterpretation, and historical myopia." In addition to asking sensible queries about the use of the term, Chickering offers damning examples of the nonsense it inspires, e.g. "total war becomes less total." He notes both that the total war paradigm spawned in limited war "a caricature" of 18th-century warfare and that total war has not proved a useful analytical tool for understanding war since 1945.[87]

After neatly eviscerating the concept, Chickering evokes a "formidable" historiography in defending its use. Since we are stuck with it, Chickering calls for "more critical employment of this evidently indispensable tool" and repeats that "historians evidently cannot dispense with the narrative of total war."[88]

Five volumes later, Chickering concedes that the project failed to "produce a definition of total war that can command general assent." Still unresolved since the first conference is the debate over whether total war is best analyzed in realist or nominalist terms. Either total war is a Weberian ideal type, a theoretical idea which individual wars more or less approach, or it is "a discrete historical phenomenon that was confined in the first half of the twentieth century – an era that the Second World War brought to a close."[89]

Total warriors are untroubled by the failure of the total war project even to define its subject. Reviewing some of the resulting volumes, William Mulligan acknowledges Chickering's concession but offers the reassurance that so many years of work have not been wasted. If the essays failed to reach their definitional objective, "the journey has been

---

[87] Roger Chickering, "Total War: The Use and Abuse of a Concept," in Manfred F. Boemeke, Roger Chickering, Stig Foerster, eds., *Anticipating Total War: The German and American Experiences, 1871–1914* (Cambridge: G.H.I and Cambridge University Press, 1999), 13, 16, 21 (Quoting Shaw, *Dialectics of War*), 44

[88] Ibid., 23, 28.

[89] Chickering and Foerster, "World War II and the Theory of Total War," in *A World at Total War*, 2, 13.

stimulating" and the work demonstrated "the richness, variety, and sophistication of military history."[90]

Mulligan does not consider whether this intellectual stimulation came at the moral cost of encouraging allegiance to the notion of total war nor observes that adding "totality" does not enrich our understanding of events. To take one example, Michael Howard's observation that it was not in the "nature" of the United States "to fight anything less than total war" and that "everything it did was on a gigantic scale…" will gratify American readers convinced that size is everything, but did 15 years and 100 essays fail to make a point as elementary as the difference between "big" and "total?"[91]

To Chickering's argument that the solecisms committed in the name of total war do not override the weight of historiography devoted to the subject, one can only reply that bad ideas can and must be challenged. Although, for example, few ideas are as firmly entrenched in the modern psyche as that of race, biological study suggests that whole social orders have rested on a cultural idea with little biological basis and a history of causing considerable political, social, economic, and moral harm.

Indeed, that most of the essays produced by the project would remain interesting for the material they cover after the removal of the analytical superstructure belies Chickering's suggestion that historians cannot dispense with "total war." The concept is indispensible only to those who are intellectually invested in it. While it is easy to find works of scholarship marred by the emotionally charged phrase and important scholarship eschewing it, one would be hard-pressed to find a book to which the concept of total war makes a positive analytical contribution.[92]

The real question is not whether the concept of total war could be abandoned but why we are so loathe to do so.

---

[90] William Mulligan, "Total War," *War in History* 15 (2008), 221.

[91] Michael Howard, "Total War: Some Concluding Reflections," in Chickering and Foerster, *A World at Total War*, 282, 283.

[92] If total war were a useful category, one would expect it to feature in Hugo Slim, *Killing Civilians: Method, Madness and Morality in War* (New York: Columbia University Press, 2008) and to get more than a passing and critical reference in Azar Gat's comprehensive *War in Human Civilization*, Azar Gat *War in Human Civilization* (Oxford: Oxford University Press, 2006), 525, 527–8.

Part IV: Clinging to Total War

Mulligan's praise of the total war project as "stimulating" adumbrates the strongest reason for the concept's survival. Logical efforts to eradicate the empty concept ultimately fail because the discussion itself becomes part of Bell's "quasi-erotic celebration of violence." It is even possible that some theorists of total war are staking a claim to superior toughness by their willingness to emulate Hermann Kahn in "thinking about the unthinkable." There is a competitive element to historians' efforts to see their favorite wars categorized not only as total but as more total than rival wars. In any trial of "total war," the best evidence for the prosecution would be video recordings of military historians apparently speaking enthusiastically of total war to excited audiences of West Point cadets.[93]

How can the prospect of mobilizing an entire nation to exploit all possible means in an effort to annihilate an enemy without discrimination between combatants and non-combatants—and the acceptance of reciprocal action by the enemy—arouse enthusiasm rather than horror? Surely total war is exciting only because it is powerful and inchoate fantasy. Were it plausible, such fantasy would be appalling rather than stirring. It is worth wondering whether total war is simply the extreme case of a more general human inability to comprehend in peacetime the experience of war.[94]

But the contemporary conflicts that best illustrate conflict without limits are generally denied the dignity of being called war, let alone "total war." The murderous events in Rwanda in 1994 had many parallels with David Bell's "first total war."[95] The rhetoric of annihilation was there, as were the mobilization of killers and the procurement of

---

[93] To those of my West Point colleagues angered by this suggestion, I can only say that I reported what I have observed and continue to observe. At the risk of alienating others, it is fair to point out that, although the phrase "total war" does not appear, Stanley Kubrick's *Dr. Strangelove or: How I Learned to Stop Worrying and love the Bomb* (1964) catches the sexual undertones of nuclear theory. General Buck Turgidson's (George C. Scott's) excitement over the prospect of destroying the Soviet nuclear arsenal at the cost of "no more than 10 to 20 million [Americans] killed, tops…" suggests the absurdity of embracing the concept of mass annihilation.

[94] For a discussion of the problem of grasping war, see Eugenia C. Kiesling, "What Were They Thinking? France before the Great War," a paper presented at the Royal Military College, Kingston 22 March 2007.

[95] Bell, 4, mentions Rwanda without calling it "total war."

weapons. Hutu machetes performed more efficient extermination than French muskets, and what could be more total than murder preceded by rape, torture, and mutilation? However, since speaking of a Rwandan total war would besmirch the concept, Rwanda becomes, except to those constrained by the legal implications of the term, "genocide." Once again, total war turns out to be what one wants it to be, and *want* is a telling verb. Desiring to capture the label for the Wars of the French Revolution, Michael Broers calls studying the term total war "a matter of some urgency."[96] What is actually urgent is its relegation to its proper and limited role.

Future historians will puzzle over the complacency, nay enthusiasm, with which so many people speak of the "century of total war." We could ease their task by investigating the motivations behind our investment in such language. And then it would be best to bury this twentieth-century phenomenon along with its millions of victims.

---

[96] Michael Broers, "The Concept of "Total War" in the Revolutionary-Napoleonic Period, *War in History* 15 (2008), 247.

ENGLAND'S "DESCENT" ON FRANCE AND THE ORIGINS OF BLUE-WATER STRATEGY

Robert McJimsey

War may be too important to be left for generals alone to manage, but politicians who venture into areas of strategic planning often make even less enviable records. By the end of the seventeenth century English political society had divided over the issue of the nation's proper strategic relationship to the Continental powers. On one side stood a band of Whig politicians who espoused the preference of their Dutch-born sovereign, King William III, for policies that linked their nation's security to the military fate of his anti-French coalitions. Opposing these advocates of close alliances and continental warfare was a gathering of Tory and country party politicians who championed a "blue-water strategy." The proponents of this strategy sought a limited commitment to land warfare, stressed the importance of the navy as the guardian of the nation's security and prosperity and emphasized the independence of England in any alliance system her sovereign might negotiate. The existence of this dispute is not in doubt.[1] The story of how it came into being remains to be told. A crucial part of this story is the effort of William III's government to launch, in 1692 during the Nine Years' War (1689–97), a seaborne invasion or "descent" upon France.

The origins of the blue-water strategy and its contest with the Williamite position did not rest solely upon the descent. From its beginning in 1689 until 1694 most observers would have agreed that for England the war against France had not gone well at all. By 1691 only the war in Ireland showed any sign of coming to a satisfactory conclusion. In Flanders Anglo-Dutch forces suffered a series of minor reverses, but showed no sign of recouping. In 1691 the English fleet had narrowly avoided a major defeat at French hands, leaving the threat of an invasion to restore the deposed James II hanging over the scene for the next two years. All the while expenses were mounting and criticism of the allies' performance (William's Grand Alliance included the

---

[1] Geoffrey Holmes, *British Politics in the Age of Anne* (New York, 1967), 64–81.

Dutch, the Emperor, Spain, Savoy and certain German states) became commonplace. These signs of adversity were so clear that by 1692 William himself had turned to thoughts of peacemaking.

Nourishing these perceptions were certain concepts of English foreign policy, concepts which supplied much of the motivation for the government's critics. Since the latter part of Charles II's reign, the ideal of an independent English nation "holding" a balance among the Continental powers had become reasonably well defined.[2] Proponents of this ideal stressed England's insularity and the nation's ability to intervene in Continental affairs when it suited her to do so. Clearly this ideal stood at variance with William III's insistence that his new kingdom assume the obligations of an ally in a mutually interdependent set of strategic relationships. Moreover it is known that two proponents of this conventional ideal, the Marquis of Halifax and Sir Thomas Clarges, carried over into William's Parliaments, and that Clarges was a central figure in assembling the government's critics into a "new country party."[3]

The foregoing events and attitudes might seem sufficient to account for the emergence of a blue-water strategy. When we consider the position of the government's critics, however, difficulties with this explanation arise. These difficulties were partly constitutional and partly political. Constitutionally the control of foreign policy and the command of the military fell to the monarchy alone. Parliament had no right of petition on such matters and could not form committees to discuss war policy. The politicians consistently faced the bald choice of either funding or rejecting their King's conduct of the war. Such a choice created an even more serious political liability. One set of critics, the Jacobite faction, opposed the entire constitutional settlement of 1689 and wished to restore James II, presumably with the aid of French firepower. Any critics of William's war policy, therefore, ran the risk of being tarred with the brush of Jacobitism, a fate which might well lead to a traitor's end. Advocates of an alternative war strategy would have to follow a pathway leading somewhere between the cliffs of the royal prerogative and the slough of Jacobitism. The story of how this band of malcontented pilgrims made their way through these perilous

---

[2] The Marquis of Halifax gave this position a clear summary in his "The Character of a Trimmer." J. P. Kenyon (ed.), *Halifax: The Complete Works*, (Baltimore, 1969), 86–98.

[3] Keith Feiling, *A History of the Tory Party, 1640–1714*, (Oxford, 1924), 292–3.

channels to arrive in the land of respectable opposition is the story of the descent on France.

The genesis of the descent went back to 1689 when William III wrote to Prince Waldeck of his desire to create a "considerable diversion" in France. In 1690 the King told Halifax himself that "he would land in France to save Ireland."[4] A discussion of the descent came up early in 1691 at the conference of the allies at The Hague, though it was clear that any commitment to the design depended upon the freeing of ships and troops from the Irish campaign.[5] Throughout June and July William, Secretary of State the Earl of Nottingham, the Secretary of State for Ireland Viscount Sidney and the Lords Justices of England considered the feasibility of transporting troops from Ireland to carry out the descent.[6] Although the lateness of the year rendered the design impractical, the project did receive a considerable political boost from Lord President of the Council the Marquis of Carmarthen. Writing to William on July 18, 1691 Carmarthen presented a painfully accurate assessment of the descent's political significance:

> Your Majestie knows very well that a litle thing done upon France itselfe will not only please better than a very great one done in Flanders, and might perhaps force the French to send some of theire troops out of Flanders, but the Parliament would certainly continue any support for that service, which I feare they will hardly do to maintaine them in Flanders, where they do already grumble at the charge.[7]

As Carmarthen anticipated the descent was an attractive alternative to the Flanders campaign. Its full importance was yet to be realized.

The descent became a public issue when William opened the parliamentary session of 1691–92 with a promise to deploy English troops "in order to annoy the common enemy, where it may be sensible to them." The precise meaning of this phrase became clear in the House of Commons' debate on supplies for the land forces. In response to demands to know the disposition of these forces and the nature of England's treaty obligations, a Court spokesman replied that the King

---

[4] P. L. Müller (ed.), *Wilhelm von Oranien und Georg Frederick von Waldeck*, (The Hague, 1880), II, 210. "The Spencer House 'Journals'," H. C. Foxcroft, *The Life and Letters of George Savile, Bart., First Marquis of Halifax*, (London, 1898), II, 218.

[5] Historical Manuscripts Commission, *Report on the Manuscripts of the late Allan George Finch, Esq.*, (London, 1957), III, 17.

[6] Ibid., III, 99, 129, 141, 165, 182–3, 188, 191, 202, 281, 397, 402.

[7] Andrew Browning, *Thomas Osborne, earl of Danby and duke of Leeds, 1632–1712*, (Glasgow, 1951), II (Letters), 202–3.

intended to employ his forces either for home defense or "beyond the sea, either by making a descent into France, or otherwise to annoy the common enemy."[8] The next day, amid complaints about the number and cost of these troops, Sir John Thompson, a consistent critic of the Court, singled out the descent as a ruse designed to gain support for a large standing army.[9] Thompson's opinion, however, should be compared with the privately expressed thoughts of such critics as Clarges and Sir Christopher Musgrave. Although both these men decried the large sums devoted to the war on land, in 1691 each of them looked forward to a speedy end of the Irish war and to a major effort against France.[10] Moreover, looking back on this session, Secretary Nottingham recalled that, upon learning of the King's intention to launch the descent, the House of Commons "broke thro' the rules and forms of Parliament to add 12,000 men to the army."[11] Thompson's voice may have been that of a lone dissenter; more likely his opinion was directed not against the descent, but against the effort of the Court to manipulate Parliament by proposing a popular plan.

The descent was such a plan. Its popularity with both Court and country may be gleaned from a pamphlet published in 1691 under the title *A Project of a Descent upon France*. In 1690 the pamphlet's author, Sir Edward Littleton, had distinguished himself by writing critically of the expensive and ineffectual siege warfare in Flanders.[12] Now Littleton proposed to break that deadlock. Claiming that the French could not guard their coastline with strength sufficient to repel a mobile landing force of 20,000 men, he foresaw this force establishing several garrisons which, when reinforced by additional landings, could live off the countryside. The troops would be recruited, as earlier government plans had envisioned, from forces serving in Ireland, or, if necessary, from those serving in Flanders itself. The troops would assemble in England, and while awaiting transportation to France, would serve as a home guard. Payment for the enterprise Littleton assigned to a variety of

---

[8] Henry Horwitz (ed.), *The Parliamentary Diary of Narcissus Luttrell, 1691–1693*, (Oxford, 1972), 26–7 (hereinafter P.D.).

[9] Ibid., 30.

[10] H. M. C., Fourteenth Report, Appendix, part ii, *Report on the Manuscripts of His Grace the Duke of Portland*, (London, 1894), III, 461, 472.

[11] H. M. C., *Report on the Manuscripts of the late Allan George Finch, Esq.*, (London, 1965), IV, 231 (hereinafter Finch, IV).

[12] [Sir Edward Littleton], *The Management of the Present War against France Consider'd in a Letter to a Noble Lord*, (London, 1690).

measures, taken apparently in descending order of political popularity: reduction of subsidies to the allies, an excise tax and a land tax. The composition of the forces he decreed to be English, or at least foreign Protestants serving under English officers. Supervision of the project he would entrust to a parliamentary committee. The result of the descent, he claimed, would be the diversion of French troops from their frontier engagements, a diversion which would allow allied forces to "bear in upon France: Since therefore the Confederates then would not, and now cannot, find the way into France by Land, We must do it by sea."[13]

The Project of a Descent offered a solution of appealing simplicity to battlefield adversity and rising war costs. An English force, unlikely to spend its money abroad, would do double duty of home defense and assault troops. The grand fleet would control the Channel, protecting shipping and supporting the descent. Troops seasoned in living off the Irish countryside would support themselves at French expense. Monies destined to prolong the stalemate in Flanders would now contribute to breaking that deadlock. It was all there: sea power, patriotism, cheapness, victory. England would intervene in European affairs in her own peculiar fashion and tilt the balance of forces decisively in her own favor. To both Court and country the descent offered the prospect of ending the war quickly; to the country gentlemen the plan also held out the prospect of a cheaper and more limited commitment to the Grand Alliance.

For William III the descent was an adjunct to his policy of Continental warfare; for the country gentlemen the descent offered a potential substitute for that policy. At this starting point it is doubtful if anyone appreciated this divergence of intention. The country gentlemen were not accepting a wise strategy; they were simply for the King. It is noteworthy that being for the King conferred a benefit. Endorsement of the royal policy relieved the country gentlemen of the burdens of opposition. Again, it is doubtful if anyone made much of this benefit; at least the evidence for such an awareness is lacking. The descent was simply, as the Marquis of Carmarthen had predicted, a popular strategy. All the government had to do was carry it through successfully. Only a failure to do so would bring these potential problems into play.

---

[13] [Sir Edward Littleton], *A Project of a Descent upon France*, (London, 1691), 27.

Unfortunately for the government the shadow of that failure had reached its doorstep.

By February of 1692 the descent's planning had gotten under way. A landing either at Brest or St. Malo would take place either in late May or early June. By early March an outline for the supply of troops had been drawn up. This called for five regiments of Irish infantry and five regiments from England to be joined by ten battalions taken from Flanders. Horses would come out of Ireland, ships and sea victuals would come from Flanders. The English would provision their own land forces. Troops, horses and ships would rendezvous at the end of April. The drawing up of battle instructions fell to the Admiral of the Fleet, Edward Russell, and the English army commanders. Administrative oversight of the project rested with Secretary Nottingham. Such was the state of the descent's planning when William left England for Flanders on March 5th.

Six days later the first problem developed. Apparently plans for the descent had been kept secret; now they were communicated to the Council. Broadening the base of decision-making, in turn, led to a rehash of the project's pros and cons. Several councilors objected that the descent was too expensive and hazardous. Some of them claimed that the ten battalions from Flanders could not be spared (a claim which proved to be prophetic). Against these objections the project's proponents pointed out the King's promise to Parliament and Parliament's subsequent vote of supplies. They argued that plans were already advanced and that the strategy might at least succeed in destroying a few coastal towns and perhaps draw out the French fleet for a battle (arguments which also proved to be prophetic). The Council then voted to continue the plan, but its critics asked that the King be informed of their reservations. Despite this vote, the dispute apparently delayed preparations by ten days while William's reply was awaited. Only by March 22nd did Nottingham report to the King that the Council had received his decision to proceed and that its plans had been taken up again. This episode prefigured the descent's twisted course: whenever a snag developed, the councilors went to the King and appeared to depend upon his will. The result was delay after delay.[14]

---

[14] British Library, Additional Manuscripts 37,991 (Nottingham-Blathwayt Correspondence), ff. 5–6.

ENGLAND'S "DESCENT" ON FRANCE 249

While this discussion proceeded, the King began to intervene with his own suggestions. On March 15th the King's private secretary, William Blathwayt, wrote to Nottingham questioning orders for the transportation of horses and troops out of Ireland. The King thought the embarkation date of April 15th was much too early. One week later, upon receipt of this communication, Nottingham replied explaining that a lead time of six weeks was needed to allow for the possibility of contrary winds. On March 28th William accepted this explanation, but added two cautions: first, that the troops might spend too long a time aboard ship; and second, that the contingent from Flanders might not be ready until the end of May. Nottingham received this letter on April 3rd, less than two weeks from the scheduled embarkation. To this exchange Blathwayt appended a letter from Viscount Galway, William's Dutch commander in Ireland, to the effect that no troops could be sent from Ireland before May.[15] On April 5th Nottingham replied that Galway had written to him that the troops would be ready for embarkation on April 15th. But they were not. April 15th, embarkation day, had come and gone; much correspondence had been exchanged, but no troops had moved.[16]

The King and his Secretary of State played a concurrent and identical scene over the transportation of horses out of Ireland. On March 25th Nottingham reported that the horses chosen for the expedition were too ill to travel. He estimated that they would not be fit until the end of May. On March 29th he wrote that he planned, upon the King's approval, to purchase fresh horses.[17] On April 8th Nottingham received William's reply accepting his proposal with the familiar caveat that the embarkation time seemed too early and suggesting that the sick horses might be well by a suitably later date.[18] Nottingham went ahead with arrangements to purchase 100 horses in England and have 150 shipped from Ireland. The Secretary informed Blathwayt of his decision on April 15th, embarkation day. While these preparations lumbered on, outside of Whitehall one observer reported that "nothing is talked of" except the descent into France.[19] Before the divergence between

---

[15] Ibid., f. 9v. Finch, IV, 53.
[16] Finch, IV, 83.
[17] Ibid., 50.
[18] Ibid., 58.
[19] B. L., Add. Mss. 29,578 (Hatton-Finch Correspondence), f. 316.

expectation and performance became clear, the descent's course was to take an unexpected turn.

Throughout March and into April, reports of French preparations to invade England had moved in parallel with the English design. On April 19th, the day before the last report on the movements of the Irish troops, Nottingham confirmed to William the immediate danger of a French descent and undertook to halt any further dispatch of troops from England to Flanders.[20] There now followed an interlude of one month during which preparations for home defense preempted the descent. This interlude ended on May 22nd, when the Anglo-Dutch fleet, under Admiral Russell's command, dispersed the main French fleet at the Battle of Barfleur. In addition to postponing the descent, the invasion scare had one material effect on its planning. To provide for home defense William had ordered three regiments from Scotland and three from Flanders into England.[21] These forces, along with the Irish contingent which had finally arrived in England on May 23rd, now made up the force available for the descent.[22] The invasion scare thus provided an opportunity to regroup; it also provided an opportunity to overcome the problems which had dogged earlier efforts.

In Whitehall this fresh round of preparations got off to a brisk start. Nottingham and William's general of the land forces, Friedrich Schomberg, Duke of Leinster, were busy moving troops to Portsmouth.[23] From St. Helen's Admiral Russell wrote of his desire to press the descent as quickly as possible. On May 28th a conference of the land and sea officers took place at Portsmouth. Leinster apparently was still under orders to secure a landing area, fortify a garrison and otherwise disturb the countryside.[24] Other parties favored either concentrating on destroying the ships at St. Malo or carrying through an invasion. Still, the main thrust of opinion was clear enough: the design should be pressed forward.

This happy consensus prevailed until June 11th, when Nottingham received a letter from William saying that no more troops would be sent from Flanders and asking that all horses sent from Flanders be

---

[20] Finch, IV, 79–81.
[21] Ibid., 124.
[22] Ibid., 180–1, and Introduction, xxi–xxii.
[23] Ibid., 180–1.
[24] N. Japikse (ed.), *Correspondentie van Willem III en van Hans Willem Bentinck eersten graff van Portland*, (The Hague, 1928), First Series, II, 32–3 (hereinafter Correspondentie).

returned.[25] This letter occasioned a long reply which Nottingham addressed to William's Dutch confidant, the Earl of Portland. The Secretary spelled out the damage William's decision would do to the descent and warned of its "fatall consequence to his Majesties affairs and government."[26] He reviewed the circumstances under which the descent had been approved, the expectations which the parliamentarians held of its success and the political consequences which a failure to carry it out would have. It is worth paying specific attention to Nottingham's argument on these latter two points:

> I fear that unless the King by keeping his whole army can this year so beat the French as to reduce them to the necessity of agreeing to such a peace as will be firm and secure, which I take to be impossible, both England and Holland must be undone; and therefore, I press that the King would please to take some other method as I propose, which might immediately be more prejudiciall to France then any thing which can be done in Flanders, and thereby engage Parliament to continue the warr which may be then carryed on with half the expence, and with almost a certainty of a good event. But otherwise I may venture to fortell that the Parliament will not be induced to maintain an army abroad.

Nottingham's case for the descent here is twofold: first, it is politically necessary; and second, it is the only way to break the stalemate in Flanders and hasten peace as cheaply as possible. For the King and his Secretary of State a moment of truth had arrived. Now it became clear that William regarded the descent purely as an adjunct to his war in the Low Countries. Nottingham, on the other hand, was urging that the descent should become a substitute for that policy. The line between the Secretary and the King was sharpening; that between the Secretary and the country gentlemen was beginning to blur. Later on we can observe something of the handing down of this moment of truth along the political hierarchy.[27]

At this particular moment the issue lay between William and Nottingham. Their discussion dragged on throughout June, William holding to the necessity of reinforcing his Flanders army, Nottingham pleading not to compromise the descent. Finally, at the month's end, William relented and allowed the descent to receive priority, though he criticized the delays.

---

[25] Finch, IV, 209.
[26] Ibid., 231.
[27] Ibid., 245, 263–6.

The King's criticism did have a point. Administrative and sailing delays had stretched out the embarkation schedule well into July. In fact, by the end of June, everyone connected with the project was growing restless, defensive and ill-tempered. Nottingham found himself defending his loyalty to the Dutch alliance as well as his management of the preparations.[28] Leinster had begun to worry, and continued to do so throughout July, that the French would fortify their coastal towns and that his own forces were too small to accomplish anything of importance.[29] These concerns, however, paled before the mounting wrath and skepticism of Admiral Russell. In what became the *cause celebre* of the whole affair, Russell fell into a dispute with Nottingham, which consumed the rest of July and eventually finished off the project. Russell objected that St. Malo presented too many technical problems: the soundings and fortifications had not been properly assessed, the weather and tides were threatening. To these objections Russell appended his own charge of continual delays, which had put the project back until too late in the season. Russell's objections could not be overborne: the Council, acting through Queen Mary, made some attempts to win Russell back to the descent, but a final conference at Portsmouth on August 1st failed to persuade him and the project was given up for the year.[30] When William learned of this decision, he gave his grudging consent, indicating that had he been privy to the dispute, he would have intervened to save the descent.[31] At best it was an ironic end to a lackluster episode.

For the politicians it was also a moment of truth. The Court ministers were the first to face the probable consequences of the descent's failure. In August Nottingham, Carmarthen, and the Lord Privy Seal, the Earl of Rochester, submitted assessments of the political situation. Each foresaw Parliament ill-disposed to spend more on the Continental war. Rochester argued that William should propose more money for the fleet, less for Flanders, saddle the Dutch with the main cost of the land forces and generally show himself better disposed to care for English interests.[32] Nottingham and Carmarthen argued that only a

---

[28] Ibid., 268–9, 295.
[29] Correspondentie, II, 33–6.
[30] John Ehrman, *The Navy in the War of William III, 1689-1697: Its State and Direction*, (Cambridge, 1953), 405–7.
[31] Finch, IV, 373–4.
[32] Sir John Dalrymple, *Memoirs of Great Britain and Ireland from the Dissolution of the last Parliament of Charles II until the Sea-Battle off La Hogue*, (London, 1873), appendix, part ii, II, 241–2.

firm commitment to another attempt at the descent could appease Parliamentary opinion. Nottingham, in particular, stressed that renewal of the descent would require sufficient troops, a considerable number of which must be drawn from Flanders.[33] Clearly the Secretary's opinions had not changed since June. Now he had the support of two of the principal Tory members of William's Council.

Outside the Court the news of the descent's cancellation spread slowly. In early August Sir Christopher Musgrave and Sir Thomas Clarges wrote to Robert Harley of their good hopes for the descent.[34] On August 6th Musgrave noted the return of the transport ships and wondered "what charge this hath been and no advantage by it. Surely the Lords that are gone to the fleet will enquire what had occasioned not proceeding on their voyage."[35] By September this mood of wonder had changed to suspicion. Harley received a letter claiming that the flag officers were so busy concocting a defense of their conduct that they had allowed French warships to go "basking" in the Channel.[36] Musgrave, Clarges and Harley's father-in-law, Paul Foley, were also writing of the war's great expense, its lack of progress in Flanders and of complaints of great losses by merchants. Clarges was especially concerned to take up the "quality of our foreign subsidies" at the next session of Parliament.[37] From another quarter of the political spectrum Henry Guy, the associate of the great would-be adviser, the Earl of Sunderland, wrote to Portland urging the maintenance of a strong force for home defense, and less money for the Continental war.[38] Foley summed up the situation in a letter to Harley of September 17th. He foresaw three possible courses for the government to follow. The first was Guy's alternative: reduce the army to a home guard and strengthen the navy. The second was to increase the army to carry out the descent. The third course would be to continue the present muddle in which the Court and Parliament struggled to work out a policy piecemeal. This third course, Foley thought, amounted to no agreement at all.[39] Two features of Foley's letter are remarkable. The first is its presentation of two alternatives to the present policy of land warfare: a sharp move in

---

[33] Finch, IV, 427–8.
[34] H. M. C., Portland Mss., III, 495, 499.
[35] Ibid., 496.
[36] B. L., Loan Manuscripts (Portland Mss.) 29/186, f. 119.
[37] Ibid., f. 124.
[38] Correspondentie, II, 37.
[39] B. L., Loan (Portland) 29/137, f. 7.

the direction of the blue-water strategy, the option of Guy and Rochester, or a tilt toward the blue-water strategy, the descent. The second noteworthy point is Foley's agreement with the forecasts of William's Tory ministers. From August to October of 1692 a discernable interest in the blue-water strategy as an alternative to the Williamite war policy had emerged.

The parliamentary session upon which these issues converged proved to be one of the most volatile of the war years. So vehement and consistent was the criticism of the government's failure to carry out the descent that it quite overshadowed the victory at Barfleur. Even William's pledge to launch the descent the following year failed to appease the country gentlemen. Both the Lords and Commons conducted investigations into the failure. These ran along two lines. The main business was to inquire into the management of the descent; the secondary concern was to voice discontent with government policy. As is usual in these matters, the bulk of the documentation comes from the House of Commons, particularly with respect to the criticisms of government policy.

The principal line of investigation – into the management of the descent – turned out to be a debate over men rather than measures, a debate between Whig and Tory rather than between Court and country. In the Commons the Whigs turned the inquiry into an attack upon Nottingham. The Commons passed resolutions requesting that "the management of the fleet should pass through the hands" of the Admiralty Commissioners and that "one cause of the miscarriage of the descent was for want of giving timely and necessary orders by such persons to whom that matter was committed."[40] The Whigs fleshed out these slaps at Nottingham with speeches criticizing the loyalty of some of William's ministers to the Revolution Settlement.[41] In the Lords this story was reversed: Nottingham's friends rallied to transfer blame from the Secretary to the cantankerous Russell. The result of this sharp division of loyalties was that William removed both Nottingham and Russell from control of naval affairs. They thus became the descent's first casualties.

The other potential casualty of this winter of discontent, William III's Continental war policy, survived; though not without considerable

---

[40] P. D., 294.
[41] Ibid., 274–7.

bruising. As they debated the failure to launch the descent, the spokesmen for the country gentlemen delivered a broad attack upon the war effort. Theodore Bathurst summarized this criticism as he listed the requirements for a successful descent: trade should be carried on in fleets to avoid convoy expenses; the Dutch must keep up the entire Grand Fleet, a landing force provided numbering 30,000 foot, 10,000 horse and dragoons and an escort of twenty men-of-war. It was a familiar list: expenses trimmed, allies shouldering more of the war effort and a substantially larger force than last year's 12,000 troops. The session saw other spokesmen make similar points. Clarges said that too much effort had been spent on the Flanders war and too little on the navy. Harley argued that England should strive for mastery of the sea. And Foley married the descent to the conduct of the allies, charging that the allies not only failed to press the fight against France, but also traded with the enemy. Only an English descent, he concluded, could sufficiently damage the French war effort.[42] This concerted attack on behalf of the descent and the blue-water strategy had an effect: the Commons did not increase the land force and by the end of the session William was complaining that it would be impossible to accomplish any more in Flanders than he had done last year.[43] At the same time the country gentlemen showed themselves willing to support increases in the fleet. This was a position William came to expect as 1693 revolved toward another parliamentary session.[44]

With the session of 1692–93 the descent had made its most important contribution to the evolution of the blue-water strategy. The rest of its tale may be briefly sketched in. The effort of 1693, though begun two months earlier, had to be aborted in favor of a vain rescue mission to save the Smyrna merchant fleet. The next year the project reappeared, this time in conjunction with the sailing of the main fleet into the Mediterranean. These preparations William supervised himself until departing for the continent, leaving orders for weekly reports on its progress. This time there were a few delays, but, aside from some ministerial faint-heartedness, no interruptions. On June 8th a landing party of 7,000 troops, supported by a squadron of twenty-two ships, put

---

[42] Ibid., 242, 271–2. Anchitell Grey, *Debates of the House of Commons from the year 1667 to the year 1694*, (London, 1763), X, 274–5.
[43] F. J. L. Krämer (ed.), *Archives ou correspondence inédite de la Maison d'Orange-Nassau*, (Leiden, 1907), Third Series, I, 313–4.
[44] Ibid., 333.

ashore at Camaret Bay next to the port of Brest. The troops met with stiff resistance from newly-fortified positions and withdrew after sustaining 2,000 casualties. After bombarding some coastal towns, the expedition made its way home. The darling hope of both King and Parliament had ended in a fiasco.[45]

It was, however, not quite the end. Like a ghostly Ahab, the descent now beckoned from amid its ruins. William III wanted another attempt. The Williamite journal, *The Present State of Europe*, hailed the landing as causing an important diversion of French forces from Flanders. Discussion of the strategy hung on into 1696 when Sir Edward Littleton offered it as an antidote to the shortage of coinage, claiming that no money spent on the descent would leave the kingdom.[46] These opinions rang more than a bit hollow. Despite his interest in the enterprise, William refrained from mentioning the descent to Parliament and the scheme disappeared from the Admiralty's planning boards.

Parliament's reaction to the failure of 1694 is difficult to measure. For one thing, the records of the sessions after 1693 are much scantier, depending mainly upon reports of foreign observers. Apparently the government's critics in the Commons mounted an effort to investigate the losses at Brest and voiced displeasure at the expedition's handling. This, however, created only a brief flurry. The descent seems to have lost its allure for the advocates of the blue-water strategy. Harley, and perhaps his colleagues, had become interested in the establishment of a council of trade. Also the sailing of the main fleet into the Mediterranean drew a large share of attention.[47] The attack on Brest did contribute to a notable political event which took place in the Lords. On February 25th, the Earl of Nottingham, an ex-Secretary of State since 1693, rose to denounce government policies. Nottingham criticized the sending of large amounts of money out of the kingdom. He decried the Brest expedition as foolhardy and argued that the expedition into the Mediterranean left England's coasts unprotected.[48] He was followed in support by Rochester, the Marquis of Halifax and the Tory Admiral Torrington. This was the moment at which prominent Tory

---

[45] Ehrman, Navy, 509–15.
[46] *The Present State of Europe or, the Historical and Political Monthly Mercury*, No. 6, (June, 1694), V, 204–5 and No. 8, (August, 1694), V, 273. William Coxe (ed.), *Private and Original Correspondence of Charles Talbot, Duke of Shrewsbury*, (London, 1821).
[47] B. L., Add. Mss. 17,677 (OO) (Netherlands Transcripts), ff. 136v.-8, 174v.-6.
[48] Henry Horwitz, *Revolution Politicks: The Career of Daniel Finch, Second Earl of Nottingham*, (Cambridge, 1968), 152.

politicians moved into the camp of the blue-water strategists. No one knew better than Nottingham that, from the broken measures of 1692 to the landing of a minor force of 7,000 men at Camaret Bay, a chief stumbling block to the descent had been the King's preference for a war fought in Flanders. The disparity between the pronouncements of William III and his government's performance had now become part of the controversy between Whig and Tory as it already had been an argument between Court and country.

By 1695 it was fairly clear that the blue-water strategy had not only been defined, it had also become a politically respectable position for the government's critics to espouse. It should also be clear that the descent had made an important contribution to the emergence of this strategy. As a popular scheme to hasten the war's end it had provided a rallying point for the government's critics, particularly during its first year's trial, when its apparent mismanagement had disappointed all of its supporters. The descent also supplied the Court's critics with something their investigations into peculation and inefficiency could not provide: the outline of a war policy. Whereas William III saw the descent as an adjunct to his commitment to the war in Flanders; Harley, Clarges, Foley and their associates saw the descent as an alternative to fruitless and expensive support of feckless allies. To them the descent represented a way to maximize English naval skill and strategic position to protect English interests. Even the Court ministers recognized this appeal and took up the descent as the political and military salvation of the war effort. If anything, the course of the descent's planning revealed the disparity between William III's interest in the Flanders war and his support of a blue-water strategy. It was this disparity which invigorated the foreign policy disputes which closed William's reign and informed the partisan quarrels which beset the political and military managers of Queen Anne's reign. Like Caesar's ghost the abortive descent of 1692 cast over these years a long and menacing shadow.

CONCLUSION

Dennis Showalter

My late colleague Bob Mc Jimsey was once confronted by a concerned parent. "My daughter is graduating with a history degree," she declared. What can she do with history?" Bob reflected for a moment, then replied, "What can't she do with history?"

That response can be applied as well to the specific field of military history. The company of military historians includes five of Edmund Burke's "little platoons." Each makes a unique and necessary contribution. The students include college professors, tenure-trackers and the *goliardi* who fill itinerant adjunct slots. They include the secondary teachers who keep pace in the field, and communicate their conclusions as classroom alternatives to the orthodoxies of class, race, and gender. Finally, students incorporate the commercial writers whose works often contribute significantly to human and institutional dynamics that defy archival analysis. What students have in common, and what they contribute, is time. Students are paid, directly and indirectly, by the community to read, research, reflect—and communicate. Their challenge is to do those things well and honestly.

Soldiers contribute rootedness. Military history has avoided floating off into postmodernist abstraction because it is fact-centered. It is impossible to make a case for the Pacific Fleet attacking Yokosuka on December 6, 1941. As much to the point, since the days of Thucydides and Xenophon men of war have sought to understand war. It may be in terms of retrospection: coming to terms with decisions and experiences. It may be in terms of projection: seeking guides to the future by evaluating the past. It is always instrumental: soldiers study war for the purposes of war. Their challenge is to move outside the matrices of applicability, to see history as more than a source of metaphors and templates.

Public military historians are too often the field's "lost platoon." But government work on assigned projects is more than a mere alternative to a "real" job usually defined as academic. From the command historians tasked to produce "accurate, thorough, and objective" accounts of administrative institutions, to Ph.D.s sent into harm's way with a "field historian's pack" of a scanner and a laptop, to the high-end teams working on high-end and controversial projects, these historians provide contact between official institutions, self-referencing by nature and experience, and wider audiences unfamiliar with the complex, contradictory specifics of war in any era. Anyone who has tried to reconstruct even a company-scale battle or a modest amphibious operation owes a debt to colleagues on public payrolls.

Aficionados of military history provide passion—on their own time. They range from experts in one subject to those who wonder what History Book Club will offer this month. What they have in common is day jobs. For them the field is a source of pleasure. There is no trick to military history, no secret knowledge available only to those with doctoral degrees or discharge papers. To call aficionados buffs or hobbyists is to dismiss the energy they bring to their chosen approaches. It also invites dismissing the perspectives that non-professionals can bring to a subject that, while complex, is not rocket science.

The war-gamers, the modelers, the reenactors are military history's craftsmen. Their numbers are suggested by their well-attended events. For craftsmen, the opportunity is in the details. These range from appropriate underwear for a weekend with the Civil War to board games and computer simulations that compel analytical approaches and quantitative dimensions to events and situations otherwise frequently described in heroic/narrative fashion. The craftsmen's temptation is concentrating on details in a context of abstraction. Their contribution is immediacy, a hands-on, minds-on sense of events that, appropriately contextualized, highlights war's ultimate reality as a human experience.

Theodore Ropp, the doyen of military history studies in the United States, once said "we're a small tribe, and nobody loves us." But to look beyond fashionably pessimistic descriptions of military history's "marginalization" is to see a discipline that in the past quarter-century has reshaped and redefined itself internally while simultaneously filling external niches with the enthusiasm of Charles Darwin's finches.

Beginning in the 1950s a "new military history" challenged the traditional format of "a battle a day and a war a week" by emphasizing social, cultural, and institutional contexts that eventually incorporated ethnicity and gender. Beginning in the 1990s, what is sometimes called "the new new military history" reintroduced the operational aspects of war and created a three-way synergy with war's human and cultural aspects.

Thus revitalized, military history has reasserted itself in the classroom, as any survey, on any scale, of its course enrollments will demonstrate. Arguably even more important, military history has moved to reclaim a traditional position. Since Thucydides history has been part of the public sphere and a contributor to public debate. That role has been deemphasized as historians in general commit increasingly to abstract, hypertrophied specialization. In a fundamental contrast, military history does not equate solipsism with profundity and scope with superficiality. It encourages breadth, and honors practitioners who can cover the field from Attica to Afghanistan: the Michael Howards and Russell Weigleys. Contemporary military history brings perspective and balance to issues otherwise too often defined by present-mindedness. Specifically, it demonstrates war's central role in the development and survival of states, societies, and cultures. Generally, it helps explain how we reached the present, and helps understand the behaviors of other times and places.

Small wonder that military history attracts correspondingly high levels of public interest and public support. Mainstream publishers and academic presses alike find that its printed version has a wide audience with an increasingly sophisticated appetite. In an unusual reversal of Gresham's Literary Law, good work across the spectrum, from illustrated periodicals to thousand-page monographs, is displacing the superficial and the slipshod on magazine racks, bookstore shelves, and internet ordering sites—a development easily demonstrated by comparing early titles of Osprey Publishing with a random sample from their current list. Military history has been in the forefront of reaching audiences and opportunities exponentially expanded by television. Internet-based sites and forums with a military history focus are multiplying and improving. Military history contributes disproportionally to the online degree programs that bid fair to reshape fundamentally American higher education. What, indeed, isn't being done with military history?

The Society for Military History provides a big and welcoming organizational tent. But what integrates this diffuse field and its diverse membership is a correspondingly broad-gauged, wide-ranging body of learning. The essays in this volume are bench marks and fulcrums for an ongoing process whose foci and approaches differ widely, but which has carried military history into a new century and given it unprecedented prospects for future development. The contributors have individually and collectively been central to this process. Mike Neiberg stands as an archetype. He has taught in academic and military systems, inspiring undergrads and mentoring doctoral candidates. His first academic book dealt with the ROTC and the US ideal of the citizen-soldier. Since then he has done a standard general history of the Great War and a prize-winning study of one of its battles. He has written on soldiers' lives in the nineteenth century, and surveyed twentieth-century war. He has published in general-audience magazines, edited anthologies, helped launch the new International Society for First World War Studies, and put together this volume. With the possible exception of that last, Mike stands for what we are, and what we are becoming.

Kelly DeVries's essay leads the work chronologically and epitomizes the work conceptually. His lever is medieval military technology. This piece is part of the fulcrum applying that lever to the larger issues of war and society in the Middle Ages. "The Question of Medieval Military Professionalism" is worth reading for its bibliography alone. Its long-term value, however, is its demonstration that the relationship between professionalism and chivalry is not inevitably a dichotomy. Professionalism involves two skills: knowing how and knowing when. Medieval war repaid that knowledge well enough to make it valuable—especially in the context of technological development important enough to bring base-born gunners to the same high end of armies' payment scales as belted knights. Kelly's work demonstrates the centrality of competence in medieval societies. The results have extended well beyond the academy. Kelly's presence is regularly sought alike by museums and by the History Channel. As a young scholar he sought to make a difference. He has helped define and publicize a field.

Bob McJimsey's academic forte was the high-end, well-crafted conference paper. He could say more in eighteen pages than many can do in twice the length, especially when mining his primary field of political-military relations from the Glorious Revolution of 1688 to the mid-eighteenth century. Like many scholars who contribute to military history, Bob never considered himself a military historian. But his ability to synergize parliamentary maneuvering, foreign policy decision-making, and military-naval operations makes him an honorary—and honored–member of the guild.

Bob's untimely passing left it to me to select his contribution. I chose this one because of its demonstration that tactics can indeed determine strategy and policy appropriately—when conditions at the sharp end are sufficiently changed. A limited seaborne invasion of France, a "descent," had become an issue in England's strategy with the reign of William III. The problem was that an increasingly effective French coast defense made the forces required and the risks incurred higher than was realized when the widely-popular Descent of 1692 was planned and prepared. Cancelled before a boat hit the shore, the abortive operation encouraged developing an alternative approach. By 1695 the emerging "blue water strategy" was a respectable alternative to William's continuing support for a continental commitment. The rest of the story is the history of a "British way of war" that owed much to an external contingency.

Rob Citino established his expertise in modern mobile warfare in a series of specialized monographs admired by other specialists. He demonstrated it in four seminal volumes published in five years that attracted general attention. He has expanded it by developing an initial operational matrix into a comprehensive framework for analyzing "ways of war" by synergizing their military and cultural aspects.

Rob's focal point is Germany, but his methods and his approach are not system-specific. Neither is his admonition that studying ways of war facilitates understanding the past, but is an unreliable guide to the present and no guide at all to the future. Those are the subtexts of his essay on Erich von Manstein and the Battle of Kharkov in early 1943. Most accounts depict Manstein's genius in restoring a front ruptured by the Red Army's earlier Stalingrad offensive. Citino, masterfully shifting among perspectives, presents two armies trapped in and victimized by doctrines, by "ways of war" that led both of them to the edge of the abyss, and eventually, the Germans over that edge into catastrophe.

I find one fault with Citino's paper—I did not write it. Certainly the essay sets the stage for Bill Astore's extended question: why has the German model of war making, specifically the World War II version, remained so attractive to a United States whose social and political systems are essentially diametrically opposite from those of the Third Reich? Bill makes a persuasive case that the goal of rapid, decisive victory through method as opposed to mass has generated a case of what John Mearsheimer called "Wehrmacht penis envy." This admiration for a sanitized version of the Wehrmacht, however, produced an armed force separated from society, a warrior elite that has become an instrument of perpetual war because of its ability to protect the homeland from war's realities. Americans, he concludes, have bought into a vision selective, immature, adolescent—a wet dream from which it is vitally necessary to awaken.

Rich DiNardo develops the concept of a German way of war in a different direction and a different context. His zone of operations is the Great War's Eastern theater, which only in recent years has moved from obscurity to a major source of information and analysis. And a central figure in that process has been an almost forgotten Imperial field marshal, August von Mackensen. He never made it to the center stage of the Western Front. Even his appearance, bedecked in the military regalia of a bygone era, is against him. But DiNardo shows Mackensen was an adept field commander and a skillful coalition warrior. He was able to control large-scale combined operations and utilize cutting edge technology, aircraft, artillery, motor transport, with finesse and panache.

Above all Mackensen was flexible. He profited from experience. And he was almost 65 in 1914: an age when most who reach it, historians as well as soldiers, tend to think they know everything worth knowing. DiNardo aptly calls Mackensen an old dog able to learn new tricks. In that latter quality August von Mackensen is more an archetype of the successful soldier than his ever-present busby might suggest. He is also a useful model for aging academicians.

Holger Herwig's essay demonstrates that the United States is not alone in pursuing illusions. Germany in August 1914 staked its existence on a mirage. But this analysis of a "forgotten campaign" on a secondary front challenges two major stereotypes. The first is that the abandonment of the Schlieffen Plan threw fatal levels of grit in a German war machine that should have been an instrument of victory. The second stereotype depicts a Second Reich whose structural flaws were a recipe for disaster no matter how well its forces might perform in battle.

Herwig instead shows that the German army's structural defects in command and communications, combined with its failure to understand the "next war" in terms of material rather than maneuver, were quite enough to secure immediate defeat in the West. The same points are made on a wider scale in his *The Marne, 1914*. In conception and execution the book is a model of the three-way synergy I described earlier as characteristic of contemporary military history. It is also part of an *ouevre* that illustrates that synergy's development. Herwig's early work on the dynamics of the German navy and its officer corps was a seminal contribution to the new military history. He found increasing room for operations in such studies as *The First World War: Germany and Austria-Hungary, 1914–1918*. He is now as well a master of the sharp end of war, without having limited his earlier, broader perspectives. As for reaching non-academic audiences, filmmaker James Cameron describes Holger's co-authored *The Destruction of the Bismarck* as "always next to my bunk" on the expedition that explored the battleship's wreck.

Bob Doughty's essay complements Holger's in its analysis of French strengths and weaknesses in 1914. Doughty describes a French army "surprisingly flexible and responsive, "able to overcome the mistakes generated by doctrinal and institutional commitment to a "short-war illusion." In 1940 as well the French fought within the constraints of their pre-war preparation. This time, however, they lacked the flexibility to regain a lost initiative. Doughty's three seminal monographs on the Pyrrhic victory of 1914–18, the interwar development of French army doctrine, and the 1940 Battle of Sedan, link those three situations from three perspectives: strategic/operational, intellectual, and operational/tactical.

The work's quality and their professional soldier's perspective highlight General Doughty's two decades as professor and head of the US Military Academy's history department. From start to finish he played a seminal role in strengthening the academic and personal relationships of civilians and uniforms, recognizing both and privileging neither. The solid links between the field's primary human taproots owe more to Bob's mature and unobtrusive presence than most of us realize or understand.

Kathy Barbier has published general-audience books on infantry tactics and the battle of Kursk. She is the author of a standard work on Allied deception plans for the invasion of Europe in 1944. Her contribution to this volume shifts professional gears again by using micrometric research to address a broad question: what happens when a democratic government's key agencies lock horns over policy or procedure in the context of a total war? On one level the complex story of an individual caught between Great Britain's intelligence services and its justice system seems an account of road kill in a total war. On another it invites categorization as overkill: an example of the kind of moral equivalence that describes war, even the "good" World War II, as a comprehensively immoral process in which all participants are somehow victimized and all belligerents are somehow morally culpable.

What Barbier presents instead is a case study in cultural flexibility. The conditions of 1940 did not obtain by 1942. As a result, what author John Mortimer might call the "golden thread" of British justice, restrained the heavy hand of British administration. And what Kathy demonstrates is that though war seldom offers clear contrasts between good and evil, concern for decent, lawful conduct often survives. What Great Britain did for one of its marginal citizens in the depth of World War II was not perfect. It was good enough, and preferable to the alternatives offered by Germany and Japan.

Jennie Kiesling's work epitomizes an ability and a quality central to contemporary military history. The ability is range. Jennie's publications handle the ancient world as smoothly as the twentieth century. She has taught military history in Afghanistan. Case for range? Prima facie. Jennie's quality is courage: courage that tackles the tough questions. And to military historians none is more fundamentally controversial than the subject of total war. As someone with three articles' worth of skin in the international project for the study of total war Jennie describes, I can affirm the ambivalence that underlay those meetings and the carefully qualified conclusions they drew. Jennie, by contrast, takes no intellectual prisoners, even in her own department. Her intellectual breadth adds weight to her case for "total war" as at best a trope or metaphor rather than a functional analytical concept. Her position can be disputed; it cannot be dismissed. And like the other contributions to this anthology, "Total War, Total Nonsense" is a synergy of substance and style. Jennie's concluding riff, describing historians' competitive efforts to bring "their" wars as close as possible to the "total" archetype, leaves the aftertaste, and the sting, of good Scotch.

It is an honor for me to receive this Festschrift. It is a pleasure to be alive to express my gratitude. And it is sheer joy to respond to the nice things said of me by colleagues and friends by discussing their achievements, their contributions to our common enterprise. Military historians are a diverse and fractious group. But when we cooperate, borrowing from Frederic Manning's Great War classic *The Middle Parts of Fortune*: "we're a bloody fine mob." I cannot think of a better way to have spent my academic life than being a military historian. I know I could never have found better company.

LIST OF BOOKS BY DENNIS SHOWALTER

Hitler's Panzers. The Lightning Attacks that Revolutionized Warfare (New York: Berkeley, 2009). History Book Club selection.

Railroads and Rifles: Soldiers, Technology and the Unification of Germany (Hamden CT: Archon Books, 1975. Reprint, Helion Books, 2007).

Soldiers' Lives through History. The Early Modern World. Co-authored with William Astore (Westport, Ct.: Greenwood, 2007).

Patton and Rommel: Men Of War in the 20th Century (New York: Berkeley, 2005) History Book Club selection, BMOC selection, Military Book Club selection.

The Wars of German Unification. (London: Arnold, 2004).

Tannenberg: Clash of Empires. Revised edition (Washington D C: Brasseys, 2004. (History Book Club selection). (Original: Hamden, CT: Archon Books, 1990. Military Book Club Selection; Paul Birdsall Prize, AHA. Polish edition, 2005).

The Wars of Frederick the Great (London: Longmans, 1996).

Voices from the Third Reich: An Oral History, co-authored with J. Steinhoff, P. Pechel (Washington: Regnery Gateway, 1989; New York: DaCapo, 1994) (History Book Club Alternate Selection). (German edition: *Deutsche im Zweiten Weltkrieg. Zeitzeugen Sprechen* (Munich: Schneekluth, 1989).

SELECT BIBLIOGRAPHY

Aron, Raymond. *The Century of Total War*. Boston: Beacon Press, 1955.
Atkinson, Richard. *The Day of Battle: The War in Sicily and Italy, 1943–1944*. New York: Henry Hold, 2007.
Bacevich, Andrew J. *The New American Militarism: How Americans Are Seduced by War*. Oxford: Oxford University Press, 2005.
Bacevich, Andrew J. *The Limits of Power: The End of American Exceptionalism*. New York: Metropolitan Books, 2008.
Bartov, Omer. *Hitler's Army: Soldiers, Nazis, and War in the Third Reich*. Oxford: Oxford University Press, 1991.
Bartov, Omer. *The Eastern Front, 1941–45, German Troops and the Barbarisation of Warfare*. New York: Palgrave, 1985, 2001.
Bell, David A. *The First Total War: Napoleon's Europe and the Birth of Warfare as We Know It*. Boston and New York: Houghton Mifflin, 2007.
Black, Jeremy, *Naval Power: A History of Warfare and the Sea from 1500 Onwards*. London: Palgrave Macmillan, 2009.
Black, Jeremy, *The Age of Total War, 1860–1945*. London: Rowman & Littlefield, 2010.
Boemeke, Manfred F., Roger Chickering, Stig Foerster, eds., *Anticipating Total War: The German and American Experiences, 1871–1914*. Cambridge: G.H.I and Cambridge University Press, 1999.
Broers, Michael. "The Concept of "Total War" in the Revaluation-Napoleonic Period," *War in History* 15 (2008), 247.
Browning, Christopher. *Ordinary Men: Reserve Police Battalion 101 and the Final Solution in Poland*. New York: HarperCollins, 1998.
Bruce, Robert B. *A Fraternity of Arms: American and France in the Great War*. Lawrence: University Press of Kansas, 2003.
Chickering, Roger and Stig Foerster, eds., *Great War, Total War: Combat and Mobilization on the Western Front, 1914–1918*. Washington, DC and Cambridge: German Historical Institute and Cambridge University Press, 2000.
Chickering, Roger, Stig Foester, and Bernd Greiner. *A World at Total War: Global Conflict and the Politics of Destruction, 1937–1945*. Cambridge: German Historical Institute and Cambridge University Press, 2005.
Citino, Robert M. *Death of the Wehrmacht: The German Campaigns of 1942*. Lawrence, KS: University Press of Kansas, 2007.
Citino, Robert M. *Quest for Decisive Victory: From Stalemate to Blitzkrieg in Europe, 1899–1940*. Lawrence: University Press of Kansas, 2002.
DiNardo, Richard L. *Germany and the Axis Powers: From Coalition to Collapse*. Lawrence, KS: University Press of Kansas, 2005.
DiNardo, Richard L. *Breakthrough: The Gorlice-Tarnow Campaign 1915*. Westport, CT: Praeger, 2010.
Doughty, Robert A. and Ira Gruber, et al.,eds. *Warfare in the Western World*. 2 vols. Lexington MA and Toronto: D. C. Heath and Company, 1996.
Foerster, Wolfgang, ed. *Mackensen: Briefe und Aufzeichnungen des Generalfeldmarschalls aus Krieg und Frieden*. Bonn: Wahlband der Buchgemeinde, 1938.
Germany, Reichsarchiv. *Der Weltkrieg 1914 bis 1918*. 14 Vols. Berlin: E. S. Mittler und Sohn, 1925–1944.
Frieser, Karl-Heinz. *The Blitzkrieg Legend: The 1940 Campaign in the West*. Trans. John T. Greenwood. Annapolis, Maryland: The Naval Institute Press, 2005.

Fritz, Stephen G. *Frontsoldaten: The German Soldier in World War II*. Lexington: The University Press of Kentucky, 1995.
Fussell, Paul. *Wartime: Understanding and Behavior in the Second World War*. Oxford: Oxford University Press, 1989.
Glantz, David M. *From the Don to the Dnepr: Soviet Offensive Operations, December 1942–August 1943*. London: Frank Cass, 1991.
Herwig, Holger and Richard Hamilton. *Decisions for War, 1914–1917*. Cambridge and New York: Cambridge University Press, 2005.
Herwig, Holger. *The First World War: Germany and Austria-Hungary 1914–1918*. London: Edward Arnold, 1997.
Herwig, Holger. *The Marne 1918: The Opening of World War I and the Battle That Changed the World*. New York: Random House, 2009.
Kier, Elizabeth. *Imagining War: French and British Military Doctrine Between the Wars*. Princeton: Princeton University Press, 1997.
Klemperer, Otto. *The Language of the Third Reich*. London: Continuum, 1957, 2006.
Legro, Jeffrey W. *Cooperation under Fire: Anglo-German Restraint during World War II*. Ithaca, NY: Cornell University Press, 1995.
Ludendorff, Erich. *Der totale Kriege*. Munich, 1936.
Ludendorff, Erich. *The Nation at War*. Trans. A.S.Rappoport. London and Melbourne: Hutchinson & CO., 1938.
Manstein, Erich von. *Verlorene Siege*. Bonn: Athenaeum Verlag, 1955.
Melvin, Mongo. *Manstein: Hitler's Greatest General*. London: Weidenfeld & Nicolson, 2010.
Neely, Mark E. Jr., "Was the Civil War a Total War?" *Civil War History* 37 (1991): 434–458.
Nelson, James, ed. *General Eisenhower on the Military Churchill: A Conversation with Alistair Cooke*. New York: W. W. Norton, 1970.
Rosen, Nir. *Aftermath: Following the Bloodshed of America's Wars in the Muslim World*. New York: Nation Books, 2010.
Sadarananda, Dana V. *Beyond Stalingrad: Manstein and the Operations of Army Group Don*. Mechanicsburg, PA: Stackpole, 2009.
Scheibert, Scheibert. *Zwischen Don und Donez*. Neckargemünd: Kurt Vowinckel Verlag, 1961.
Schoenbaum, David. "The Wehrmacht and G.I. Joe: Learning What from History?" *International Security*, Vol. 1, #8 (Summer 1983), 201–07.
Shepherd, Ben. *War in the Wild East: The German Army and Soviet Partisans*. Harvard: Harvard University Press, 2004.
Showalter, Dennis E. *Tannenberg: Clash of Empires*. Reprinted Edition. Washington, DC: Brassey's 2004.
Smelser, Ronald. *The Myth of the Eastern Front: The Nazi-Soviet War in American Popular Culture*. Cambridge: Cambridge University Press, 2007.
Stein, Marcel. *Field Marshal von Manstein, a Portrait: The Janus Head*. Solihull, UK: Helion, 2007.
Sumida, Jon Tetsuro. *Decoding Clausewitz: A New Approach to On War*. Lawrence, Kansas: University Press of Kansas, 2008.
Taylor, Telford. *Sword and Swastika: Generals and Nazis in the Third Reich*. New York: Simon and Schuster, 1952.
Terkel, Studs. *"The Good War: An Oral History of World War II*. New York: Ballantine, 1984.
Turse, Nick, ed. *The Case for Withdrawal from Afghanistan*. New York: Verso, 2010.
Van Creveld, Martin. *Fighting Power: German and U.S. Army Performance, 1939–1945*. Westport, CT: Greenwood Press, 1982.
Wagener, Carl. *Heeresgruppe Süd: Der Kampf im Süden der Ostfront 1941–1945*. Bad Nauheim: Podzun, 1967.

Walters, John B. "General William Tecumseh Sherman and Total War," *Journal of Southern History* 14 (1948): 447–80.
Weigley, Russell F. *The American Way of War*. New York: Macmillan Publishing, 1973.
Wette, Wolfram. *The Wehrmacht: History, Myth, Reality*. Harvard: Harvard University Press, 2006.

INDEX

Afghanistan, 12, 17, 19, 28, 79
Albright, Madeleine, 17
Alsace-Lorraine, 169–170, 173–174, 184–185, 188, 190–191, 193–213
American Exceptionalism, 65
Anderson, Sir John (Viscount Waverly), 38, 60
Auftragstaktik, 6–7, 11, 13–15, 85, 211
Austria, 11, 226
Austria-Hungary, 132, 134, 136–152, 154–155, 160, 162–166

Badanov, Vasily M., 98, 106, 112
Belgium, 16, 33, 61, 170–175, 181–183, 186, 190, 194–195, 201, 208, 212, 225
Blitzkrieg, 5, 7, 13–17, 27, 224–225, 233
Blue-Water Strategy, 243–244, 254–257, 263
Bonaparte, Napoleon, 7, 83–86, 223–235, 227, 230–231, 237
Bradley, Omar N., 13
Britain, 67, 69, 73, 75, 79–80, 82; Nine Years' War era, 243–258, 263; World War I era, 131, 149–150, 163, 170, 175, 182, 185; World War II era, 16, 31–62, 172, 175, 183, 227, 234, 265–266
British People's Party (BPP), 42–45, 47, 53, 57, 61
Brusilov, Alexei, 132, 140, 154
Bulgaria, 146–148, 150–155, 163, 166
Bush, George W., 15–16, 79

Carmarthen, Marquis of, 245, 247, 252
Charny, Geoffroi de, 122–123
Cheney, Richard "Dick", 15
China, 64, 72–73, 81
Churchill, Winston, 131, 234–235
Clarges, Sir Thomas, 244, 246, 253, 255, 257
Clausewitz, Carl von, 6, 7, 11–14, 17, 27, 77–78, 85, 101, 107, 111, 199, 225, 230–232
Clinton, William J., 26
Cold War, 17, 78
Crusades, 119, 121–122

De Castelnau, Edouard, 193–194, 202–204, 208, 210
Desert Storm, 11

Detention during wartime, 5–6, 38–39, 44, 51–52, 60–62
Domesday Book, 125, 129
Dommes, Wilhelm von, 201–202, 211
Dubail, Yvon, 193–194, 203–204
Duke of Wellington, 85
Dunkirk, 48, 61

Edward I, 115, 118, 121
Eisenhower, Dwight D., 8–9, 27
England in the medieval era, 113–130
Enlightenment, 72, 76

Falkenhayn, Erich von, 133, 138–142, 144–146, 151–154, 156–157, 162–166, 207, 211
Fascists, 37–38, 44, 47, 61
Fifth Column, 32–33, 35, 61
Flanders, 131, 243, 245–253, 255–257
Foch, Ferdinand, 185, 189, 191, 202–204, 209
France, 7–8, 16, 223–226, 232–233, 242; Nine Years' War era, 243–258, 262–263; in World War I, 131, 148–151, 169–187, 188–192; in World War II, 31, 33, 48, 54, 61, 76, 84–85, 117, 169, 171–175, 178–184, 186–192
Franks, Tommy, 16
Frederick II, 224, 226, 237
Frederick the Great, 13–14, 84
French, Sir John, 170, 186, 191–192

Gaertner, Fredericka Stattinger, 45–50, 52–54, 56–58, 60, 62
Gamelin, Maurice, 171–172, 175, 179, 183–186, 192
Germany; military 5–24, 26–30, 218; militarism, 5, 13, 20, 24, 26–27; in World War I, 169–187, 188–192, 193–213, 221, 227, 232; in World War II, 32–35, 38–49, 51–55, 62, 84–85, 87–112, 169, 171–175, 178–184, 186–192, 218, 221–226, 229, 233–235
Goebbels, Joseph, 233–234
Greece, 71–72; Salonika 148–154, 160, 162
Greene, Benjamin, 32, 34–43, 45, 48–53, 55–62

Greene, Edward, 39, 52, 56
Guderian, Heinz, 16, 21, 171–173, 175, 187

Haig, Douglas, 131
Halifax, Marquis of, 244–245, 256
Harley, Robert, 253, 255–257
Hastings, Battle of, 124–129
Hickson, Oswald, 52, 55–57, 60
Hindenburg, Paul von, 18, 136–137, 145, 154, 156–157, 166
Hitler, Adolf, 18–19, 21–22, 27, 42, 44, 50, 90–91, 95, 100–105, 108, 171–172, 223–224, 233–235
Hötzendorf, Franz Conrad von, 132, 137–140, 142, 144, 146, 151–152, 154, 163, 165
Hussein, Saddam, 15–16

India, 72–73
Iraq, 11–12, 15–17, 19, 28, 78–79, 225
Ireland, 34, 243, 245–246, 248–250
Italy, 35, 54, 71, 91, 94, 96–99, 117, 129, 138, 145–146, 221–223, 226

Jackson, Thomas "Stonewall", 84–85
James II, 243–244
Japan, 67, 72, 75, 213
Joffre, Joseph, 169–175, 177, 182, 184–186, 188, 191–195, 197, 199–203, 208–211

Kell, Sir Vernon, 42–43
Kharkov, 83, 100, 102, 104, 106–107, 109, 111, 263
Knight, Charles Henry Maxwell, 36–37, 44–47, 55, 58, 61–62
Korea, 66, 215, 237
Krafft von Dellmensingen, Konrad, 195–196, 199–202, 209, 211–212
Kurtz, Harold, 43–45, 48–50, 52–60, 62

Lee, Robert E., 84–85
LeQueaux, William, 32–33
Liddell, Guy, 54–55
Littleton, Sir Edward, 246, 256
Louis IV, 226, 237
Ludendorff, Erich, 131, 133, 137, 145, 154, 157, 164–166, 221–222, 228–230
Luxembourg, 170–172, 190, 194–195, 201, 208–210

Mackensen, August von, 131, 133–167, 264
Maginot Line, 172–173, 179, 181
Manstein, Erich von, 87–91, 95–96, 98, 100, 102–106, 108–112
Marne, First Battle of the, 169–170, 172, 174–176, 178, 182, 185–186, 188, 191
McClellan, George, 7, 237
Medieval Era, chivalry, 117, 119–120, 122–123; military obligation, 117–118, 123–126; military professionalism, 113, 115–119, 122–130; generalship, 113, 115, 117, 120–122, 126
Menzies, Sir Stewart, 45–46
Meuse, 169, 171, 173, 175, 183, 186–188, 190–192
Moltke, Helmuth von (the Elder), 84–85, 103
Moltke, Helmuth von (the Younger), 173, 175, 186–186, 195–197, 199, 201–202, 207–212

Nazism, 5, 8–10, 12–13, 19–20, 22–23, 28–29, 32–33, 37–38, 41–42, 44–45, 48, 56, 61, 68
Netherlands, 16, 19, 33, 61, 243–244, 249–252, 255
Normandy, 46–47
Nottingham, the Earl of, 245–246, 248–254, 256–257

Obama, Barack, 19–20
Operation Blue, 89–91, 106
Operation Saturn, 96, 98–99, 106
Operation Star, 97, 100, 102, 109
Operation Winter Storm, 93–95, 98
Ottomans, 71–73, 121–122

Palestine, 42, 45
Patton, George S., 8, 13
Paulus, Friedrich, 90, 92, 95
Peace Pledge Union, 37, 40–41
Poincaré, Raymond, 193–194
Poland, 132, 136–137, 144–146, 163, 166, 171, 174, 180
Przemysl, 137, 140–142, 162, 164

Quakers, 39–40

Reagan, Ronald, 65–66
Revolution in Military Affairs (RMA), 69–70

Romania, 90–94, 96–97, 99–100, 118, 133, 138, 145, 154–157, 159–162, 165–166
Rommel, Erwin, 8, 16, 30
Roosevelt, Franklin Delano, 26, 235
Rumsfeld, Donald, 15–16
Rupprecht, Crown Prince, 156, 195–196, 198–205, 207–212
Russell, Edward, 248, 250, 252, 254
Russia, 224, 226; *see also Soviet Union*

Schlieffen, Alfred von, 195, 197, 201, 209, 212
Schuster, Sir Claude, 35, 43, 60
Sedan, 11, 169–173, 183–184, 186–187, 189–190, 192
Seeckt, Hans von, 133, 139, 141–145, 149–151, 153, 157, 164–166
Serbia, 146–152, 159–160, 162–163, 165–166
Seydlitz, Friedrich von, 84
Sherman, William T., 12
Sledge, Eugene, 25
Somme, Battle of, 212
Soviet Union, 8, 14, 21, 31, 89–93, 95–109, 112, 132, 135–146, 154–155, 159–163, 170, 175–176, 233–237, 241, 263; *see also Russia*
Spain, 220, 226
Stalin, 107
Stalingrad, Battle of, 87, 89–98, 100, 104–105, 109, 111, 233, 263

Tannenberg, Battle of, 132, 135–136, 142, 146, 158, 161, 166
Tavistock, Lord, 41–42, 45, 53, 57
Thucydides, 225, 259, 261
Tory Party, 243, 254, 256–257
Total War, 215–242, 266
Trapp, Wilhelm, 23
Truman, Harry S., 8

Unconventional Warfare, 219
United States Air Force, 1–2, 6, 13–14, 24, 216
United States Civil War, 64, 216–217, 237
United States Military Academy, 215–217, 219–220, 236–238, 265
United States, 64–66, 69–70, 76–79, 82, 107; military, 6–21, 23–29, 221–222, 234–238, 240, 263; all-volunteer force, 7, 10, 12–13, 25–26

Verdun, Battle of 153–154
Vietnam War, 10–14, 16–17, 25–26, 29, 66, 78, 215, 236–237

Wehrmacht, 5, 7, 9–10, 12, 17–18, 20–23, 29, 68, 87–88, 90–94, 98, 103, 107, 112, 263
Western Way of War, 66–67
Weygand, Maxime, 180, 186
Wheatley, Dennis, 37, 46–47
Whig Party, 243, 254, 257
Whiggism, 63, 74, 77–78
Wilhelm II, Kaiser, 13, 18, 27–28, 134, 143–146, 165–166, 204, 207, 211
William III, 243–257, 263
William the Conqueror, 124–126, 128
Winters, Richard, 25
World War I, 7–8, 11, 14, 18, 24, 27, 29, 32, 34, 131–167, 169–186, 188–192, 215–216, 221, 227, 231–232, 264
World War II, 6–9, 11–15, 18–19, 23–29, 31–62, 67, 87–112, 169, 171–175, 178–184, 186–192, 216–218, 221–223, 225, 231–237, 239, 265

Xylander, Rudolf von, 203, 205, 209